TROUBLED NEIGHBORS

TROUBLED NEIGHBORS

*The Story of
US–Latin American Relations,
from FDR to the Present*

HENRY RAYMONT

A Century Foundation Book

A Member of the Perseus Books Group

Published in the United States of America by Westview Press, A Member of the Perseus Books Group. Find us on the world wide web at www.westviewpress.com.

Westview Press books are available at special discounts for bulk purchases in the United States by corporations, institutions, and other organizations. For more information, please contact the Special Markets Department at the Perseus Books Group, 11 Cambridge Center, Cambridge, MA 02142, or call (617) 252-5298 or (800) 255-1514, or email special.markets@perseusbooks.com.

Library of Congress Cataloging-in-Publication Data
    Raymont, Henry.
    Troubled neighbors: the story of US–Latin American relations, from FDR
to the present / Henry Raymont.
        p.   cm.
    Includes bibliographical references and index.
    ISBN 0-8133-4303-8 (pbk. : alk. paper)
    1. Latin America—Foreign relations—United States. 2. United States—
Foreign relations—Latin America. 3. United States—Foreign relations—20th
century. 4. Latin America—Foreign relations—20th century. I. Title.
F1418.R39 2005
327.8073'09'045—dc22   2004021687

10   9   8   7   6   5   4   3   2   1

THE CENTURY FOUNDATION

The Century Foundation, formerly the Twentieth Century Fund, sponsors and supervises timely analyses of economic policy, foreign affairs, and domestic political issues. Not-for-profit and nonpartisan, it was founded in 1919 and endowed by Edward A. Filene.

CONTENTS

FOREWORD

During the second half of the twentieth century, World War II and the Cold War defined the central interests of US policy in the Americas. "Our own backyard," in this context, was an arena where our view of the world should be paramount, with other, more local considerations relegated to secondary status. From time to time, when an issue, an insurrection or a dictator forced special concern, the US response would be swift and usually heavy-handed. Roosevelt's Good Neighbor policy, Kennedy's Alliance for Progress, Bush's Enterprise for the Americas Initiative and other forward-looking enterprises sometimes seemed to offer the hope that there would be a permanent shift in approach, but all proved to be temporary. With tiresome certainty, American policy would slip back into the unfortunate mix of inattention, rigidity and occasional insistence.

Since the end of the Cold War, however, there have been significant changes in relations between the United States and its southern neighbors. Unencumbered by the potentially life-and-death imperatives of the struggle against a hostile Soviet Union, American political leaders have been eager, at least sometimes, to rebuild relationships based on questions that go far beyond the former emphasis on undermining regimes seen as too "soft on communism" and supporting those governments, whatever their other characteristics, that were staunchly pro-American. Over the same decade and a half, the movement of many of the countries of Central and South America from military or one-party rule to civilian and democratic government has made progress on broader economic and political matters more practical and likely. Overall, for the first time, widespread and enduring democracy coupled with steady and broad-based economic growth seems likely to become the norm for most nations in the Americas.

The adoption of the North American Free Trade Agreement by the United States, Canada and Mexico, of course, is the outstanding example of a breakthrough in policy of real substance. On a more rhetorical but still important front, the advocacy by both the Clinton and Bush (II) administrations of freer trade with several South American nations has signaled a possible long-term agenda for wider cooperation. Still, much of American policy toward Latin American nations can be characterized as a patchwork approach. The simple fact is that, most often, statesmen in the United States more or less intentionally want to keep the region off the list of high-priority areas.

While the relationship between the United States and its southern neighbors has been and is of considerable scholarly interest, the subject remains evergreen for attention. Geography is inescapable, and so is the shared destiny of the New World's peoples. This work, by Henry Raymont, a knowledgeable observer of the region, builds on that premise to provide fresh insights into the past and important advice about the future.

Raymont, currently a syndicated columnist for a number of Latin American papers, has been a journalist specializing in Latin American issues for five decades, first with the United Press and then with the *New York Times*. In addition, he has served as director of cultural affairs at the Organization of American States; been a senior fellow at the Joan Shorenstein Center on the Press, Politics, and Public Policy; and received a Nieman Fellowship for his reporting from Cuba.

Ultimately, the question that Raymont explores is that of leadership. He asks, in effect, given particular conditions, to what extent did each president choose to pursue constructive policies with regard to the Americas. In this sense, explanations of US policy that, for example, assert that preoccupation with Cold War concerns accounts for the behavior of this administration or that one miss a key question. For, even within the limits imposed by the particular urgencies of the global contest with the Soviet Union, there were real choices to be made, questions of emphasis, calculations of long-term interests, beliefs about what works and what does not. Strong leadership in foreign policy, Raymont would argue, can change the calculus of the possible, reshape the public (and media) agenda and overcome the forces of the status quo and the resistance of partisan opposition.

The fact that leadership and competence matter may seem a commonplace observation. But, in these times of relative political timidity, it is a point well worth remaking. Moreover, presenting solid evidence of the abiding significance of policymakers, as Raymont's book does, provides an important reminder that we have the right to hold them accountable. In other words, our leaders, our nation and our neighbors are not in the grip of uncontrollable international forces. We can do much to shape our common destiny.

This book adds to The Century Foundation's long-standing interest in American foreign policy. It is a major contribution to our list of studies of

Latin America, which includes such landmark books from the late 1960s and early 1970s as Albert O. Hirschman's *Journeys Toward Progress: Studies of Economic Policy-Making in Latin America* and Jerome Levinson and Juan de Onis's *The Alliance That Lost Its Way: A Critical Report on the Alliance for Progress*, as well as our series on Latin American debt in the mid-1980s and studies of individual nations in the region over the next two decades, including Lincoln Gordon's *Brazil's Second Chance: En Route Toward the First World*. It also meshes with our examinations of democracy and the making of foreign policy in such studies as Tony Smith's *America's Mission*, Walter Russell Mead's *Special Providence: American Foreign Policy and How It Changed the World*, Henry Nau's *At Home Abroad: Identity and Power in American Foreign Policy*, Robert Art's *A Grand Strategy for America* and Kathryn Sikkink's *Mixed Signals: U.S. Human Rights Policy and Latin America*.

On behalf of the Trustees of The Century Foundation, I thank Raymont for his thoughtful description of US–Latin American affairs. His insights into how American policy choices have shaped those relations is a special contribution to our understanding of these matters.

Richard C. Leone, President
The Century Foundation

PROLOGUE

Our first and fundamental maxim should be, never to engage ourselves in the broils of Europe. Our second, never to suffer Europe to
intermeddle with cis-Atlantic affairs. *America, North and South, has a
set of interests distinct from those of Europe, and peculiarly her own.* She
should therefore have a system of her own, separate and apart from
that of Europe. While the last is laboring to become the domicile of
despotism, our endeavor should surely be, to make our hemisphere
that of freedom.

THOMAS JEFFERSON, LETTER TO PRESIDENT MONROE,
OCTOBER 24, 1823 (EMPHASIS ADDED)

Rarely have two consecutive periods of US foreign relations been more
starkly delineated than the decade of hemispheric friendship generated by
President Franklin D. Roosevelt's Good Neighbor policy toward Latin America
and its subsequent erosion as succeeding administrations became absorbed by
the Cold War. Indeed, never have successive US administrations been so consistent in squandering such a reservoir of goodwill. Yet the story of the unraveling of US–Latin American ties, beginning almost immediately after FDR's
death, has received very little attention in our time.

Since the end of World War II, Roosevelt has been hailed as the architect of
the New Deal and a great wartime leader. But historians and even some of his
most notable biographers have shown little interest in the legacy of the Good
Neighbor policy, a neglect that is all the more surprising when one considers
the importance FDR accorded it, how vivid an imprint that policy left south of
the border and the abundant Latin American sources that remained untapped.

There is a plausible reason for this neglect: the prevailing theme of inter-American relations during the postwar years was one of tragedy—missed opportunities, divergent perceptions, unrequited friendship, errors and misconceptions. It was not testimony to creative policy. The Cold War swung the US foreign policy focus away from the principles of the Good Neighbor, subordinating the idealistic goal of spreading democracy to the pragmatic decision of fighting communism, by any means. That resulted in the often counterproductive tendency to succor autocratic regimes as a handy political expedient in the increasingly dirty war to contain "Sino-Soviet expansion."

To Latin Americans their abrupt displacement from postwar US strategic cosmology was stunning, the more given that the region had been at the core of FDR's foreign policy. It most certainly was not what Latin America had envisioned: the end of the war was to have been a moment for the American republics to celebrate the restoration of the Good Neighbor to the core of US foreign policy so that the hemispheric community could jointly face the uncertainties of the postwar era. The unsung demise of FDR's reforms is one of the most futile, self-defeating chapters of US diplomatic history. My experiences and observations as a journalist reporting from Latin America and Washington on the state of inter-American relations for almost half a century, roughly corresponding to the period under review, leads me to conclude that these years deserve closer examination. Apart from the drama and romance, the tragedy and pathos, the unraveling of the Good Neighbor offers a textbook example of what Harvard economist John D. Montgomery describes as "the tarnished outcome" of US foreign policy initiatives containing "traces of US idealism." However, "the follow through was deplorably inadequate" and "indifference again succeeded noble beginnings."[1]

The Roosevelt era was unparalleled in taking hemispheric relations to the most constructive level in the twentieth century. The relationship between 1933 and 1945 indicates that when the United States applies thoughtful diplomacy to hemispheric affairs and uses multilateral institutions to promote democracy, US and Latin American interests are well served. The question today is, Is the inter-American system still viable, and does it serve US interests in a post–Cold War world?

Current Latin American attitudes and policies reflect the historical forces that formed them. The statecraft, learned over a period of more than a century, first through the Pan American movement, then the inter-American system, offers important precedents and lessons. How early must collective measures be used to contain a government that threatens its neighbors or commits human rights violations? How wise is a policy of economic sanctions and/or military force, even if it is approved by a multinational body? How can we minimize miscalculation and misperception? Can international and regional organizations take the place of traditional balance-of-power politics? This book attempts to overcome Washington's chronic tendency to overlook its own best antecedents.

A reappraisal of many events and public figures in US–Latin American relations is in order. Few, if any, of the recent popular biographies of US presidents even mention Latin America. By contrast, this work makes an effort to bring a Latin American perspective to the assessment of the presidencies that followed Roosevelt's. Thus, some statesmen we have been taught to respect will appear in these pages in sorry roles, whereas some neglected personalities were quite important from a Latin American vantage point. Josephus Daniels, Roosevelt's ambassador to Mexico, was important for his steadfast advocacy of nonintervention in opposition to Sumner Welles's conventional "Big Stick" diplomacy in Cuba; George Kennan was extremely persuasive in warning against the communist threat to Latin America and overwhelmed such State Department specialists as Louis Halle, who struggled to keep alive the Good Neighbor policy and pleaded with Truman to address the region's postwar social and economic distress; Brazilian President Juscelino Kubitschek's 1958 hemispheric development plan, Operation Pan America, was an imaginative "wake-up call" to restore hemispheric cooperation, which, had Washington been more cooperative, might well have forestalled the anti-American sentiment that a year later rallied around the Cuban revolution.

Events such as the Chapultepec, Rio de Janeiro, Bogota and Punta del Este conferences, which were major building blocks in the construction of the inter-American system, are not covered extensively in this volume because they are dealt with elsewhere. Nor do issues and events in Latin America that by and large conformed to the East–West perspective that animated Washington and caught the attention of the media and scholarship require detailed treatment here. In the case of hemispheric events that achieved global significance, such as the Cuban missile crisis of October 1962, the Falkland/Malvinas war of 1982 and President Reagan's Central American policy and the invasions of Grenada and Panama, an abundance of memoirs and strategic analyses are now available. They are, therefore, treated here only chronologically and in less detail than they deserve.

This work may indicate some of the conditions necessary to provide more effective, viable policy alternatives and stimulate a wider debate on US–Latin American relations. Is it desirable and feasible for Washington to recover the Good Neighbor spirit and modernize and revitalize the inter-American system? Is it in the mutual interest of the United States and Latin America?

The discrepancies between doctrine and practice in US policy toward Latin America deserve attention, perhaps because they are not greatly different from the discrepancies that prevail in international relations as a whole. To illustrate these divergences takes only a comparison between the ritualistic protestations of Latin American fraternity and regional unity as they disappear when they clash with national interests. But most importantly, we must address the question of what makes Latin America such a difficult, elusive subject for the United States to understand. The North American Free Trade Agreement (NAFTA) and other economic relations draw the United States and Latin America ever more together, but the awareness of historical and cultural commonalities lags far behind. The arguments underscoring the importance of a regional market in terms of trade and investments have recently received much media attention. Future relations might be greatly enhanced if our appreciation of our neighbors went beyond immediate objectives.

A reassessment of hemispheric relations is especially significant at this juncture, when a new political topography suggests a world organized not so much by antagonistic ideologies as by the emergence of economic blocs, such as NAFTA, the European Union and a Pacific Rim dominated by Japan. With a younger, more vigorous leadership and a concerted effort to reform the Organization of American States (OAS) as well as national governments across the hemisphere, we are approaching the twenty-first century as a time of promise and uncertainty not unlike the 1930s, when all the American republics, the United States included, were in the midst of great flux and renewal.

Henry Raymont

NOTE

1. John D. Montgomery, *Aftermath: Tarnished Outcomes of American Foreign Policy* (Dover, Mass.: Auburn House, 1986), p. xii.

ACKNOWLEDGMENTS

Newspaper writers, particularly those who learn the trade in the trenches of the wire services, can pound out at least half a dozen stories in less than half a day. So when I first approached what was then called the Twentieth Century Fund and promised to have the book ready in "a year, if not before that," I received a knowing smile from the Fund's then director, Murray Rossant, a former financial writer I had met when we both worked at the *New York Times*. He went on to say, "Better give yourself a little more time—books are different from daily journalism." Almost twenty years later, I must thank Murray for his advice, as well as thank his successor, Richard C. Leone, the current president of The Century Foundation; a procession of editors; and a long list of my own family members and friends who were unflagging in their encouragement.

My wife Wendy was amazingly stalwart in her trust in me, and our children, Daniel, Sarah, and Adam, helped with taunts that at the present pace the book might be finished "when we become grandparents." Putting "finis" to the book manuscript was not exactly helped by my daily newspaper column in Spanish or my teaching a course on US–Latin American relations at the Freie Universitaet in Berlin. In fact, there was a well-founded suspicion abroad that some of that activity was undertaken precisely to ward off completing the book.

That said, I hasten to recognize how greatly indebted I am to Jason Renker, my most recent editor at The Century Foundation, who has so diligently improved my tenses and smoothed out Latinate words where Anglo synonyms were available. I am also thankful that Westview Press decided to publish the book.

I should particularly stress my debt to Beverly Goldberg, the director of publications at The Century Foundation, and to Arthur M. Schlesinger, Jr., a member of the board, who never faltered in their trust that at the end of the road there would be a valuable book on Latin America, an area that receives little enough attention from the US mainstream.

And a few lifelong friends who thoughtfully cajoled and prodded to get the manuscript off the drawing board—the late Paul Hirsch and Arturo Frondizi of Buenos Aires, and Ambassador Felipe Seixas Correa and his wife Marilu. Similarly, my conservative friend, Allan Gerson, and Tad Szulc, my colleague in the four corners of the globe, first at the United Press and then at the *New York Times* and eventually our neighbor in Washington. Also, Daniel Samper and Carlos Fuentes, who have brightened both journalism and the literary scene of Latin America with their sardonic humor and uncompromising criticism.

My appreciation also to the inspiration and friendship of Jorge Batlle, the former president of Uruguay; Celso Lafer, Gabriel Valdes Subercasseaux, and Oscar Camilion, former foreign ministers of Brazil, Chile, and Argentina, respectively; Ambassadors Carlos Portales of Chile, and Enrique Cantoni of Argentina, the dean of the Latin American envoys in Berlin; Samuel Lewis Navarro, the foreign minister of Panama, and his late father, Gabriel Lewis Galindo.

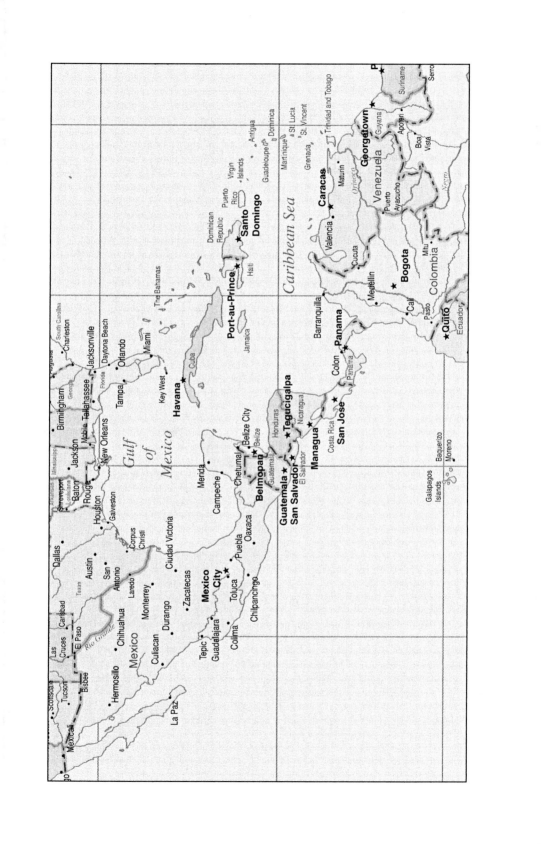

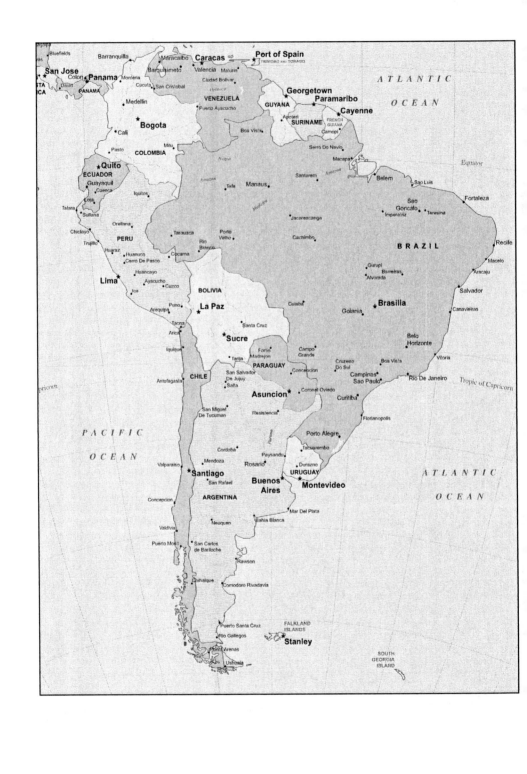

Chapter One

INTRODUCTION

Misunderstanding of the present is the inevitable consequence of ignorance of the past. But a man may wear himself out just as fruitlessly in
seeking to understand the past, if he is totally ignorant of the present.

MARC BLOCH, 1942

The societies that cannot combine reverence toward their symbols
with freedom of revision, must ultimately decay either from anarchy,
or from slow atrophy of a life stifled by useless shadows.

ALFRED NORTH WHITEHEAD

The history of relations between the United States and Latin America is
marked by contradictions and an erratic course. US policy on the one
hand has been described as idealistic, the reflection of a benign nation willing
to share its democratic experiment with the rest of the world, and on the other
hand as seeking to impose on its neighbors to the south some of the colonial
policies it has repudiated since the time of the Revolutionary War.

Latin America continues to be a singularly elusive, perplexing subject for
US policymakers. In five decades of reporting on inter-American affairs, the
question I have encountered most frequently and puzzled over most often is,
Why does Latin America seem to be such an impenetrable subject in the
United States? Or, to put it another way, why has Latin America been considered such a marginal subject by practically every administration in Washington
after Franklin Delano Roosevelt? Sometimes the question is aired in ceremonial speeches by a momentarily puzzled secretary of state and a few ritual

newspaper editorials in the midst of a crisis; more often it is repeated by frustrated Latin American leaders.

The much reiterated thesis that the New World was scattered geographically and developed by two predominant and rival cultures—Iberian Roman Catholicism and northwest European Protestantism—should not obscure, as it frequently does, its common characteristics and the unity of force it exerted on the rest of the world. When differences become overdrawn, it is useful to remember the origins of those settling the New World, as simply described by the Colombian historian German Arciniegas: "The peoples of the Americas were commoners—plain Perezes in the Hispano-Indian colonies, plain Smiths in the English. Europeans who had been docile vassals in Europe emigrated to America as bold adventurers."

Was not post-Columbian America settled by people seeking new frontiers and status in a hemisphere free of the oppressiveness of the old order? Did not both North and South America wage fierce wars to free themselves from the royal autocrats of Europe? Is not a measure of the New World's identity the convergence of Indo-American, European, African and Asian cultures that produced the American miracle?

Aside from certain elements derived from the traditional Amerindian societies, Latin America's social institutions, cultural values and norms and economic and political systems have been fundamentally Western in character. With these antecedents, there came to be a New World version of Western civilization, best characterized by the hemisphere's unique mestizo culture. A sense of our New World commonalities was shared, if sometimes tenuously, by the founding fathers of the United States and the Latin American patriots alike. Clearly the experiences of the United States and Latin America over the past two centuries have an abundance of differences and divergences. But they also have enough similarities as New World nations to require a more balanced view about one another, a sense of proportion and context that makes comparison fruitful and exciting.

And yet since World War II, when the two halves of the hemisphere confronted each other in international forums, it has become increasingly evident that they have almost ceased to communicate. As recently as the 1980s, Washington and most Latin American capitals held differing views on everything from Central America to Cuba, from the foreign debt, illegal drug traffic and immigration to the invasions of Grenada and Panama and the role of the OAS. For years hemispheric divergences were so frequent that they were considered normal relations. This is tragic in view of the period of friendship and cooperation that preceded the Cold War and was haltingly revived by John Kennedy.

Those old enough to remember the presidency of Franklin D. Roosevelt from 1933 to 1945 know that there can be convergence, that differences and divergences are not inexorable but tend to be cyclical and that they need not always dominate US–Latin American relations. Roosevelt's Good Neighbor policy was unparalleled in taking hemispheric relations to the most constructive level in this century. It fashioned an unprecedented regional alliance recalling the unifying vision of Simón Bolívar and the democratic convictions of the founding fathers that there is something distinctive about the way of life and the ideals of the societies this side of the Atlantic. A whole new spirit of cooperation sprang into being. For the first time in a hundred years hemispheric solidarity actually existed.

But, as often seems to happen in history, every golden age is finite, followed by decline and, hopefully, resurrection. World War II had barely ended, just weeks after FDR's death, when the Cold War began and the Good Neighbor policy was cast aside by the zeal with which Roosevelt's successors, beginning with Harry S. Truman, turned the containment of communism on a global scale into the exclusive priority of US foreign policy.

Having accepted Washington's official wartime rhetoric about inter-American "friendship and cooperation" as a genuine sentiment, perhaps mistaking a spiritual goal for a geopolitical reality, Latin Americans reacted restlessly and with dismay at Washington's postwar tendency to dismiss them as practically irrelevant to the East-West power equation. True, Latin Americans had not suffered the devastation of World War II; nonetheless, their frustration was understandable. During a time of unchallenged US supremacy, Washington possessed the leverage to push for democratic reform rather than deal with opportunistic dictatorships. And a small fraction of Marshall aid might have been applied with great profit to meet Latin America's looming economic and social problems.

During the 1950s, as Latin America was battling the effects of a worldwide recession and a gathering storm of social discontent, ancient anti-US attitudes enlivened the political scene. There was widespread resentment over the fact that while the Eisenhower administration devoted enormous economic resources to counter communism in Europe and Asia, in Latin America the primary emphasis was on lecturing fiscal conservatism. A *New York Times* survey reflecting the prevailing mood in 1956 recognized that

> Latin Americans feel slighted because they consider themselves neglected economically and point out bitterly that this fiscal year the Eisenhower Administration has earmarked only $96,000,000 for the region compared to nearly $5 billion asked for global aid. . . . On the political side nationalism is

producing noticeable restiveness in regard to United States' leadership and there is much talk these days about ending economic and political dependence on the "Colossus of the North.[1]

By early 1958, it could have been foretold with mathematical certainty that if Washington failed to respond to democratic stirring and economic grievances across the region, the hemispheric solidarity that had prevailed during World War II would be in mortal danger. Latin America was now looking for urgent remedies, preferably in cooperation with the United States but no longer in awe of Washington's latest word. Had it not been for Washington's obdurate indifference, the deterioration of the hemispheric relationship would have been neither so acute nor irreversible. Cuba's spiteful embrace of communism might have been averted.

The stage had been set, unnecessarily, for confrontation by two blocs, of which one would turn to a Third World strategy and the other to the industrialized nations; both seemed prepared to forgo an inter-American system that had been in the making since 1898. Few events in hemispheric history have made a deeper impression on contemporaries or on posterity than the striking reluctance of postwar US administrations to respond to Latin America's appeals for greater attention in terms of political influence and economic needs.

Consequently, hemispheric solidarity faded fast and with it the importance of hemispheric alliance. The inter-American system, once confidently hailed as a model for the free world, no longer offered viable solutions to the hemisphere's profound political, economic and social problems. Instead, it became the object of derision. Not long ago, a Mexican foreign minister and Nobel Prize laureate called the regional system "a disgrace to the memory of Bolívar." In the United States, a former undersecretary of state said the regional alliance was "obsolete" and suggested that Washington consider withdrawing from the OAS.

During the four decades I spent in Washington, where I arrived in the final year of the Truman administration in 1951, I encountered an intellectual climate indifferent to Latin America, in sharp contrast to the preceding decades. Even the most intelligent internationalists, when talking about Latin America, sounded much like Isaiah Berlin's description of certain British attitudes: "there generally is something curiously remote and abstract about their ideas."

When these internationalists think about the neighbor republics at all, they think of them in terms of their treatment by the United States and Europe and discuss them "as wards or victims, but seldom if ever in their own right, as peoples with histories and cultures of their own; with a past and present and future which must be understood in terms of their own actual character and circumstances." The price that is paid for this treatment—spiritually, intellectually and politically—cannot be overestimated. That is what Gabriel García Márquez meant in his Nobel Prize speech when he said: "The interpretation of our reality through patterns not our own serves only to make us ever more unknown, ever less free, ever more solitary."

Yet the founding fathers of the US republic, just as much as the independence leaders of Latin America, predicated their struggle on the conviction of the New World's uniqueness—that it was something new in geography, history, experience and people that separated republican America from monarchical Europe. In the general way of life there was less to differentiate North Americans from Latin Americans, compared to the differences between the monarchies of the Old World and the republics of the new. One needs only roam the streets of any major US city today to realize how Latin American culture is permeating US society, from what we read and eat and listen to the barrios of New York, Los Angeles, San Antonio, Chicago, Washington and Boston.

The more I ponder the inconsistencies and misunderstandings that have marked US–Latin American relations during the past half century, the deeper it seems to me the mystery of something like a mental block that keeps Latin America outside the US weltanschauung. The contradiction of their uniqueness as siblings of the New World, compared to other regions, on the one hand, and of a curious tendency to obscure commonalities by belittling their importance and stressing divergences, on the other, is startling.

There is a strange historical irony here. In the first century of their independence, and again in the Roosevelt era, the United States and Latin America defined their identity partly, if not mainly, by affirming that they were not Europe. But during the postwar years the US–Latin American dialogue became so estranged that each was casting not the Old World but the other as a negative reference point. This is one of the great anachronisms of our time and deserves closer examination.

It is therefore useful to remember that exclusion of and divergences with Latin America were not always the rule in US–Latin American relations. During World War II and the early years of the Cold War, most Latin American governments supported Washington on every major foreign policy issue. The US global agenda was accepted, if at times grudgingly, in the name of hemispheric solidarity.

To understand current Latin American attitudes and preoccupations, we must understand the forces that have shaped them. Since independence, Latin America's quest for self-identity has taken place mostly in the form of a constant dialogue with the United States. As Octavio Paz put it: "The US image is always present among us, even when it ignores us or turns its back to us; its shadow covers the entire continent." Under the impact of every new phase in their shared history—frontier, colonial, independence, civil war, manifest destiny, the Big Stick policy, dollar diplomacy, the Good Neighbor policy, Peronism—the peoples of Latin America and the United States set about reinterpreting the meaning of their existence and the mystery of their fate.

The idea of hemispheric cooperation continues to exert far from negligible appeal in Latin America, especially in an era of economic interdependence that no country can hope to face in isolation.

NOTE

1. Tad Szulc, "Latin Nationalism Challenges Policy of U.S., Survey Shows," *New York Times*, April 13, 1956, p. 6.

Chapter Two

THE PAST AS PROLOGUE
The Old World's Vision of the New

En general el américano está hecho para sufrir en silencio los desdenes del europeo. . . . Así, amigos de Europa, no hay por que alarmarse ante las novedades de América, que también tienen su vejez.
[As a rule, the Americas are sentenced to suffer in silence the disdain of the European. . . . So, my European friends, there is no need for alarm in the face of America's novelties, which are also ancient history.]

ALFONSO REYES[1]

La libertad del Nuevo Mundo es la esperanza del Universo.
[The New World's freedom is the hope of the universe.]

SIMÓN BOLÍVAR

Amerika, du hast es besser
Als unser Kontinent, das alte. . . .
Dich stört nicht im Innern,
Zur lebendiger Zeit,
Unnützes Erinnern
Und vergeblicher Streit.
Benutzt die Gegenwart mit Glück!
[America, you're better off than
our Continent, the old one. . . .
You have no inner qualms,
to distract vital time with
useless Memories
And vain strife.
Utilize the Present with felicity!]

JOHANN WOLFGANG VON GOETHE, *Faust*

Latin America is the only one of the world's great subdivisions where the human being is still entirely human. . . . The South American continent may prove some day to be the last repository and custodian of humane Christian values that men in the European motherlands and in North America—overfed, overorganized, and blinded by fear and ambition—have thrown away.

GEORGE KENNAN, *Memoirs*

The history of US–Latin American relations since the New World colonies emancipated themselves from the European monarchies in the late eighteenth and early nineteenth centuries shifts uneasily from moments of lyrical friendship to long stretches of acrimony and misunderstandings. It is a history that can be treated as the history of New World self-awareness, applying equally to both halves of the hemisphere: every change in the socioeconomic and political-cultural constellation would give rise to another version of the New World phenomenon.

Nonetheless, one of the most persistent questions heard these days in the northern and southern halves of the Western Hemisphere is, What do we have in common? The obvious and immediate reply is, both belong to the New World. If one common denominator was more powerful than any other, it was that the American continent was not Europe but something new in history, in people, new in nature and in experience.

Since independence two profoundly rooted but conflicting strains have existed in the way North Americans view their neighbors to the south—as siblings born of the same New World roots or as an alien culture brought to the hemisphere by a decadent, imperial Spain in opposition to the progressive, virtuous, Anglo-American north. Sometimes these two strains battle each other in the same North American breast; more often large segments of opinion lean decisively one way or another, with the result that each strain has had its period (or periods) of ascendancy in US public life.

Ambivalence and uncertainty have plagued the hemisphere since Christopher Columbus sailed into the Caribbean in 1492 and thought he was in Asia. "It seemed to me that these people are very poor in everything," he wrote to the Spanish sovereigns of the indigenous tribes he encountered on the island he named Hispaniola. And yet elsewhere in his diaries Columbus describes them as "gentle, kind and guileless."

Deeply embedded prejudices have conspired to keep Latin America remote from the US intellectual mainstream. School textbooks used in the United States may have something to do with it; until very recently, many of the standard textbooks used in the United States depicted Spain and Spanish influence in the New World as something undesirable, reflecting ancient Anglo-Saxon antipathies toward "obscurantist" Spanish colonialism and holding it responsible for the region's "backwardness." For example, the enduring popular edition of Julian Hawthorne's turn-of-century history of the United States contains such gems as "whatever Spain has done in America has, from the first, been evil," and "The Mexicans were a semi-barbarous people, with whom no civilized association was possible; they were a cross between Spaniards and Aztec Indians, combining the least attractive features of both."[2] Additionally, many US textbooks tend to deal with history as if it were a European invention. From that perspective, anything that is not northern European or its direct, unspoiled offspring is exotic.

With few exceptions, textbook writers do not know how to handle Latin America in the scheme of world history or even their own national history. As a result, the region often rates only an aside. Nevertheless a series of images has become fixed. When dealing with ancient times there is an appreciation of the rich pre-Columbian civilizations of Mesoamerica and Peru; a far less objective and benign treatment is accorded to the Spanish conquest and colonial period, leading to the popular, simplistic interpretation that after independence Latin America became a relic of Spanish feudalism, violent and fractious, bypassed by modernity and progress and lacking in intellectual accomplishment.

The Latin American version of the region's identity has produced its own biases, ranging from conservative criticism that juxtaposes Spain's "spirituality" with Anglo-Saxon "materialism" to liberal denunciations of the absence of democracy in the Spanish heritage. Many Spanish and Latin American historians tend to characterize the Anglo-American colonies as the heartland of "primacy and heresy," of godlessness and imperial pretensions. More thoughtfully, Mexican historian Leopoldo Zea has pointed out that Latin America, in its attempts to reject Europe and seek an original identity, placed itself outside history. "The Spanish and Portuguese colonies in America were a part of that [European] past. The peoples who emerged from them were tainted with the sin of belonging to a bygone stage of history."[3]

Conversely, few in the United States, Howard Mumford Jones reminds us, realize to what extent their history "lies in the sunlight or shadow of the Renaissance and Spain." Spanish was the first European language spoken in what today is the United States in 1513, when Ponce de León discovered, baptized and explored Florida, or La Florida. During the following half century, other such noted Spaniards as Alvar Núñez Cabeza de Vaca, Hernando de Soto and Francisco Vásquez de Coronado arrived on the North American coast and explored and colonized the south, southwest and west of the United States. During the seventeenth, eighteenth and nineteenth centuries more than 1,500 cities and missions were founded, which still have their Spanish names. The names of Arizona, California, Colorado, Florida, Montana, Nevada, New Mexico, Oregon and Texas reveal their Spanish origins and underscore the Spanish component in US history.

"The Portuguese influence was least, the Spanish influence the richest, the English influence the most immediate of these formative contacts," writes Jones.

> Historians have abandoned notions prevalent in the nineteenth century that the Spanish Empire in the New World was the product of cruel, unenlightened, lazy, or ineffectual men, albeit there were cruel, unenlightened, lazy and ineffectual Spaniards, including some highly placed officials. The Spaniards invented a system of colonial administration unparalleled since the days of ancient Rome; in religion they launched the most sweeping missionary movement since the Germanic tribes accepted Christianity; and in the matter of race relations, though the Indians were unquestionably exploited and occasionally so oppressed that they rose in bloody rebellion against their conquerors, the Spanish government, in harmony with the church, adopted a theory, and often succeeded in practicing a policy more enlightened than that of any other European power except Portugal.[4]

Nonetheless, few regions in the world seem to pose more confusion, frustration, periodic hope and despair and sheer perplexity to US policymakers than its neighbors to the south. But as long as US policymakers, blinkered by enduring Hispanophobic clichés, see Latin America primarily in terms of incompetence, corruption and disregard for the sanctity of life and private property, they are, perhaps unconsciously, also depriving the region of cultural property.

Beginning with Columbus's fabulous accounts of his encounters with the "Indians" and the exotic flora and fauna of the Western Hemisphere, European chroniclers assiduously wrote down their observations. Nevertheless, they were, in the words of one scholar, "prisoners of their ecological lexicons." John Elliott's description of the psychological confusion provoked by the first encounters between the Old and New Worlds suggests the problems that have continued to distort cross-cultural communication to this day:

Their [European] minds and imaginations were pre-conditioned so that they saw what they expected to see, and ignored or rejected those features of life in the southern lands for which they were mentally unprepared. They found (because they expected to find) the inhabitants barbarian and ape-like and the tropical landscape unalluring. No doubt the tendency to think in cliches is the eternal hallmark of the official mind. . . . For the obstacles to the incorporation of the New World within Europe's intellectual horizons were formidable.[5]

Incidents in the New World, such as those recounted in Peter Martyr's *Decades,* Las Casas's *Brief Account of the Destruction of the Indies* (first published in Spain in 1552) and Girolamo Benzoni's racy *History of the New World* (issued in Venice in 1565), provided new images on which national and religious hatreds could thrive. Horrific illustrations in the Dutch artist Theodore de Bry's new editions of Las Casas at the end of the century stamped an indelible image of Spanish atrocities on the European consciousness—just as Drake's atrocities entered the collective mentality of the Castilians. The propaganda warfare between the rival imperial powers of Europe had reached proportions close to the more refined disinformation skills of the twentieth century. "Against propaganda warfare on this scale," writes Elliott,

Spain's official chronicler of the Indies could offer no more than feeble resistance. A weapon had been forged in those years of European crisis which would render invaluable service to generations of enemies of Spain. The suffering of the Indians even figured in the pamphlet campaign of the Catalans against the tyrannical government of Olivares in the revolt of 1640, and it was in Barcelona that Las Casas received the accolade of his first Spanish reprint, in 1646. For the first time in European history, the colonial record of an imperial power was being systematically used against it by its enemies.[6]

With time, the national contests became secularized. Nationalistic fervor, that contagious hysteria of all nineteenth-century Western society, gave it a far wider currency than it had ever before enjoyed. The United States survived the Civil War, which to many appeared as evidence that the "experiment" of American nationhood had been successfully completed.

To a remarkable degree, the distorted interpretation of New World phenomena of five centuries ago intrudes into much of what is written about Latin America today. Many Latin Americans, and the handful of US officials and scholars concerned with hemispheric affairs, blame the press for deforming the region's image by concentrating mainly on crises and disasters and failing to give a balanced picture. Yet it hardly could have been otherwise, since much of the reporting reflects dominant US cultural assumptions about the neighbor republics: we are success, they are failure. Frank Tannenbaum, the father of Latin American studies at Columbia University, put it candidly when he wrote:

> The most serious of our [US] difficulties is the treatment of Latin Americans as inferiors. . . . Our difficulties with Latin America are not merely economic and political. They are moral. We treat the Latin Americans as lesser people. We cannot help ourselves and we cannot conceal our feeling. Latin Americans sense it in every gesture and attitude, even when we are condescendingly egalitarian.[7]

The obstacles to mutual understanding have not changed much since the voyages of Columbus or the virulent racism of Corneille DePauw in the eighteenth century. Abbott DePauw, the man Benjamin Franklin charitably called "ill-informed and malignant," wrote, "Europeans who had migrated to America had visibly degenerated. Through the whole extent of America, *from Cape Horn to Hudson Bay,* there has never appeared a philosopher, an artist, a man of learning" (emphasis added). Unflattering European views of America continued well into the nineteenth century as monarchists and conservatives feared that the New World's experiment in democracy would contaminate the Old and result in anarchy and chaos. Certainly there is a burden of proof on the New World that does not apply to the Old.

In 1826, the great satirist Sidney Smith, writing in the respected *Edinburgh Review,* asked these mordant questions about the United States: "In the four quarters of the globe, who reads an American book? Or goes to an American play? or looks at an American picture or statue? What does the world yet owe to American physicians or surgeons?" Rather than openly find fault with the American democracy, which English conservatives detested, he reminded Americans that their intellectual achievements were nil and that the world owed them little in those domains where civilized people generally tried to excel. The barb was meant to wound; it did. Today, European bookstores, theaters, opera houses, museums and hospitals are the best testimony to refute him, DePauw and the other detractors of the New World's incipient vitality and creativity!

In the meantime, however, the disparaging European clichés and barbs caused great mischief, not the least because of the disconcerting psychological impact such demeaning portraits have on their subjects. Daniel Boorstin recognizes this when he writes, "Our intellectual insecurity, our feeling of philosophical inadequacy, may be explained at least in part by our failure to understand ourselves. This failure is due in some measure by our readiness to accept European clichés about us."[8]

When postwar Washington strategists remitted Latin America to a new category known as "developing countries" (a diplomatic euphemism invented to replace the term "underdeveloped countries") along with Africa and Asia, they pointedly disregarded the fact that for almost five centuries the region had been an integral part of Western civilization. For generations the accepted political context for the Latin American republics had been the Western Hemisphere; they were perhaps the weaker members of an inter-American alliance they shared with the United States, but partners with equal rights nonetheless. Then, almost immediately after World War II, they were unceremoniously removed from their historical moorings and dispatched into a new category with not only economic but also geopolitical and ethical connotations. Perhaps it is even a natural development—or an exquisite irony in history—that the United States should today bestow on Latin America some of the same reckless clichés it had to endure from conservative Europeans, even though time has proven them to be nothing but prejudice and direful nonsense. Unquestionably, in great measure the negative attitudes that exist in the United States about Latin America can be traced back to the pervasive influence of Britain with its ingrained biases against the Spanish empire of the sixteenth and seventeenth centuries. Edward Hayes, advancing a rival imperial English vision of the world, in his narrative of 1583 describing Sir Humphrey Gilbert's last voyage, argued that "the countreys lying north of Florida, God hath reserved the same to be reduced unto Christian civility by the English nation." This, he thought, was made "very probable by the revolution and cause of God's word and religion, which from the beginning hath moved from the East, towards, and at last unto the West where it is like to end."

By the closing decades of the sixteenth century it was clear that the Spaniards were not the only people in the world to cherish the vision of a mission, and an empire, in the west. Even during the subsequent centuries after the New World patriots had sundered the shackles of colonialism, opinions about the fate and place of the Americas in the world continued to be sharply divided.

Simón Bolívar's vision of the Americas as united, independent and democratic where the noblest aspirations of humanity would find their fullest expression was shared by Henry Clay's proposal for an "American League." Other US statesmen, having inherited England's Black Legend about the abuses of the Spanish empire, were contemptuous of Latin America's Spanish heritage. However, when Bolívar convened the Amphictyonic Congress of Panama in 1826, the US delegates, mindful that in Washington there was no desire to undertake international commitments while the nation was still seeking to consolidate, failed to arrive.

In an early example of diverse goals and visions of inter-American relations, when Secretary of State James G. Blaine convened the First International Conference of American States in 1889, half a century after the Panama convocation, his approach was fundamentally different from Bolívar's grandiose "amphictyonic" plans modeled after the leagues established by the Greek states to guard their common spiritual, religious and security interests. Instead, the conference, held in Washington, dealt essentially with problems of commerce and transportation, aside from the subject of arbitration of international disputes, a burning contemporary issue. Blaine in effect set the tone of future US approaches to inter-American relations: it was to be focused on practical propositions such as defense and trade, generally leaving unattended Latin American aspirations for a more equal and relevant political partnership with the United States.

In the more romantic spirit of the independence struggles, the prescient Jefferson, observing events in Latin America, wrote to his friend, the distinguished German philosopher-scientist and Latin American expert Alexander von Humboldt:

> But in whatever governments they will end, they will be American governments, no longer to be involved in the never ceasing broils of Europe. . . . America has a hemisphere to itself. It must have its separate system of interests which must not be subordinated to those of Europe. The insulated state in which nature has placed the American continent, should so far avail that no spark of war kindled in the other quarters of the globe should be wafted across the wide oceans which separate us from them and it will be so.[9]

The doctrine of the two spheres was stated with Jefferson's characteristic lucidity and eloquence. It echoed the Bolivarian belief in a common interest among the recently independent nations of the Western Hemisphere. Both men assumed that there is something distinctive about the way of life and the ideals of the countries on this side of the Atlantic. But this vision would soon be challenged by narrower parochial interests, both in Latin America and the United States. In Latin America the unifying spirit of the *libertadores* was challenged by local caudillos, who cleverly turned popular revolt against Spanish centralism into suspicion against their neighbors across the newly drawn national boundaries.

In the United States, the two poles—continentalism versus seclusion—were best represented by Henry Clay and John Quincy Adams. Henry Clay of Kentucky, the speaker of the House of Representatives, was one of the earliest and the most outspoken advocates of an American alliance with the United Provinces of the Río de la Plata, which had achieved independence by 1812. He hectored the House into granting them early recognition, animated by an American feeling and guided by an American policy. They would obey the laws of the system of the New World, of which they would compose a part, in distinction to that of Europe. "At the present moment," he told the House,

> the patriots of the south are fighting for liberty and independence—for precisely what we fought for . . . the moral influence of such a recognition, on the patriots of the South, will be irresistible. . . . Of us they speak as of brothers having a similar origin. They adopt our principles, copy our institutions, and, in many instances, employ the very language and sentiments of our revolutionary papers.[10]

However Clay's oratory may have stirred the House, it was not convincing enough, and his plea for recognition was effectively blocked by the more moderate and global views of Secretary of State Adams, his eventual rival for the presidency. The motion on recognition was defeated by 115 votes to 45. Still, recognition came in 1822, and by 1889 the First International American Conference in Washington launched the movement known as Pan Americanism, the forerunner of the inter-American system founded at the Inter-American Conference at Bogotá in 1948, which adopted the Charter of the Organization of American States.

After the Latin American independence movement asserted itself without US help, Adams gave a remarkably candid explanation of his dilatory stance to Clay:

> I have never doubted that the final issue of their [the revolted provinces] present struggle will be their entire independence of Spain. It is equally clear that it is our true policy and duty to take no part in the contest. . . . So far as they are contending for independence, I wish well to their cause; but I have

not yet seen and do not now see any prospect that they will establish free or liberal institutions of government. . . . They have not the first elements of good or free government. Arbitrary power, military and ecclesiastical, is stamped upon their education, upon their habits, and upon all their institutions.[11]

Writing in 1820, three years before the Monroe Doctrine, Adams said,

The political system of the United States is . . . extra-European. To stand in firm and cautious independence of all entanglement in the European system, has been a cardinal point of their policy under every administration of their government from the peace of 1783 to this day. . . . It may be observed that for the repose of Europe as well as of America, the European and American political systems should be kept as separate and distinct from each other as possible.[12]

The differences between Clay and Adams offer an interesting antecedent to two conflicting currents in US policy toward Latin America: an idealistic belief in the commonality of New World exceptionalism, which evolved into Pan Americanism, and the more universal and pragmatic approach infused with the notion that the New World basically replicates in this hemisphere the European divisions between a relatively liberal north and an autocratic south.

The next US president, James Monroe, swung toward the latter position, an early New World realpolitik, in his famous message of December 1823. He formally set forth the concept of the special identity of the New World and its distinct separation from Europe, echoing a sentiment held widely in Latin America as well as the United States. America, it was believed, had a historic mission in civilization to achieve the aspirations of humanity for a life of peace, liberty and justice, which the prevalence of power struggles and reactionary social systems had made impossible of attainment in the Old World.[13]

Beyond these inspirational links, since the early days of the republic, the United States clearly recognized that its security was intimately linked with the independence of the countries that emerged from the former Spanish and Portuguese empires. The Monroe Doctrine expressed the major concern of the United States against the threat of the European powers seeking to regain their colonies. Not surprisingly, the rise of the United States as a world power and the Monroe Doctrine's assumption that superior power endowed it with a hegemonic mission in the hemisphere made Washington's advocacy of Pan Americanism deeply suspect to the other American republics.

Seventy-six years after the Monroe Doctrine was enunciated, Theodore Roosevelt, who epitomized the idea of manifest destiny and his nation's "civilizing mission," turned what was meant to be a shield against European interdiction in the hemisphere into a justification for direct US intervention. The United States should assume the role of an "international police power," he contended, in cases of "wrongdoing or impotence," especially in Central America and the Caribbean.[14]

Having assumed the right to serve as protector of the Americas, the United States took the logical, easy step of becoming their mentor as well. This attitude was based on the conviction that the form of government of a foreign nation is a matter of international concern that other countries may and should try to influence. This constituted the juridical foundation of the policy of intervention adopted by the United States in the aftermath of World War II. Meanwhile, the protection of dollars, combined with an idealistic urge to teach less favored nations to elect "good governments" eventually led presidents Roosevelt, Wilson, Taft, Harding and Coolidge to send troops into Mexico, the Dominican Republic, Cuba, Haiti, Nicaragua and Panama. The Caribbean and Central America were now staked out as exclusive spheres of US influence, where policy was sustained by the belief that US investment was the recipe for political stability in the region. This was the rationale of dollar diplomacy. The protection of dollars led to President Woodrow Wilson's intervention in Haiti—the most drastic intervention of this period. There his secretary of state (Robert Lansing) expanded the Monroe Doctrine into the claim that Central America would have to be reserved exclusively for US capital if European powers were to be prevented from exercising undue influence in the nation's "backyard." Curiously, President Wilson was able to combine this view with a passionate belief in self-determination. He was convinced that such interventions as he made in Mexico, Haiti or Santo Domingo were no more than the creation of the necessary conditions of "constitutional liberty," and, therefore, only formally in conflict with the doctrine of self-determination. Since the government of the United States remains the final judge, it might well appear, not merely to the country in whose affairs the United States intervenes but even to an external observer, that "constitutional liberty" means something like accepting the principles of political behavior and institutions that are regarded with most favor in the United States.

Two other elements in the pattern of manifest destiny deserve attention. The first is the theory of the United States wielding international police power by which it preserves law and order in its general sphere of interest; in the

Western Hemisphere, the United States must regard itself as responsible to Europe for the fulfillment of this obligation. As an international policeman, the United States may quell revolution, restore governments of its choice, reorganize a country's financial arrangements, and insist on the fulfillment of what President Wilson called "certain moral values of Pan Americanism"—values that the United States, as more advanced and more experienced than other American nations, has a duty to define.

A second aspect of manifest destiny is the view that the United States is fated to be the leader of the world. Many diverse streams have contributed to the formation of this outlook. From the sense, at the outset of its national history, that the United States is not like other peoples comes the conviction that it is superior to them. From that superiority came the ardent faith of men like senators Albert J. Beveridge and Henry Cabot Lodge that God had "marked the American people as His chosen nation to finally lead in the regeneration of the world." President George W. Bush is only the latest exponent of this conviction.

———————

By 1926 the US government believed that revolutions in Central America resulted from the machinations of foreign financiers, not social conditions or local political traditions. Accordingly, US intervention in Nicaragua was justified not by fear of foreign intervention but on the grounds that Bolshevism, ostensibly exported by Mexico, was seeking to control the country.[15]

The reaction was not slow in coming; Latin American nationalism flourished, already nurtured by the Mexican–US War of 1848 and the subsequent interventions by the US Marines in Nicaragua, the Dominican Republic and Haiti. Anti-US sentiment was not confined to politics but acquired romantic literary proportions: Rubén Darío, the Nicaraguan poet laureate, Enrique Rodo of Uruguay, Manuel Estrada of Argentina and Machado de Assis of Brazil, among others, became the heroes of the Latin American intelligentsia. However, their lyrical denunciations of the "gross materialism of the Colossus of the North" often ended in the cultural embrace of Europe, creating new contradictions with their simultaneous assertion of Latin American uniqueness. In Mexico, for example, José Vasconcelos sketched an idealistic vision of America's future in his books *La Raza Cósmica* and *Indología*. But after his ambitions to become president were thwarted, he became a bitter, belligerent pessimist. Although he had raised the standards of the Indians, he changed his beliefs and held that Catholic Spain and its heirs knew the formula that could save America, honeycombed with Freemasonry, Protestantism and capitalism—the three demon sons of the Yankees.

Indifferent to these sentiments, the United States often seemed to hold a blithe faith like that of William Jennings Bryan that the whole world, but especially the rest of the hemisphere, would accept the United States as the natural arbiter of its disputes. Sometimes, as with President Taft, the finance capitalism embodied in dollar diplomacy was thought to differ from all other finance capitalism because Washington's motive was international philanthropy. And sometimes, as with Woodrow Wilson and Franklin Roosevelt, it rejected territorial expansionism in order to secure international cooperation against aggression, above all to secure stability in the relation between states.

Infused with this firm conviction, US presidents from Monroe to Theodore Roosevelt could argue the case for US predominance in the affairs of Latin America without moral equivocation. Moreover, it was held to be a political and economic necessity for a great nation to possess colonies or their equivalent; this benefited the colonized as well, providing them with orderly government and progressive reform. Social Darwinism, an important intellectual force at the time, said that young, "manly" nations had a natural right to expand and conquer others in decline—that there is an organic progression in the lives of nations that is futile to resist. This led to a moral and historical dilemma that the advocates of manifest destiny were no more attentive to than the advocates of more recent efforts by the United States to resume its role as the gendarme of the hemisphere. But contradiction it nonetheless is, and its corrosive effect on relations with Latin America was everywhere evident. "American imperialism," the historian Dexter Perkins correctly wrote, "has been imperialism with an uneasy conscience."

When the Republicans returned to power with Warren Harding in 1921, there was evidence of an uneasy conscience over the clumsy imperialist pretensions of William McKinley, Theodore Roosevelt and William Howard Taft. Charles Evans Hughes, Harding's secretary of state, suggested a new mood by stressing the nation's "deep interest in the prosperity, the independence, and the unimpaired sovereignty of the countries of Latin America." Accordingly, he sought to moderate the abuses accompanying the occupation of Haiti and Nicaragua and terminated that of the Dominican Republic. However, with Calvin Coolidge and his secretary of state, Frank Kellogg, interventionism got another boost as the government sent 5,000 troops into Nicaragua, charging that Russian Bolshevik interests in Mexico were encouraging Nicaraguan rebels.

In foreign affairs, twelve years of consecutive Republican rule meant isolationism with a vengeance. A separate peace treaty was made with Germany in

August 1921. The League of Nations was first ignored, then grudgingly recognized as an irreducible fact; the United States pledged to enter the World Court but never followed through. The ill-fated intervention in Russia of 1918–1920 was abandoned, but diplomatic recognition was sternly refused to the Soviet government. Immigration was cut off, and almost insurmountable tariff walls were erected, for isolationism and economic nationalism were opposite sides of the same coin.

Dollar diplomacy in the Caribbean was continued in the best tradition, but Latin American sensibilities were soothed with assurances that the United States had no imperialistic designs and that the Monroe Doctrine was not what it seemed to be. The exclusive pursuit of US national interests was again couched in terms of long-established principles and policies.

The Monroe Doctrine and the Treaty of Rio de Janeiro, two outstanding innovations in US foreign policy more than a century apart, reflect this deep, continuing concern with the security and independence of the Western Hemisphere. Yet the US view on intervention, though opposed by many leading Latin American jurists and strong elements of US public opinion, had a strong basis in international law at that time. Charles Evans Hughes put it in succinct terms when he said: "What are we going to do when government breaks down and American citizens are in danger of their lives? Are we to stand by and see them killed because a government in circumstances which it cannot control, and for which it may not be responsible, can no longer afford reasonable protection?"[16] This view resurfaces as a rationale for US interventions in the 1960s, and again in the 1980s.

Hughes expounded this doctrine valiantly at the Sixth Inter-American Conference at Havana in 1928, succeeding in having the issue of nonintervention postponed, to the chagrin of the Latin American delegates. It was a Pyrrhic victory, for it soon became clear to the US government that continuation of its intervention policy would worsen the badly damaged state of inter-American relations and render virtually impossible the maintenance of any useful regional association.

Behind these limitations on each country's perception of the other lay a deep-seated fundamental difference in their view of the international community and their role in relation to it. In 1920 the United States had opted out of the evil "balance of power" problems that beset Europe, while Latin America looked first to Europe and then the League of Nations as a counterpoise to US influence in the region. It is worth stressing this basic factor—the divergence of international strategies affecting the nature of the US–Latin American relationship that began in 1933 and consolidated itself in the years thereafter.

Herbert Hoover, determined to improve relations with Latin America, made a preinaugural trip around South America and helped in the final arbitration of the Tacna-Arica dispute between Chile and Peru. In his inaugural address, President Hoover confidently announced that "we have no desire for territorial expansion, for economic or other domination of other peoples." His secretary of state, Henry L. Stimson, further reassured the Latin American republics when he showed a willingness to accept the narrow interpretation given to the Monroe Doctrine by Undersecretary J. Reuben Clark, who maintained that "the Doctrine states a case of the U.S. vs. Europe, and not the U.S. vs. Latin America."

These promising assurances were given a severe test when an epidemic of revolutions broke out in Latin America, largely a by-product of the worldwide depression. Yet while the depression also contributed to a less aggressive attitude by the Washington government toward the smaller nations south of the Rio Grande, the Hoover administration's protectionist policies, exemplified by the Smoot-Hawley Act, contributed to the region's economic dislocation and rekindled Latin American resentment.

As elsewhere in the world, in Latin America too the depression brought in its wake political upheaval and a new rash of dictators who portrayed themselves as saviors of civilian mismanagement. Getúlio Vargas installed himself in Brazil at the end of 1929. Bolivia, Peru and Argentina became dictatorships the following year; Chile followed in 1931. In 1932 Bolivia and Paraguay, ignoring the appeals of the League of Nations, embarked on a long, bloody war. The financial collapse of October 1929 was followed by political disarray across the Southern Hemisphere and the rise of state-controlled economies, as laissez-faire was considered to have brought ruin to the world's wealthiest country, the United States. People in the great northern republic had less money; much of that which they had invested abroad, particularly in Central and South America, had been lost, and US citizens were bringing less pressure on their government to intervene.

President Hoover and the Republican party had so consistently claimed credit for American prosperity that they could not escape responsibility for the disaster; when the stock market crashed under Hoover, the last vestiges of US prestige collapsed with it. The Republicans were dismissed in 1932 by an electorate that would not forgive them for two full decades.

Ironically, it would fall to Franklin Roosevelt, who, as Wilson's assistant secretary of the navy, was the embodiment of a resolute interventionist, to repudiate the idea that the United States must act alone in the exercise of this authority. FDR's assumption of the presidency in 1933, with his determination to heal the rifts that had torn the inter-American community and given Pan Americanism a bad name, marked a fundamental turning point in Latin American attitudes and policies.

NOTES

1. Alfonso Reyes, *Memorias de Cocina y Bodega,* p. 12.

2. Julian Hawthorne's partial *United States: From the Landing of Columbus to the Signing of the Peace Protocol with Spain* (New York: Collier, 1898) states, revealingly, "whatever Spain has done in America has, from the first, been evil. Her influence has always been exerted on the side of oppression and against enlightenment and liberty; it has been marked by cruelty and selfishness. . . . Every nation of Europe owed her a grudge; she obstructed commerce and industry, and lay sullen and inert before the path of progress" (p. 3). Another contemporary work comes from the English historian Robert Mackenzie (*The Nineteenth Century: A History of the Times of Queen Victoria* [London: Nelson, 1887]): "When the thirteen English colonies of the Northern Continent gained their independence, they entered upon a political condition for which their qualities of mind and their experience amply fitted them. . . . With the Spanish settlements on the Southern Continent it was altogether different. The people were entirely without education; the printing press was not to be found anywhere. . . . They were of many and hostile races" (p. 511).

3. Leopoldo Zea, *América en la Historia* (Mexico City: Fondo de Cultura Económica, Universidad Nacional Autónoma de México, Centro de Estudios Filosóficos, 1957), p. 7.

4. Howard Mumford Jones, "O Strange New World," in *American Culture: The Formative Years* (New York: Viking, 1964), pp. 78–79.

5. John H. Elliott, *The Old World and the New, 1492–1650* (Cambridge: Cambridge University Press, 1970), p. 17.

6. Elliott, *Old World,* p. 96.

7. Frank Tannenbaum, *Ten Keys to Latin America* (New York: Vintage, 1966), p. 176.

8. Daniel J. Boorstin, *America and the Image of Europe: Reflections on American Thought* (New York: Meridian, 1960), p. 13.

9. Quoted in Saul K. Padover, *A Jefferson Profile: As Revealed in His Letters* (New York: John Day, 1956), p. 224.

10. Quoted in Samuel Flagg Beamis, *The Latin American Policy of the United States* (New York: Harcourt, Brace, 1943), p. 41.

11. W. C. Ford, *Writings of John Quincy Adams* (New York: Macmillan, 1913–17), 4:46–52.

12. Ford, *Writings of John Quincy Adams*, 4:46–52.

13. John C. Dreier, *The Organization of American States and the Hemisphere Crisis* (New York: Harper & Row, 1962), p. 15.

14. Dexter Perkins, *A History of the Monroe Doctrine* (Boston: Little, Brown, 1955), p. 267.

15. Perkins, *History of the Monroe Doctrine*, pp. 267–269.

16. Quoted in Ann V. Thomas and A. J. Thomas, *Non-Intervention: The Law and Its Import in the Americas* (Dallas: Southern Methodist University Press, 1956), p. 60.

Chapter Three

CONVERGENCE

The Roosevelt Era

A RELATIONSHIP TURNED UPSIDE DOWN

On a bright, sunny Monday, November 30, 1936, more than a million Argentines took to the streets of Buenos Aires to give a clamorous welcome to Franklin D. Roosevelt, the first US president to visit their country. The day had been declared a national holiday. People were in a festive summer mood, eager to catch a glimpse of the man who had been widely praised by their government and press as the leading advocate of democracy in the world and the devoted friend of Latin America. Chants of "Viva Roosevelt! Viva la democracia!" surged from the crowds as the presidential motorcade wound its way through the packed avenues of the Argentine capital. Roosevelt, riding in an open sedan seated next to his Argentine colleague, President Augustín P. Justo, flashed his famous smile and waved at the cheering crowds.

The outpouring of friendship from the hemisphere's southernmost nation that for a century had cast itself as Washington's rival for leadership in the hemisphere was a measure of the change in the nature of inter-American relations that occurred even before Roosevelt's first term had ended. The *New York Times*, in a dispatch from Buenos Aires, noted that the reception was the largest, most jubilant the country ever extended.

The hemispheric relationship was turning upside down. During his four terms in office—including the darkest moments of the war—Roosevelt gave the American republics a status both inside and outside the United States that they never enjoyed before. From the moment he took office Roosevelt was determined to dispel the suspicions and misunderstandings that had brought US–Latin American relations to the verge of collapse and to transform a wary, languishing Pan American movement into an effective continental alliance

25

based on mutual respect and the recognition of the New World's shared goals of renovation and revolution, of freedom, democracy and social justice.

His impact on hemispheric relations was almost instantaneous. It came from several sources: the thrall his domestic reforms held for many Latin Americans and the effective implementation of his campaign vows to cease interventionism and give priority attention to Latin America, as well as from his appealing, energetic oratory style and engaging personality. Perhaps most of all, however, it came from his recognition of past mistakes and misjudgments and his awareness of the need for a coherent conception of the world and the place of US relations with Latin America in it. He was able to translate that conception into a policy that he named Good Neighbor. For Roosevelt the Good Neighbor policy was more than a political device, it was a personal mission.[1] Good-neighborliness to him was a practical application of the Golden Rule.[2]

From the day of FDR's inaugural speech on March 4, 1933, when he pledged to "dedicate this Nation to the policy of the good neighbor," to his re-election in November 1936, Latin America occupied a preponderant place on Roosevelt's foreign policy agenda. Realizing that the turbulent situation in Europe and Asia and the depressed domestic economic situation created limitations on its exercise of power, the Roosevelt administration early on decided that a most effective policy course would be to concentrate on the Western Hemisphere. In the State of the Union message of January 3, 1936, Roosevelt could tell Congress with justifiable satisfaction:

> Among the nations of the great Western Hemisphere the policy of the good neighbor has happily prevailed. At no time in the four and a half centuries of modern civilization in the Americas has there existed—in any year, in any decade, in any generation in all that time—a greater spirit of mutual understanding, of common helpfulness and of devotion to the ideals of self-government than exists today in the twenty-one American Republics and their neighbor. The policy of the good neighbor among the Americas is no longer a hope, no longer an objective remaining to be accomplished. It is a fact, active, present, pertinent and effective.[3]

Thus the stage had been carefully set before he embarked on his momentous trip to the opening ceremony of the Inter-American Peace Conference, which he had proposed for Argentina almost a year earlier. Fresh from the triumph of his re-election in November 1936, Roosevelt decided to make the long ocean voyage on the cruiser USS *Indianapolis* to underscore his continued dedication to hemispheric solidarity. He also wanted to send a message to the rest of the world that the Americas stood together at a time when the clouds of war were casting an ominous shadow on Europe and Asia.

The exertion of the trip, which included one-day stopovers in Brazil and Uruguay, was well rewarded. His twenty-five-minute speech at the opening session of the conference was interrupted fourteen times by standing ovations. It set the tone of his visit. He referred to the twenty-one representatives as "the American family" united in "common purpose" and in the "glories of independence." His faith in the hemisphere's unity and its message to the rest of the world was unequivocal: "Can we, the Republics of the New World, help the Old to avert the catastrophe which impends? Yes, I am confident that we can."[4]

Yet the troubled past was not entirely forgotten. The tumultuous acclaim that greeted the president in the Argentine congress also elicited a single anguished cry: "Death to the US fascists!" The protester was a political radical—the son of President Justo. It was, however, the sole discordant note.[5]

The president's agenda indicated an unequivocal US commitment to New World solidarity: full ratification of peace machinery, inter-American economic amelioration, strengthening of cultural ties to reinforce political solidarity, measures to protect this side of the oceans from the disastrous effects of strife in the Old World. The conventions and agreements adopted by the Inter-American Conference for the Maintenance of Peace were proof, Roosevelt reflected afterward, that "in a world which is beset with rumors and the threats of war, governments determined to keep alive the spirit of peace and willing to renew mutual trust and faith in treaties can move together in a cooperative search for the means of enduring peace."[6] The agreements, the president observed, provided "a complete consultative system intended to meet the menace of conflict by the quick and active cooperation of the 21 Governments."[7]

Thus culminated a new and momentous chapter for the Western Hemisphere, replacing the unilateral Monroeism and Big Stick policy that had disrupted inter-American relations and domestic politics in former years. The Monroe Doctrine was "continentalized" and "multilateralized." Buenos Aires became the great landmark in relations between the two parts of the hemisphere, the principle of equality was fastened onto Pan Americanism and the feared Colossus of the North finally became the admired Good Neighbor.

Even contemporary commentators who contended that Roosevelt's trip yielded little other than persuasive oratory conceded that the conference, which had been his initiative, had alerted the world to one overriding message: that the United States was determined to consolidate hemispheric relations and that it could count on Latin America's leaders for help. Four years of reconstruction efforts had passed into a new phase—affirmative action in political consultation on mutual security, economic cooperation and cultural exchanges.

The morning of Roosevelt's arrival in the Argentine capital, the influential newspaper *La Nación* summed up Latin America's high expectations for the conference:

> A new epoch is about to begin, and our continent—which has none of those tenacious hates nor that insurmountable spirit of revenge that exist in other continents—is preparing to assume its destined role as monitor in the world community.
>
> Even if this objective is not immediately attainable, even if conditions in Europe and Asia are such as to prevent the acceptance of the Americas' message of peace, nothing can detract from the historical importance of these meetings of the next few days to work out the development of President Roosevelt's suggestion.[8]

The editorial captured two essential features of the Good Neighbor policy. Foremost was a recognition of the importance Roosevelt attached to US ties with Latin America, as expressed, for example, in his instructions to the US delegation at the 1933 Montevideo conference: "Among the foreign relations of the United States as they fall into categories, the Pan American policy takes first place in our diplomacy."[9] A second and related feature, not always understood in the United States, was the widespread impression created in Latin America that through the new partnership with Washington the region was gaining a more significant role in the world arena. These features were of great importance to the self-esteem of a proud people who before the advent of the Roosevelt era had widely perceived themselves as marginal to Washington's concerns, victims of "Yankee imperialism."[10]

Roosevelt was delighted with the results of his South American trip. Returning home on the battle cruiser USS *Independence*, he expressed his satisfaction in a brief note to his wife, Eleanor: "There was real enthusiasm in the streets. I really begin to think the moral effect of the Good Neighbor policy is making itself definitely felt."[11] To James M. Cox, the former governor of Ohio who was the Democratic party's presidential nominee in 1920 with FDR his running mate (they were defeated by the Republican Harding-Coolidge ticket), he wrote: "I think the trip has been worth while and here is no question of the excellent reactions in South America. That, after all, was the primary objective because three years ago Latin American opinion was almost violently against us and the complete change is, I hope, a permanent fact. Nevertheless, I am still most pessimistic about Europe and there seems to be no step we can take to improve it."[12]

Roosevelt might have added that in a mere four years his new policy had won the overwhelming support of Congress and the American people. There was practically no major inter-American treaty or convention that did not win universal acceptance. This represented a striking change from the decades the major Latin American nations had recoiled from Pan Americanism, suspecting it of masking their northern neighbor's imperialist impulses, the dollar diplomacy of its businessmen-rulers, or the outright military interventions of the Big Stick policy.

Roosevelt appreciated that the best way to silence Latin Americans' criticism and allay their suspicions was with effective gestures, such as the renunciation of US interventionism, the abrogation of the odious Platt amendment and other measures that had been seen as violating the sovereign rights of the neighbor republics. On the home front, he took advantage of every possible occasion to emphasize the vision of hemispheric solidarity and to make it more than a diffuse, remote concept. It was as if in the 1930s the Roosevelt presidency was determined to realize the dreams of Simón Bolívar and Henry Clay a century earlier—a voluntary association of New World nations dedicated to peace, freedom, justice and mutual respect, capable of offering "a beacon of democracy and hope" to a troubled Old World.

Through an unquenchable faith in the US system and a masterly exploitation of propitious domestic and international circumstances, Roosevelt set up an effective juridical network of collective security arrangements, peacemaking machinery, liberal trade arrangements and cultural exchanges to infuse new life into the inter-American system long before the storms of war threatened the shores of the New World. As the first US president to set foot on South American soil and cross the Panama Canal, Roosevelt gained distinction among Latin Americans as "the world's best good neighbor."[13]

The strategic yield of FDR's efforts came in the wake of Japan's attack against Pearl Harbor when the Latin American republics stood ready and united to defend the hemisphere from the perils abroad. For years to come, FDR's triumphal South American trip epitomized the constructive transformation of the Good Neighbor policy—just as the violence directed against Vice President Richard M. Nixon in the streets of Lima and Caracas in 1958 marked its unraveling. These two landmarks can also be read as evidence of a fundamental difference between the Roosevelt era's conception of Latin American policy and that of most of the administrations that followed it.

Historians and political commentators have interpreted the Good Neighbor policy in a variety of ways. To some, it has seemed simply a clever, sophisticated attempt to tighten up and extend US dominance in the Western Hemisphere.[14] Others have accepted it at face value as an idealistic yet realistic effort by a powerful nation to treat its weaker neighbors with understanding, tolerance and restraint.[15] If in the process the United States made friends and achieved a measure of political and commercial influence, these were the natural, well-deserved rewards of an essentially unselfish policy.

Most likely, the Good Neighbor policy was a little of each—clever, idealistic, effective and self-serving. Never precisely formulated or defined, over the years it was applied by the Roosevelt administration quite haphazardly, though with a good deal of pious drumbeating. Some in the administration construed neighborliness as a tool to promote US interest, just as others stressed idealistic impulses. At times even President Roosevelt himself seemed unclear as to which aim was primary. If its conception developed consistently and in step with Roosevelt's own maturing political philosophy, then neither in its motivation nor in its application was the Good Neighbor policy a simple, consistent doctrine.

One of the earliest formulations of Roosevelt's Latin American policy, which significantly foreshadowed the Good Neighbor and signaled a drastic change in his own earlier views, was his famous article in the July 1928 issue of *Foreign Affairs* stating the Democratic foreign policy platform for the candidacy of Al Smith. In it Roosevelt argued that unilateral US intervention had become intolerable.

It was a striking reversal of the positions Roosevelt held as an imperious young assistant secretary of the navy during the Wilson administration, when he boasted his interventionist and annexationist views in Latin America.[16] Focusing on the most recent, unpopular, expedition to Nicaragua, he attacked the Republican interventions, contending, correctly, that "never before in our history have we had fewer friends in the Western Hemisphere than we have today."[17]

To remedy the situation he urged the renunciation "for all time" of "arbitrary intervention in the home affairs of neighbors."[18] Roosevelt was already hinting at restoring the Monroe Doctrine to its original interpretation by repudiating the corollary enunciated by Theodore Roosevelt to justify unilateral intervention—almost three years before the Hoover administration published the celebrated memorandum written late in 1928 by J. Reuben Clark, the undersecretary of state, declaring that the doctrine "states a case of United States vs. Europe, not of United States vs. Latin America." In that connection, Roosevelt wrote:

> After the general peace of 1815, the newly-won independence of the Central and South American nations provided frequent opportunities for reconquest and disturbance; our response was the Monroe Doctrine, a policy aimed not

only at self-protection but, in the larger sense, at continental peace. Promulgated by a Democratic Administration, it was our countermove against the desperate attempt of the Holy Alliance to curb the rise of liberalism by interfering in the internal affairs of government and by crushing revolting colonies desirous of setting up democracies.[19]

Roosevelt remained cautious in his open advocacy of the renunciation of the so-called right of unilateral intervention. His ideas on this topic are worth quoting in full, since they clearly foreshadow plans he later put in practice as president:

> The time has come when we must accept not only certain facts but many new principles of a higher law, a newer and better standard in international relations. We are exceedingly jealous of our own sovereignty and it is only right that we should respect a similar feeling among other nations.
>
> The peoples of the other Republics of this Western world are just as patriotic, just as proud of their sovereignty. Many of these nations are large, wealthy and highly civilized.
>
> The peace, the security, the integrity, the independence of every one of the American Republics is of interest to all the others, not to the United States alone. It is possible that in the days to come one of our sister nations may fall upon evil days; disorder and bad government may require that a helping hand be given her citizens as a matter of temporary necessity to bring back order and stability. In that event it is not the right or the duty of the United States to intervene alone.
>
> It is rather the duty of the United States to associate with itself other American Republics, to give intelligent joint study to the problem, and, if the conditions warrant, to offer the helping hand or hands in the name of the Americas. Single-handed intervention by us in the internal affairs of other nations must end; with the cooperation of others we shall have more order in this hemisphere and less dislike.[20]

There is at least an implied recognition of the need for some inter-American system of collective consultation, the kind he later proposed to the Buenos Aires conference in 1936 and was eventually enshrined in the Inter-American Treaty of Peace and Security signed at Rio de Janeiro in 1947, two years after his death. In this piece Roosevelt articulated the two main elements destined to be the core of the Good Neighbor policy of the Roosevelt administration—renunciation of unilateral intervention by the United States and the multilateralization of the responsibility for the maintenance of peace, order and stability in the hemisphere.

Though none of these phrases may have seemed particularly original or stirring in the United States, they had a strong impact south of the border. Commenting on the *Foreign Affairs* article, Antonio Gómez Robledo, a philosophy professor and one of Mexico's leading diplomatic historians, wrote retrospectively:

> Noble words from that generous spirit, written before he aspired formally to the highest office and the world was not yet plunged into the economic and political crisis that would impel the United States to seek a more cordial understanding with the rest of America on other levels; words that simply betrayed the felicitous internal evolution of the president's mind.[21]

The importance of Roosevelt's article cannot be exaggerated, for it practically offered a blueprint of what Roosevelt's Latin American policy would look like after he became president in 1933. In every major statement on the subject before and after he took office can be found the same watchwords—spirit, good neighbor, hemispheric solidarity, mutual respect—and calls for common political, economic and cultural cooperation to help promote world peace and closer understanding among the sister republics. It also contradicts the belittling argument by US and Latin American critics of FDR claiming the Good Neighbor was nothing more than a scheme to draw the region into World War II; there were no intimations of war in 1928.

The *Foreign Affairs* article testifies to a remarkable consistency and continuity in Roosevelt's thoughts about the hemisphere; for example, he ended the 1928 article with an exhortation to the spirit, influenced as he was by his grade school German courses where he learned the words of Goethe, "It is the spirit which fashions the body to itself."[22] The same hortatory device resurfaced in the conclusion of his address before the Inter-American conference at Buenos Aires nine years later:

> The faith of the Americas, lies in the spirit. The system, the sisterhood, of the Americas is impregnable so long as her Nations maintain that spirit. In that faith and spirit we will have peace over the Western World. In that faith and spirit we will all watch and guard our Hemisphere. In that faith and spirit may we also, with God's help, offer hope to our brethren overseas.[23]

From the mid-1920s on there is a clear continuity of thought and feeling, of plans and deeds that gave Roosevelt and the United States new stature in Latin America. Throughout his presidential campaign of 1932 the recurring themes of his foreign policy platform reflected the egalitarian and anti-imperialist aspects of Roosevelt's thinking and his resolve to improve relations with the neighbor republics to the south.

The age of Roosevelt set a new standard for US–Latin American relations, one that soon developed into a paradigm of harmony and cooperation against which all subsequent US administrations were measured. What were these new conceptions? What did it take to resurrect the Pan American movement just years after it had been largely discredited as a vehicle of US economic and political domination? How did Roosevelt sell the Good Neighbor policy to the North American people so that practically every new Pan American treaty and convention received unanimous Senate ratification?

FROM GRIM INHERITANCE TO GOLDEN AGE

Roosevelt's assumption of the presidency in 1933 with his determination to heal the rifts in the inter-American community marked a fundamental turning point both in Latin American attitudes and policies. The gulf between the United States and Latin America was possibly deeper than at any time since the war with Mexico almost a century earlier; there existed an unrelenting hostility toward anything that remotely suggested US intervention or hegemony. Cordell Hull recalled, "Our inheritance of ill-will was grim."[24]

The new chapter in hemispheric relations began, remarkably, while Roosevelt's main energies were directed to the formidable task of leading the country out of the Great Depression, and while he sought European cooperation for a new and better world in which there would be peace and economic recovery through free commerce. From the moment he came into office, Roosevelt pursued a course of deliberate rapprochement with Latin America. It was manifested in a succession of major policy decisions and speeches as well as in less noted gestures that indicated a keen sense for Latin American sensibilities. Even though at first the Democratic administration was engrossed in domestic problems arising out of the Depression and the prevailing mood of the country was manifestly isolationist, Roosevelt began considering ways to lead for the cause of world peace. He was determined to reverse the drift toward international anarchy and to unify the Western Hemisphere, while at the same time pressing ahead in whirlwind fashion with his domestic New Deal program of social and economic reforms.

At the same time, far from neglecting foreign affairs, as some commentators have argued, Roosevelt urged action in both the disarmament talks that were dragging on in Geneva and the World Economic Conference scheduled to begin that summer in London at the time he was preparing to unveil his Good Neighbor plan at the Pan American Union. By the spring of 1933, events in

Germany and Japan had already eliminated the possibility of effective disarmament; the prospects for economic cooperation in London were no better. By late May, after desultory discussions between the new administration and the debtors revealed no basis for agreement and following a particularly frustrating meeting with German Finance Minister Hjalmar Schacht, Roosevelt told Treasury Secretary Henry Morgenthau that he was "in an awful jam with Europe," that European salesmen were "a bunch of bastards" and that he saw "a very strong possibility of war with Germany." Small wonder, perhaps, that under the circumstances relations with Latin America, despite their troubled history, loomed as more promising.

The evolution of the Good Neighbor policy began with great deliberation and little fanfare. Roosevelt had been swept into office to lift the nation out of the confusion and despondency caused by the Great Depression. Domestic reform received overarching priority. As frequently noted, foreign policy occupied a mere paragraph in the inaugural address of March 4, 1933:

> In the field of world policy I would dedicate this Nation to the policy of the Good Neighbor—the neighbor who resolutely respects himself and, because he does so, respects the right of others—the neighbor who respects his obligations and respects the sanctity of his agreements in and with a world of neighbors. We now realize as we have never realized before our interdependence on each other; that we cannot merely take, but must give as well.[25]

Yet already in his Pan American Day message on April 12, 1933, just a month after his inauguration, Roosevelt endowed the "Good Neighbor" with its special hemispheric significance when he said:

> In my inaugural address I stated that I would dedicate this nation "to the policy of the Good Neighbor. . . ." Never before has the significance of the word "good neighbors" been so manifest in international relations. . . . Your Americanism and mine must be a structure built of confidence, cemented by a sympathy which recognizes only equality and fraternity.[26]

Nine months later, in December 1933, he stunned even the most critical of Latin Americans by authorizing Secretary of State Cordell Hull to sign a convention at the Seventh Pan American Conference in Montevideo proclaiming that "no State has the right to intervene in the internal affairs of another."

Within a few days, the president himself announced in a speech before the Woodrow Wilson Foundation in Washington that "the definite policy of the United States from now on is opposed to armed intervention."[27] In the words of Sumner Welles, "no more heartening statement, insofar as our relations with the rest of the republics of the continent are concerned, had ever been made by a President of the United States."[28] The distrust of US hegemony was not entirely removed. But the general picture was highly favorable.

Before the year was over, Roosevelt had managed to give his inaugural pledge to be a good neighbor to the world a special meaning for the Western Hemisphere. The prospect of turning the US record of interventionism and dollar diplomacy into actions by a neighbor who "respects others because it respects itself" was received with a mixture of hope and skepticism. But the skepticism quickly began to dissolve as action lent credibility to Roosevelt's inspiring rhetoric. And FDR's overtures were not just confined to the comparatively tranquil peacetime years. A decade later, in the middle of the war, Roosevelt, returning from North Africa in early 1943, met with President Getúlio Vargas in Brazil to discuss South American defense. In April of that year, when Roosevelt conferred with the Mexican head of state, Avila Camacho, he became the first US president to meet with a Mexican president on Mexican soil.

Still, the Good Neighbor did not evolve altogether smoothly—there was the early Cuban crisis, the challenge posed by Mexico's expropriation of US-owned land and oil companies, the vexing wartime dispute with Argentina, and a host of unresolved economic problems. However, compared to the profound political frictions of the previous decades—and those that were to follow—these difficulties seem like family squabbles.

Roosevelt's accomplishments were impressive. In addition to his momentous pledge to observe the principle of nonintervention in hemispheric affairs, within a year after taking office he had withdrawn the last marines from Nicaragua and signed an executive agreement to remove the marines from Haiti; initiated negotiations to end the US protectorate over Panama; and abrogated the Platt amendment, renouncing Washington's rights to intervene in Cuba's internal affairs. Other problems were to be addressed within the context of the Good Neighbor policy. There was the continuing Chaco War between Bolivia and Paraguay and the Leticia dispute between Peru and Colombia.

By May 1934 there were ominous rumblings of civil war in Cuba, compelling immediate action. Consultation with the Latin American allies on major world issues was a constant preoccupation of Roosevelt's, just as he had anticipated in his 1928 *Foreign Affairs* article. It was an issue that surfaced regularly, as illustrated in this dispatch from Josephus Daniels, the ambassador to Mexico, in a cable to Secretary of State Cordell Hull:

> In the past Latin Americans had rightly objected because we tell them in-
> stead of consult with them. There is a world of difference, particularly to
> sensitive nations or individuals.[29]

The desire on the part of Latin America, which had long felt itself discrimi-
nated against by history, to be a more active part of the international community, to be at one with the respected members of the concert of nations, was
naturally overwhelming. Roosevelt knew that. For example, on April 5, 1933,
a week before his historic Pan American Day speech, Roosevelt saw to it that
the State Department invited Mexico, Brazil, Argentina and Chile, along with
the European powers, Canada and China, to send representatives to Washington for high-level talks on the international debt problem, preliminary to the
London conference. He also included most Latin American heads of state in
the letters he sent to fifty-four world leaders pleading for a renewed effort to
halt the armaments race.

In November 1933, just nine months after assuming office, he named Secretary of State Cordell Hull to head the US delegation to the Seventh Pan
American Conference at Montevideo. It was not only the first time that a secretary of state attended such a meeting but, on his way to and from Montevideo, Hull visited a dozen Latin American countries to dramatize the new
spirit of the Good Neighbor policy. Significantly, at the time the United States
was negotiating bilateral trade agreements—one of Hull's favorite methods of
consolidating ties—with Colombia, Brazil, Cuba and Argentina.[30] Roosevelt
wrote some years later that his aim was to dispel the ill will inherited from past
administrations and start afresh:

> The first objective of our delegates was to tear down what was left of the wall
> of misunderstanding and prejudice between ourselves and the other Re-
> publics, and to eliminate entirely any traces of enmity and resentment by
> their people toward us.[31]

As Hull remembered the mission in his memoir,

> we had to pave the way for gradual restoration of confidence and friendli-
> ness and steadily increasing cooperation on the part of all the Latin Ameri-
> can nations—not only with us, but also among themselves. Actually, our
> task was to create a whole new spirit.[32]

Indeed, "a whole new spirit" was already stirring in the Americas, inspired by
the élan, careful planning and skillful execution of the Roosevelt administra-

tion's relations with the region. The leaders of the hemisphere, who for years felt largely ignored by Republican administrations, believed the Good Neighbor policy had assumed a central position in Washington's foreign policy—the external counterpart in importance to the New Deal. During the opening years of the Roosevelt administration this impression was by no means farfetched. "Our domestic values and energies will determine the course in foreign affairs," the president often said.

IMPACT OF THE NEW DEAL

The shift in US policy toward Latin America was not the only (and perhaps not even the primary) cause of Latin America's favorable disposition toward the Roosevelt administration. Important as these steps were, Roosevelt ultimately won Latin America's confidence and admiration in other significant ways. One was the New Deal, the program of social and economic reforms that became the model for most of the hemisphere's progressive leaders. The other was Roosevelt's magnetic style of leadership.

It was in this internal policy, plainly animated by a humanitarian purpose, that Roosevelt first won the recognition of Latin American leaders and their peoples. They had seen three Republican administrations, imbued with the idea reflected in Coolidge's famous pronouncement, "the business of America is business," leave behind an economic and social debacle. Photographs and news stories chronicling the ruins—hunger marches, Hoovervilles, men selling apples and emaciated children and women begging in the streets of New York—did little to enhance the image of the businessman as statesman. After the unbridled individualism promoted by Harding, Coolidge and Hoover, which led to such widespread misery, Roosevelt was seen as seeking to establish new rules of social justice, the kind Latin America had been yearning for as well. And yet Roosevelt was trying to do this without forcing the country into a doctrinaire straitjacket, whether socialism or state capitalism. "History may record that he did more to advance democracy than any president since Lincoln," the historian Henry Steele Commager has observed, "and as much to strengthen capitalism as any statesman since Hamilton."[33]

With Roosevelt's accession to power not merely a new Democratic administration but a new social and economic vision began to develop in the United States. Certainly the Latin Americans had no difficulty in distinguishing the new tone and character of Roosevelt from past administrations. "Our domestic values and energies will determine our course in foreign affairs," he told Congress in his first State of the Union address. Nothing else would have accounted for the president's ability to push more legislation through Congress during the legendary first one hundred days of his administration than others had during their entire presidency.

Early innovations included the Agricultural Adjustment Act to force up farm prices by reducing production and the National Industrial Recovery Act, which attempted to overcome industrial paralysis by persuading employers to observe "codes" raising wages, shortening hours, improving conditions and banning child labor. Far different from the road mending that had previously been dignified with the title of public works, Roosevelt launched the Tennessee Valley Authority, which set out to control a destructive river and proved to be the greatest and most successful example of regional planning in a free country. Flood control was only one of its benefits; cheap and universal electricity, reforestation and the restoration of eroded land, and the introduction of new industries completely changed what had been a poverty-stricken and despairing area.

Moreover, they could identify with Roosevelt's conviction that the communal effort was a basic idea of the American past. If the history of the Americas was a history of pioneers seeking to establish New World democratic societies based on republican principles of freedom and equality, the New Deal loomed as an exemplary effort to restore the sense of civic responsibility envisioned by the founders of the American republics. It was a vision far more congenial to a majority of Latin Americans than that of the previous Republican administrations with their entrenched defense of the status quo and hegemonic impulses toward the neighbor republics.

Franklin Roosevelt came to be regarded as the friend of the forgotten and the downtrodden. The people of Latin America had, for many generations, listened to empty phrases about Washington's commitment to Pan Americanism and democracy; now they were seeing the accomplishment of deeds. A wholly new spirit of cooperation sprang into being. For the first time in a hundred years hemispheric solidarity actually existed. By the time World War II broke out, almost all of the twenty-one American republics were prepared, to an unprecedented degree, to present a common front to dangers from abroad. If it is true that democratic alliances prosper best when they rely on the will of the people, then there can be no better example.

Roosevelt's achievements in restoring the nation's domestic health and fashioning victory in World War II have been the subject of many biographies and historical works in the United States. His extraordinary transformation of US relations with Latin America and the enduring impact of his Good Neighbor policy are less well known, especially in his own country. Yet in the rest of the hemisphere he is remembered as the only US statesman of genius in the twentieth century, a man who has continued to occupy the imagination of the Latin American peoples.

Like much of the rest of the world, Latin Americans could not help but be impressed by Roosevelt's optimism and resolve. From the moment of his inaugural address with its promise of bold leadership to combat economic depression and injustice with the vigor of warfare, he kindled a new spirit of national unity and purpose.

> This great nation will endure as it has endured, and will revive and prosper . . . the only thing we have to fear is fear itself. The nation asked for action and action now. I shall ask Congress for broad Executive power to wage a war against the emergency, as great as the power that would be given to me as if we were in fact invaded by a foreign foe.[34]

Here was a president who did not make excuses for inaction.

THE IMPACT OF ROOSEVELT'S LEADERSHIP STYLE

Roosevelt's personal magnetism, as much as anything else, is what projected the Good Neighbor policy beyond the confines of government offices and the high-level rhetoric of inter-American conferences to become practically a mass movement of continental dimensions. It affected not only foreign policy but also popular emotions. And it contributed as much to Latin America's own sense of identity and importance as it did to the improvement of inter-American relations. There can be no satisfactory analysis of the impact of the Roosevelt era on Latin America without taking into account these psychological factors.

Quick to personalize, Latin Americans saw Roosevelt fight economic paralysis and social injustice in the same indomitable way he had fought to overcome the infirmity of his paralyzed legs with resolute willpower. For them the president and the New Deal represented the victory of action over inaction, of change against the status quo, of experimentation over rigidity. Even some of the most doctrinaire critics of the United States had to acknowledge Roosevelt's impact. The Marxist historian Alonso Aguilar of Mexico wrote,

> The Good Neighbor Policy, because of its very nature, contained insoluble contradictions. While on the one hand, it showed respect, previously nonexistent, for the Latin American nations, on the other hand, it manifested itself as an effort to further subordinate them to United States economic needs.[35]

Nonetheless, he then went on to concede that under Roosevelt's presidency "a promising outlook for improved inter-American relations seemed to be in view."[36]

A more representative view of the Latin American mainstream is offered by Victor Andrade, who was Bolivia's ambassador to the United States for almost two decades and later foreign minister. In his 1976 memoir, *My Mission for Revolutionary Bolivia,* he wrote,

> Franklin Roosevelt deserves full credit for repudiating the "big stick" policy formulated by his cousin Theodore. In doing so he swept aside a century of fear and distrust which had divided Latin America and the United States. In a sense, by the Good Neighbor policy, the United States established itself as champion to liberate the masses from need, oppression and slavery.[37]

Many US historians, especially those contemporary to the Good Neighbor policy, concur with this view, though there are a handful of skeptical commentaries.[38] "The United States," wrote Edward O. Guerrant, "has never had a foreign policy toward any area that was more successful than the Good Neighbor Policy was from 1933 to 1945."[39] According to J. Lloyd Mecham, "the reverence for Franklin Roosevelt was responsible for the most extraordinary *entente cordiale* ever achieved between the peoples of the hemisphere."[40] What informed his Latin American policy, what led Roosevelt to innovate? What were the new conceptions he brought to bear on inter-American relations? What did it take to resurrect the Pan American movement after it had been discredited as a vehicle of US economic and political domination? How did Roosevelt sell it to the American people and Congress? From the beginning, Roosevelt made a point of playing up the theme of the New World idea. He noted that Latin America, like the United States, was emancipated under the great banner of independence and self-determination that led the common people to rise against the monarchies of Europe and their nobility, ignorance and privilege.

Drawing on history, as he did in his Pan American Day speech, the president cast his Good Neighbor policy as a continuation of a tradition and a civilization born from their common past of differences with the Old World, looking toward a common destiny in the regeneration of the New World. Along with such high-sounding transcendental goals, he never forgot the less lofty gestures, such as issuing strategic invitations to ensure Latin American participation in major international consultations. Similarly, he spared no effort to enhance the Latin American image on the home front by directly involving his top aides in the formulation and execution of hemispheric policy.

Following the failure of the London and Geneva talks, Roosevelt and Hull were ever more determined to make the Montevideo conference a major foreign policy success. In this they took a great risk, given the disastrous results of the previous hemispheric meeting at Havana in 1928 with its acrimonious clashes between the United States and Argentina over the nonintervention issue that led many observers to conclude that Pan Americanism had come to an end.[41] But the new atmosphere created by Roosevelt's Good Neighbor proclamations and the significant concessions made on this point, combined with Hull's skill as a negotiator, turned the conference into a major landmark in hemispheric relations, ushering in a new and more wholesome era. On January 20, 1934, on his return to Washington, Cordell Hull penned this assessment of the Montevideo conference:

> When our delegates figuratively took off their coats . . . and dispensed with all possible formality in applying work of conference, an immediate response was evoked. When the President, supported [by] the action of the delegation, emphasized the assurance that the United States disavows and despises all the old themes of conquest and armed intervention, it became evident that solidarity of purpose of all the Americas could be attained. For the first time in the history of such conferences, there was no imposing block arranged against us.[42]

Even allowing for the heady climate left by the closing speeches in the heat of the Uruguayan summer, Hull's self-congratulatory tone corresponded to the overwhelmingly optimistic assessments the conference received in both Latin America and the United States. The meeting was deemed to have opened a new era in relations between north and south. Latin Americans hailed the end of interventions in the Caribbean area.

The obvious sincerity of President Roosevelt's expressed wish to make the inter-American community a model of his Good Neighbor policy and the earthy cordiality of Secretary Hull deeply impressed the Latin Americans, with whom personality counts for so much. The patrician demeanor and willingness to compromise of the Secretary made him a favorite both of the Latin American delegates and the press. Marquis Childs, the respected columnist, referred to him as "the sainted man from Tennessee."[43] Still, the value of the Montevideo conference lay not so much in actual measures that went into effect as in a practical test, in the limelight of an international conference, of reoriented US policy toward Latin America under the first Roosevelt administration.[44] Sharpening this image was the historical context of the Pan American conferences. Only five years before Montevideo, at the Havana Conference, the most acrimonious debates that ever occurred in the history of the Pan American conferences took place around the nonintervention issue. Here is the nonintervention clause of a draft for a Convention on the Rights and Duties of States, which prohibited intervention and contained a very broad definition that would have forestalled almost any action by one government that might have domestic repercussions in another state:

> Any act of a State, through diplomatic representation, by armed force or by any other means involving effective force, with a view to making the State's will dominate the will of another State, and, in general, any maneuver, interference or interposition of any sort, employing such means, either directly or indirectly in matter of obligations to another State, whatever its motive, shall be considered as Intervention, and likewise a violation of International Law.[45]

The proposed article amounted to a pledge of absolute noninterference by individual states and reflected the gravity with which Latin American governments viewed the issue in the context of their history and as central for their future developments as modern, independent states. It was nonetheless rejected by the US delegation, which was willing to bind itself to its own traditional nonintervention doctrine, which was oriented more to relations with the Old World but no further. A new article was substituted and became Article 8 of the Montevideo Convention on the Rights and Duties of States. It provided simply that "no state has the right to intervene in the internal or external affairs of another state."

The United States ratified it but reserved the right to interpret the terms of the pledge in the light of the previous policies of President Franklin D. Roosevelt and in the terms of what it considered to be general international law. As Hull told the conference:

> Every observing person must by this time thoroughly understand that under the Roosevelt Administration the United States Government is as much opposed as any other government to interference with the freedom, the sovereignty, or other internal affairs or processes of the government of other nations . . . I feel safe in undertaking to say that under our support of the general principle of nonintervention as has been suggested, no government need fear any intervention on the part of the United States under the Roosevelt Administration.[46]

Roosevelt wasted no time in bringing the events in distant Uruguay to the forefront of national attention. Even before the conference adjourned, on December 29, he again expounded on his Latin American policy before the prestigious Woodrow Wilson Foundation in Washington, portraying his efforts as a sequel to the task Wilson left uncompleted. Recalling Wilson's pledge that "the United States will never again seek one additional foot of territory by conquest," Roosevelt observed:

> We know that largely as a result of the convulsion of the World War and its after effects, the complete fruition of that policy of unselfishness has not in every case been obtained. And in this we, all of us, in all of these American Nations have to share the responsibility . . . the time has come to supplement and to implement the declaration of President Wilson by the further declaration that the definite policy of the United States from now on is one opposed to armed intervention.[47]

He then quoted almost verbatim from an earlier article he had written for *Foreign Affairs*:

> The maintenance of constitutional government in other Nations, is not a sacred obligation evolving upon the United States alone. The maintenance of law and the orderly process of government in this hemisphere is the concern of each individual Nation within its own borders first of all. It is only if and when the failure of the orderly process affects the other Nations of the continent that it becomes their concern; and the point to stress is that in such an event it becomes the joint concern of the whole continent in which we are neighbors. It is the comprehension of that doctrine—comprehension not by the leaders alone but by the peoples of all the American Republics—that has made the conference now concluding its labor in Montevideo such a splendid success.[48]

The accomplishments of the Montevideo conference were the centerpiece of Roosevelt's annual report to Congress a week later. He emphasized the meeting not only to help build confidence in the hemisphere but also to alert Congress and the nation to the importance the administration was placing on inter-American relations. Roosevelt cited the Seventh Pan American Conference as "the greatest accomplishment" in foreign policy thus far in his administration and announced that his first trip abroad as president would be a cruise to Haiti, Colombia and Panama. He had already met with the presidents of Haiti and Panama late in 1933. In June, on the eve of the trip, he was visited at the White House by the president-elect of Colombia, Alfonso Lopez Pumarejo.

By the time the Buenos Aires conference was held three years later, the confidence that Roosevelt's policies inspired in Latin America knew no modern parallel. He was one of the few statesmen who in the midst of the national and world anguish of the mid-1930s seemed to have no fear of the future. While confidence in liberal democracy was everywhere in crisis, he believed in his own strength and ability to forge ahead, he believed in the economic and political resilience of the United States, and he believed in the common destiny of progress and liberty of the New World.

When Roosevelt in January 1936 launched the idea of holding a peace conference in the Argentine capital, he immediately won a warm response from the Latin American leaders. Their replies uniformly suggested the favorable impact created in 1933 when he committed the United States to abide by the noninterventionist clauses signed at Montevideo. Colombian President Lopez Pumarejo, one of the hemisphere's most respected democratic leaders, spoke for most of them in a message welcoming the prospective conference:

> In World Councils and Assemblies . . . we have been playing a role subordinate to the conveniences of the great European nations, which accept our adherence to anti-war pacts, which solicit our effective cooperation . . . to give them weight . . . but do not consult our will when they consider it possible to dispense with them. . . .
>
> A very appropriate continental atmosphere now exists for the strengthening of relations of the other American Republics with that republic over which Your Excellency worthily presides. . . . We Colombians understand the policy which the present President of the United States is developing to be a radical and favorable modification of the policy which formerly aroused uneasiness and mistrust among the Latin American peoples.[49]

Like Roosevelt, Lopez and other democrats in Latin America sought to lead their peoples in founding a new society in which the principles of equality and social justice enshrined in their constitutions would be translated into reality and not compromised by powerful oligarchies manipulated by special interests.

Years later, John Gunther rightly characterized Lopez as a man who "greatly admired FDR and wanted to emulate the New Deal," and who sought "to grab Colombia by the neck and bring it to modern times. He set up a social security system that is still one of the best on the continent, encouraged labor to organize, and did more for education than any Colombian in a generation."[50] He might have added that Lopez was one of many Latin American leaders whose earlier anti-Yankeeism had been converted by Roosevelt's policies.

FDR'S CUBAN DILEMMA

At times the "new era," as Roosevelt liked to call it, ran into impediments erected by the past. Just months after his inauguration in March 1933, the growing underground war against the detested eight-year-old tyranny of General Gerardo Machado of Cuba posed the first major foreign policy crisis for the young Roosevelt administration. Significantly, the Cuban crisis offers a scenario of divergent views, misperceptions and missed opportunities that would be repeated numerous times over the next five decades. Because this 1933 event has been largely forgotten, the episode deserves detailed attention. The rise and fall of the Machado regime prepared the ground not only for the rule of Fulgencio Batista but also the subsequent events that led to Fidel Castro and US–Cuban estrangement less than three decades later. Hugh Thomas, in his encyclopedic history of Cuba, properly recognized the Castro revolution as a sequel to the events of 1933: "an act which cast long shadows over events in the 1950s a generation later."[51]

On a broader canvas, the Cuban crisis of 1933 offers a look at an endemic Latin American drama in which power and liberty, the idea of progress and resistance to change, are locked in a remorseless struggle, with the United States invariably playing a decisive, if at times unwanted and unwilling, role. Cuba's internal factional disputes cannot be minimized; but given the pervasive influence of the United States, some crucial turning points can be identified that, if different attitudes and policies had prevailed, might have decisively altered the history of Cuba and its relations with the United States.

The paradigmatic question posed by the consequences of the downfall of Machado and subsequent dictatorships is whether it could not have been otherwise. Were alternatives available that could have avoided events that led to Batista's ascent? Had the incipient social revolution of 1933 been allowed to run its course, might it have forestalled the radical explosion Fidel Castro brought to the island in the 1950s? An insight into another option is provided by one of the most intensive epistolary duels in the annals of US diplomacy, that between Josephus Daniels and Sumner Welles.

They were two powerful contenders: Welles, the debonair foreign service officer and Roosevelt family friend whom the president had dispatched to Havana, and Daniels, the veteran seventy-two-year-old Raleigh newspaper publisher, staunch New Dealer and former secretary of the navy and Roosevelt's superior in the Wilson administration, whom the president had appointed ambassador to Mexico. Their sharply contrasting positions emerge poignantly, and often full of contradictions, in what might be called the "war of missives." From Havana come Welles's reports urging the president and the State Department to intervene to "stabilize" the Cuban situation and then, when FDR would not listen, to withhold diplomatic recognition from the revolutionary junta that replaced Machado, foiling, in the process, a popular movement demanding social justice. From Mexico, we have Daniels's unrelenting warnings against any form of intervention, citing the distress of not only the Mexican government but most of the Latin American diplomats posted in the capital. The polemic reached its climax when a revolutionary junta ousted the conservative civilians Welles helped install after the fall of Machado.

The revolutionaries, so Welles's argument goes, were a handful of incompetent "communistic" radicals who were incapable of establishing efficient government and public order and were a threat to US investments and commercial interests. Daniels, in contrast, pleads to give them a chance; he reports that not only the Mexican government but most of the diplomats in the Mexican capital who knew anything about the Cuban situation considered the university professors and lawyers who emerged as leaders of the revolutionary movement to be liberals and "honorable men." "They are very tense down here," Daniels told Hull. "They feel that if we intervene it will destroy the Montevideo Conference," the inter-American meeting scheduled for the coming December.[52]

If only the Roosevelt administration had recognized them, things might have turned out better in the end.

Welles's role in Cuba in 1933—and Daniels's emphatic dissent—constitutes a perfect study of the dilemmas confronting a brand new administration when it is forced to answer anew fundamental general questions about relations with Latin America: How to deal with revolutionary situations? What kind of allies does it want to have? Must it stand by and tolerate oppression and rioting in the name of respecting sovereign rights? Is it prepared to risk the rise of a revolutionary regime likely to imperil US property and investments?

"MORE A PROCONSUL THAN AN AMBASSADOR"

On the day before Roosevelt's enunciation of the Good Neighbor doctrine on March 4, the State Department received a report from the US embassy in Havana calling attention to "the increasing state of unrest prevailing in Cuba." The unrest of course had been building for years. A succession of violent disorders arose from the Depression and from the murderous, corrupt rule of Machado. By 1932, Hoover's ambassador, Harry F. Guggenheim, heir to a family mining fortune in South America, was recommending abrogation of the Platt amendment. He wrote the State Department, "I am in complete agreement with the dictum that it is far better for Cuba to make her own mistakes than to have our government make mistakes for her."[53] But in an election year nobody in the Hoover administration was particularly interested in raising the Cuban issue before Congress. Consequently Guggenheim's enlightened position became known only in 1934, after he published a book.

On being alerted that the Machado regime was tottering, Roosevelt at first sought to ignore the problem. He had been assured by the State Department that Cuba was more secure than most other neighbor nations, since Machado had the backing of the military. Like most official assessments in Latin America, it failed to appreciate the intense popular hatred the dictator generated alongside mounting anti-American nationalism. When it finally became obvious that the Cuban dictator, once favored by the Hoover administration, was about to be overthrown, Roosevelt dispatched Welles to Havana as his special ambassador with express instructions to mediate between the rival factions in such a way as to ease Machado out. But the wily dictator, as might have been foreseen with a man who had ruled his country with an iron fist since 1929, refused to oblige. Welles's handling of the Cuban crisis exposed the perhaps unconscious prejudices of a man who had been raised in the class-conscious parameters of New York aristocracy and the professional foreign service. His background made him vulnerable to pitfalls that Welles, unlike Roosevelt, could never overcome. Like someone who never personally experienced the brutality of a repressive regime, he ignored the depth of hatred and alienation it generated. He clearly identified with the Cuban elite of conservative politicians, landowners and sugar barons as a kind of honorary fellowship, the only ones capable of ensuring order and stability. In so doing, of course, he lifted the actual political situation out of its historical setting. By all accounts, during his first three months in Havana he became, in the words of Hugh Thomas, "the arbiter of Cuba's destinies. . . . More a Proconsul than an ambassador."[54]

After eight years of Machado's brutal rule, Cuba's political scene had become too polarized for the kind of expedient compromises the United States wanted. When friendly persuasion failed, Welles rallied Machado's more moderate opponents with the incentive of trade concessions and liberal loans once a democratic government was installed, thereby reverting to the old and much resented pattern of intervening in the island's internal affairs. Curiously, the expert Welles was willing to sacrifice relations with the rest of Latin America for the sake of resolving the Cuban imbroglio, whereas Daniels, the newcomer, argued from the broader perspective, mindful of Latin American opinion as a whole and bearing in mind long-range US strategic interests.

Welles was supremely confident of his ability to persuade Machado to accept a peaceful transition to a civilian government. Other foreign diplomats in Havana were more skeptical; they suspected that the Cuban dictator was simply using the US mediation effort to preserve his power. Indeed, it soon became clear that Machado would resort to all the maneuvers and ruses that have since become a familiar pattern for Latin American dictators dealing with

Washington. His main argument was the classic one—that he was the best and only guarantee for law and order and the protection of US investments.

In their determination to stay in power, the dictators, when pressed by Washington, would even consent to some of the trappings of democracy while their goon squads continued (perhaps more discreetly) to sow terror in back alleys and rural hamlets away from the presence of foreign diplomats and inquisitive newsmen. If local embassies or the State Department didn't always fall for this choreography, the dictator would rely on somebody in Congress, the US business or banking communities or a national columnist to argue his case. Over the years this routine became an endless pas de deux.

In the case of Machado, months of frantic efforts by Welles led only to frustrating deadlocks until the Cubans took matters into their own hands: a general strike and popular outrage at a massacre of students finally led to general uprisings culminating in Machado's flight from the country on August 12, 1933—practically writing the script for the similar demise of the dictatorship of Fulgencio Batista a quarter century later. To force Machado's hand, Welles had threatened to bring the US Navy to Cuban ports—a move that was in keeping with the provisions of the Platt amendment, which made the United States responsible for maintaining internal peace on the island. Such actions, the Cubans were told, were not intervention but "measures intended to prevent the necessity of intervention."

Under a plan devised by Welles, Machado finally yielded power to a provisional government headed by Carlos Manuel de Céspedes, a colorless veteran diplomat and the patrician grandson of one of Cuba's independence heroes. By choosing the conservative Céspedes, the United States turned a deaf ear to the popular forces that were at the heart of the revolutionary situation building up in the Caribbean island. The new government was not able to cope with the wave of political revanchism and anarchy that was the Machado legacy: a thousand former Machado officials and policemen were killed and hundreds of homes were sacked. Within days the popular disaffection culminated in a mutiny of the rank-and-file of the army, the bloodless "sergeant's revolt" that launched the political career of a sergeant-stenographer named Fulgencio Batista, who would dominate Cuban politics for the next quarter century.

Welles's experience in Latin America made it even more puzzling that he failed to grasp the legitimacy of the revolutionary stirrings among the Cuban people provoked by the brutal Machado regime. Nor did he understand that policies advocated by the conservatives, and even the moderates he supported as successors to Machado, were obsolete. This inability to gauge bitter popular resentment led to short-term solutions that invariably unraveled into long-range disasters for Cuban and US interests alike.

THE PENTARQUÍA AND A
SERGEANT NAMED BATISTA

On September 5, the rank-and-file of the army led by Sergeant Batista mutinied and installed a revolutionary junta of five civilians, known as the Pentarquía, as the provisional government. The junta was headed by Dr. Ramón Grau San Martín, dean of the medical faculty in the university of Havana who had lived in exile during the last half of the Machado regime. Other members were a banker, a journalist and two prominent lawyers. The revolution was carried out with no bloodshed and comparatively little disorder, a testimony to the ousted government's lack of popularity.

A new nationalist fervor, including the rejection of Welles's intrusive role, was in the air. The Directorio Estudiantil, Cuba's most prominent university students' association, declared itself "against the whole unhappy business of mediation and the inanimate government named by the U.S. Ambassador" and came out in favor of the revolution. Sergio Carbó, a prominent editor who prepared the Proclamation of the Revolutionaries, told the *New York Times*: "At daybreak on September 5, 1933, the Republic came of age and, with cries of joy, escaped from the American embassy." Raúl Róa, another former exile and professor of law, wrote that with the Pentarquía for the first time Cuba had "an authentically revolutionary government backed and nourished by the great popular masses without the previous authorization of Washington and its agent in Cuba." Less than three decades later the same Róa, blaming the United States for thwarting the reformist revolution of 1933 in favor of an impending Batista dictatorship, embraced the communist regime of Fidel Castro to become its foreign minister.

The day after it was installed in power, the "de facto revolutionary government" announced it would guarantee the lives and property of foreign citizens and recognize foreign indebtedness. None of these assurances diminished Welles's hostility or surprise. Reporting on the coup at 1:00 A.M. on September 5, a shocked Welles informed Washington: "The action taken has been fomented by the extreme radical elements." At 8:00 A.M. he added, "A sergeant named Batista has been installed as chief of staff." Within a few days Batista promoted himself to colonel, won US confidence by turning against his former allies, and became the most powerful political force in Cuba for the next twenty-five years.

After the coup, Welles suggested that a small detachment of Marines be landed to protect the US embassy and the National Hotel in Havana, where he, other US citizens and 500 armed senior army officers opposed to the coup were living. He argued that "the government of Cuba today is an undisciplined group of individuals of divergent tendencies representing the most irresponsible elements of the city of Havana."[55]

GRAU SAN MARTÍN'S RESILIENCE

A superficial observer in the last months of 1933 might have had the impression that the revolutionary government headed by Dr. Ramón Grau San Martín had essentially solidified its control over the country. A number of attempted coups by the deposed army officers were put down and the conservative parties seemed too divided among themselves to represent a serious danger. In reality, however, the revolutionary regime was moving relentlessly toward its demise, largely because it failed to win recognition from the United States.

While Washington's manifest hostility fueled the nationalist zeal of intellectuals and students, it eventually cost the regime the support of Batista and his troops—leading to the installation of the army as a powerful political force for the first time in Cuban history. Why was the United States so steadfastly opposed to the revolutionary junta and Dr. Grau? For one thing, Welles actively supported the counterrevolutionary forces seeking to restore the Céspedes regime he considered to be the constitutional successor of Machado. Thus he rigidly maintained that the United States could not recognize a government that had seized power illegally. In addition to Welles's personal resentment, there was also an ingrained preference in the State Department for dealing with established institutions and preserving stability, and a corresponding fear of the political consequences of social upheaval. With these personal, political and cultural biases coloring the news from Cuba, it was difficult for the president to obtain impartial information from his envoy in Havana.

No sooner was the junta sworn in than Welles began a bold exercise of what a few decades later became known as destabilization—a campaign of covert and overt pressure aimed at destroying a regime considered inimical to US interests. He peremptorily told junta representatives that any new bloodshed would at once lead to US intervention. Simultaneously, he was in constant touch with members of the ousted government and other political leaders.

Most importantly, he deliberately maneuvered to separate Sergeant Batista from the revolutionary movement with seductive entreaties that he was the only one in Cuba powerful enough to take over, broadly hinting that a more conservative government would immediately win important political and economic concessions from the United States.

On September 5, Welles called on Washington to send a detachment of marines to protect the US embassy and the Hotel Nacional in Havana. He also sounded out Washington on the idea of sending a larger force to maintain order until an acceptable government was formed. Roosevelt and Hull wisely did not follow Welles's suggestions. Though they agreed to send warships in case US citizens had to be evacuated, they did not want to send troops.

Meanwhile from Mexico Ambassador Daniels pleaded fervently for absolute restraint of US interference in the internal affairs of the other American republics. In a private letter written on September 9, the same day Welles had requested the dispatch of warships, Daniels urged Hull to consider the adverse psychological effect on Latin America if the United States intervened in Cuba under the Platt amendment. "Something ought to be done to get rid of Machado," he conceded, but Washington should not do the job alone. "Would it not be better," he asked, "for us to ask the cooperation of the ABC [Argentina, Brazil, Chile] countries or a representative of Mexico and nearby Latin American countries, with a view to securing peace in Cuba than to act alone?"

After again conferring with the Mexican foreign minister, Daniels telegraphed an additional warning that Mexico believed unilateral intervention by the United States not only "would not be approved by Latin American countries," but might indeed militate against agreements by the [Pan American] Montevideo Conference" which was scheduled for December. Thus began an extraordinary behind-the-scenes diplomatic disputation between two ambassadors, each trying to persuade Washington to follow a different course, each using his personal relationship with the chief executive to sway the State Department, each in his own way deeply devoted to the cause of US–Latin American friendship. Unfortunately, these seminal polemical exchanges have been only sporadically recorded in general accounts of US diplomatic history of the period.

"INTERVENTION BY INERTIA"

The president basically agreed with Daniels; he knew that landing troops in Cuba would wreck his long-range plans for the Good Neighbor policy to advance hemispheric cooperation. Accordingly, Roosevelt and Hull were crystal clear in their instructions to Welles—they decided to permit the envoy to order the landing of marine guards only if he and his staff were in actual danger, but otherwise they thought such a move would be imprudent.

Hull, drawing on the lessons of past US interventions, decried the use of troops and asserted, "We will never be able to come out and we will have on our hands the trouble of thirty years ago." At the same time, Roosevelt admonished the press "to lay off this intervention stuff. . . . That is absolutely the last thing we have in mind. We don't want to do it." Roosevelt's statements reflected a concerted effort by the administration to ward off criticism, both domestic and foreign, of Welles's intrusive diplomacy.

The US government thus reacted with supreme caution when on September 10, Cuba's revolutionary Executive Committee chose one of its members, Dr. Grau San Martín, a distinguished surgeon and former dean of the Havana University Medical School, to the office of provisional president. Grau was enthusiastically supported by the Student Directorate and the junior army officers. But Welles had already described Grau as "communistic," "utterly impractical" and an "extreme radical."

Few if any knowledgeable Latin Americans shared the envoy's assessment, least of all the Mexicans who were closely following the internal developments in Cuba as well as Welles's wheeling and dealing. Within a few days of Grau's selection, the Mexican government concluded that the new president had succeeded in forming a stable regime capable of maintaining order. Mexico consequently abandoned its mediation efforts and suggested privately that the time had come for the United States to withdraw its naval forces from Cuban waters lest their presence encourage counterrevolutionary moves. Ambassador Daniels refrained from giving official advice on this point, but he left no doubt that he sympathized with the Mexican view that Cuba was undergoing a healthy social revolution that deserved Washington's approval.

Welles, after unsuccessfully trying to induce the Roosevelt administration into military intervention that would force the reinstatement of Céspedes, turned to another Wilsonian tactic: refusing to recognize the revolutionary government on the grounds that it was unconstitutional and could not prove it had the support of the governed. He suggested a public declaration that the United States could not and would not recognize anything but a legitimate and constitutional government in Cuba unless there was conclusive evidence that it represented the will of a majority of the people. In a significant aside, he prognosticated that "no government here can survive for a protracted period without recognition by the United States."

Welles had deliberately trapped the Cuban regime in a vicious circle—without a stable government there would be no recognition, and without recognition there could be no stability. Many Cubans felt that the United States had refrained from armed intervention and official diplomatic action only to take up the equally serviceable weapon that Grau, in an interview with the *New York Times*, aptly called "intervention by inertia." Welles listened mostly to his conservative friends, as so often happened with what Daniels sarcastically called the "old-style" US diplomats in Latin America.

Just as some three decades later US intelligence officers fed on similar sources to become convinced of their predictions of the imminent collapse of the Castro regime, so Welles sent Washington the bleakest possible reports about the prospects of Dr. Grau's provisional government. Economic and political conditions were "verging upon complete prostration," he informed the State Department. Despite Welles's wishful thinking, the Grau regime withstood being cold-shouldered by the United States as well as repeated attempted coups, partly inspired by Washington's policy of nonrecognition, and remained in power until January 1934.

Judging from Roosevelt's notes explaining the administration's response to the Cuban troubles, it was Welles's analysis from Havana that prevailed. If the Roosevelt administration had recognized the Grau administration as a caretaker government, things might have turned out better in the end. After meeting with Welles at Warm Springs, Georgia, Roosevelt publicly reaffirmed US intentions not to accord recognition to a regime it claimed lacked popular support. Latin Americans were outraged, feeling that nonrecognition was an invitation to Grau's enemies to overturn his rule—which of course was the point. For his part, then, Daniels could take satisfaction in winning the war for Roosevelt's rededication to the doctrine of nonintervention.

In retrospect, it would appear that the Cuban experience removed any lingering doubt Roosevelt might have retained from his headier manifest destiny days about the wisdom of renouncing the right to unilateral interventions. As it turned out, in January 1934, after more than four months of nonrecognition from the United States, Grau resigned—under pressure of Washington's latest ally, "a sergeant named Fulgencio Batista." The new interim president, Carlos Mendieta, a moderate conservative, was recognized by Washington within five days.

Daniels had accurately measured the true nature of the Grau regime: it represented nationalist forces seeking to establish a new social order, not part of a communist conspiracy. Soon Welles himself acknowledged this popular nationalism as a key factor in twentieth-century Latin American politics and became one of the most zealous and eloquent advocates of the nonintervention policy. However, the switch came too late to ingratiate the diplomat with the Raleigh editor.

FDR AND THE GOOD NEIGHBOR:
A BALANCE SHEET

The English political scientist Harold Laski, a friend and mentor to many high-ranking New Deal officials, probably came closer than any analyst of his day to an intellectual premonition of the fate of the Good Neighbor policy and what the future had in store for inter-American relations. Already in 1948, only three years after Roosevelt's death, he gave this penetrating account of the US policy toward Latin America in his popular work, *The American Democracy*,

> Broadly speaking, the record of the United States as an international power is better than that of most other great nations. It has not, indeed, been an especially good record in Latin America; there it has continuously used authority backed by force to impose its will upon States with which it has disagreed; and while it is true that the settlement with Mexico over the latter's oil nationalization policy was an admirable example of what President Roosevelt called the attitude of the "good neighbor," the attitude is new, and it is far too early to assume that it has become a permanent part of the American outlook.
>
> Yet it is far from easy to be certain if this is any more than a temporary stage in America's view of its place in the world. Above all to secure peace and stability in the relations between states leading the world to a rational scheme of organization.[56]

In a scant twelve years, the Roosevelt administration developed a coherent, long-range hemispheric policy that effectively dispelled Latin American mistrust, won overwhelming congressional support, and substantially improved and consolidated the inter-American system. The extent of the transformation brought about by Roosevelt's New Deal and Good Neighbor policies was reflected in the drastically changed attitudes of the region's liberal democratic movements previously opposed to Pan Americanism.

It was, foremost, a period that saw the credibility of the United States enhanced by coherence between goals and means, self-interest and principles— with words always being followed by accomplishments. As we have seen, by 1941 virtually all the American republics rallied around the United States in defense of hemispheric security—a stupendous achievement compared to the picture of disarray that the inter-American community presented in the 1920s and early 1930s. How did this come about, considering that in previous administrations Latin America had generally been a contentious, ill-defined theme?

As president, Roosevelt grew through his experiences in Latin America to achieve new stature. He went there in touch with the realities of the Latin American situation and he began to understand them and their implications long before many of his countrymen did. In the address he delivered after his return from South America in December 1936, he presented a compelling argument about the common goals and values that unite the New World.

But it is unlikely that Roosevelt would have secured Latin American support so swiftly and with so little contention for so many measures without chemistry and credibility. This was partly the result of Cordell Hull and Welles's attempt to build the Western Hemisphere idea through the Good Neighbor diplomacy. Far more, it was the outcome of the force of Roosevelt's vision and personality. Accordingly, it is not merely sentimentality or anecdotal interest that makes this Roosevelt style such an attractive model right now. Nobody can easily understand his attitude toward intervention, for example, without reflecting on the remarkable fact that in his youth, fascinated by the example of cousin Theodore, he was one of its most determined advocates—before experience taught him that as a foreign policy practice it more often than not is counterproductive.

The great accomplishments in the 1930s and 1940s, such as the renunciation of interventionism, the annulment of the Platt amendment and the constant attention Roosevelt bestowed on hemispheric affairs, were part of a larger scheme of things; their forms, idiosyncratic though they may have been, were woven successfully into a whole foreign policy pattern. After two generations of post-Rooseveltian departures from such principles and styles that have resulted in the United States practically standing alone and aloof from the rest of the hemisphere like minimalist sculpture, such values seem important once again.

Today more than ever the most convincing attribute of adhering to the principle of nonintervention enshrined in our treaty obligations both within the inter-American system and the United Nations is not nostalgia for the Roosevelt era, but sensible policy. The vital danger inherent in the American position is the simple one that its drive to expand may come to be regarded as a mission—the manifest destiny of the United States—at this turning point in the history of civilization when the power and authority of America are at their zenith. No student of the history of the United States can afford to omit this element from his assessment of the future.

Franklin Roosevelt repudiated the idea that the United States must act alone in the exercise of this authority. He urged that "when the failure of orderly processes affects the other nations of the continent . . . it becomes the joint concern of a whole continent in which we are all neighbors." But Mr. Roosevelt was not then president, and he gave no guide to the institutional method by which he would have translated his approach into action.

STALWART NONINTERVENTION, DICTATORS INCLUDED

Surely to have expected Roosevelt to use the Good Neighbor policy for the primary purpose of rooting out autocratic governments is to misconstrue its most important theoretical underpinning: the recognition of nonintervention, self-determination and multilateralism as fundamental principles of the inter-American system. Clearly this was based on the conviction that US policy was best served by recognizing that each country had to be left to resolve its own internal problems. Furthermore, to criticize Roosevelt as bland on principle because he continued to deal with undemocratic regimes, even in wartime, implies a moral absolutism that would hold him to standards completely at variance with his political pragmatism.

Some criticism of Roosevelt's toleration of dictatorships early in his administration came from liberal historians, such as Frederick Schuman, who were riled by his failure to adopt more forceful action against Hitler and Mussolini. Attributing the president's caution to a character flaw rather than to his sense of what the American people were prepared to accept, the noted historian observed, "Since he liked being liked, and feared being hated, he was ever tempted to trim his sails to the shifting winds of opinion, despite his earnest desire to build a better American society and a free world order."[57]

They also passed over the extraordinary confusion that existed on the domestic and international scenes at the time Roosevelt entered the White House. Indeed, as noted earlier in this chapter, nowhere were his international problems more immediate and complicated than in Cuba. Popular upheaval was threatening the entrenched Machado dictatorship, whose brutality the Hoover administration had tolerated for years.

Roosevelt's determination to respect the autonomy of America's neighbor republics enunciated in his *Foreign Affairs* article of 1928, so antithetical in spirit and practice to the policy of his predecessors, requires further consideration. The circumstances frequently cited by chroniclers of his first term in office are the absorption of the nation in domestic problems, popular aversion to military involvement abroad—or isolationism—and the president's historical memory of the adverse effect in Latin America of past interventions. Yet critical domestic problems are frequently an incentive, rather than a deterrent, encouraging leaders to resort to foreign adventure in order to divert the public from intractable issues at home. Why did Roosevelt not consider resorting to this political expedient? For one thing, the Roosevelt revolution rejected many old practices, especially those that in the long term had proved disastrous in national as well as international affairs. Possibly Roosevelt, the student of Turner, was imbued with the spirit of innovation and exploration so characteristic of the westward movement.

Roosevelt's sensitive reaction to the menace of totalitarianism in the twentieth century stands in memorable contrast to the obtuse and dull reactions of nearly all other leaders of the democratic nations. A shrewd recognition of the dangers to democracy in the modern world enabled him to identify the key elements of a positive democratic government. Nowhere were these beliefs more forcefully presented than in his numerous Pan American addresses, for he consistently identified the fate of his nation with that of the whole hemisphere, the New World. Fascism, communism and national socialism were concrete realities of decisive importance; his understanding of their decisive importance enabled Roosevelt to suggest the proper course of action at home. The task confronting American democracy was not to lead a crusade against communism. The first duty was to create within the country, and later in the hemisphere as a whole, the conditions that would make communism impossible.

HOPE AND THE SEEDS OF DISAPPOINTMENT

Paradoxically, the same attitudes and policies that brought harmony and cooperation to the inter-American scene from the early 1930s to the mid-1940s contained the ingredients of the disillusionment and alienation that followed the passing of the Roosevelt era. Roosevelt kindled hopes and expectations that none of his successors, perhaps with the exception of President John F. Kennedy, seemed able to fulfill. Latin America became frustrated with US absorption in its commitments to Europe and Asia, even before the war ended, at the expense of what the Latin Americans regarded their just dues, given the general cooperation they extended to the Allies and the promises made by Washington during the war.

Few foresaw that the goodwill generated by the Roosevelt era would also be eroded by the wholesale impoverishment of the region as a result of plummeting commodity prices. Many were disappointed and some felt betrayed. From the world of Roosevelt and Hull to the world of Eisenhower and Dulles, the United States had regressed in less than a decade from the vigorous assurance of the Good Neighbor policy to something like the frustration and angry confrontation of the dollar diplomacy of the 1920s and, after the Guatemala episode of 1954, to something reminiscent of the Big Stick policy.

Still, the guidelines Roosevelt brought to US policy toward Latin America were so revolutionary that fifty years later they are still hard to grasp and should be counted among his greatest and earliest foreign policy successes. Roosevelt undertook, and to an unprecedented degree accomplished, the task of building, without resort to force or intimidation, a continental community out of diverse countries in size, cultural traditions and economic conditions; he established a self-governing regional system in which the tiniest state had equal juridical voice and vote with the largest. For a dozen years and more the policy was a permanent part of hemispheric relations.

However, no policy could undo in a few months or even years the negative legacy of the four previous decades. Despite the renovation, recovery and reform Roosevelt had brought to the inter-American scene, his Good Neighbor policy was not without its critics, both at home and abroad. To domestic conservatives the new doctrine's renunciation of intervention—the protection they had enjoyed under dollar diplomacy—was tantamount to betrayal. Radical US progressives, on the other hand, complained that the reforms were neither deep enough to change the inequities of the region's economic and social structures nor effective as a weapon to remove the dictatorships that tarnished the hemisphere's political geography.

Although in Latin America the significance of Roosevelt's Good Neighbor policy has retained a vivid meaning, it has had a distinctly checkered career in US historiography. At first the juxtaposition of the cordiality that marked inter-American relations during Roosevelt's presidency and the distrust and animosity that preceded it led to reductionism and even self-congratulatory bombast, as the memoirs of Hull and Welles can attest. During the postwar years, the old images were blurred by successive interpretations, the absorption with the Cold War and global politics, and a corresponding decline of interest in Latin America by foreign policy experts, except as it intersected in the global struggle against communism. Occasionally enthusiasts of realpolitik focused on the security advantages that wartime unity had brought to the United States, while revisionists tended to consign the Good Neighbor policy to the realm of nostalgia or myth, belittling its impact on hemispheric relations or ignoring it altogether. According to Humphreys, the proclamation of the Good Neighbor policy in 1933 was

> more than a realization that the Caribbean policy of the United States had outlived its usefulness and was in fact menacing the political and economic relations of the United States with the Latin American states. It was an expression of American idealism at its best, and it was a recognition also of the increasing maturity of the Latin American states.[58]

The Good Neighbor policy was a policy, according to historian Bryce Wood, in that it was "principled action, demonstrating in promise and behavior over a period of time such evidence of continuity that assumptions of stability may with confidence be based upon it."[59] Furthermore, it would easily have passed all the tests currently applied to differentiate rhetoric and sporadic tactical steps from what constitutes real policy. What will be its place in history? In the words of James McGregor Burns, author of a two-volume biography of Roosevelt,

The crucial test of excellence in this kind of leadership is the capacity of the President not simply to represent the voters in the narrow sense, but to move ahead of them, to ignore their more transient and petty interests—in a sense to misrepresent them, at least until the next presidential election comes around. At the same time, however, the President is a constitutional officer elected by the people, accountable to them, and dependent on them for support. On the President's understanding of when he must directly respond to the fleeting interests of the people, and when he must transcend them, turns his ultimate success as a political leader.[60]

The positive side of the Good Neighbor policy was reflected at successive Pan American conferences, emphasizing multilateralism, mutuality of interests and the evocation of reciprocity in trade and economic matters. In the six meetings of foreign ministers held between 1933 and 1940, the idea was accepted that threats of aggression from abroad or within the hemisphere would be dealt with through consultation among all American states.

The seventh Pan American conference at Montevideo in December 1933, at which the United States accepted a resolution denying the right of intervention by one state into the internal or external affairs of another, infused new life into the Pan American movement. Three years later almost to the day at Buenos Aires, the Inter-American Conference for the Maintenance of Peace, opened by Roosevelt, was to adopt a still more sweeping protocol against the right and practice of intervention. Its consultative part recognized the joint responsibility of the American nations to prevent hostilities among themselves and provided for consultation in the event of a threat to the peace of the hemisphere from within or without its borders. At the eighth Pan American conference at Lima (1938) and the ninth one at Havana (1940), these pledges were renewed in a more specific form and machinery was devised to implement the procedure of consultation agreed on at Buenos Aires and to act as a unit in dealing with the rest of the world. Despite Argentina's initial objections, that integrating principle became the central purpose of the Pan American Union, the flagship of the regional system, which in 1948 would become the Organization of American States (OAS).

The innovations Roosevelt brought about through the Good Neighbor policy and the effective and compelling form in which he executed them are relevant issues today, and have become, if anything, more critical than they were in his own lifetime. Above all, they provide a case study of how ancient antagonisms can best be overcome by understanding the problems of others, exercising some empathy and balancing national interest with the interests of the Pan

American community at large. Significantly, Roosevelt found that while isolationism and isolationist tendencies prevented him from following an activist foreign policy in Europe and Asia, there was no opposition to building closer ties with Latin America, culminating with the conclusion at Rio de Janeiro in 1942 of a regional defense pact in the interest of hemispheric security. Each convention, each treaty Roosevelt submitted to Congress binding the nation more closely to the other American republics was approved by the Senate without a dissenting vote.

By November 1936, Roosevelt could confidently declare in an address to the Brazilian Congress: "There are, it is true, conflicts of interest between the American States, but they cannot be called serious or difficult of solution when compared with the deeply rooted hates of other continents." Less than two years later, in April 1938, in his annual Pan American Day message, he went further:

> The twenty-one American Republics present proudly to the rest of the world a demonstration that the rule of justice and law can be substituted for the rule of force, that resort to war as an instrument of policy is unnecessary, that international differences of all kinds can be solved through peaceful negotiation; that the sanctity of the pledged word faithfully observed and generously interpreted offers a system of security with freedom.
>
> The three hundred millions of citizens who live in the American Republics are not different from other human beings. We have the same problems, the same differences, even the same material for controversy which exists on other continents. Yet we have undertaken contractual obligations to solve these normal human differences by maintaining peace; and that peace we are firmly resolved to maintain. It shall not be endangered by controversies within our own family; and we will not permit it to be endangered from aggression coming from outside our hemisphere. This, a common objective of all of us, forms a lasting foundation for the maintenance of an international understanding that is unique in the world.[61]

The significance of FDR's Good Neighbor policy and the era of good feeling it brought to inter-American relations can be measured best by their sense of loss. The postwar era cruelly eroded the faith in hemispheric solidarity that had been created during the dozen years of his presidency, leaving Latin Americans confronting complexities they were unprepared to deal with. But if the impact of Roosevelt's international thought on the lasting conduct of US foreign policy is in some doubt, there can be none about the influence and effect it had as a positive phenomenon on inter-American relations. The architects of the Good Neighbor policy were fully aware that perfecting this relationship would take years.

With the history of the years between independence and 1933, the inherent differences between the evolution of the two economic systems were too great for any assurance to exist that a perfect collaboration was possible. But an actual start in the right direction had been made. Foundations had been laid. Indeed, Roosevelt lent the prestige of his great name and that of his nation, and in fact gave much heart, to the rekindling of the Western Hemisphere idea and the inter-American system. No matter how wide his travels and deep involvement in the war, he never seemed to lose touch with Latin America.

Yet by mid-1946 the Good Neighbor policy was foundering in a welter of broken promises and crushed expectations. Cracks in the Good Neighbor edifice became apparent as early as 1943, two years before Roosevelt's death, most notably with the resignation of Undersecretary of State Sumner Welles, his longtime family friend and a principal architect of the administration's Latin American game plan. As is wont in a democracy, there were occasional contradictions and missteps and internal discrepancies between senior officials and various executive departments. And there was always the intractable problem of Argentina—how to deal with a dictatorship who repressed civil liberties and was friendly to the Axis Powers without reverting to the interventionism Roosevelt had abjured.

Unfortunately, within twelve months after Roosevelt's death those foundations had been shaken and the old frictions, misunderstandings and suspicions between Latin America and the United States had again intruded in inter-American relations.

What led to the rapid demise of the Good Neighbor policy after Roosevelt's death? As Laski foresaw already in 1948, the period of friendship was destined to be brief, considering the previous record of US policies in the region. Moreover, as the war drew to a close in 1944 and early 1945, there is increasing evidence that the president wished to distance himself not so much from the Good Neighbor policy as from the emphasis on regionalism it implied for US global policy. The operational fact for the purpose of this chapter, however, is that for a long time his administration's exceptional relationship with the republics of the south prevailed.

It is interesting (this emerges from personal correspondence as well as from his policy papers) that the Good Neighbor policy may have reached its zenith in 1943—after the principle of hemispheric solidarity had become consolidated in the mutual security arrangements all but Argentina and Chile had undertaken in the face of the threats of the expanding world war. By then, the Moscow declaration of October 1943 pledged the four Big Powers to establish a new world organization and set machinery in motion for the Dumbarton Oaks meeting and the San Francisco Charter. Accordingly, the emphasis on hemispheric regionalism gradually came to be challenged within the State Department by those who were involved with laying the groundwork of the United Nations Organization based on the principle of universalism, rather than regionalism. Notable among them was the Polish-born Leo Pasvolsky, who can be said to be emblematic of the intensely Eurocentric inclinations of the senior State Department staff.

An effective argument from this camp was that by continuing the special relationship with Latin America, Washington would give Moscow a powerful excuse for creating a hegemonic bloc in Eastern Europe, which it eventually did anyway—but that is a theory that requires further explanation. On a more popular level one could say that the US media and public were captivated by an emerging, if prematurely optimistic, "one world" vision, after the book written by Republican internationalist Wendell Willkie, in his vigorous campaign against a return to US isolationism.

Still, the Roosevelt era was unlike any other in the twentieth century; even after the president died the vitality of the Good Neighbor policy was far from exhausted, and the goodwill it generated in Latin America continued to keep US–Latin American relations on a relatively friendly level and ensured the continued support in the region for the US postwar policies for another decade. Why, then, does so much of the literature insist on slighting Roosevelt's formulation and management of foreign policy during his first two terms? Adjectives such as "inconsistent," "neglectful," "hesitant," and even "superficial" recur with striking frequency.

Perhaps what made these years so important to Latin America is exactly what evoked so much criticism from those accustomed to measuring the effectiveness of US foreign policy in terms of relations with Europe or Asia. F. A. Bemis, in his often caustic treatment of Roosevelt, after questioning the president's general knowledge of Latin America, contends that as president it was only

under the counsel of Secretary of State Cordell Hull and his professional advisers in the Department, including the experienced Sumner Welles . . . the Good Neighbor Policy rapidly developed, through speeches of the President, by successive steps of policy, and in inter-American conferences, to accept the Doctrine of Nonintervention. That Latin American doctrine eventually became the capstone of the Good Neighbor Policy.[62]

Elsewhere, Bemis refers to Roosevelt's Caribbean trip of 1934 with a sardonic sideswipe, stating that the president "showed a very great interest, manifested in fishing trips on naval ships, in the strategic waters and islands that guard the [Panama] Canal." Yet Bemis makes no mention of the political significance of the trip—the visits to Colombia, with stops in Puerto Rico, the Virgin Islands, Haiti and Panama, nor the fact that he was the first sitting US president to set foot on South American soil.

If the Wilson administration tried to shake the pillars of discord and prejudice on which US–Colombian relations rested since the Panama incident of 1903 by paying compensation, Roosevelt tried to smash them through sheer force of personality. Roosevelt played host to Colombian president-elect Alfonso Lopez Pumarejo in Washington and hit it off extremely well with him, and consequently the political circumstances for the trip could not have been more auspicious. Even a decade later, in the middle of the war, Roosevelt met with President Getúlio Vargas in Brazil and the Mexican head of state, Manuel Avila Camacho. Vice President Henry Wallace made an impressive, widely acclaimed tour of Latin America from mid-March to late April 1943 and returned to Washington more committed to strengthening the Good Neighbor policy.[63] Roosevelt entrusted a similar goodwill tour to his wife, Eleanor.

Despite the negative characterizations of Roosevelt's foreign policy performance early in his administration, most biographers and historians agree that few presidents came to office more propitiously prepared to guide the country's foreign affairs. A firsthand account by Sumner Welles helps provide a better perspective, stating that during the years preceding his inauguration, President Roosevelt had "studied every aspect of foreign relations." Welles added:

> The general lines of policy . . . included an attempt to create a system within the Western Hemisphere through strictly co-operative methods, . . . the conception of the New World as a hemisphere group of sovereign states.[64]

Yet Roosevelt and his aides understood, perhaps better than their critics, that they had come only part of the way. Henry Wallace remarked, "We are children of the transition—we have left Egypt but we have not yet arrived at the Promised Land."[65]

More recently, revisionist historians have added another wrinkle to FDR's hemispheric defense policies, contending that he deliberately exaggerated fears of Axis aggression and even political infiltration in order to consolidate US economic penetration in the region. This argument, a favorite of English revisionism, is incongruously based on Nazi documents suggesting that Berlin never planned to invade any Latin American countries—which tell little about subversive efforts to undermine democratic governments while carrying out an effective program of political, military and economic penetration and sabotage.[66] Suffice it to recall the cautioning message Roosevelt received from his ambassador to Chile, Claude Bowers, a renowned journalist and historian: "It is commonly thought here that the Germans, who are numerous, are thoroughly organized with the view of a coup d'état."[67]

In fact, Roosevelt's first line of defense against fascism in the hemisphere was the wartime continuation of the Good Neighbor policy.[68] Between the enunciation of the policy in 1933 and the end of World War II in 1945, seventeen Latin American presidents and presidents-elect were welcomed to Washington and given state receptions. Numerous leaders, including not only heads of state but also journalists, physicians, professors, musicians, chiefs of police, businessmen and many others from all the Latin American countries, were brought to the United States on goodwill missions or for technical training. Still, Roosevelt has been called an isolationist up to his "quarantine" speech of 1941. This can be said with justification, perhaps, from the narrow and specific point of view of his initial prudent reluctance to committing the United States to exceedingly risky positions in the menacing European conflicts at a time when the country had still not recovered from its internal economic distress and lacked the necessary self-confidence for a strong international posture. But from the larger historical point of view, Roosevelt cannot be classified as an isolationist, for he constantly and consistently had a clear idea of what US democracy had to do in order to be true to itself and to keep afloat in the face of the crisis of democracy throughout the world. Nowhere was this stance more evident than in his policy toward Latin America.

NOTES

1. "It was one of his achievements in which he took the most pride" (Frank Freidel, *FDR: A Rendezvous with Destiny* [Boston: Little, Brown, 1990], p. 211); "The Rooseveltian phrase will go down in history as a dictum of American policy more important to the Hemisphere than any related to Washington, Jefferson, or Monroe" (Luis Quintanilla, Mexican diplomat, in *A Latin American Speaks* [New York: Macmillan, 1943], p. 157).

2. "There was nothing particularly new about these sentiments. What was new was their immediate *translation* into practical effect" (Lawrence Duggan, Chief of the Division of American Republics, *Public Affairs Bulletin* 7 [1941]: 1).

3. *The Public Papers and Addresses of Franklin D. Roosevelt* (New York: Random House, 1938–1950), 5:8–9 (hereafter *Public Papers*).

4. *Public Papers*, 5:602.

5. "Cry of 'Down with Imperialism,'" *New York Times,* December 1, 1936, p. 11.

6. *Public Papers,* 2:463.

7. *Public Papers,* 2:463.

8. *La Nacion* (Buenos Aires), November 30, 1936, p. 1.

9. Cordell Hull, *Addresses and Statements* (Washington, D.C.: Government Printing Office, 1935).

10. For an especially keen assessment of the Roosevelt policy's impact in Latin America, see Randall Bennett Woods, *The Roosevelt Foreign-Policy Establishment and the "Good Neighbor": The United States and Argentina* (Lawrence: Regents Press of Kansas, 1979): "Latin America welcomed the Good Neighbor policy as much for its apparent spirit as for its substance. It seemed to many that at last the United States intended to treat the American republics as a community of nations, each with a unique culture and political heritage and each possessed of the right to formulate domestic and foreign policies absolutely free from outside interference" (p. 6). A British diplomat put it more succinctly: "Mr. Roosevelt is giving up hope in the old world and is turning his attention to the new" (D'Arcy Osborne, British chargé in Washington, to Sir Robert Vansittart, permanent secretary of foreign affairs, August 27, 1933; quoted in Frank Friedel, *FDR: Launching the New Deal* [Boston: Little, Brown, 1973], p. 498).

11. Elliott Roosevelt, ed., *FDR: His Personal Letters, 1929–1945* (New York: Duell, Sloan, 1950), pp. 634–635.

12. Roosevelt, ed., *FDR,* p. 637.

13. Bryce Wood, *The Making of the Good Neighbor Policy* (New York: Columbia University Press, 1961), pp. 98–112.

14. Waldo David Frank, *America Hispaña: A Portrait and a Prospect* (New York: Scribner's, 1931); Carleton Beals, *Latin America: World in Revolution* (New York: Abelard-Shulman, 1963); David Green, *The Containment of Latin America: A History of the Myths and Realities of the Good Neighbor Policy* (Chicago: Quadrangle, 1971).

15. Frank Burt Freidel, *Franklin D. Roosevelt: A Rendezvous with Destiny* (Boston: Little, Brown, 1990); Freidel, *Franklin D. Roosevelt* (Boston: Little, Brown, 1952); Arthur M. Schlesinger, *The Crisis of the Old Order, 1919–1933* (Boston: Houghton Mifflin, 1957); Schlesinger, *The Coming of the New Deal* (Boston: Houghton Mifflin, 1959); and Schlesinger, *The Politics of Upheaval* (Boston: Houghton Mifflin, 1960); James McGregor Burns, *Roosevelt: The Soldier of Freedom* (New York: Harcourt, Brace, Jovanovich, 1970).

16. Frank Freidel, *FDR: The Ordeal* (Boston: Little, Brown, 1954), pp. 237–241; Robert Dallek, *Franklin D. Roosevelt and American Foreign Policy, 1932–1945* (New York: Oxford University Press, 1979), pp. 13–14.

17. F. D. Roosevelt, "Our Foreign Policy: A Democratic View," *Foreign Affairs,* July 1928, p. 584.

18. Roosevelt, "Our Foreign Policy," p. 586.

19. Roosevelt, "Our Foreign Policy," p. 574.

20. Roosevelt, "Our Foreign Policy," p. 584.

21. Gomez Robledo, *Cuadernos Americanos*, March 1953; interview with the author, Mexico City, March 1992.

22. Emil Ludwig, *Roosevelt: A Study in Fortune and Power* (New York: Viking, 1938), p. 65.

23. "The People Approve," in *Public Papers*, 2:610.

24. Cordell Hull, *Memoirs of Cordell Hull* (New York: Macmillan, 1948), p. 308.

25. *The Year of Crisis* (New York: Random House), 2:14.

26. *Public Papers*, p. 130; address before the Woodrow Wilson Foundation.

27. *Public Papers*, p. 130; also quoted in Hull, *Memoirs*, p. 339.

28. Sumner Welles, *The Time for Decision* (New York: Harper, 1944), p. 240.

29. October 4, 1933.

30. Herbert Feis, memorandum to Cordell Hull, in *Franklin D. Roosevelt and Foreign Affairs*, ed. Edgar B. Nixon (Cambridge: Belknap Press, 1969), 1:441.

31. FDR, note, in *Public Papers*, pp. 463–464.

32. Hull, *Memoirs*, 1:334; Hull, "Some of the Results of the Montevideo Conference," February 10, 1934; Official File, FDR Library, Hyde Park, New York.

33. Henry Steele Commager, *The American Mind: An Interpretation of American Thought and Character Since the 1880s* (New Haven, Conn.: Yale University Press, 1950), pp. 354–355.

34. Inaugural Address, March 4, 1933, *Public Papers*, 2:11.

35. Alonso Aguilar Monteverde, *Pan-Americanism from Monroe to the Present: A View from the Other Side* (New York: Monthly Review Press, 1968), pp. 69–70.

36. Aguilar Monteverde, *Pan-Americanism*, pp. 69–70.

37. Victor Andrade, *My Mission for Revolutionary Bolivia, 1944–1962* (Pittsburgh: University of Pittsburgh Press, 1976), p. 54.

38. For most thoughtful skeptics, see David Green, *The Containment of Latin America: A History of the Myths and Realities of the Good Neighbor Policy* (Chicago: Quadrangle, 1971); Beals, *Latin America*.

39. Edward O. Guerrant, *Roosevelt's Good Neighbor Policy* (Albuquerque: University of New Mexico, 1950), p. 212. He also wrote, "This policy of the Roosevelt Administration was designed to gain the co-operation of the 20 nations to the South of the Rio Grande and to follow an economic and social policy calculated to bring material benefits to the entire Hemisphere."

40. J. Lloyd Mecham, *A Survey of United States and Latin American Relations* (Boston: Houghton Mifflin, 1965), p. 465.

41. The distinguished Mexican diplomat Luis Quintanilla writes, "Anti-American sentiment was climaxed when the Sixth Pan American Conference was held in

Habana in 1928. How could such a conference stand on any solid ground when the government in Washington was still pursuing a policy of systematic official interference and military intervention in the weaker countries south of the Rio Grande?" (*A Latin American Speaks* [New York: Macmillan, 1943], p. 143).

42. Hull, *Memoirs*, p. 342; also Department of State press release, December 20, 1933; *The U.S. in Foreign Affairs* (New York, 1933), p. 200.

43. Marquis Childs, *I Write from Washington* (New York: Harper, 1943), p. 150.

44. John Child, *Unequal Alliance: The Inter-American Military System, 1938–1978* (Boulder: Westview, 1980), p. 82.

45. Declaration of Havana, 1928.

46. Hull, *Memoirs*, p. 334.

47. Roosevelt, speech at the Woodrow Wilson Foundation Dinner, Mayflower Hotel, Washington, December 28, 1933; *Franklin D. Roosevelt and Foreign Affairs* (Cambridge: Harvard University Press, 1969), pp. 559–560.

48. *Franklin D. Roosevelt and Foreign Affairs,* p. 560.

49. Republica de Colombia, *Política Internacional,* 1936, p. 130.

50. John Gunther, *Inside Latin America* (New York: Harper, 1941), pp. 167–168.

51. Hugh Thomas, *Cuba: The Pursuit of Freedom* (New York: Harper, 1987), p. 627.

52. Memorandum of telephone conversation, September 9, 1933, *Foreign Relations* 5 (1933): 412–413.

53. Harry F. Guggenheim, *Cuba and the United States: A Study in International Relations* (New York: Macmillan, 1934), p. 235.

54. Thomas, *Cuba*, pp. 639–642; also see Thomas's characterization of Welles as "behaving more as if he were the leader of the opposition than an ambassador" (p. 616).

55. Thomas, *Cuba,* p. 627: "an act which cast long shadows over events in the 1950s, a generation later."

56. Harold Laski, *American Democracy* (New York: Viking, 1950), p. 540.

57. Frederick L. Schuman, *Design for Power: The Struggle for the World* (New York: Knopf, 1942), p. 243.

58. Humphreys, *The Evolution of Modern Latin America* (New York: Oxford University Press, 1946), p. 132.

59. Bryce Wood, *The Making of the Good Neighbor Policy* (New York: Columbia University Press, 1961), p. 356.

60. Stephen R. Graubard and Gerald J. Holton, eds., *Excellence and Leadership in a Democracy* (New York: Columbia University Press, 1962), p. 153.

61. "The Continuing Struggle for Liberalism," *Public Papers,* p. 219.

62. Samuel Flagg Bemis, *The Latin American Policy of the United States* (New York: Harcourt Brace, 1943), pp. 257–258.

63. John Gunther, *Inside Latin America* (New York: Harper, 1941), p. 172; author's conversations with Harry Frantz, United Press correspondent who covered the Wallace trip, Washington, D.C., 1952.

64. Welles, *Time for Decision*, p. 192.

65. Quoted in William E. Leuchtenburg, *Franklin D. Roosevelt: A Profile* (New York: Hill & Wang, 1967), p. 253; author's interviews with New Dealers Rexford Tugwell, Paul Porter and Thurman Arnold.

66. See Dallek, *Franklin D. Roosevelt,* p. 233: "Few issues gave Roosevelt more concern in the summer of 1940 than the threat to Latin America. As Hitler's armies swept across Western Europe in May and June, Roosevelt received repeated warnings of Nazi subversion in Brazil, Chile, Uruguay, Colombia, Ecuador, Venezuela, Panama, and Mexico."

67. Bowers to FDR, May 14 and 25, 1940; President's Secretary's File, FDR Library, Hyde Park, New York.

68. Dallek, *Franklin D. Roosevelt,* p. 175.

Chapter Four

TRANSITION
Harry S. Truman

The presidential succession in the United States has almost always presented a problem for Latin America. A change of party frequently meant abrupt, unpredictable shifts in foreign policy—as from Taft to Wilson or Hoover to Roosevelt. Although Vice President Harry S. Truman's sudden accession to the presidency after Roosevelt's death kept the Democrats in power, few successions were as fateful for inter-American relations. Roosevelt had deliberately cultivated and won the admiration and confidence of the leaders and the peoples of Latin America; Truman was unknown to them. Throughout the hemisphere the president's death was perceived as a personal and political catastrophe: the loss of a trusted friend and, with him, the priority place he had accorded to the region in the overall scheme of US foreign policy.

Of critical importance to the hemisphere was the fact that with the change in Washington also came the failure of the victors of World War II to maintain their wartime cooperation and the consequent ushering in of what came to be known as the Cold War. Though distant from its European epicenter, Latin America was not spared from the ideological aftershocks of the East–West confrontation that sundered the world for the next four decades. Important global issues remained unsettled, and the new position of the United States as a major postwar power required major policy decisions.

The Roosevelt administration, having anticipated that Europe would need US help after the war, had already steered the country away from isolationism to victory against the Axis powers; now it was up to Truman to lead US participation in world affairs commensurate with its strength in the coming nuclear age. For the new president and his advisers, Washington's principal objective was the containment of Soviet expansion and international communism. That, and not Roosevelt's prewar drive to consolidate the hemispheric alliance, moved postwar US policymakers and the US public.

Another element that contributed to Latin America's diminished profile in Washington was more subjective. When Truman found himself elevated to the presidency he had no particular ideas on hemispheric relations; in fact, it was not until 1947, almost two full years after he took office, that he became personally involved in Latin American affairs by making a state visit to Mexico and Brazil. Until then he let the State Department take care of hemispheric problems to allow the United States to concentrate on the big international issues. Where Roosevelt had insisted on being his own secretary of state, Truman restored the primacy of foreign policymaking from the White House to the State Department.

Truman's worldview was greatly influenced by Undersecretary of State Dean Acheson, who won the president's total confidence early on. Unfortunately Acheson had little interest in Latin America, and by mid-1945 most of the senior officials who had built the Good Neighbor policy had left the State Department.

The perils of this shift for Latin America were not long in making themselves felt. For example, when it came to drafting the United Nations Charter in San Francisco, the department's globalists, led by Leo Pasvolsky, a Polish-born senior policy planner, were in control and predictably counseled Secretary of State Edward Stettinius Jr. to oppose Latin American desire to retain a regional bloc "completely free of world arrangements." The secretary's inclination was to override the Latin American pretension with a firm Big Three opposition. He was nonetheless thwarted by the firm opposition of two influential senators, Arthur H. Vandenberg and Tom Connally, prodded by Nelson A. Rockefeller, the assistant secretary for inter-American Affairs, that rescued the inter-American system from being smothered by the new international organization.[1]

Four years later, however, the globalists won the day when President Truman clustered Latin America with Asia and Africa in his Point Four program offering to make the benefits of US scientific advances and industrial progress available for the improvement of the world's "underdeveloped" countries. With a remarkable disregard for the political and cultural bonds created by the Good Neighbor policy that may not have been intended, Truman tacitly voided the region's conviction that it enjoyed a distinctive relationship with the US government.

The enunciation in March 1947 of the famous Truman Doctrine to defend Greece and Turkey from communism and the announcement of the Marshall Plan two months later established new foreign policy priorities and laid the groundwork for a postwar order that would last almost a half century. The message accompanying the Marshall Plan recognized that "the rehabilitation of the economic structure of Europe quite evidently will require a much longer time and greater effort than had been foreseen," signaling to Latin America that its role as a cornerstone of US foreign policy, in Welles's phrase of 1932, was ended. The temporary displacement of the Good Neighbor policy due to wartime conditions steadily acquired a more permanent status.

Accordingly, grant aid to Latin America was insignificant compared to the aid given to Europe and Asia. From 1949 through 1952, the twenty republics of Latin America received $79 million in net grant aid. The rest of the world received $18 billion—228 times what Latin America received. The figures do not tell the whole story, but they illustrate why Latin Americans felt they were not being fairly treated. They thought their contribution to the Allied war effort entitled the region to a more substantial share of US economic assistance as well as a larger role in Western councils.

Countries such as Brazil, Colombia, Mexico, Uruguay and the Central American republics, which had collaborated intimately with Washington in the war effort, looked eagerly to the entente with the United States to continue. But these expectations gave way to the perception that Washington was reverting to pre-Rooseveltian indifference, just when the region had been stirred into undertaking major social and economic changes, some of them directly inspired by the New Deal.

The State Department met criticism of the meager postwar effort by noting that Latin America had suffered no war damage and by expatiating prosaically on the superiority of the private over government investments for the achievement of economic and social purposes. A retrospective congressional study of this period acknowledged that there was considerable resentment in the region on the grounds "that the United States takes Latin America for granted and that the United States is not concerned for the welfare of the people."[2]

By all reckoning, at a time when US supremacy was unchallenged, the leverage was there for Washington to succor democratic reform. A small fraction of Marshall aid might have been applied profitably to meet Latin America's looming economic and social problems. Instead, Truman did not move beyond including the region in his global Point Four program of concessionary technical assistance to the "underdeveloped" regions of the world; he encouraged private investors to meet the major demands of Latin America's development needs.

Confronted with the challenge of the Soviet Union, the United States responded with an unprecedented aid program for the reconstruction of Europe, with enormous consequences for its stance in the hemisphere. Washington deferred serious consideration of Latin America's economic needs until Europe was in a stronger position.

Preparatory conference documents show that State Department specialists in hemispheric affairs were keenly aware of the kinds of problems that would arise unless the US government acted decisively. Three weeks before the meeting, a memorandum commenting on the absence of a defined economic policy for the region cautioned that "it is in this field, and this field only, where we feel the thinking in Washington has not crystallized."

> Yet it is this section of the agenda upon which the success or failure of the Conference, both politically and economically, depends. If the U.S. cannot meet the relatively simple problems presented by economic readjustments in the Western Hemisphere, its leadership in world affairs will prove to be more dangerous than helpful. The Conference will not only be a test of the sincerity of the United States with respect to the inter-American system, but a test of the ability of the United States to assume practical and constructive leadership.

As early as March 1948, the State Department policy planning staff was pressing to establish a US policy regarding "anti-Communist measures which could be planned and carried out within the Inter-American system." No specific plans were made, however, to confront the economic and social conditions that could have made some Latin American countries vulnerable to revolutionary movements and exploitation by the communists.

In the economic field, one of the Truman administration's greatest problems in tackling the postwar relationship with Latin America was inadequate preparation for peace during the final phase of the war. Private interests gave some attention to postwar economic relations with Latin America, reflecting the renewed prestige and influence that the business community was beginning to acquire in the high councils of government, from which Roosevelt had tended to exclude it.

This made itself felt from the very first day Truman came to office and set out to reconstruct the leadership of the federal government by appointing his old banker friend, John W. Snyder, federal loan administrator. With this appointment, the new president indicated that he was concerned with fiscal responsibility and an expanded role for the private sector, especially in Western Hemisphere affairs. The problem was that the shift came at a time when most of the Latin American governments believed that they could achieve rapid economic development, their first postwar requirement, through public ownership and centralized planning. By 1946, many of the nonautocratic governments in Latin America were emulating the economic and social reforms of the New Deal, which meant a major role for the government in planning economic development.

Suddenly it seemed that the US heirs of the New Deal were leaving them in the lurch. Latin American leaders noted the new direction of Truman's policy with alarm. "You evidently do not perceive the depth of our economic crisis," wrote President Getúlio Vargas of Brazil.[3]

Despite such warnings, Truman decided to subordinate regional political interests to the emerging anticommunist global strategy, thus emphasizing hemispheric security considerations over and above economic ones. The Latin Americans accepted it, if grudgingly, rather than countenance a bruising break with the new administration in Washington.

Underscoring the importance of these transactions, Assistant Secretary of State Nelson Rockefeller testified before a House committee that during the war Latin America had sold strategically vital rubber to the United States for about one-fifth of what it would have cost under normal market conditions.

No sooner was the war over than Allied purchases of strategic materials dropped precipitously. To compound the problem, essential imports of capital goods and consumer goods from the United States, still in short supply, demanded higher prices. A run on foreign exchange reserves accelerated inflation. Combined with rising populations and endemic opposition to entrenched authoritarian governments, these economic dislocations produced social unrest and deep nationalist stirrings.

If the Truman administration had recognized the seriousness of Latin America's economic problems by 1947, it did not develop an action plan until January 1949, when Truman unveiled his Fair Deal along with its international component, the Point Four program of technical assistance: "a bold new program for making the benefits of our scientific advances and industrial progress available for the improvement and growth of underdeveloped areas." By contrast with the Marshall Plan, however, technicians and private investors, rather than official funds, were to be encouraged to carry the burden, in a manner suggestive of President Taft's dollar diplomacy.

Well intentioned as it may have been, the Point Four program had some unforeseen consequences by globalizing what heretofore had been an exclusive, regional focus—the Americas. Since their independence the American republics were generally regarded as New World siblings of the United States.

Then, abruptly, a new postwar geopolitical thesis, predicated on income and population statistics, indifferent to history or culture, remitted the region to the new category of "underdeveloped nations." Besides appealing to US idealism, the idea served to give a more humane counterpoise to the Cold War character of the Truman Doctrine.

Nonetheless, for Latin America it did not work out quite that way. The "sister republics" were suddenly plucked out of Western history and transplanted to an alien, timeless economic zone. Remarkably, little notice was given to just how misguided the move was from the viewpoint of the negative psychological and geopolitical implications it held for Latin America. Turning adversity to their advantage, subsequent nationalist and revolutionary movements in Latin America seized on the notion of Third World solidarity as a strategy to exact concessionary aid from the industrialized nations.

Norman Armour, Louis Halle and other Latin American specialists at the State Department repeatedly argued that the absence of a hemispheric economic recovery program "would seriously weaken our friendly relations," which indeed it did. Nonetheless, Washington's effective wartime propaganda campaign, portraying the United States as leading the worldwide struggle for democracy, had kindled hopes of swift social and economic reforms to help the Latin American masses. What emerged instead was a Truman administration program that was committed to the Good Neighbor rhetoric but retained little of its substance or spirit.

From the Latin American viewpoint, the policy that Roosevelt had so diligently worked to consolidate, putting hemispheric interests at the center of Washington's foreign policy agenda, was fading fast. Many Latin American diplomatists, most notably the Mexicans, feared that the Good Neighbor spirit of hemispheric solidarity based on the principles of nonintervention and respect for sovereignty was being undermined for reasons having little to do with specific hemispheric interests. Ironically, as Cold War tensions heightened, the Truman administration soon seized on the nonintervention principle as a rationale for tolerating dictatorships such as the Peronist regime of Argentina, reasoning that they could be best trusted to protect the continent against communist subversion. Democratic governments were deemed less orderly, subject to ceaseless internal polemics and therefore more vulnerable to radical leftist infiltration.

The president told Congress that "it must be the policy of the USA to support free peoples who are resisting attempted subjugation by armed minorities, or by outside pressures."[4] The message, intended to reassure the noncommunist governments of Europe, was interpreted in Latin America as formal and unequivocal notice that in certain circumstances it was in the interests of the United States once again to interfere anywhere in the world. This put the fate of the Good Neighbor policy, with its emphasis on nonintervention, in doubt.

The State Department was soon criticized for abetting Latin American dictators by extending diplomatic recognition to any regime, regardless of its undemocratic qualities, as soon as it had effective control of the country. It responded with the traditional argument (as much honored in the breach as in the observance during the twentieth century) that recognition implied no approval whatsoever.[5]

Thus surfaced the dubious proposition, increasingly accepted by an emerging official consensus in Washington, that in order to defend democracy from communism it was sometimes necessary to align US interests with Latin America's antidemocratic forces. These included the military as well as right-wing political parties whose elastic definition of communism often included democrats who had espoused the Allied cause during World War II.

Predictably, the defensive atmosphere generated by the Cold War and articulated in apocalyptic language by Acheson, George Kennan and the War Department not only created an effective crisis climate in the United States but also spurred passage of the National Security Act, which called for the unification of the armed forces and the creation of the Central Intelligence Agency and the National Security Council.

As the Cold War intensified, economic discussions were subordinated to security concerns. Three men contributed critically to this debate, despite their dissimilar power and viewpoints: Acheson, who in 1949 became secretary of state; Kennan, the retiring head of Policy Planning; and Halle, the Policy Planning staff's Latin American specialist. An examination of their roles may provide insight into the intellectual climate in the administration and how it affected Latin American policy.

Having been appointed secretary of state in January 1949, Acheson waited until December 1952, a couple of months before the Truman administration came to an end, to make his first visit to Latin America, and then only to Brazil. In the words of biographer Smith:

> He had little personal interest in the history or culture of the region or fondness for the hollow pomp of Latin American political and diplomatic style. He saw nothing in Latin America which threatened the security of the United States and much that was trivial compared to the great issues of war, peace, and the balance of power in Europe, Asia and the Middle East.[6]

Not surprisingly, under Acheson senior officials in policymaking positions viewed Latin America in a new framework that cast it as a sideshow to the Cold War confrontation. Acheson's first major statement on the subject of inter-American relations came on September 19, 1949. It was contained in a speech addressed to the Pan American Society of New York. The story of that speech demonstrates the marginal interest of the nation's top officials in hemispheric affairs, and how quickly Latin America was relegated to the proverbial "back burner" of the policy-making establishment.

Paradoxically, at a time when the main motivating impulse for congressional action in foreign aid seemed to be the threat of communism, an internal State Department memorandum deprived policymakers of that critical argument when it said: "During the last six months Communist penetration does not appear to have made gains in Latin America and we believe these efforts have lost ground."[7]

Approved by the National Security Council as NSC-68, it became the first formal statement of US policy setting forth the guidelines for the Cold War world. The document called for a massive, coordinated worldwide anticommunist program including defense, propaganda, aid, domestic security and intelligence activities. It also confronted the United States with the need to rally Latin America to another collective security effort.

KENNAN: CONTAINMENT, DISDAIN, VISION

A very different picture was drawn a few months later in a remarkable secret document prepared for Acheson by Kennan, the author of the historic "long memorandum" urging that US policy must be that of "a firm and vigilant containment of Russian expansive tendencies." Kennan's formulation marked a turning point of fundamental importance in the history of US foreign policy, prompting the US anticommunist crusade culminating in the Vietnam War.

Much less known, but of considerable importance, was Kennan's assessment of Latin America's vulnerability to communist penetration and his recommendations for dealing with it. The report, based on a 1950 tour of Latin America just after he resigned as director of the department's Policy Planning staff, provided a theoretical framework for thrusting US–Latin American relations into a new Cold War context. Insofar as it also provided the rationale for a renascent interventionist policy, the Kennan report represented a decisive departure from the Good Neighbor policy and was in line with the Cold War guidelines set by Truman and Acheson. In an odd way, the veteran diplomat seemed to accord Latin America a greater significance than did the president or the secretary of state. Kennan saw that the region could fit into the general pattern of postwar US policy in two ways: (1) as an important part of the noncommunist international system and (2) as "an important element of our strategic position in the event of war."[8] He wrote in one of his more prescient observations,

We will not be able to say that we have coped creditably and successfully with postwar problems in the noncommunist world unless we are able to assure a fairly successful economic relationship between the peoples and resources of Latin America and those of other noncommunist areas.[9]

The most striking aspect of the report was Kennan's negative and lurid description of the region's culture and political history. Latin America was a paradox he characterized as "fortunate and tragic almost beyond anything ever known in human history." At times he seemed to drawn into an amateurish but florid discourse on human geography, as when he theorized that it seemed to him unlikely that there was another region on earth in which nature and human behavior could have combined to produce a more unhappy and hopeless background for the conduct of human life than Latin America.

"As for nature," he added,

one is struck at once with the way in which South America is the reverse of our own North American continent from the standpoint of its merits as a human habitat. . . . South America, on the other hand is wide and vast in those portions of it which are close to the equator and are least suited to human habitation.[10]

After contrasting a salubrious "human habitat" of North America with a South American geography deleterious to "the possibilities for a vigorous and hopeful development of human society," Kennan draws equally inauspicious comparisons of their respective histories.

"The Spaniards," he observes,

came to Latin America as the bearers of a national and cultural development which was itself nearing its end; a development in which many of the more hopeful origins had already died and little was left but religious fanaticism, a burning, frustrated energy in addition to the most merciless cruelty.

Elsewhere in Latin America, the large scale importation of Negro slave elements into considerable parts of the Spanish and other colonial empires, and the extensive intermarriage of all these elements, produced other unfortunate results which seemed to have weighted scarcely less heavily on the chances for human progress.

In these circumstances, the shadow of a tremendous helplessness and impotence falls over most of the Latin American world. The handicaps to progress are written in human blood and in the tracings of geography.[11]

Kennan's scornful comments on Spanish America, especially his observations on race, so shocked Edward Miller, the assistant secretary for inter-American affairs, that Miller prevailed on Acheson to immediately classify the memorandum and restrict its circulation. "I was never told just what passages had occasioned this drastic measure," Kennan allowed a decade later, "but I have an idea they were ones in which I dwelt on what seemed to me to be the tragic nature of human civilization in all those countries to the south of us."[12]

By the 1960s, however, Kennan had discounted much of the negative load of history he attributed to the region's Iberian heritage in 1950. In fact, he came close to sanctifying the Latin American world as a possible future savior of Western civilization. In his celebrated *Memoir*, written in the early 1960s, Kennan acknowledged with remarkable candor that he had second thoughts about Latin America, perhaps influenced by the Kennedy administration's keen new interest in hemispheric relations. Thus after reflecting on the 1950 report, he included this significant caveat:

> I think I should add, lest a false impression be created, that despite the emphasis on the tragic element in Latin American civilization, I have in another sense a high opinion of it and even look to it as perhaps humanity's best hope for the future.[13]

Endowing his observations with a perspective that had been conspicuously absent in his original report, Kennan mused that with human existence being "everywhere tragic," that of Latin America seemed to him "only tragic in its own manner; and this is a manner in some respects less menacing, certainly less apocalyptic, than that in which tragedy threatens to manifest itself elsewhere."[14]

Notwithstanding Miller's ostensible disavowal of Kennan's original report, the document could not have failed to have some impact, not only through the force of his own prestige but also because it largely coincided with the negative attitudes prevailing in the highest reaches of the State Department. Nonetheless, beyond confirming the Truman administration's well-developed fears of communism and recommending a no-holds-barred policy against it, in the annals of US foreign policy the report is likely to make more of a mark for its literary quality than for any comprehensive fresh guidelines for dealing with the region as a whole.

Within the bureaucratic process, however, the Kennan report evidently inspired Acheson to seek out Louis Halle of the Policy Planning staff to write an anonymous article on Latin America for *Foreign Affairs*, the same journal that published Kennan's famous essay, "The Sources of Soviet Conduct," under the pseudonym "X" in July 1947.

HALLE: DON'T SCORN THE GOOD NEIGHBOR

The Halle article, entitled "On a Certain Impatience with Latin America," appeared in the July 1950 issue of the prestigious quarterly under the anonymous signature "Y." On August 7, Miller forwarded a copy of the magazine to Acheson with a cover letter urging, "I hope that you will have time to read this excellent restatement of our Latin American policy."

The implied endorsement actually masked significant divergences between the regional division and the policy planning adviser over the quality and direction of the administration's policy toward Latin America. These differences were aired later that year in a series of top-secret memoranda in which Halle subjected the Truman policy to a strict Rooseveltian critique. The administration, he said, should recapture "some of the initiative in inter-American relations that should be associated with its leadership but has in some degree been allowed to lapse because of urgent preoccupations in other areas."

Specifically, Halle criticized the exclusion of the region from decisions of the US-led Western alliance and criticized inadequate US support for efforts to strengthen democracy and economic development in Latin America. The central question Halle posed was, "Is the relationship of the United States to the Latin American nations in fact paternal? Or is it fraternal?" "The distinction," he correctly pointed out, "is fundamental to the question of what the United States ought to do about the state of democracy in Latin America." Paternalism, he recalled, was exemplified in Theodore Roosevelt's corollary to the Monroe Doctrine and the military interventions of the early century when US policy was apt to treat the neighbor republics as "irresponsible children." The turning point that recognized Latin Americans as "adults" came between 1928 and 1936, with the abandonment of intervention and the adoption of the Good Neighbor policy.

> The development of a wise foreign policy can take place only in terms of the historical perspective. The historical view shows us a group of 21 separate nations striving for democratic self-realization, and also working for the development of a community to regulate their affairs.[15]

One of Halle's goals, already anticipated in the 1947 memorandum to Marshall, was to have the administration increase economic development assistance and generally have Washington viewed once more a willing hemispheric partner. Like Woodrow Wilson and Franklin Roosevelt, Halle was convinced that "we North Americans, by our nature, feel better when we are conducting ourselves in a broad and generous way than when our behavior in the world is mean, quarrelsome and niggardly. That is our natural instinct."

Unfortunately the Halle memorandum came at an inopportune moment. Just as he was urging the administration to shore up hemispheric relations, events were pushing Washington toward another portentous decision—to counter the North Korean invasion of the South by military means, opening a new and more acute phase in the Cold War. In 1951, after North Korea had invaded South Korea, the United States tried to get Latin America to accelerate the struggle against international communism and join the US-sponsored UN police action to roll back the North Koreans and their communist Chinese allies and to supply raw materials for the US stockpile. Once more to underscore hemispheric cooperation, the United States summoned a special conference of foreign ministers under the OAS Charter.

While the conflict turned the United Nations into a diplomatic battleground, Washington called for an emergency meeting of the OAS foreign ministers. The express purpose of the conference was to consider "prompt action by the Republics of this Hemisphere for common defense against aggressive activities of international Communism." After two weeks of deliberations, from March 26 to April 7, 1951, the conference concluded that communist activities tended to "disturb the tranquillity of the peoples of this Hemisphere and endanger the liberty and democracy on which their institutions are founded." It was a proposition hardly likely to provoke strong dissent. On a rhetorical level, therefore, agreement had been comparatively easy.

Beneath the harmonious surface, however, currents of opposition ran deep. The fact that all delegates recognized the theoretical danger from international communism did not mean that they agreed on the best ways of combating it or even on the necessity of combating it at all. The United States, in line with the current emphasis of its general policy, had hoped to persuade the Latin American governments to participate more fully in the defensive mobilization of the noncommunist world. Only Colombia's conservative President Laureano Gomez agreed to send an army battalion, the Batallón Colombia, to join the UN force, after Washington failed to get Brazil to take the lead. Finally, the Korean War caused Acheson to give slightly more attention to Latin America, not because he became suddenly aware of the region's needs but because he wanted as many countries as possible to contribute to the UN war effort.

Under the circumstances it was easy for Assistant Secretary Miller to dismiss Halle's paper as "somewhat uneven" and as demonstrating "in parts an excessive tendency to put on the hair shirt." What had occurred in US–Latin American relations, he maintained, is "not so much that we have left undone what we should have done in regard to this part of the world, but rather that we have assumed more duties in other parts of the world." Not surprisingly, Halle's recommendations were adopted only where they conformed to already established policies. That eliminated the crucial economic segment of his paper. Nor was any serious attempt made to demonstrate Washington's capacity for leadership in the inter-American field comparable to what had been demonstrated in Europe. Thus the debate over a correct Latin American policy continued.

Since the United States had announced its plans for European reconstruction, agitation for a Marshall Plan for Latin America was expressed in a plethora of official statements, editorials and columns in the Latin American daily press and journals. President Truman, asked at a press conference on the eve of the Rio meeting if the United States was taking any notice of the Latin American demands, came up with an original, if evasive, answer:

> I think there has always been a Marshall plan in effect for the Western Hemisphere. The foreign policy of the United States in that direction has been set for one hundred years, known as the Monroe Doctrine.[16]

Not surprisingly, some commentators interpreted the remark as mockery.[17] It must be recalled that at Chapultepec in 1945 the United States had agreed to a "reorganized" inter-American system based on a balance between security and economic considerations. As the Cold War intensified, however, the economic provisions were persistently subordinated to security concerns. Thus for Latin America the timing of the Rio Conference could not have been less favorable.

RIO DE JANEIRO: STRUGGLE OVER PRIORITIES

At Montevideo in 1933 the United States had pledged to abide by nonintervention and take steps to build real regional cooperation, inaugurating a new chapter with the aim of sheltering the continent from a conflict-ridden world. At Rio in 1947 the United States played almost an opposite role—urging Latin Americans to back the United States in its new role as bulwark of the democratic world. The inter-American system was no longer the fulcrum of hemispheric security—as the argument went, a red epidemic was threatening Western civilization so that it was now the turn of the Americas to help the most exposed and vulnerable flanks—Europe and Asia. It was also the Rio meeting that defined the military versus economic-social-political issue in the open for the first time.

Despite the decline of the thrall of wartime alliance, at Rio there was a substantial residue of cooperative spirit. It is doubtful that as strong a treaty could have been achieved from any similar conference held after 1948 or 1949. For already in 1947 US–Latin American differences in terms of worldview and policy priorities were very evident.

Interestingly, the recently declassified record of Marshall's private conversations with different delegates shows that some were not beyond pandering to US fears about communist subversion. Argentine Foreign Minister Atilio Bramuglia, for example, began the conversation noting that his government viewed communist infiltration "with great concern" and offered to sign a secret "anticommunist" pact with the United States. Lieutenant General Goes Monteiro of Brazil spoke of the communist danger, "which he felt was more serious than the Fifth Column had been during World War II."[18]

President Truman, in his address to the closing session of the inter-American Defense Conference, dealt only casually with the major accomplishment of the conference, the Rio Treaty, preferring to focus on the global task that lay ahead and emphasizing the great responsibility that rested on the New World: "The sick and the hungry cannot build a peaceful world. They must have the support of the strong and the free." It is a theme President George W. Bush would emulate fifty-five years later.[19]

To the great dismay of the Latin Americans it was not the dispossessed of the hemisphere that Truman had in mind but those of Europe and Asia. Reiterating the central point of Marshall's earlier speech, Truman stressed that the United States alone could not carry that global burden. There had to be cooperation of all the nations of the Americas, "each according to its ability and in its own manner" if the goal was to be achieved.

Commenting on Truman's undiplomatic remarks to the effect that winning World War II had imposed on the United States the responsibility of leading the world, Narciso Bassols, a Mexican jurist and political commentator, fired back a political broadside:

> The Latin American people support continental defense. But on a specific condition—that this idea should not be used to shield any sort of expansionist adventures on other continents or struggles aimed at the violent conquest of world domination. . . . The gravest aspect of the alliance entered into in Rio de Janeiro . . . lies in that with one stroke of the pen, Latin American countries are transformed into the compulsory automatic allies of the United States.[20]

From the standpoint of consolidating the Rooseveltian legacy of US–Latin American cooperation, the year-long delay in holding the Rio conference diluted key wartime attitudes. One was that the Latin Americans, realizing their numerical strength in the United Nations, partially abandoned their earlier emphasis on regionalism and the concomitant willingness to play a subordinate political and military role to the United States. Conversely, the United States, having had its initial enthusiasm for universalism dampened by the exercise of the Soviet veto in the Security Council, began to see advantages in regionalism that had not been obvious to the policymakers at Chapultepec. Clearly the two halves of the hemisphere were again beginning to march to different drumbeats.

From Chapultepec on, several countries, most notably Mexico and Colombia, waged a muted struggle on three major issues: (1) to prevent the militarization of the inter-American system, (2) to remedy the failure to incorporate economic goals to the agenda, (3) to subordinate the secretariat of the Pan American Union to the will of Permanent Council. Unless this last point was accomplished, it was feared that the secretariat in Washington would continue to be vulnerable to US pressure, as it had been in the sixty preceding years.

In turn, the Latin American governments were unprepared to take Washington's cataclysmic global view seriously. Consequently, except for the region's military regimes, they indicated fundamental disagreement with the US inclination to place primary emphasis on building military security to counter external and internal subversion; the US military, seizing on the growing difficulties with the Soviet bloc and Communist China, took the Rio Treaty as a signal for an enlarged military role in inter-American relations.

To Marshall fell the unenviable task of telling the Latin American delegations that the United States was so thoroughly committed to helping the reconstruction of Europe that it was unable to give much assistance to them. But his friendliness and candor with the foreign ministers and his description of Europe's desperate economic plight, with stress on Latin American benefits from economic recovery in Europe, prevented their outspoken hostile disappointment.[21]

It is likely that economic aid for Latin America would have encountered congressional opposition, as military aid did—though in 1947 and 1948 that was by no means certain. Failing to meet Latin American needs had the effect of dampening the friendly atmosphere among the hemispheric governments and instilling frustration and dissent into the inter-American community just as it was consolidating its juridical structure.

THE 1948 BOGOTA CONFERENCE:
FOUNDING THE OAS

The consummation of modern Pan Americanism came at the Ninth International Conference of American States at Bogota, Colombia, March 30 to May 2,

1948. In effect, it codified much of the juridical and practical experience accumulated in the half century since the first steps toward structuring a hemispheric community were taken at the First International Conference of American States convened by the United States in Washington in 1889.

An outbreak of popular violence sparked by the assassination of the Colombian liberal leader Eliezer Gaitan, just as the delegations were assembling in Bogota, almost forced the cancellation of the conference and clearly hampered its work. Marshall and the Colombian authorities dismissed the riots as communist inspired. However, in Latin America the Bogotazo, as the event became known, was widely deemed to be emblematic of the grievances of the region's poor and voiceless and an apt portent of the difficult path that lay ahead for the regional organization.

As might have been expected, the divergences left unresolved at Rio resurfaced to haunt Bogota. From the outset, Marshall remained adamant against committing the United States to even discuss economic assistance. Predictably, he again incurred the wrath of the Latin American delegates, who had been waiting for economic measures since they were promised at Chapultepec three years earlier. In the style of the early postwar inter-American meetings, the delegates made their views known in the constrained language of diplomacy. But the Latin American press allowed the full expression of its almost unanimous disappointment.

To Marshall the Latin American displeasure could not have come as a surprise. He had clearly been forewarned, as revealed in an internal State Department memo dated February 19, 1948, prepared by the Policy Planning Staff:

> To Latin American countries economic developments is a foremost objective of national policy. The US has repeatedly stated its desire to assist in their development programs, but in their eyes performance by the US has been disappointing. . . . Their dissatisfaction has been increased by the US occupation with [European Reconstruction] and other foreign aid programs which they feel were crowding out consideration of their needs and will delay still further their plans.[22]

The unsigned memorandum, most likely drafted by Louis Halle, special policy adviser to the Division of Inter-American Affairs, went on to make four specific recommendations: (1) liberalize the policies of the Export Import Bank; (2) establish machinery to study development problems; (3) expand grants for health, sanitation, education; (4) provide wider technical aid.

Notwithstanding these recommendations and Marshall's own promises at Rio that Latin America's economic grievances would be dealt with at Bogota, the US approach was again preeminently oriented toward security. Its primary objective was to get the strongest possible structural support for the Inter-American Treaty of Reciprocal Assistance at the lowest economic price. Inman quotes an anonymous US State Department official as saying, "The immediate problem which we have before us is to determine how high is the price we must pay. . . ." Another ill-conceived off-hand remark that became public was John McCloy's admission that he had been advised to "leave his checkbook at home before departing for Bogota."

Marshall, mindful that the full range of the incipient US–Latin American Cold War differences were present, made plain again and again the administration's conviction that "the reconstruction of Europe was a matter that directly concerned us, and we could not turn our backs on it without directly jeopardizing our national interest." An editorialist in the Mexican newspaper *El Universal* was quick to take the secretary up on this point.

> In one case Marshall seems to favor an attenuated economic liberalism, and in the case of Europe, he shows the greatest confidence in government planning of the economy. If Latin America were to play the role which Marshall would assign them, what would happen?
>
> The United States as supreme director of European economy would constitute a block of buyers of the only thing that Latin America can sell—raw materials; and on the other side, Latin America would be a group of economically weak countries in avid competition, trying to sell their products to the United States and to a Europe controlled by the United States.[23]

In terms of hemispheric relations, the Bogota Conference revealed, even more sharply than Rio, the US–Latin American divergences that were developing in the wake of the Good Neighbor policy. Wartime acquiescence and cooperation by Latin America was reaching an end; the Latin American nations had seen US largesse directed toward Europe, felt they were entitled to their share as good allies in World War II, and were determined to hold the United States to its promise that it would consider economic matters at Bogota. As Sumner Welles put it:

> the feeling against this country at the Bogota Conference was more bitter than at any Inter-American meeting since the Havana Conference in 1928. The United States had failed to show any comprehension of our neighbors's most vital problems.[24]

TRUMAN FROM THE
LATIN AMERICAN VIEWPOINT

While a central objective of the Roosevelt era had been to put to rest the old interventionist impulse of the United States, under Truman US policy was advancing simultaneously toward an apparently contradictory process of seeking hemispheric solidarity while applying Washington's global strategy to "immunize" the region against communism, which to many in Latin America signaled a return to hegemonic interventionism.

As a contemporary, but in no sense a key, participant in the New Deal, Truman was suitably reverent to the memory and contribution of Franklin D. Roosevelt. But the private papers edited by his daughter Margaret and published in 1989 reveal that Truman did not include Roosevelt's name when he noted that Jefferson, Jackson and Wilson "served as models for me when I was president." It was not until 1947, two years after becoming president, that Truman himself became more seriously involved in Latin American affairs. Commenting on an impending trip to Mexico, Canada and Brazil, his daughter Margaret wrote, "With Russia threatening aggression in Europe and Asia, Dad felt it was vital to build friendship on our borders."[25] The friendship, of course, had already been built by Roosevelt.

As far as Latin America was concerned, Truman seemed to lack the kind of political antennae Roosevelt used to such a great advantage in forging a sense of community and common interest around the Good Neighbor policy. Indeed, his episodic attempts to recapture the Pan American spirit often seemed to have been mere afterthoughts.

In his *Memoirs*, Truman records that his earliest concerns with Latin America came in relation to the impending San Francisco conference called to draft the UN charter. "We were particularly anxious," he recalled, "to be sure that the Western Hemisphere nations and the British Commonwealth were in agreement. We felt that if we had that sort of backing we would get almost anything we wanted to build an international organization that would work."[26]

Few aspects of the Truman presidency have been more harshly criticized than its failure to retain the spirit and substance of the Good Neighbor policy. A typical scholarly assessment came from Armin Rappaport, a professor of history at the University of California–San Diego:

> Affairs in Europe and in Asia in the years following the close of the war occupied the attention of the American people and their leaders so completely that other parts of the world suffered neglect. Latin America was one of

those places despite the fact that its problems were grievous and its position in the struggle against international communism crucial.[27]

A declassified National Security Council document provides explicit evidence of Truman's concern over reconciling a desire to be Latin America's good neighbor with a commitment to preventing the spread of Soviet influence. Written in 1952 and referred to by one of its authors as "the intellectual last will and testament in this area of security policy of the Truman Administration to the Eisenhower Administration," the document, known as NSC-141, delineated the task in Latin America.

> In Latin America we seek first and foremost an orderly political and economic development which will make the Latin American nations resistant to the internal growth of communism and to Soviet political warfare. . . . Secondly, we seek hemisphere solidarity in support of our world policy and the cooperation of the Latin American nations in safeguarding the hemisphere through the individual and collective defense measures against external aggression and internal subversion.[28]

In sum, the Truman administration marked a clear retreat from the guidelines and spirit of the Good Neighbor policy in two important ways. One, perhaps the most significant, was to endow military cooperation with its great powers. And two, spurred by the fear of communist expansion, it displayed an increasingly tolerant attitude toward nondemocratic regimes.

In fairness, the Truman administration must not be faulted too harshly for giving a lower priority to hemispheric relations in the postwar environment, fraught as it was with new and unpredictable dangers. Almost immediately after Truman took office, a defensive atmosphere gripped Washington, fueled by the dire warnings of Marshall, Acheson and Kennan, that unless the noncommunist West countered Soviet moves resolutely, the tide of history would turn against it.

Latin America, after learning to regard itself as sharing center stage with other major US foreign policy concerns, suddenly saw itself unceremoniously shunted aside. What time the new team in Washington had for hemispheric affairs was mostly devoted to security considerations. A retrospective commentary by the Mexican political scientist Ruben Salazar Mallen reflects much of the contemporary Latin American reaction to the shift away from the Roosevelt era.

> Anti-communism came to substitute [for] the Good Neighbor policy which had fallen into decay and was left without substance when Franklin D. Roosevelt

died in April of 1945. Anti-communism, or the defense against the communist threat, for that is how it was called, had as its father president Harry S. Truman and culminated with the "witch hunts" carried out by Senator Joseph McCarthy.[29]

Appropriately, University of Chicago economist Rexford G. Tugwell, assessing Roosevelt's impact twenty-five years after his death, observed:

> Whether anyone is indispensable is not an abstract question. What has to be asked is: how much will he be missed? is there no one else? is his work done? . . . There is momentum in events themselves, but is there reason for apprehension that with him gone there may be a slowing down or even that courses may be altered?
>
> This is what happened when Roosevelt died. His plans died with him. The war went on to its prepared end—so much for momentum; but what happened after that was drastically different than it would have been if he had lived. He survived in people's memory, a standard for his successors; but, much as they might be granted for effort, they failed.[30]

Nowhere was this gloomy, perhaps overstated analysis of the implications of Roosevelt's death and succession better exemplified than in relations with Latin America. To depreciate Truman's Latin American policy is not, however, to underestimate the difficulties the neophyte president faced so unexpectedly, which he best expressed when he said, "The sky fell in."

What would have happened had Roosevelt lived is impossible to say, given his style of personal diplomacy. It is unlikely, however, that after investing more than a decade in building inter-American friendship and witnessing its practical results in terms of wartime collaboration, he would have discarded it so swiftly and unceremoniously. Truman had no such commitment nor any such hemispheric vision.

NOTES

1. Townsend Hoopes and Douglas Brinkley, *FDR and the Creation of the U.N.* (New Haven, Conn.: Yale University Press, 1997), pp. 195–196.

2. House of Representatives, Subcommittee on Inter-American Affairs, *Report on United States Relations with Latin America* (Washington, D.C.), May 11, 1959.

3. March 20, 1951; partial translation quoted in *Foreign Relations, 1951* (Washington, D.C.: U.S. Government Printing Office, 1979), 2:1196.

4. Message to Congress, March 12, 1947; quoted in Donald R. McCoy, *The Presidency of Harry S. Truman* (Lawrence: University Press of Kansas, 1984), p. 121.

5. Draft memorandum briefing material for the secretary, *Foreign Relations, 1950* (Washington, D.C.: U.S. Government Printing Office, 1976), 2:592.

6. Gaddis Smith, *Dean Acheson* (New York: Cooper Square, 1972).

7. *United States Foreign Affairs, 1950*, 2:592.

8. *United States Foreign Affairs, 1950*, 2:598.

9. *United States Foreign Affairs, 1950*, 2:599.

10. *United States Foreign Affairs, 1950*, 2:599.

11. *United States Foreign Affairs, 1950*, 2:601.

12. George F. Kennan, *Memoirs, 1925–1950* (Boston: Little Brown, 1967), p. 480.

13. Kennan, *Memoirs*, p. 483.

14. Kennan, *Memoirs*, p. 483.

15. Y [Louis Halle], "On a Certain Impatience with Latin America," *Foreign Affairs*, July 1950, p. 574.

16. Harry S. Truman, press conference, Washington, D.C., August 14, 1947.

17. Ruben Salazar Mallen, *El pensamiento politico en America* (Mexico, 1973), p. 284.

18. *Foreign Relations of the United States, 1947*, vol. 8, *The American Republics* (Washington, D.C.: U.S. Government Printing Office, 1972), p. 55.

19. Nevertheless, Halle, a State Department adviser during the Roosevelt and Truman administrations, provides a vivid description of the importance of the Rio Treaty as a model for NATO: "It must have been sometime in 1948 that Mr. Dean Rusk, then Director of the Office of United Nations Affairs in the State Department called a meeting to consider an undertaking with which he had been charged by Secretary Marshall. The Secretary, he announced in opening the meeting, wanted the Department to address itself to the question of preparing a treaty, *modeled on the Rio Treaty*, that might be entered into by such countries all around the world as were disposed to resist the expansion of the Soviet Union. The meeting is worth mentioning here simply because what eventuated from it after many months was, rather than a worldwide alliance, the North Atlantic Treaty."

20. N. Bassols, *Cuadernos Americanos* (Mexico), p. 15.

21. Forrest C. Pogue, *George C. Marshall: Statesman* (New York: Viking, 1987), p. 383.

22. *Foreign Relations of the United States, 1948*, vol. 9, *The Western Hemisphere* (Washington, D.C.: U.S. Government Printing Office, 1972), p. 5.

23. *El Universal* (Mexico), April 3, 1948.

24. Sumner Welles, *The Time for Decision* (New York: Harper, 1944).

25. Margaret Truman, *Harry S. Truman* (New York: Morrow, 1973), p. 372.

26. Harry S. Truman, *Memoirs* (Garden City, N.Y.: 1955–1956), 1:279.

27. Armin Rappaport, *A History of American Diplomacy* (New York: Macmillan, 1975), p. 445.

28. Richard H. Immerman, *The CIA in Guatemala: The Foreign Policy of Prevention* (Austin: University of Texas Press, 1982), p. 11.

29. Mallen, *El pensamiento politico*, p. 267.

30. Rexford G. Tugwell, *The Diary of Rexford G. Tugwell: The New Deal, 1932–1935* (New York: Greenwood, 1992).

Chapter Five

THE EISENHOWER ERA

STORM WARNINGS

Rarely has a US election campaign produced a thorough or enlightening national debate on Latin America. Obligatory promises by the candidates to nurture and cherish hemispheric relations invariably turn to dust as soon as the campaign is over. Nonetheless, the theme comes up routinely and sometimes acquires peculiar twists, as in 1952, when inter-American affairs were brought into the campaign not by Democrats, as was habitual, but by Republicans. Though the GOP campaign strategy on foreign affairs was centered on blaming Truman for "losing China," candidate Dwight D. Eisenhower and the party's foreign policy strategist, John Foster Dulles, contrived to add the Western Hemisphere to the list of "Democratic failures."

Truman's "neglect," Eisenhower charged in his campaign speeches, had made Latin Americans lose confidence in the United States. During World War II "we frantically wooed Latin America," Eisenhower recalled, but after the war the Truman administration "proceeded to forget these countries just as fast," creating "terrible disillusionment" and making the region vulnerable to communist subversion.[1] The fact that a Republican-dominated Congress had done its level best to dissipate the legacy of the Good Neighbor policy was discreetly omitted.

Once in office, the Eisenhower administration forgot the criticism and in many ways sustained and expanded the foreign policy course begun under Truman. This course, as could be expected, was remarkably at variance with the election campaign rhetoric professing deep concern for Latin America. During most of the eight years Eisenhower occupied the White House, the administration often seemed determined to demolish what was left of the Good Neighbor legacy. Only during his last years in office did the president show any interest in Latin America, capped by a head of state conference in Panama, which he attended grudgingly, and a trout fishing trip to the foothills of the Argentine Andes. What caused this decline? What were the formative influences and qualitative differences that led to such a sharp deterioration of US relations with Latin America?

Oswaldo Aranha, Brazil's wartime foreign minister and perhaps Latin America's most ardent advocate of alliance with the United States, was one of the first to reflect this disenchantment in his memorable opening speech of the UN General Assembly meeting in 1957:

> We are puzzled and dismayed by the fact that while the nations that suffered most of the impact of the [Second World] War, have been entirely rebuilt and even exceeded the levels enjoyed before the conflict, other nations are suffering a decline in their public and private revenues.[2]

Aranha's remarks echoed a widespread resentment in Latin America elicited by the Eisenhower administration, which devoted enormous economic resources to counter communism in Europe and Asia while lecturing the Western Hemisphere on fiscal conservatism. Since Latin America during the 1950s was battling the effects of a worldwide recession and a gathering storm of social discontent, it was not surprising that ancient anti-US attitudes were again enlivening the political scene.

The UN Economic Commission for Latin America and a stream of friendly democratic leaders vainly warned Washington that the alternative to democratic reforms and far-reaching economic development efforts was revolutionary upheaval and an interventionist reaction on Washington's part. In 1956, when the United States could boast of the richest collection of global alliances and security arrangements any power had ever accumulated since the Holy Roman Empire, Latin America's problems were left to wither on the vine.

Latin American restiveness increased conspicuously after Eisenhower's reelection in 1956. Allowing for an initial erosion in US–Latin American relations following Roosevelt's death, under Truman there was still the occasional apologetic note about the dethronement of hemispheric preeminence, suggesting a glimmer of guilt, or at least nostalgia, over the waning of the Good Neighbor policy. If the Latin Americans were no longer considered siblings, they at least remained somewhere in the US consciousness as distant cousins.

Except for Nelson Rockefeller, who was considered too "liberal" to wield much influence in the GOP, the Eisenhower administration was without any experienced officials of any prominence associated with Latin American affairs during the war years. Compounding its inattention to the region was the administration's conspicuous tolerance of dictatorships so long as they were anticommunist. Occasional editorials would appear deploring this trend, but to little avail. Thus the *New York Times* wrote, "It cannot be emphasized too often that the answer to the Communist threat in Latin America is democracy and not the military-fascist dictatorships of Venezuela, Colombia, Nicaragua and the Dominican Republic."

Calling on foresight and historical memory, policymakers might have met Latin America's legitimate political aspirations and economic grievances without significantly detracting from the European reconstruction effort. During the first postwar decade the United States, at the peak of its power, certainly had the resources. Also the mood of Congress and the American people remained sufficiently influenced by the Roosevelt era to augur goodwill toward the neighbor republics.

What was lacking was an attempt to enlist presidential leadership on behalf of actions more sympathetic to Latin American needs, as well as a high-level team experienced in inter-American affairs and knowledgeable about the region's culture and history, not only about the economic opportunities it offered to US investors, which seemed to be the paramount, if not the exclusive, interest of the Eisenhower administration. Had these existed, they would most likely have been able to forestall the rapid erosion of the inter-American alliance.

For example, when the president was asked at his first press conference March 1952 if he was considering a trip to Latin America, his answer did little to encourage such an idea. "I have stated many times how terrifically interested I am in that region," he began,

> I believe we can do much to improve our relationship with them; but whether or not the President of the United States can find time these days to make one of those trips with their physical drain and other features that go with them, I am not so sure.[3]

More critical was the role of Secretary of State John Foster Dulles with his zeal to stem and even "roll back" communism in Europe and Asia. From the first day he assumed office with his ambitious plans to forge "free world" alliances to ward off "Sino-Soviet" expansionism in every corner of the globe, Dulles did not take kindly to diversions, including Latin America's perennial demands for special consideration and sizable economic development assistance, from an almost messianic mission. He admonished the State Department staff to "stop coddling the Latins." At the same time he warned the hemispheric allies against becoming seduced by the "neutralism" that was spreading in Asia and

Africa and lectured that a denial of the communist hazard offered no protection against it. Democracy was on trial and he was prepared to meet the test with his celebrated "brinkmanship."

Dulles sought to refute growing Latin American complaints that the United States continued to neglect neighbor republics at a press conference, arguing that in recent months he had met regularly with Latin American representatives

> to discuss with them world problems in which they are interested—and I have met with them before the summit conference, after the summit conference, the subsequent Meeting of Foreign Ministers, the Suez Canal crisis— things which they are vitally interested in, because they know that, if a war occurs, a general war occurs, they are going to be in it.[4]

He either ignored, or chose not mention, the fact that the Latin Americans no longer were satisfied with being "informed" of events they had already read about in the newspapers; they now were demanding consultation with Washington before decisions affecting their future were sealed and delivered. Still, Dulles concluded his remarks with the lofty assertion, "I believe that we are giving a very great attention, in fact, an unusual amount of attention, to our relations with all the American States."

Undoubtedly something more than fiscal conservatism colored the Eisenhower administration's approach toward Latin America, just as it did Truman's. Most senior Washington officials were grounded in a deeply held belief in the superiority of US institutions and culture—the values, the irresistible onrush of advanced industrial civilization as a role model for the "underdeveloped" nations of the south. They had no doubt that the spread of private capital and US managerial and technological skills would quickly result in substantial economic and social improvements in the rest of the hemisphere, if only the Latin leaders would learn to use them.

It was the rationale Eisenhower, Dulles and Humphrey used to ward off insistent Latin American demands for US assistance to their weakened economies. Moreover, they considered it useless to increase public loans to Latin America without at the same time introducing severe austerity measures such as curbing public expenditures to combat inflation. Since as a general rule the Latinos, as Dulles was wont to call the neighbor nations, could not be trusted to enforce these restraints, the supervisory role of the International Monetary Fund and the World Bank in applying a free market orthodoxy was considered a sine qua non for US economic cooperation.

Believing that Latin America had to be grateful to the United States for assuming the lion's share of hemispheric defense responsibilities, US officials and bankers were prepared to guide the region away from statism toward the economic practices of unregulated competition of a free market system. Administration officials seemed incapable of perceiving how most Latin American governments regarded such arrangements as unfair and destructive to weaker and unequal partners.

Likewise, US policymakers tended to overlook the fact that state control over natural resources was in part a legacy of the early 1930s, when the calamitous world depression set in motion widespread nationalistic programs designed to abolish economic colonialism promptly and definitively. It would not do, two decades later, for the economic planners of the Eisenhower administration, whether right or wrong, to counsel the Latin Americans that most of their problems would be solved if only they would adopt the free market model. Nor did it help matters when an able assistant secretary of state for Inter-American Affairs (Henry Holland), who had been urging governments to relinquish control over the petroleum industry, left his post to join one of the big US oil companies as a lobbyist-consultant.

Though signs of disenchantment surfaced as early as the early 1950s, at first slowly and sporadically, then with growing impetus and stridency, outright public criticism of US foreign policy was rare. Typical of an early and milder brand of criticism was a statement contained in a 1954 speech by former Ecuadorean President Galo Plaza, one of Latin America's more ardent admirers of the United States and a close personal friend and adviser of the Rockefeller brothers.

Latin America's frustration occasionally received spiritual comfort from critics in Congress led by Senators Mansfield, Aiken, Humphrey, Morse and Smathers, who skewered the administration for failing to grasp the explosive social and economic conditions confronting the neighbor republics. But with the Cold War coloring much of US thinking, they were voices crying in the wilderness. In Washington those who felt that the legacy of the Good Neighbor spirit would best be served if Washington balanced its global anticommunist crusade with promoting democracy in its own hemisphere were no longer a majority.

It was not easy in the early years of the Eisenhower administration to identify any significant action to justify the campaign promises to reverse the "neglect" of the Truman administration. Until public discontent turned into violence in 1958, making the "communist threat" more plausible, the region's pleas for attention and assistance were almost ostentatiously ignored. Latin Americans saw the new policy as peremptorily demoting the region from center stage to a peripheral role without consultation or even explanation. In short, the United States made plain that at a time of global threats, the hemispheric alliance could be taken for granted. If anybody in Washington noticed Latin America's mounting anger, it did not seem to trouble the Eisenhower administration.

Beyond a brief salute to the Americas in the inaugural address and his first message to Congress, Eisenhower's first move on the Latin American front came with the announcement in his Pan American Day speech on April 12, 1952, that he intended to send his brother, Milton Eisenhower, the president of Pennsylvania State College, on a fact-finding mission to ten neighbor republics. The momentary goodwill generated by the mission raised expectations about the ability of the president's brother to influence US policy but did little to improve the root social and economic problems that afflicted the region.

A year later, having completed his first mission to the region, Milton Eisenhower warned of growing Latin American discontent with US economic policies. But the administration's fiscal conservatism was so entrenched that neither Eisenhower's report nor the prodding of some of the president's top foreign policy advisers (Paul G. Hoffman, C. D. Jackson and Henry Cabot Lodge) for US support of low-interest regional development agencies had the slightest effect. Indeed, Dulles had condescendingly referred to Milton Eisenhower's mission to Latin America as little more than a goodwill gesture toward the Latin American governments, "to pat them a little bit."[5]

Though the secretary of state originally seemed to favor a more flexible policy, he refrained from using his considerable influence to oppose Humphrey's determined protectionism or promote multinational funding agencies, fearing that such actions would weaken his ability to bargain for bilateral programs and imperil congressional approval of the global Mutual Security Program, which was his highest priority. When Dulles made plain that he had practically committed the United States to endorse Latin American demands for a regional development bank in return for votes at the Caracas conference to condemn the Arbenz government of Guatemala, he found Humphrey's opposition to be adamant, with Eisenhower's backing.

Five years passed before President Eisenhower realized that Humphrey's formula did not address the realities of US–Latin American economic relations (culminating with US endorsement of the Inter-American Development Bank in 1960), and then only after Secretary of State John Foster Dulles and others warned of Soviet competition.

Ironically, the first country to call attention to itself by using the trading with the Soviets ploy was the conservative, pro-US government of Chile led by General Carlos Ibañez del Campo. Faced by a budget crisis largely caused by the accumulation of more than 130,000 tons of surplus copper, Chilean officials warned that they might have to sell the excess holdings to the Soviet government unless the United States agreed to make purchases for its strategic stockpile. Humphrey opposed the purchase, but Dulles, fearing Soviet penetration, decided to challenge the powerful Treasury secretary. "We can't prevent them from selling to the Russians if we refuse to buy," he told Humphrey in a telephone conversation. "No matter how stupid they may act we must remember that we have to deal with them." The purchases were made.[6] The lesson was not lost on the rest of Latin America. Fiscal conservatism, they learned, would be suspended, at least temporarily, when Cold War imperatives were deemed to threaten US national security interests.

The specter of communism was more effective in drawing US attention to Latin American nations than the dire economic and social conditions confronting most of them. It was an argument that would be deftly used in years to come by advocates of a more liberal economic foreign policy within the administration and in Congress. As early as September 1954, on the eve of an inter-American conference in Rio de Janeiro, a National Security Council policy paper advocated a "more liberal lending policy" to stop communist gains in the region.[7]

Secretary Dulles soon put that new modality to his own advantage; henceforth US assistance would be doled out on a country-by-country basis. Having mastered the classical divide-and-conquer strategy in international relations, the impression left with hemispheric leaders was that the time he gave Latin America was devoted more than anything to its Balkanization. For that he displayed a talent Latin American commentators compared favorably to Metternich's. Drawing on the remnants of Latin American goodwill, the secretary of state stifled criticism with the argument that any sign of divisiveness helped the communist enemy.

AD HOC DIPLOMACY

Not willing to make major economic concessions, but dimly aware of Latin American discontent, Dulles tried a series of improvised cosmetic moves in the hope of assuaging the ruffled feelings of the neighbor republics. But his efforts were public relations stratagems rather than serious political initiatives, and in each instance they were brusquely rebuffed. To his good fortune, the secretary's gestures barely received any mention in the US media; however, accounts of their failure were emblazoned on the front pages of the Latin American press.

Dulles's first ad hoc move came in December 1957, when he proposed to link the North Atlantic Treaty Organization (NATO) to the OAS, despite the misgivings of such key countries as Argentina, Brazil and Mexico. The idea, advanced at a NATO ministerial meeting in Brussels, took most Latin American governments by surprise. It was not long before the determined opposition of Mexico, arguing that the European defense alliance and the OAS were incompatible, led to its demise.

Another US initiative was executed more diplomatically, though it suffered a similar inglorious end. In March 1958, while Costa Rican ambassador Gonzalo Facio was president of the OAS Council, he proposed a far-ranging regional disarmament plan, having been previously assured of US backing. The plan was predicated on the sensible assumption that with the United States committed to the protection of the hemisphere, there was no need for the Latin American countries to engage in costly armament races. Costa Rica itself had no army. But both Facio and the United States failed to take into account the deep nationalistic stirrings a proposal that publicly acknowledged the region's military dependence on Washington would arouse. Mexico again took the lead in torpedoing the plan, this time causing considerable resentment among such countries as Chile and Uruguay, which had consistently denounced the senseless drain caused by the costly armament programs on the already strained Latin American economies.

Finally, and ironically for an administration that took pride in its manipulation of public relations, Washington showed great clumsiness and poor timing in a series of economic and political moves that would have disastrous consequences for Vice President Nixon's prospective goodwill tour to South America in May 1958. On April 24, exactly three days before the vice president's departure, the Tariff Commission increased duties and import quotas on zinc and lead, further imperiling the depressed exports of Peru, Mexico and Canada. The economic move came shortly after the US government offended democrats across the hemisphere first by decorating Venezuelan dictator Marcos Perez Jiménez's hated police chief, Pedro Estrada, and then granting the two political asylum after they were deposed—further inflaming suspicions about Washington's excessive friendliness toward military dictatorships. Only months before Perez Jiménez's overthrow, the Eisenhower administration had bestowed the Order of Merit on the odious dictator in recognition of his anticommunism. These events, perceived as insults to the democratic yearnings of the Venezuelan people, no doubt fueled the anti-Nixon demonstrations as much as the vaunted communist agitation the Eisenhower administration held mainly responsible for the riots.

Three substantially weighty episodes stand as landmarks in the deterioration of the administration's Latin American policy: (1) the CIA-sponsored coup in Guatemala as an expression of the new interventionist impulse taking hold of Washington, (2) Venezuela's violent protests against Vice President Richard M. Nixon's goodwill tour and (3) the obstructionist response to Brazil's Operation

Pan America. In the last case Washington clearly passed up a great opportunity to reconstruct the inter-American alliance and forestall the advent of more radical challenges.

GUATEMALA

Washington's interventionist mood in the name of protecting the hemisphere from the "Sino-Soviet peril" spurred a new resolve in Latin America to prevent the continent from again falling under total US domination. It coincided with the worldwide anticolonial movement that flourished in the wake of World War II. Not much of the Latin American mood was reflected in the US mass media, which chose mainly to echo the administration's jeremiads about an imminent danger of communist subversion while reporting little or nothing of the region's resurgent nationalism. Nowhere was this more in evidence than in the Guatemalan crisis. Early in 1954, the democratically elected government of Lieutenant Colonel Jacobo Arbenz Guzmán, enacting its agrarian reform law, expropriated some 178,000 acres of the vast landholdings of the United Fruit Company, the world's leading banana grower, with a powerful public relations department whose persuasive efforts reached some of the most influential journalists of the time. The company headquarters was located in Boston, and at various times John Foster Dulles, Spruille Braden and many other influential political and financial figures graced its board. Guatemala offered to pay about $525,000, the amount at which the lands were entered in the tax books, whereupon the company presented a claim in excess of $15 million that, it said, was the true value. United Fruit's claim was supported by the State Department in a drastic departure from President Franklin Roosevelt's early pronouncement that the US government had ceased being a "collection agency" for private US businesses. The *New York Times,* which for years had been chary about the reformist efforts of the Arevalo government and then Arbenz, reported by February 1954 that "the Communists were about ready to assume outright control."[8]

Arbenz, having come to government as an avowed foe of foreign business interests, like the reformist administration of his immediate and more able predecessor, Juan José Arévalo, found natural allies in the labor unions, which included some communists. That did not mean, however, that communists had taken over the government, as the State Department's hyperbole claimed in its accusations that Arbenz was destroying democracy. The Arbenz government responded by joining the communist propaganda war and accusing the United States of using bacteriological weapons in Korea.

That a US-sponsored campaign was afoot to defame the Arbenz regime there can be no doubt. For the previous two years United Fruit had solicited and won the support of the powerful New York–based Council on Foreign Relations, an elitist organization of businessmen, bankers and retired diplomats. In October 1952, the council began a series of studies and seminars on Soviet penetration in Central America. With the discussions largely controlled by militant anticommunists including Spruille Braden and John McClintock, both former diplomats recruited to be executives of the United Fruit Company, it surprised no one when the council concluded that "the Guatemalan situation . . . is quite simply the penetration of Central America by a Russian-dominated Communist group."

The fiery Braden went further: "Perhaps we are getting to the point when actual armed intervention is the only solution. . . . I pray that moment may come soon." Eisenhower and the Dulles brothers were the answer to Braden's prayer. The new administration had been in office only six months when it began to prepare for the overthrow of the Arbenz regime. The idea that a small Central American nation had the effrontery to challenge the United States at the time when Washington saw itself waging a life-and-death struggle with "Sino-Soviet totalitarianism" was difficult for the new US leadership to stomach.[9]

Coming soon after the 1953 coup that toppled Mossadegh and returned the shah of Iran to the Peacock Throne, Guatemala bred in the CIA an illusion that it could make and unmake governments around the globe, but especially in what US officials and columnists liked to call "our own backyard." From the vantage point of an administration wedded to fiscal conservatism, the coup in Guatemala was a masterpiece of efficiency: it was inexpensive—no great armies had to be recruited—and could be conducted in secret; no exile communities tingled with rumors; no governments in exile competed for leadership. Small wonder it received the code name Operation Success.

The political climate for the coup had long been prepared by the United Fruit Company and Guatemalan conservatives who took advantage of the anxiety in Washington to fan the embers of suspicion. It spawned, at least for the Western Hemisphere, the vaunted domino theory. Guatemala was held to be the focus of communist contagion for the region, what Dean Acheson, warning against a communist takeover in Greece, had once called the "bad apple" theory.[10] With the knowledge of the Central Intelligence Agency, United Fruit had engaged the services of legendary publicist Edward Bernays, who launched a finely orchestrated campaign to portray Guatemala as a Soviet satellite. Bernays knew the media was easy prey for the sophisticated public relations and propaganda enterprise he launched in conjunction with the State Department and other agencies of the Eisenhower administration.

In April, the State Department announced it had uncovered evidence of a secret arms purchase by the Arbenz government in Czechoslovakia, which was on its way to Guatemala on a Swedish freighter. For a week the press was given a daily progress report in the State Department's noon briefings on the itinerary of the vessel, the *Alphen*, on its way to Guatemala. Not surprisingly, the briefing officers never told the press that the CIA was already mounting a military coup against Arbenz; clearly the days of the Arbenz regime were numbered.

Even while the CIA was plotting with the right-wing governments of Nicaragua and Honduras, Dulles flew to Caracas to denounce the Arbenz regime as communist before the Tenth Inter-American Conference. He stayed almost two weeks in the Venezuelan capital for the express purpose of ramming through a resolution declaring communism to be "incompatible" with the principles of the Organization of American States (OAS). In effect, the measure was to give the impending covert transgression a legal rationale within the inter-American juridical structure.[11]

The Caracas resolution advanced the novel principle that the control of any country in the Western Hemisphere by the "international communist movement" was justification for "the adoption of appropriate action in accordance with existing treaties." However, while this added the specificity of communism to the provisions of the Rio Treaty calling for collective action in the case of threats to hemispheric security, including military intervention, it did not authorize a member state to engage in covert operation against another. Many Latin American diplomats viewed the US effort with suspicion. Arbenz to them was not so much a communist as an incompetent progressive-minded colonel whose presidential boots were too big for him. They saw the US reaction to be deliberately overblown and Dulles's heated denunciations of the Arbenz government to be outright intervention into the internal affairs of Guatemala. However, all but Argentina and Mexico voted in favor of the Caracas resolution.

The Caracas meeting provided an object lesson in incongruity that was not lost to Latin Americans. In point of fact, it was the Guatemalan foreign minister, Guillermo Torriello, who emerged as the hero of the conference with an impassioned defense of his country's right to expropriate foreign properties and buy weapons abroad after the United States refused to sell it arms. Most of the assembled foreign ministers rose to give him a standing ovation. However, despite the sentimental outburst for Torriello, it was Dulles who plainly won the day: by rallying the votes to banish communism from the political spectrum, he paved the way for covert operations against any future "Soviet bridgehead" in the Western Hemisphere.

Some delegates admitted privately that they had voted against their better judgment in the hope of winning US support for the items on the conference they considered to be of primary importance—economic development assistance and trade. But by the time these reached the floor, Dulles was already flying back to Washington. As one of these diplomats put it, the US refusal to discuss the region's economic difficulties combined with the ouster of Arbenz "was like another nail driven into the coffin of the Good Neighbor policy."[12]

The causes and results of the Guatemalan intervention need to be understood because the Guatemala episode has found its way into Latin American history as the first outright violation of the nonintervention policy to which the Roosevelt administration had pledged the United States twenty years earlier. The Guatemalan crisis had unfortunate international consequences: neither the UN Security Council nor the Organization of American States responded to the Arbenz government's distress signals when it was still possible to reach a negotiated settlement, thereby suggesting that superpowers are immune to charges of aggression.

On the other hand, the Guatemala operation led Washington into a series of feckless alliances with right-wing dictators, notably Venezuela's Perez Jimenez, Cuba's Fulgencio Batista, and Nicaragua's Anastasio Somoza, as well as the various generals and colonels who at various times ruled Argentina, Colombia, Chile and El Salvador, until a popular democratic upsurge would turn them out of office. Contemporary CIA claims of successes notwithstanding, alliances with autocrats and military regimes have inescapably brought US policies in the region to grief. Over the years various sponsors and allies of Operation Success have expressed misgivings about an operation they once hailed enthusiastically.

A year after the coup Castillo Armas had become bitterly disenchanted both with the internal squabbles that were tearing apart his government and "continued meddling" by the US embassy. "I don't see how I can govern," he told me in a private interview during Vice President Nixon's visit to Guatemala in May 1955. "Most of the government functionaries who knew their job were purged along with Arbenz's followers. I was left with shit. But the authorities in Washington don't seem to care. Your government is always more interested in the earnings of the United Fruit Company than in the welfare of the Guatemalan people."[13] Guatemalan observers attributed the president's dispirited mood to the refusal of his conservative allies to consider any serious reforms, and to the impression that the United States had placed all its trust in the representatives of Guatemala's business and banking community rather than in his leadership. That was not an entirely fair assessment, though many officials in the US embassy had, indeed, become disenchanted with Castillo's rule. However, both ambassador Norman Armour and the State Department in fact favored social reforms, though they were often stymied by the US Treasury Department and the powerful financial interests that traditionally dominated the country's political scene with the exception of the Arevalo and Arbenz periods.

Castillo Armas was assassinated by a presidential bodyguard in 1957 as part of an internal military conspiracy, and Guatemala has been in turmoil since. A brutal, bloody struggle of revolution and counterrevolution has gone on to this day, leaving an estimated 100,000 dead.[14] In fact, the US-engineered overthrow of the freely elected, somewhat inept, reformist Arbenz regime—with its Hollywoodesque code name PBSUCCESS—went far toward restoring the coalition of a reactionary oligarchy backed by the overarching power of the military. As Richard Bissell, an architect of the CIA operations, put it wistfully, "I would be surprised if there was anyone at Opa Locka—or even the CIA Washington headquarters of PBSuccess—who had a thoughtful understanding of what was going on in Guatemala."[15]

Ironically, Guatemala set an irresistible precedent for future interventions, both covert and overt: the Bay of Pigs in 1961, the destruction of the constitutionalist forces in the Dominican Republic in 1965, the "destabilization" of the Allende regime of Chile in 1973, the invasion of Grenada in 1982, and the covert war against Nicaragua and Panama in the 1980s, culminating in the outright invasion of Panama in 1990.[16] Aside from further animating the US government's proclivity for covert action, the Guatemalan experience also encouraged the tightening of ties with right-wing dictatorships and the Latin American military establishments that supported them. Twenty-six years later, in a 1980 *NBC White Paper*, foreign affairs analyst Marvin Kalb concluded that "the era of the Banana Republic is over. The era of the radical Marxist Republic is now dawning, with the US watching from the side-lines."[17] To which one State Department official conceded, "What we'd give to have an Arbenz now. We are going to have to invent one, but all the candidates are dead."[18]

Aside from inciting US government's propensity for covert action, the Guatemalan experience encouraged Washington's cementing of closer ties with right-wing dictatorships and the Latin American military establishments that supported them. But more often than not the political expendiency of such alliances backfires when the CIA clients end up becoming the masters. A 1989 study for Harvard University by Sharon I. Meers revealed to what a remarkable degree right-wing Guatemalans, ostensibly in the service of the CIA, in fact used the agency to further their own interests, which often were quite at variance with Washington's. The study, based on interviews conducted in Guatemala in 1988 and 1989 with key political and military figures who participated in the coup, concluded:

> An objective inspection of Operation Success suggests that far from being a controlled exercise of US power, it was at least as disorderly and ultimately counterproductive an operation as the Iran-Contra imbroglio. . . . Lionel Sisniegas Otero put the MLN [Movimiento Liberacionista Nacional] view best: The CIA may have baptized the child, but it did not make the baby.[19]

To sum up, the Guatemala episode indicated the critical role played by Washington's Cold War assumptions and how they determined not only policy but also its perception of the New World reality. Discussing a similar alteration of facts in the case of the Dominican invasion two decades later, Hans Morgenthau has written:

> Our diplomatic representatives on the spot reported not what was actually happening, but their fantasies as to what ought to have happened in view of their assumptions about the omnipresence of Communist conspirators and the identity of leftist and Communist revolution. Thus even if one assumes for the sake of argument that it would have been in the interest of the United States to oppose a Communist revolution in the Dominican Republic, the lacking evidence of such a risk vitiates our intervention.[20]

THE REVENGE OF NEGLECTED ISSUES: THE CRITICAL 1950S

When we seek to identify the changes in the tone and substance of the US–Latin American relations that lie at the root of postwar divergences, we are carried back to 1958, the year when misunderstandings and frustrations that had been simmering for a decade boiled over. Latin American governments spoke out. Crowds took to the street to demonstrate against domestic dictators and US policies. The first major radical insurgency since the Mexican revolution of 1910 was moving toward victory in Cuba.

It was the year that can appropriately be characterized in a phrase Stanley Hoffmann used in another context, "the revenge of neglected issues." Other universal historians have accorded another significance to the year 1958—it was the year UN hegemony reached its pinnacle and simultaneously began its decline.[21] In a hemispheric context it was, perhaps foremost, the year when hostile public demonstrations disrupted Vice President Richard M. Nixon's goodwill tour in South America, stunning the US government and public alike. As a consequence, the Eisenhower administration, prodded by Brazil and Argentina, finally reconsidered its Latin American policy. The Caracas mob chanting anti-United States slogans did what Latin American leaders and newspaper editorials had failed to do for a decade: it galvanized, if only for a moment, US attention on the deteriorating hemispheric relationship. In Caracas, Nixon told reporters that the demonstrators were part of "the international Communist conspiracy," a charge he repeated in his book *Six Crises*. Willard Beaulac, a veteran career diplomat, and a political conservative, had a different opinion. "Seldom," he observed, had "so much been made of so little."[22]

No only was this not a communist conspiracy, the familiar scenario Washington had been warning about, but it was something deeper and more ominous—the explosion of large-scale popular discontent over US policies that many Latin Americans had long been anticipating. Quick to change gears, the US media, which had been generally indifferent to the affairs of the region, began to sense a perilous if still vague, inarticulate movement, like a giant stirring in its sleep.

By early 1958 it could have been foretold with mathematical certainty that, should Washington fail to respond to the democratic stirring and economic grievances that were surfacing across the region, the kind of hemispheric solidarity that had prevailed during World War II would be in mortal danger.

Latin America was now looking for urgent remedies, preferably in cooperation with the United States but no longer in awe of Washington's latest word. Had it not been for Dulles's obdurate indifference, the deterioration of the hemispheric relationship probably would not have been so acute and perhaps irreversible. The stage had been set, unnecessarily, for confrontation by two blocs, of which one would turn to a Third World strategy and the other to the industrialized nations: both seemed prepared to forgo an inter-American system that had been in the making since 1898. Few events in hemispheric history have made a deeper impression on contemporaries or on posterity than the striking reluctance of the postwar US administrations to respond to Latin America's appeals for greater attention to the region, in terms of political influence and economic needs. It is easy to place disproportionate emphasis on the unsolved economic and social problems as they had developed in the region since the end of World War II; but equally important was the awareness—prominent in the minds of democratic politicians and writers such as Rómulo Gallegos, Rómulo Betancourt, José Figueres, Luis Muñoz Marin, Alberto Lleras Camargo, Ricardo Arias, Octavio Paz, and many others—that the position of Latin America in the world was changing and would be irretrievably lost unless something was done to restore it. The pitfalls, then, to which Washington's analysis was liable are obvious.

It was no coincidence that the most violent protests happened in Peru and Venezuela, whose dictators, injudiciously decorated by President Eisenhower, had recently been deposed. The anti-Nixon demonstrations were therefore widely perceived as a rebuff of Washington's courtship of dictators in the name of maintaining order and making the continent safe from communism and its reluctance to respond to Latin America's pleas for economic assistance.

Seen against the long-range background of US–Latin American relations, the riots recalled in stark contrast the reception accorded to President Franklin D. Roosevelt during his historic trip to Argentina, Brazil and Uruguay in December 1936, when cheering millions turned out in a rousing testimony to the success of the Good Neighbor policy he had pursued since 1933, raising hopes that it would persevere for all time. Yet twenty-two years later the Good Neighbor policy lay in ruins, symbolically ravaged by the mobs that stoned the Nixon motorcade in the streets of Caracas. Rightly or wrongly, the explosion represented a report card of post-Rooseveltian policy in the region and the grade had fallen from "incomplete" to "failed."

Aroused by the Nixon trip, Congress held hearings to determine what had gone wrong in the US–Latin American relationship. Administration critics such as Senators Morse, Mansfield, Fulbright, Humphrey and Smathers had long favored an upgrading of inter-American relations as Kubitschek was proposing in terms of political and economic cooperation. Yet important elements in the Eisenhower administration were loath to accept a policy that would inevitably conflict with the established fiscal orthodoxy or the primacy of Europe and Asia in the Cold War. Dulles continued to oppose long-term aid, the central economic goal of the Brazilian plan; nor was he entirely freed of his reservations about "coddling the Latins."

"THE RUDEST SURPRISE SINCE SPUTNIK": 1958

The year 1958 opened with turbulence and bitterness in Latin America. The recession that had made itself increasingly felt during the previous years had by now reached serious dimensions. Even Venezuela, which had fared well in 1957, was affected by the contraction of world oil consumption and by the imposition of further import restrictions by the United States. The state of the Venezuelan economy was described as "nothing but disorder and deficits."[23] The situation in Argentina and Brazil was no more enviable. Countries such as Bolivia that mainly depended on mineral exports were desperate.

Against this background Vice President Nixon was dispatched on a good-will mission that exploded into violent mass demonstrations in Lima and Caracas. The violence shook Washington as it had not been shaken since Sputnik, the Soviet satellite that drove home the uncomfortable realization that the United States was no longer the world's leader in space research. State Department officials, Congress, academic experts and public affairs commentators exhausted themselves analyzing and discussing the origins and depth of the anti-Nixon, anti-Yankee feelings in Latin America. Then, typically, the alarm was superseded—at least temporarily—by crises elsewhere. But in a report on 1958, the Council on Foreign Relations, which generally reflected the State Department's official view of the world situation, was forced to acknowledge that hemispheric events that year gave the United States "the rudest surprise since Sputnik."[24]

The anti-Nixon riots took official Washington and the US public completely by surprise. The Eisenhower administration's immediate reaction to the demonstrations in Caracas was to blame communism and order the marines to Puerto Rico in case it became necessary to evacuate the vice president and his entourage from Caracas. Justified as the order may have been as a strictly precautionary measure, especially in view of the ominous tones of news accounts emanating from the Venezuelan capital, it nonetheless exacerbated Washington's already strained relations with the young Venezuelan democracy.[25]

A few months before the Nixon trip, Roy R. Rubottom, the assistant secretary for Inter-American states, blandly told the Senate Foreign Relations Committee that "relations were never better." He had been summoned by chairman William Fulbright to respond to a United Press report citing deep dismay among Latin American diplomats over US policies. Soon thereafter, an annual publication of the influential Council on Foreign Relations observed, "Everyone in Washington agreed on the importance of Latin American affairs" and quoted Dulles's exculpatory, patently inaccurate remark, "I suppose we devote as much time and thought to the problems of the Americas as we do to the problems of any other region in the world."[26] Yet with remarkable candor, the council conceded that

> despite this unique concern, and despite the long-established tradition of fellowship among the 21 republics of the Western Hemisphere, few observers would have contended that United States–Latin American relations were in satisfactory condition at any time during the postwar period. For the United States there seemed to be no logical way of fitting Latin America into a foreign policy that had come to be so completely dominated by the Soviet-Communist threat in the opposite hemisphere. . . .

With the benefit of hindsight, contemporary observers recognized the violence that greeted Nixon as an explosion that had been lying in waiting. Newspaper editorials, columnists and congressional critics suddenly came awake to the familiar Latin American complaint that Washington had for too long been guilty of "neglect" and "taking the Latinos for granted." Conservatives joined in the criticism, belatedly resurrecting the Republican campaign issue of 1951, arguing that US inaction had made the hemisphere vulnerable to the communists, whom they naturally blamed for the violence.

Brazilian President Juscelino Kubitschek, having long experience with US indifference, saw in the "violent shock" and confusion that followed the Nixon riots an opportunity to press ahead with a major initiative—something like a Marshall Plan for Latin America. In a hortative message to President Eisenhower, he held that the violent demonstrations were not directed against Nixon but were "the product of years of neglect" to which neither the United States nor Latin America could remain neutral. The time was now, he pleaded, to turn the ill-fated Nixon trip into an opportunity to call on all American republics for a sweeping reassessment of hemispheric relations, an eleventh-hour move to restore the tone and substance of inter-American relations that had dominated the alliance during the Good Neighbor era. Unfortunately it would take almost three more years and another administration in Washington before the United States absorbed the full meaning of the message. From the vantage point of the Eisenhower administration, OPA turned out to be a *rendezvous manque*.

KUBITSCHEK AND OPA

The reputation of Juscelino Kubitschek, perhaps the most remarkable political leader of Latin America in the 1950s, yet hardly remembered in the United States, seems ripe for reassessment. Those who recognize his name most likely associate it with the visionary construction of Brazil's new capital, Brasília. In addition to that bold, controversial initiative, which opened the country's vast hinterland for generations to come, "Juscelino," as he was popularly called, left an indelible imprint on hemispheric diplomacy as the author of Operation Pan America (OPA).

Even though it never quite made headlines in the United States, OPA promised to be something of a watershed in hemispheric relations; it did not merely incarnate the aggregate of the region's frustrated expectations but signaled the passing away of Latin American acquiescence to Washington's political and economic strictures. It also produced high drama, staged in large measure by Kubitschek's confidant, Augusto Federico Schmidt, a poet with a consummate sense of occasion, aided by a team of unusually qualified diplomats and young technocrats prepared to usher in a more equitable era in US–Latin American relations.

Perhaps in Washington's postwar relations with Latin America there are few better examples of misunderstanding and lost opportunities than the Eisenhower administration's dealings with the Brazilian leader; the effects of that misunderstanding remain stamped on the hemisphere's political topography. It clearly carried the potential of reversing the deterioration US–Latin American relations had suffered since FDR's death.

Kubitschek assumed office on January 31, 1956, with a pledge to bring about "fifty years of progress in five." The new president was a tall, dignified man whose grandparents had emigrated from Czechoslovakia to the state of Minas Gerais. He had studied to become a surgeon but turned to politics after graduating from medical school. Elected president on the conservative Social Democratic ticket, his alliance with Joao Goulart, who ran as his vice presidential candidate, coupled with communist support in the elections, earned him the distrust of Washington. Despite attempts to allay suspicion that his administration might be sympathetic to communism, the suspicion lingered for years to come.

Two days after he was sworn in, Kubitschek publicly emphasized to Vice President Nixon, who headed the US delegation to the inauguration, the unity of the two countries in the fight against foreign oppression, for an improved Brazilian living standard and a hemispheric "struggle in favor of freedom."[27]

Having projected himself and Vice President Joao Goulart as the avowed champions of the poor, it was widely believed that the new government would return to the pro-labor policies of the Vargas regime—one of the factors that added to Washington's distrust of the new government. Yet Brazil needed US assistance, especially at a time when coffee prices were sagging.

Kubitschek's vision was not hampered by economic realities. He focused on such grandiose projects as the creation of a new capital city, Brasilia, in the uninhabited central region of that vast country. His expansionist policies aroused bitter opposition, both at home and abroad; his "developmental" mentality was anathema to conservative economists who fought Brasilia on the grounds that it was chimerical and inflationary. Similarly, senior officials of the Eisenhower administration made no secret of their belief that his foreign policy was poorly conceived, designed to rally Latin Americans to "gang up" on Washington. Not infrequently some irate State Department official would mutter that OPA was little more than a device to "blackmail" the United States.

Considering the recent history of inter-American relations, OPA can be considered visionary, timely and practical, just as Roosevelt's Good Neighbor policy had been two decades earlier. It was the first major initiative to come from a Latin American head of state since Juan Perón sought to lead the region toward a "third position" between capitalism and communism, the last before Fidel Castro called on the United States to grant Latin America $30 billion in aid and then took his Cuban revolution into the communist camp.

Along with Brazil, four other nations played major roles in OPA: Argentina, Colombia, Peru and Honduras. On June 18, Kubitschek wrote Argentine President Arturo Frondizi stressing that Brazil was not seeking to push itself into the leadership of a South American bloc but hoped to march in lockstep with Argentina toward achieving a continental consensus. Frondizi, whose own government program was centered on the promise of economic development, especially in the industrial sector, swiftly assured his Brazilian colleague that Argentina would view with favor any initiatives to strengthen hemispheric economic cooperation.

On a continent where it was considered axiomatic that Argentine and Brazilian cooperation was needed for any meaningful collective Latin American effort, there was a unique coincidence of temperament and outlook between Kubitschek and Frondizi that endured throughout the initial efforts to implement OPA. Indeed, there was no need to press the point, for the Argentine and Brazilian teams became such intimate interlocutors that it was hard to say where one man's train of thought ended and the other's began. "No comparable relationship between the two countries had existed until then or until the present," observed Oscar Camilion, Frondizi's undersecretary of foreign affairs who would become Argentina's ambassador to Brazil two decades later. Confident of growing Latin American support, Kubitschek pressed ahead with OPA, pleading with Eisenhower for a more "understanding and realistic" approach to hemispheric problems in economic and political terms. He also placed OPA squarely within the Western camp in the ideological conflict with the Soviet Union, in the understanding that this was clearly the most effective way to win the support of Washington. "We in Latin America," he wrote Eisenhower,

> continue to believe that the people of the Western Hemisphere stand in so close a relationship to one another, that it sets us apart from the rest of the world, but we fail to accept that since the close of World War II, the Western World concept has replaced Latin America as the key of United States foreign policy. . . . We hope that the people of the United States realize that continued economic development of the Western Hemisphere is vital to the winning of the "Cold War," that no matter how strong our bastions are at the "Iron Curtain," they will not provide sufficient protection from the dangers we are guarding against if the great masses in Latin America continue to live in poverty and disease.[28]

OPA's major conceptual contribution was a strategy that predicated an upgrading of the Pan American alliance—a radical political rethinking of Latin America's place in Washington's foreign policy—as a precondition for economic reform. This was the plan's major miscalculation, for it was based entirely on the assumption that the Eisenhower administration would reassess its postwar strategy to restore Latin America to a position of priority. If it didn't, it could not be expected to endorse the kind of massive economic and social effort envisioned in the Brazilian initiative.

Kubitschek might have anticipated Washington's rejection of OPA as overly ambitious, in the light of an antecedent: Eisenhower's cool response when he first raised the prospects of such a plan during a breakfast meeting the two had late in 1955. At the time Eisenhower made a vague counteroffer of bilateral aid, nowhere near the scale the Brazilian leader contemplated in his hemispheric plan. There was no reference to the Brazilian initiative in the sparse US news accounts of the Key West meeting.

Yet Milton Eisenhower, who attended the breakfast, later wrote that Kubitschek "talked of a program to be called 'Operation Pan-America,'" which was the formation of a massive development fund with the United States putting up the bulk of the capital." Despite the cool official reaction to the Brazilian's plan, at least one of its features intrigued the Eisenhowers: the formation of a committee of presidential representatives to study the hemisphere's most urgent problems and recommend remedies to the Organization of American States.

Six months later, in June 1956, President Eisenhower advanced a strikingly similar proposal before the meeting of hemisphere heads of state at Panama. In what turned out to be the only substantive step of a largely ceremonial meeting, the president called on each of his colleagues to name "a special representative to join in preparing for us concrete recommendations" with the aim of finding "ways which will enable our people to combat the ravages of disease, poverty, and ignorance." To the acclaim of the conference, the president announced he would designate his brother Milton to represent him on the committee. But the hopes aroused by this high-level gesture soon led to bitter disappointment. Before long, both the presidential committee and the effectiveness of the OAS became objects of derision. The president's strangely facile reflections about the Panama meeting, the first inter-American conference of heads of state in several decades, was contained in a single entry in his diary:

July 25, 1956—So far as I am concerned, the meeting just concluded at Panama gave me a chance to pay my respects in a single conference to each of the republics lying to the south of us. . . . It was a great success from the standpoint of public relations. Each of the Presidents that I met seemed to consider my visit to Panama practically as a personal visit to his particular country. It had, of course, been my hope to inspire this feeling. As individuals I thought the Presidents of Paraguay [Stroessner] and Nicaragua [Somoza] stood out. I was also quite taken with President Ibañez of Chile. Kubitschek of Brazil is smart, quick, but I am a little unsure as to his stamina if he gets into a real battle. All in all I would class the meeting as a very successful affair in the promotion of good will.[29]

It is odd that Eisenhower characterized as "outstanding" the three military presidents, two of whom were notorious dictators despised across Latin America, while expressing unease about Kubitschek's leadership. It was Kubitschek who wrote Eisenhower when a new Middle East crisis developed in Lebanon requiring the landing of US troops, to suggest that Latin America should participate in a UN Security Council summit meeting to deal with the crisis in July 1958. This kindled Eisenhower's interest. He replied that he had "long ago been convinced of the need and urgency that the voice of Latin America should be heard with greater strength in the world," and reiterated his view that there should be closer ties between the Organization of American States and the North Atlantic Treaty Organization. That was not exactly a priority on Kubitschek's Pan American agenda.

Once more the Eisenhower administration demonstrated that while it seemed prepared to give Latin America a bigger voice in world affairs, participation depended on the region's willingness to focus on Cold War issues. Kubitschek, on the other hand, sought a much broader objective: ending the region's cultural and historical isolation from the Western alliance and accelerating the march toward modernization by focusing on economic development. Washington was especially sensitive to Kubitschek's warning that the Cold War was beginning to show its "first symptoms" on the South American continent. Yet it could find no logical way of fitting Latin America into a foreign policy that under Secretary of State Dulles had come to be almost entirely dominated by the task of containing the Soviet and Communist Chinese expansion in Europe and Asia.

But by 1958 Washington was beginning to realize that this difficulty, so long evaded, would have to be faced. Criticized for its sluggish reaction to the destabilizing impact of the 1957 recession and the impact on Latin America of the falling commodities prices, the Eisenhower administration had become somewhat more sensitive to the hemispheric predicament, especially in the face of a series of Soviet overtures to intensify trade and cultural relations with the region. Indeed, some analysts made a point of juxtaposing the amicable reception given to Vasily Kuznetsov, the Soviet deputy minister for foreign affairs, with the hostile reaction toward Nixon.

As a result Secretary Dulles, who at the beginning of the year had dismissed Soviet penetration of Latin American markets as unimportant, abruptly reversed himself and declared that the Kremlin aid-and-trade drive was a greater danger to the Americas than an armed attack. Hence the Eisenhower administration began moving, gradually and cautiously, to adjust its economic policies to meet some of Latin America's demands—and to use the shift as leverage to stem any pro-Soviet tide by exacting new anticommunist measures.

It was clear from the outset, however, that the warm public endorsement the White House gave Kubitschek's initiative concealed serious reservations within the administration. Thomas C. Mann, the assistant secretary for economic affairs, distrusted Kubitschek's emphasis on social reform and was largely responsible for derailing OPA, exacerbating Latin American frustrations and leading many failed reformists to look with sympathy to the more radical solutions that within a year would become the stock in trade of the enthusiasts of the Cuban revolution.

That Mann was able to make as much headway as he did in holding the conservative line depended, of course, on much more than his own personal abilities. He was, for instance, buttressed by an equally conservative fellow Texan, Robert Anderson, Eisenhower's influential secretary of the Treasury. Besides, Mann had the support of the conservative leaders in Congress who feared, rightly, that the fundamental economic objective of Brazil's plan was to secure long-term government assistance, which would require a drastic overhaul of the administration's foreign economic policy.

Neither Eisenhower nor Dulles had to be reminded of the political consequences of such a move, particularly in an election year, for an administration committed to promoting private capital and a balanced budget. Little wonder, then, that while Assistant Secretary Roy Rubottom was sent off on a mission to pay lip service to the Brazilian initiative, he simultaneously carried confidential instructions to do his utmost (1) to dissuade Kubitschek from pressing ahead with a summit conference that could be embarrassing for Washington and (2) to prevent OPA from snowballing among the other republics.

A follow-up visit by Secretary Dulles early in August, publicly billed as further evidence of Eisenhower's support of the Brazilian initiative, was not much more encouraging. Though some accounts suggest that Dulles and Kubitschek "agreed that a meeting of the presidents of all the countries of the American continent should be convened," it actually led to a compromise whereby the Brazilian president settled for a meeting of foreign ministers, leaving the idea of a summit for the future.[30] Indeed, for the next six months Washington's diplomacy concentrated on keeping the Brazilian initiative in check through a series of obstructionist maneuvers.

OPA: A LAST BEST CHANCE

The feverish diplomatic activity that accompanied Kubitschek's OPA proposal reflected the Brazilian government's determination to organize and energize the rest of Latin America for a vigorous effort to forge the region into a more cohesive, influential entity. No sooner than Dulles departed, three days later to be exact, on August 9, the Kubitschek government pressed ahead with its campaign by circulating an aide-mémoire to all the American republics. As a practical starting point it proposed the appointment of a committee of special presidential representatives, to be known as the Committee of Twenty-one, which would be charged with establishing goals, priorities and other tasks necessary for the implementation of the multilateral plan.

If Kubitschek had agreed to a foreign ministers meeting at Dulles's suggestion, it was in the expectation that a summit conference would follow. For a time Washington appeared ready for a new look at, if not a radical reappraisal of, some of the sources of Latin America's discontent. A first indication was its decision to participate in the twenty-three-nation international coffee study group, thus discarding its long-standing opposition to international commodity negotiations. Under the pressure of events, Washington also began to shift its ground on what many Latin Americans considered the most fundamental question of all—the creation of an inter-American development bank. The bank was eventually created and became known as the Inter-American Development Bank. But the OPA summit never took place.

In the aftermath of the Nixon trip debacle, the administration had to act to mollify Latin American grievances and congressional and editorial criticism. OPA seemed to offer the opportunity for negotiating a compromise, especially since the proposal purported to aim at strengthening western security. These considerations helped Milton Eisenhower and C. Douglas Dillon, the undersecretary of state, press ahead with plans for an Inter-American development fund and more flexible policies on commodity arrangements. But as far as a new political dialogue was concerned, all that could be expected was an exchange of words, and that is mainly what occurred.

While the State Department viewed the informal foreign ministers conference as an expedient way to forestall the summit meeting Kubitschek had been pushing for, OPA proponents publicized it as an effort to raise the project's political significance and give it a multinational character. By the close of the conference, however, it was apparent that further negotiations at some level were almost certain to follow, if nothing else than to work out some of the significant differences that had surfaced. During the next two years there were additional ministerial meetings in Bogota and Buenos Aires, but by then Cuban Premier Fidel Castro dominated the political scenario and not the more middle-of-the road Brazilian delegate Augusto Frederico Schmidt.

However, it was significant that even on the eve of the conference, the State Department made no attempt to come up with some new thinking. Speaking in an interview a few days before the meeting, Rubottom reiterated that the United States would "simply listen" to the Brazilian proposals. Openly displaying their frustration, Kubitschek's team, led by Schmidt, opted for a change in tactics.

WAITING FOR GODOT

On September 23, 1958, the Latin American foreign ministers gathered in the ornate Hall of the Americas of the Pan American Union in Washington for a special two-day conference—their first in five years. Its primary objective was to begin the joint effort of implementing Operation Pan America. For this purpose the ministers established the Special Committee to Study the Formulation of New Measures for Economic Cooperation, better known as the Committee of Twenty-one, with three main objectives: (1) to intensify economic cooperation, (2) to create an inter-American development institution and (3) to develop Latin American regional markets.

The foreign ministers approved a Brazilian aide-mémoire as a working paper that outlined an ambitious twenty-year economic development program for the region, with the objective of pushing the 1957 per capita average income from a bare $270 to a level equal to or above $480. An annual rate of increase in the gross national product of 4.5 percent per annum by 1980 was envisioned as a tentative target. In its final paragraphs, the memorandum intimated that something more than a routine examination of economic and social problems had to take place if OPA was to be a success. It required a "well-planned program" based on equality of opportunity and social justice—values behind which "the governments and peoples of the Hemisphere should rally."

Whatever agreement there was on matters of principle, considerable divergence surfaced between the US and the Latin American positions when it came to applying principle to practice. Differences ranged from the desirability and practicability of long-range planning such as the Brazilian program envisaged and the role to be played by the proposed "lending institution" the United States had agreed to establish for the promotion of Latin American economic development, to what each side meant by closer consultations on major global decisions.

After the obligatory bureaucratic delays, the Committee of Twenty-one opened its deliberations at the Pan American Union on November 18, 1958, with the election of the chief of the Colombian delegation and a former president of Colombia, Alfonso Lopez Pumarejo, as chairman. Ambassador Guillermo Sevilla Sacasa, the veteran envoy from Nicaragua, was elected vice chairman in what seemed an obvious overture to the United States, given his long and close support of Washington's foreign policy and the special regard he enjoyed in the State Department.

The cordial note on which the meeting of foreign ministers ended dissolved rapidly in the wake of the opening speech to the Committee of Twenty-one by the titular head of the United States delegation, Undersecretary of State C. Douglas Dillon. Welcoming the committee members on behalf of President Eisenhower, Dillon reiterated US willingness to cooperate with Latin America in achieving higher standards of living but quickly stressed that the Latin American nations must play their part by resolute measures to curb inflation and by providing a more hospitable climate for private foreign investments. It was the very argument nationalist governments equated with forfeiting control over their economies and making their countries vulnerable to foreign domination.

The speech baffled many delegates. In mid-August Dillon had been hailed for his announcement that the United States was discarding its long-standing opposition to a regional development bank. In mid-November, Dillon seemed to fall back on the rigid formulas of the past. Private initiative and private capital, he insisted, "must in the United States view still play a major role." He was suggesting that Washington believed that Latin America's immediate financial needs were adequately covered by existing agencies—the Export-Import Bank, the Development Loan Fund, and the World Bank—and that the only role envisaged for the new institution was to "make it possible" for "existing institutions to increase their participation in development." In a concluding remark, before departing and leaving the chair of the US delegation to his deputy, Thomas C. Mann, he sounded a note of caution against "unrealistic expectations or quick solutions."

This provoked a caustic remark from Chairman Lopez that it would be "absurd" to expect quick results when for ten years "Latin America's pleas for development assistance fell on deaf ears." As if on cue, the Brazilian delegate, Augusto Federico Schmidt, rose to interject that the postwar dialogue between Latin America and the United States might have been written by Samuel Beckett. "It is called 'Waiting for Godot,'" he quipped.

From the opening session on it was clear that the chief Brazilian delegate, Augusto Schmidt, Kubitschek's personal adviser and close friend, intended to use Operation Pan America to change drastically the terms of the dialogue with the United States, demanding a "new deal for the Americas." Actually, Schmidt was the intellectual author of OPA; he was an unusual character, as well as one of the most influential foreign policy strategists of the Kubitschek era.

Before achieving a political reputation through his columns in the newspaper *O Globo* and his influential connections, he had distinguished himself as a lyrical poet, being considered by some critics as the most eminent exponent of modern Brazilian romanticism. He also taught French literature at the University of Rio de Janeiro and was praised by Camus for his knowledge of Stendhal and Rimbaud. In addition he was the extravagantly wealthy owner of petrochemical industries and a chain of supermarkets. For years Schmidt was viewed by the officials as a master strategist; because of his close friendship with Kubitschek, he regularly ignored protocol, which did not endear him with the senior foreign service staff. But the younger diplomats assigned to work on OPA were devoted to him. Many US officials regarded Schmidt as at best somewhat bizarre, at worst as a communist sympathizer—the way many bureaucrats in the 1950s invariably suspected intellectuals of being radical leftists.

Before the first working session, which was closed to the public, Schmidt gave a press conference to express his disappointment over Dillon's speech. He also took the occasion to air his frustration over the scant attention OPA and the Latin American position at the foreign ministers meeting had received in US news accounts. Suggesting that the Eisenhower administration was manipulating the news, he charged that "a wall of silence" was separating the conference from US public opinion. "I cannot believe that this is simply an accident," he declared, "when all I read are the speeches of the representatives of the State Department."

The Brazilian's complaint was not without foundation. Reports focusing on Dillon's speech and some Latin American dissatisfaction were only the visible tip of the iceberg. What was conspicuously omitted from the few accounts published in the United States was the basic theme of the meeting, contained in Kubitschek's initial message: "A state of misery and the absence of a minimum of comfort for human beings are not phenomena that should be viewed in purely economic terms; there is a political definition and an ethical one too, for underdevelopment." This theme was repeated in multiple and eloquent variations by Schmidt before the committee in open and closed sessions. But it was rarely, if ever, conveyed in US media coverage.

Schmidt was frustrated with the media coverage because he knew that in the US democratic system, any change in policy was unlikely without the backing of Congress and therefore public opinion. The administration, however, was not about to agree to any meaningful change in policy and had so informed the reporters who covered the State Department.

The objective of Schmidt's strategy was to elicit a US response commensurate to the magnitude of the problem: the drastic upgrading of Latin America as a priority on Washington's foreign policy agenda. That explains his obsessive concern with a blackout from the US mass media. But it was a challenge that the Eisenhower administration clearly was not ready to accept. Yet the Brazilian delegate made plain he would be satisfied with nothing short of a resounding, long-range US commitment to the paramountcy of Pan Americanism as envisioned by OPA.

From the outset Schmidt called on the United States to join the other republics in adopting a comprehensive, long-range inter-American "doctrine of development" designed to make the war on poverty their top priority. He considered such a conceptual guideline to be "an indispensable a priori" if the proposed inter-American development fund was to function effectively and meet OPA's fundamental objectives. In an acerbic reply, Mann reminded the committee that the United States had never favored "five-year or even ten-year plans," presumably a reference to the Soviet model. Furthermore, he did not think that any kind of international planning was "practical."

In contrast, he said, the United States tended to favor thinking in short-terms, "the next four or five months," and a country-by-country approach "through national rather than international or multinational" institutions.

The Brazilian position was so completely at variance with anything so far contemplated by the Eisenhower administration that it almost defied comment. By the time the working sessions got under way, the Brazilian had evidently decided to made a radical break with the previous conciliatory approach and to embark on what he wistfully called "my spiritualized barroom manner."

The Brazilian delegate's foil in the committee invariably was Mann, the granite-faced State Department official who deftly and steadfastly defended the fiscal conservatism and anticommunism of the Eisenhower administration as the last best hope of mankind. For five full weeks Schmidt used the committee as a Latin American bully pulpit in the heart of Washington. His apocalyptic warnings about the explosive consequences of the region's poverty and underdevelopment for the inter-American alliance and his attacks on US "indifference" and "incomprehension" made front-page headlines across Latin America, but, mercifully from the Eisenhower administration's point of view, were scarcely mentioned in the US media.

On November 25, Schmidt delivered a long, histrionic address before the committee in which he spelled out OPA as a twenty-year economic development plan designed to build a strong regional community by quickly transforming lagging rural societies into mixed economies with an industrial base and substantially raise their living standard. The plan predicated an annual growth rate of 2.5 percent a year aimed at raising Latin America's annual per capita income from $312 in 1958 to $480 by 1980. For the desired rate of growth to be maintained, Schmidt declared, it would have to be underwritten by a massive influx of international capital, both public and private. Plainly most of the resources would have to come from the United States, the most powerful member of the Pan American community. Brazil alone, he said, would need investments of $3 billion during the period.

If the United States refused to accept such a far-reaching political commitment—from which all the necessary economic decisions envisioned by OPA would flow naturally—it would leave the hemispheric alliance to wither on the vine. Latin America would try to negate the effects of Washington's rejection, probably not by withdrawing from the alliance, which would leave its security too vulnerable, but by multiplying its international options. The Latin American attitude toward economic problems had reached the point where "stagnation or slow development will no longer be tolerated as an alternative to catching up with the developed countries of the free world."

Brazil and the rest of Latin America, Schmidt pointed out, might have to seek markets in the Soviet Union and Communist China "as an alternative to the dangers of economic stagnation." This had become necessary because the British Commonwealth and the European Common Market "are gradually closing their doors to our production." Under these conditions "Brazil and Latin America will have to try to increase exports to markets . . . such as those of the Soviet Union and of Continental China."

After Schmidt's lengthy presentation, chairman Lopez, who had fulsome praise for the speaker, adjourned the meeting to allow delegates to consult their governments on the Brazilian plan. The recess took one week. Mann refrained from immediate public comment, but privately his first reaction was horror. Having from the start made known his distaste for OPA, claiming it was "a crass bit of economic blackmail" by the Kubitschek administration, Mann now practically damned it as a communist plot. In an apparent effort to discredit Schmidt, he confided to this writer and probably to anyone who cared to listen that he had long suspected the Brazilian delegate to be a communist sympathizer; now he said he was convinced that it was so.

If the State Department's assessment of the importance of the Brazilian initiative was inadequate, its attribution of motives was worse. Its characterization of Kubitschek and Schmidt as fellow travelers was as wrongheaded as can be.

But the United States was not alone in misjudging OPA. By the time Kennedy launched the Alliance for Progress, the move looked more like an effort to vaccinate Latin America against the Cuban revolution than a disinterested effort to help the region achieve economic and social development in the name of hemispheric solidarity. We need to try to understand what hard choices had to be made and why they were made in a way that shaped hemispheric relations for years to come.

Schmidt and most Latin American representatives denounced Mann's hesitant approach as the very negation of the basic objectives of the meeting. But Schmidt's approach was not much better. The US delegates on the committee bitterly resented Schmidt's overbearing professorial display of literary erudition, deliberately made to appear as if he were addressing naive students. Under such conditions, the anger generated among the stronger members of the alliance was bound to be exasperating for both sides.

In practical terms, Schmidt clearly underestimated how deeply embedded was the unconcern over Latin America's fate, how immovable the most influential policymakers of the Eisenhower administration were about changing the direction of their overall geopolitical scheme. He had not fully anticipated Mann's tenacity in defending the Republican administration's political and economic orthodoxy. Mann was the symbol, so to speak, for the period of great indifference, from 1948 to 1958, which had allowed the legacy of goodwill left by the Roosevelt era to dissipate in a manner best described by the popular Argentine saying, "sin pena ni gloria," without lament or glory.

A rapid postmortem offers few consolations for any of the formal principals. For Kubitschek, as well as for Frondizi and Lleras, it meant the dissolution of months and years of patient efforts, for Eisenhower a sad and inglorious exit from the inter-American scene, mitigated only by the fleeting surface acclaim of a couple of ceremonial state visits to Panama and, during his last year in office, South America, which he found most enjoyable because of the magnificent trout fishing in Argentina's Bariloche, a Swiss-style resort in the Andean foothills. What was lost was the unique opportunity that might have been won the hard way by Nixon's unfortunate experiences in Lima and Caracas.

If Schmidt's tactics were of dubious effectiveness, Mann's high-handed manner was emblematic of the treatment Latin America had received since the end of World War II. It unquestionably affected the outcome of the conference. It set a bellicose tone more properly associated with the Big Stick approach of an odious past many wished to leave buried. It exacerbated Latin American frustration with US reluctance to come up with constructive counterproposals. If Schmidt's bulldozer approach undermined six months of arduous diplomatic work and dissipated the constructive impact of the Nixon incidents, the agenda suggested by the United States offered nothing better than an exchange of generalities. A week after the conference began, it seemed to reach a dead end.

While some diplomats and reporters in Washington may have been susceptible to Mann's attempts to tar Schmidt and his team with the communist brush, it was absurd to all those familiar with Schmidt's advocacy of capitalism and decidedly pro-Western views, except to his most virulent political enemies in Brazil. The magnitude of Mann's misjudgment became obvious to the US embassy in Brazil when in 1962 Schmidt, fearing that president Joao Goulart was conspiring to bring the communists to power, emerged as one of the few intellectual militants to side with the army leaders who deposed the civilian government in 1964.

FROM OPA TO OPERATION DEEP FREEZE

When the committee reconvened on December 2 to hear Mann's response, most Latin American governments had firmly endorsed the Brazilian stand. Mann had hoped that Schmidt's vehemence and the mention of trade with communism would hurt the Brazilian's standing. Yet the signs from the Latin American capitals were that it had been bolstered. Some members of the committee, mostly Central American ambassadors accredited to Washington, confided to the State Department that they thought Schmidt had gone too far but that their governments had instructed them to continue supporting OPA anyway. The preservation of Latin American unity was considered too important to be disrupted by Schmidt's provocative statements.

In these circumstances there were obvious reasons why Mann adopted a more conciliatory tone in the first formal US response to the Brazilian position before the committee, though in substance it remained as intransigent as ever in opposition to any long-range multilateral development plan. By then Dulles had already cast cold water on the concept of a comprehensive Pan American "operation," when he told a press conference on November 26 he doubted whether anything could be achieved of "the magnitude that has been suggested by the Brazilian representative." Acknowledging that expectations for agreement had reached a low ebb the previous week, Mann again urged the committee to focus on concrete short-term measures that he said could have an immediate salutary effect on the sagging Latin American economies.

A few days later, on December 8, the US representative announced that his government would defer its final position on OPA until January 1959, when a special meeting had been called to draw up a charter for the proposed new institution for economic development. The announcement deepened the disillusionment and frustration of the Latin Americans, who felt that US participation fell far short of the vision of "a sort of new Marshall Plan" which some of them had hoped to realize. It also fell short of President Eisenhower's promise of "full co-operation in achieving concrete results." In a somber closing speech, Lopez seemed to speak for most of the delegates when he said he had come to the meeting with high hopes but was leaving with a feeling that Operation Pan America had been transformed into Operation Deep Freeze.

Kubitschek's Operation Pan America was a major event in the closing years of the 1950s. It did not merely incarnate the aggregate of frustrated expectations and signal the passing away of Latin American resentful submission to US hegemony. It marked the end of one period and the beginning of another; it was an action that cut through the continuity of events. The debate around OPA and its consequences dominated the scene for the remainder of the Eisenhower administration. It was also at times high diplomatic drama, staged with a consummate sense of occasion by an inspired Brazilian team of unusually qualified officials and their allies determined to usher in a new era in US–Latin American relations.

Ultimately, the representatives of the presidents did not resolve the hemisphere's pressing problems; far from it, and the lack of concrete results was a severe letdown from the exuberant Latin American expectations. There was no breakthrough in Washington's refusal to even discuss a hemispheric Marshall Plan and little discernible progress was made on Latin hopes for closer consultations on international issues, though some concessions were made on an inter-America lending institution and the consideration of some mechanism to prevent the wild swings of commodity prices that were rocking the region's economies.

But for the first time since the onset of the postwar differences that had virtually shipwrecked the Good Neighbor policy, high-level delegates discarded the favored diplomatic circumlocutions to speak their minds. Something was wrong. That much had been recognized in the Kubitschek–Eisenhower exchanges that led to the establishment of the committee. At issue was whether the United States recognized the gravity of the situation and was prepared to join in a major continental effort to restore the kind of harmony and cooperation that existed during the Roosevelt era. The tentative gestures by the Truman and first Eisenhower administrations seemed to have come to naught; friends and allies doubted the continued US commitment to the inter-American system and questioned its intentions. Meantime, US diplomacy had lost many painfully won positions.

Most ominous and perhaps least noticed, some of the major Latin American governments no longer regarded the hemispheric alliance as their only option: they were openly talking of expanding trade relations with the Soviet bloc and flirting with the idea of joining the nonaligned movement. A decade earlier such a situation would have been unthinkable. What emerged during the month-long discussions was that the United States seemed unable to come to grips with issues except to provide excuses of a national or global nature why the demands of the Latin Americans could not be met. A sense of helplessness, of drift, of inability to meet the challenge permeated the meeting.

"Whether we were foolish or not the historians of the future will judge," Schmidt told me some years later in Paris.

> We aimed high and looked far. Probably we were often foolish, from the point of view of opportunist politics, but at no time did we forget that our main purpose was to raise the whole level of inter-American relationship, psychologically and spiritually and also, of course, politically and economically. It was the building up of that real inner strength of the people for that vast task of getting Brazil and the other Latin American countries out of their chronic underdevelopment, knowing that all the other countries would inevitably follow if the US agreed. We were probably ahead of our time; eventually Kennedy accepted our plans, but it no longer was a strictly Latin American initiative, it had become something else.

In sum, the Nixon trip and President Kubitschek's initiative mark the end of one period and the beginning of another; it was a convergence that cut through the continuity of events. The Nixon incidents led to a moment of self-conscious examination of Eisenhower's Latin American policy, which heretofore had warranted little attention. The debate around OPA and its consequences dominated the inter-American scene for the remaining three years of the Eisenhower administration and set the stage for Kennedy.

NOTES

1. Speech in New Orleans, *New York Times*, September 14, 1952; see also Stephen G. Rabe, *Eisenhower and Latin America: The Foreign Policy of Anticommunism* (Chapel Hill: University of North Carolina Press, 1988), p. 6; likewise Dulles, when he first assumed office in 1953, had declared that the Truman administration had become "so preoccupied with . . . Europe and Asia that it had taken South America too much for granted" (Richard Goold-Adams, *John Foster Dulles: A Reappraisal* [New York: Appleton, 1962], p. 268).

2. Oswaldo Aranha, opening speech, United Nations General Assembly, September 1957.

3. *New York Times*, April 13, 1956, p. 6.

4. Goold-Adams, *John Foster Dulles*, p. 268.

5. Goold-Adams, *John Foster Dulles*, p. 274.

6. Quoted in Goold-Adams, *John Foster Dulles*, p. 161, drawn from telephone memos, John Foster Dulles Papers.

7. Louis Halle memorandum to chief, State Department Policy Planning Staff, 1954.

8. *New York Times*, February 21, 1954; in a widely quoted *New York Times* article of November 6, 1953, correspondent Sydney Gruson wrote that Arbenz had become "a prisoner of the embrace he so long ago gave the Communists."

9. Quoted in "Guatemala Is Seen as Red Beachhead," *New York Times*, February 26, 1952, p. 10.

10. "In Eisenhower's nightmare, the dominoes would fall in both directions, to the south of Guatemala toward Panama, endangering the Canal Zone, and to the North, bringing Communismo to the Rio Grande. 'My God,' Eisenhower told his Cabinet, 'Just think what it would mean to us if Mexico went Communist!'" Quoted in Stephen E. Ambrose, *Eisenhower*, vol. 2, *The President* (New York: Simon & Schuster, 1984), p. 197.

11. Policy planning official Louis Halle correctly characterized the nature of the Eisenhower and Dulles assessment of the "threat" posed by Guatemala when he wrote, "Their fears about Soviet imperialism in the Western Hemisphere drew more from inference and analogies from other areas in the world than from dispassionate analyses" (quoted in Stephen G. Rabe, "Dulles, Latin America, Cold War Anticommunism," in Richard H. Immerman, ed., *John Foster Dulles and the Diplomacy of the Cold War* [Princeton: Princeton University Press, 1990], p. 173).

12. Luis Quintanilla, Mexican ambassador to the OAS, interview with author, Washington, January 1955.

13. Sharon I. Meers, "Covert Action in Guatemala, 1954: A Lesson Never Learned" (study for Professor Ernest May's seminar, Harvard University, 1988, updated May 1989).

14. "Tortures and murders are part of a deliberate and long-standing program of the Guatemalan Government" (*Amnesty International Report, Guatemala: A Government Program of Political Murder* [London, 1981]); *Guatemala: Massive Extrajudicial Executions in Rural Areas Under the Government of General Efraín Ríos Montt* (London, 1982).

15. Quoted in Piero Gleijeses, *Shattered Hope: The Guatemalan Revolution and the United States, 1944–1954* (Princeton: Princeton University Press, 1991), p. 374.

16. "Arbenz fell. The ease with which his regime collapsed helped pave the way for the Bay of Pigs." Gleijeses, *Shattered Hope*, p. 376.

17. *Meet the Press*, NBC, September 3, 1980.

18. Quoted in Marlise Simons, "Guatemala: The Coming Danger," *Foreign Policy*, Summer 1981, p. 103.

19. Meers, "Covert Action."

20. Jerome Slater, *Intervention and Negotiation: The U.S. and the Dominican Revolution* (New York: Harper & Row, 1970), p. x.

21. Thomas J. McCormick, *America's Half-Century: United States Foreign Policy in the Cold War* (Baltimore: Johns Hopkins University Press, 1989), p. 189.

22. Willard L. Beaulac, *The Fractured Continent* (Stanford, Calif.: Hoover Institution Press, 1980), p. 162; quoted by Frederick W. Marks III, *Power and Peace: The Diplomacy of John Foster Dulles* (Westport, Conn.: Praeger, 1993), p. 150.

23. *Cuadernos Americanos* (Mexico, 1956), vol. 5.

24. Richard P. Stebbins, ed., *The United States in World Affairs, 1958* (New York: Harper/Council on Foreign Relations, 1959). In a chapter with the appropriately revealing title "The Forgotten Hemisphere," the report said: "The fiercely hostile demonstrations that greeted Vice President Nixon on a visit to Peru and Venezuela were only the most acute symptom of what appeared to be a deep seated and general discontent with United States policy in both economic and political matters—matters unrelated to the East–West struggle, for the most part, but none the less important to the numerous countries concerned. . . . In situations of this kind it not infrequently requires a violent shock to loosen the grip of habit and bring about a readjustment which conditions demand" (pp. 350–351).

25. J. A. Camacho, commenting on the "precautionary measure," wrote in *International Affairs*, "This is the sort of clumsiness that destroys much of the good done by the policy of the 'good neighbor' and by the very considerable economic aid which the United States has given Latin America" (*International Affairs*, January 1959, p. 29).

26. Stebbins, *United States in World Affairs*, p. 351.

27. "Kubitschek and Nixon Discuss Economic Policies," *New York Times*, February 4, 1956, p. 3.

28. Galo Plaza Lasso, *Problems of Democracy in Latin America* (Chapel Hill: University of North Carolina Press, 1955), p. 7.

29. Entry for July 25, 1956, in Robert Ferrell, *The Eisenhower Diaries* (New York: Norton, 1981), p. 328.

30. Goold-Adams, *John Foster Dulles*, p. 274; he optimistically reports that "in Rio de Janeiro Dulles asked for and got a frank statement from Brazil, and he was particularly disconcerted to discover the alarm which Washington's trade policies were creating all through Latin America. While talking a good deal at home about the need to keep down raw material prices, the U.S. government was nevertheless pushing them up by clamping on tariffs, and thereby hitting at some of the primary commodities on which the Latin American economies depended."

Chapter Six

JOHN F. KENNEDY

The two preceding chapters focused chiefly on the virtual collapse of the spirit of solidarity that the Roosevelt era had brought to the inter-American system, the world's oldest regional alliance. This relentless deterioration continued for fifteen years, from 1946 to 1960. The advent of the Kennedy administration brought about new hopes that the process might be reversed and the alliance's vitality restored.

The new mood became evident as Kennedy's presidency captured the imagination of a generation in his own country and beyond; it affected the entire hemisphere, radiating a promise of redemptive change. Where North Americans were given the vision of a New Frontier, an engine to drive the "revolution of rising expectations" at home and abroad, the peoples of the other American republics were told they could expect a new era of cooperation, an Alliance for Progress. Like Roosevelt, Kennedy had campaigned hard to impress the people at home with the notion that he could get the country "moving again." In his campaign speeches he also recalled FDR by insisting that Latin America was "the most important area in the world" for US foreign policy. In the light of Washington's resolute postwar orientation toward Europe and Asia, these words naturally enthralled Western Hemisphere leaders and their peoples. As is often the case in inter-American relations, the popularity of a new administration benefited from the negative legacy of the incumbent one.

The Eisenhower administration's remarkable lack of appreciation for the significance and depth of Latin American bitterness over US policy—at least until the anti-Nixon riots of 1958—had been baffling, if not frightening, to many Latin American leaders. Kennedy attempted to exploit this negative mood in the election campaign against his Republican opponent, Richard M. Nixon, with an anticommunist twist, charging that the Eisenhower administration had allowed Cuba to become "communism's first Caribbean base."

The Democratic candidate also pledged to launch a major program of development aid "in a new alliance for progress," to assist the Latin American masses to "cast off . . . their chains." He conscientiously opposed, he said, exploitation by oligarchies and big business interests. Blending idealism with Cold War realism, he touted the projected alliance as a shield against any further intrusion by the Soviet bloc in the New World. In fact, its objective was not unlike the Pax Americana of the Truman–Acheson and Eisenhower foreign policy: to provide a strong defense against communist encroachments.

Interestingly, on the Cuban issue Kennedy sounded more bellicose than Nixon, who in the critical campaign debates made statesmanlike utterances about the need to observe nonintervention, concealing the fact that he had been the administration's most vigorous advocate of the covert operations that were being activated against the Castro regime, culminating with preparations for the Bay of Pigs landings.

Kennedy, by contrast, opened his campaign late in September 1960 demanding that the United States "make clear our intention not to let the Soviet Union turn Cuba into its base in the Caribbean, and our intention to enforce the Monroe Doctrine" and that "the forces fighting for freedom in exile and in the mountains of Cuba should be assisted."

Kennedy's presidential campaign convinced North Americans as well as Latin Americans that he personified the end of an era of self-absorbed small-town Republicanism and would restore a new urbanity to Washington's style which, in the words of Norman Mailer, would end "the incredible dullness wreaked upon the American landscape" in Eisenhower's eight years. Or, as Joseph Kraft put it, Kennedy's mission was "to be an antidote to Eisenhowerism—to identify and meet problems that resisted sentimentality and required brain."

But eloquent rhetoric and vitality of style were not the only differences with the Republicans, nor the only similarities to FDR. According to one Brazilian newspaper, Kennedy's election seemed to signal "the return to Washington of the professors and the departure of the Wall Street bankers."[1] Latin Americans' reaction to Kennedy was somewhat surprising, since they were aware of his relative lack of exposure to Latin American affairs prior to becoming president.

Before his election, Kennedy's views on inter-American relations had been quite vague. As a senator, his involvement in foreign policy had concentrated mainly on Europe, Asia and Africa. During the Algerian crisis, he received media recognition as a foreign policy expert with a series of dramatic speeches on the Senate floor deploring French colonial policy in Algeria—to the chagrin of the Eisenhower administration, which had little sympathy for Third World liberation movements. He subsequently wrote an article called "A Democrat

Looks at Foreign Policy" for the October 1957 issue of *Foreign Affairs*. In it, Kennedy criticized the Eisenhower administration's hostility toward the non-aligned countries, arguing that it failed to understand "the idea that there are now social forces running through all the world which have a validity apart from the bipolar [US–Soviet] struggle." He called for a reassessment of Washington's foreign aid policies and argued that "the United States is ill-advised to chase the shadows of the past and ignore the political leadership and thinking of the generation which is now coming of age."[2]

Yet the fifteen-page article included nothing specific about Latin America. By the time he launched his candidacy in 1960, however, Kennedy had changed his order of priorities, placing Latin America roughly in the position it held during the Roosevelt campaign of 1932. Unfortunately, once in office, the new Kennedy administration proved relatively weak in Latin American affairs. The president's immediate advisers included many experts on domestic issues, defense, European and NATO affairs, Africa and India. There was no equivalent adviser for Latin America.

There was no Hull, Welles or Duggan to formulate new policies and implement them. Instead, Kennedy relied on a task force for recommendations and policy options. To lead one of these he chose the only member of his senior advisers with Latin American experience—Adolf A. Berle Jr., a former member of Roosevelt's Brain Trust, who had held the positions of ambassador to Brazil and assistant secretary of state for inter-American affairs during the 1940s. Berle represented for Kennedy not only a link to the New Deal but a liberal figure "in touch with many Latin American leaders whom the Kennedy administration wanted to support."[3] Once in the White House, he delegated Latin American affairs to two of his most trusted political lieutenants, Arthur M. Schlesinger Jr. and Richard N. Goodwin. They brought together an impressive informal network of scholars, economists and artists to deal with various issues.

If Kennedy's closest advisers had little, if any, firsthand experience in Latin American affairs, considering the track record of the experts in previous administrations, this was viewed by the president himself as perhaps an asset rather than a liability. More importantly, he knew they brought an understanding of their own country's society and history and the vitality of its culture, combined with an ability to project the Kennedy message of vision and hope.

Not surprisingly, to this day for most Latin Americans the Kennedy image remains, by and large, untarnished—unencumbered by the contradictions that plagued his policies or the analyses of revisionist historians that juxtapose his activism and good intentions with inexperience and dilettantism. Only days after Kennedy's inauguration, President Rómulo Betancourt of Venezuela, in a message reminiscent of the praise Latin American leaders had bestowed on Roosevelt, cabled him:

> Your statements during the campaign have aroused great hopes among lead-
> ers of progressive democracy. We await your actions as president with im-
> mense joys and expectation that your great democracy will join us in the
> struggle against all forms of totalitarianisms which strangle the lives of our
> peoples.[4]

Inspired by the message and the prodding of Puerto Rican Governor Luis Muñoz Marin, Kennedy promptly directed Richard Goodwin to prepare the celebrated Alliance for Progress speech to the Latin American diplomatic corps at the White House on March 13. Another reason for haste, of course, was the fact that the unfortunate Bay of Pigs invasion was already waiting in the wings; understandably, the president wanted a more attractive and positive program in place.

REVOLUTIONARY TRADITION

President Kennedy recaptured the sense of common history and common yearnings that had so profoundly marked Roosevelt's approach to inter-American relations. The long-range social and economic reforms envisioned in the Alliance for Progress were, according to Kennedy, inspired by his own country's revolutionary tradition, a common heritage, he pointed out, of all the American states that had overthrown their status of European colonies. In the formal unveiling of the alliance on March 13, 1961, less than two months after he took office, Kennedy characterized it as an attempt to "once again transform the American continent into a vast crucible of revolutionary ideas and efforts."

Though domestic critics and conservatives in Latin America decried this approach as contributing to the destabilization of the region and making it even more vulnerable to internal strife and communist penetration, it found much favor among the advocates of social change and helped remove some misgivings Latin American liberals felt about Kennedy's intentions toward Cuba. To the detractors of reform, Kennedy counseled, "Those who make peaceful revolutions impossible, make violent revolutions inevitable."[5]

The new administration offered the prospect of a substantive reversal of for-
eign policy. Arthur M. Schlesinger Jr., in a prescient essay published privately late in 1959 that may well have served as a Kennedy campaign paper, deplored

the impact of Eisenhower "passivity" on the nation's foreign policy. "In recent years," he wrote,

> our foreign policy has been defensive and unconvincing. Most of the world has come to regard us as an irrevocably conservative nation, dedicated to holding what we have, devoid of larger ideas or objectives. This should surprise no one. . . .
>
> When we are a nation on the move, our foreign policy is effective; when we are mired in complacency and indifference, our foreign policy impresses no one.[6]

Nonetheless, Kennedy found himself as if trapped by the Eisenhower administration's advanced plans to oust the Cuban regime with a CIA-trained and equipped brigade of Cuban exiles. Contrary to claims by revisionist historians that Eisenhower had not given final approval to the invasion itself, it is now known that late in 1960 he had sent word to at least one government, Argentina, that a "military action" against Castro was imminent.[7] Indeed it was this information that led the Argentine government to make a frantic bid to join Brazil and Mexico in offering its good offices to head off a US–Cuban confrontation, convinced that the impending landing operation was doomed to failure and would simply aggravate the already tense inter-American picture.[8]

The Kennedy team was clearly divided on how to proceed—whether to ignore the Cuban issue, at least for the time being, and devote all of its energies to the alliance, or to carry out the invasion plan, which the president and his most influential advisers favored in the belief that no reform movement was feasible as long as Castro threatened to subvert the governments of the hemisphere.

THE "CHARLES RIVER TECHNOCRATS"

Anticommunism was not the Kennedy administration's only reason for launching the Alliance for Progress. The cooperative program was admittedly inspired by Juscelino Kubitschek's OPA (Operation Pan America), but perhaps the idea needed the political challenge posed by Cuba to get fuller attention on the Washington scene. Though OPA had anticipated the alliance by almost two years, Washington had taken no action of consequence, as Milton Eisenhower, among others, steadfastly maintained, until after the Castro revolution made its appearance and forever changed the inter-American scene.

For the implementation of the Alliance for Progress, Kennedy tended to dismiss the vast preparatory work of OPA, though he diplomatically instructed his aides to maintain close contacts with Felipe Herrera, president of the Inter-American Development Bank, and other Latin American economists and political leaders. Instead, he relied heavily on the school of economic development theory that flourished around Max F. Millikan, Walt Rostow and Edward Mason and their Charles River Group at the Massachusetts Institute of Technology and Harvard University. Enlisting economists with Marshall Plan experience, they launched a major research program into the prospects of promoting nonrevolutionary economic growth in the Third World. Their findings were published in *A Proposal: Key to an Effective Foreign Policy* (1957). They proposed a strategy to help countries that were eager for growth, susceptible to communism and in imminent danger of concluding "that their new aspirations can be realized only through violent change and the renunciation of democratic institutions."

A vast program of "world development," led by the United States, the authors suggested, would not only save US interests abroad, but would be its moral redemption at home, saving it from the "stagnation and smug prosperity." Such a program would give fresh meaning and vitality to the historical American sense of mission—a mission to see the principles of national independence and human liberty extended on the world scene.

Kennedy and his chief advisers found the Millikan–Rostow formula tailor-made for his twin purposes of meeting the communist challenge and getting the home front "moving again." Khrushchev had recently defined his peaceful coexistence concept: communist victory would not take place through nuclear war, which would destroy humanity, nor through conventional war, which could escalate into nuclear confrontation, but through national liberation wars in Africa, Asia and Latin America, the centers of revolutionary struggle against imperialism. Kennedy was convinced that the United States could successfully compete with Soviet Russia for the allegiance of the poorer peoples by promoting the emergence of liberal, democratic regimes to serve them; it had both the material and intellectual resources required for the job.

While Millikan, the senior and most prestigious member of the Charles River team, became a consultant to the Kennedy administration in Cambridge, Rostow went to Washington to spread the gospel of economic development, first from his position as chief of policy planning at the State Department and later as White House adviser to Presidents Kennedy and Johnson. Having displayed a stunning ability to turn complex economic theory into a vastly popular book, to the dismay of some of his academic colleagues, Rostow's rise in the bureaucracy was no surprise. The book, *The Stages of Economic Growth: A Non-Communist Manifesto*, went into seven printings between 1960 and 1962. It was the outgrowth of a scholarly paper, "The Take-off into Self-Sustained Growth," which argued that a relatively small amount of seed capital, adroitly placed and carefully nurtured, could create a self-sustaining process of growth and begin to close the great gap that separates the rich from the poor.

Rostow applied his substantive knowledge and public relations skills to promote not only economic development but also counterinsurgency, increased military aid to Third World countries willing to resist communism and eventually expanded US intervention in Indochina. Rostow's tireless press briefings, public speeches and presentations to members of Congress concerning the alliance were invaluable as the administration faced the immediate question whether there would be enough time to shape and implement such an ambitious program in the face of the skepticism, impatience and mounting revolutionary spirit in Latin America. A variety of devices were developed to help advance this "action diplomacy" of the New Frontier: the Peace Corps of young volunteers to serve abroad and civic action programs by the military for winning the hearts and minds of peasant populations, as well as the counterinsurgency and internal security training of the Latin American officer corps.

Latin American radicals quickly recognized the challenge that the alliance presented to revolutionary goals. In an article titled "The Misadventures of Anticommunism," the Brazilian Pedro Motta Lima wrote:

> It must be said that modern anticommunism, for instance, the Alliance for Progress, is different from the anticommunism of John Foster Dulles. Although the strategy of imperialism actually has not changed, the Kennedy government does use a more flexible approach and employs new forms of propaganda in certain countries, such as Brazil, Mexico and Chile.
>
> This is reflected particularly in the appointment of new ambassadors to these countries. These are no longer the "dinosaurs" of the old State Department, nor are they slick operators. Now Washington is resorting to the services of professors, economists, and sociologists.[9]

The members of the Latin American task force saw themselves as the architects of a new hemispheric order and part of an exhilarating and quickly receding moment in US history that became known as Camelot. Like the young Latin American officials who worked on OPA two years before, the New Frontiersmen sensed they had the power to reshape US–Latin American relations, the energy to do so and the moral certitude to inspire their action. In this they confronted a mammoth task—to move a divided bureaucracy to support social and economic reform in defiance of private interests and an entrenched oligarchy at home and in Latin America, while countering the preaching of violent revolution emanating from Cuba. In their enthusiasm, arrogance and inexperience they clearly underestimated the odds against them.

In a more recent memoir, Kennedy adviser Richard Goodwin poignantly captured this mood in explaining how the "best and brightest" allowed themselves to be seduced into the ill-fated Bay of Pigs operation. Describing his first encounter with a CIA official who came to brief him at the White House, hinting at "vast and wondrous operations still unrevealed," Goodwin conceded he was "overwhelmed."

> Not dismayed or repelled. Far from it. I felt like an under-privileged child taken from the ghetto streets to tour the largest Toys 'R Us in distant suburbia. . . . The briefing had achieved its purpose. I was impressed, even excited.[10]

In a further attempt to delve into the question of how the Kennedy administration could have been drawn into the Bay of Pigs, Goodwin reflected,

> Admittedly we were new to government, unfamiliar with the institutions of military and foreign policy, reluctant to challenge the assertions of men who had helped conduct the Cold War since its inception. But beneath the uninformed acquiescence, there was also arrogance—the unacknowledged, unspoken belief that we could understand, even predict, the elusive, often surprising, always conjectural course of historical change. Indeed, this false certainty underlay the belief—on both sides of the Iron Curtain—that the United States and the Soviet Union were engaged in a titanic, global struggle between communism and democratic capitalism for the allegiance of the world's people. That assumption dominated, and helped explain, the first of the Kennedy years; only later would it yield to a more sophisticated awareness that the multitudinous globe could not be crammed into simple categories—friends and enemies, communists or anticommunists—that the world would go its own, unforeseeable way, not on one road or two, but along a myriad of divergent paths.[11]

And yet at times, in a culture where style seems to set the tone of relationships, it was clearly Kennedy's eloquence and charisma that often carried the day. Like Roosevelt, he stirred visions. As far as hemispheric relations were concerned, however, he could not claim the foresight and statesmanship and originality of Roosevelt as the architect of the Good Neighbor policy. Compared to the experience and years of planning that had gone into Roosevelt's approach to Latin America, Kennedy's alliance was practically an improvisation.

PARADOXES AND CONTRADICTIONS

Kennedy had done his best during the election campaign to exploit Latin American complaints that the Eisenhower administration had been indifferent toward the region's problems. One of the main attractions Kennedy held for Latin America was the belief that he was an intellectual who could understand the problems of the area.

In the circumstances of the 1960s, the Kennedy approach must be viewed in the context of both its reformist impulse and the predicament caused by the alarm that existed in the United States over Cuba as a gateway to Soviet expansionism in the Western Hemisphere. Khrushchev was perceived as testing the resolve of the new president, whom the Russian considered too young and inexperienced. With Castro preaching violent revolution, Kennedy was quick to build a new strategy of limited war that amounted to training and equipping Latin American armies in antiguerrilla warfare, intelligence, and police surveillance, civic action and other counterinsurgency techniques. Its declared goal was to marshal the hemisphere's armies into a force for progress and constitutional rule.

What was perhaps not adequately calculated was the risk that this force would be inimical to the reformist, noncommunist left parties the administration had chosen as its political partners in promoting social democracy, the "peaceful revolution" they would jointly offer the peoples of the Americas as an alternative to the violent struggle advocated by Cuba and its communist allies. Yet if the alliance was a constructive example of renewed multilateralism, of friends working together to conceive and implement an innovative policy, the framework of Kennedy's overall policy for Latin America was fraught with contradictions, inconsistencies and ambiguities that made themselves known along the bumpy road on the way to its implementation.

The problem showed up most evidently in four critical fields and in each case conflicted with his best intentions: (1) the chain of command, or lack thereof, of his faction-ridden Latin American policy team; (2) the Cuban problem and its incessant intrusion in the already complex and difficult Alliance for Progress program, at times displacing it as the keystone of his hemispheric policy; (3) the inherent paradox in training and equipping the Latin American armies in guerrilla warfare, internal security and other counterinsurgency techniques at the same time as it was relying on the region's progressive democratic parties for support of Alliance reforms; (4) the relentless, perhaps unconscious pursuit of economic development that did not always fit local needs, emerging as a hybrid between the Marshall Plan for Europe and the social reforms of the New Deal. This contrasted with the original model of the alliance, Brazil's Operation Pan America, which was a genuinely Latin American initiative.

DEMOCRACY CAN BE DISORDERLY

Kennedy's State Department saw the traditional policymaking center practically float away. In the case of Latin America the hub seemed to fluctuate between Berle's task force, McGeorge Bundy and the other presidential advisers near the Oval Office. At times policy was being formulated at three different layers at once: the speechwriters and technicians drafting the economic texts and position papers on the Alliance for Progress; historians and political advisers who excelled in hortatory prose to win the backing of Congress and the Latin Americans for the ten-year alliance program; and finally the people working in the shadows of Allen Dulles and the CIA, training and arming the Cuban exiles in complicity with the autocratic regimes of Nicaragua and Guatemala.

Some members of the first two groups believed that the third exercise was simply a contingency plan, a card to be played in case Castro got out of hand, a tactical alternative that did not merit the president's attention. Fundamental to an understanding of these contradictions in the initial stages of the evolution of Kennedy's foreign policy in general, and his Latin American policy in particular, was his keen and pervasive awareness of the need to form a team that represented a broad spectrum of political views. He considered this to be a necessary recognition of the bare margin of his electoral victory. Of nearly 69 million votes cast, Kennedy had a margin of only 120,000.

Accordingly, Kennedy considered that he could not, at least at the outset, simply entrust the conduct of defense, national security affairs and foreign policy to his select band of New Frontiersmen without jeopardizing public trust and the support of Congress. In what one commentator characterized as a "genuflexion towards financial and political conservatism," one of his first appointments included C. Douglas Dillon, Eisenhower's undersecretary of state, to be secretary of the Treasury, Allen Dulles as director of the Central Intelligence Agency and J. Edgar Hoover as director of the Federal Bureau of Investigation.[12] That may explain why a historian would write three decades later that Kennedy's national security policy

> was not marked by a surge of innovation but by forces of continuity; not by radical policies but by conservative assumptions. . . . As a Democrat,

Kennedy was influenced both by the old elites that formulated postwar foreign policy in the early years of the Cold War and by the Cold War liberals who occupied the seats of Democratic party power.[13]

To balance this ostensibly conservative slate, he named liberal stalwart Adlai Stevenson to be ambassador to the United Nations, with cabinet rank, and Chester Bowles as undersecretary of state. Perhaps more typical of the professionalism, vigor and tough-minded realism Kennedy envisioned for his administration were the appointments of Robert McNamara, a former president of the Ford Motor Company, as secretary of defense, and McGeorge Bundy, former provost of Harvard College, as national security adviser. As secretary of state he picked Dean Rusk, an experienced foreign service career officer who had moved on to head the Rockefeller Foundation in New York. Rusk caught Kennedy's attention with an article in *Foreign Affairs* that stressed that the president should be his own secretary of state and should make his own foreign policy decisions—views Kennedy shared. "The decision was taken," Goodwin would write years later,

> Rusk was appointed. And from that mistake grew the power of National Security Adviser McGeorge Bundy and the White House foreign-policy staff (as well as my own, more transient authority), essential to compensate for the deficiency of the cautious and inept secretary; while during Johnson's presidency this initial misjudgment was to have even more serious consequences.[14]

Not surprisingly, neither the Latin American left nor the right was equipped to fully understand the Kennedy brand of hard-line liberalism. It was the product of domestic circumstances, just as Latin America's national politics often seemed to elude Washington policymakers. Kennedy's foreign policy strategy was predicated on the conventional Cold War premise that Latin America and the former colonies that made up the Third World were struggling to achieve progress and freedom while communists were ready to co-opt unsuspecting reformist movements and turn their progressive impulses into totalitarian societies controlled by Moscow and Peking.

Many progressives in Latin America who enthusiastically greeted Kennedy's stand on economic and social reforms were mystified by his stand on Cuba. Convinced that the reform program would be the flagship of the new policy, they tended to dismiss his hard-line pronouncements about the Castro regime and communism as election rhetoric. This misjudgment partly accounted for the deep dismay caused among democratic governments in Latin America by the Bay of Pigs and Kennedy's relentless pursuit of the overthrow of Castro, to the point of denying aid to countries that did not join with Washington in measures to isolate Cuba. Perhaps they paid insufficient interest to Kennedy's determination not to make the mistakes of what his intimates called the "soft-headed" liberals (Stevenson, Humphrey and Bowles), whom they considered unskilled in the ways of the Cold War.

Thus Kennedy offered Latin America and other developing regions the carrot of social reform instead of the Republican formula of strengthening the old order. In matters of security he opted for a tough anticommunist stance based not on the threat of sending in the marines but on the more sophisticated weapon of counterinsurgency—of fighting subversion and guerrilla warfare with covert intelligence operations and special units trained by Green Beret veterans of Southeast Asia.

Adolf A. Berle's role as head of the Latin American task force elicited the most contradictory assessments. The press, having singled him out as one of the few men familiar with the region, consistently published laudatory reports about him, especially for what were perceived to be his internal battles with the inexperienced Kennedy aides in the White House. In addition, he was praised for his relentless efforts to persuade Latin American governments to join with Washington in opposing the Castro regime.

Berle represented that blend of realpolitik and crusading idealism exemplified in Kennedy's brand of foreign policy. The biggest mistake of that policy, which led to the Bay of Pigs, resulted from misapplied idealism—believing that the Cuban people were ready to be "liberated" by a foreign-sponsored invasion, and a reluctance to assume the full consequences of realism, the need to accord first priority to the resurgence of an inter-American consensus. Berle's own position was virtually destroyed by his involvement in the Bay of Pigs disaster, while most of the other principals remained in the administration, some sobered by the experience, others simply waiting to get even with the bearded leader in Havana.

Kennedy aides as well as a number of Latin American political leaders were critical of Berle on the grounds that he continued to rely on the magic of old formulas, acting as if a return to the policies that worked in World War II would ensure success in a very different postwar environment. Having played a key role in combating Nazi influence in Latin America during the war years, he now applied himself with the same zeal to the eradication of communism, which to him meant first and foremost getting rid of the Castro regime. Only then could the way be cleared for an orderly implementation of the reforms envisioned by the alliance.

ALIANZA PARA EL PROGRESO

President Roosevelt's Good Neighbor policy and President Kennedy's Alliance for Progress loom as the two great landmarks in the relationship between the United States and Latin America in the twentieth century. They also underscore the importance of inter-American ties and the need for the United States to respond, sooner or later, to the special requirements of each age. While history books generally portray the dozen years that spanned the Roosevelt era as a golden age in hemispheric friendship, the alliance remains the object of as many diverse interpretations as the by now legendary figure of Kennedy himself. Revisionist historians on the left mock it as a failed effort to counter the impact of Cuba's communist revolution; critics on the right denounce it as having promoted statism and undermined the stability of the free enterprise system, spurring, rather than coopting, revolutionary movements.

The alliance sought to be both a social revolution and a vehicle for rapid economic growth. On both counts US economists and political commentators have, in the main, judged it flawed. From the beginning it lacked one important ingredient that differentiated it from Kubitschek's plan—it did not carry the label "Made in Latin America." Although Kennedy never shrank from acknowledging Brazil's OPA as the model for the alliance, both in conception and practice there was never any doubt that the administration had fashioned the alliance after its own image. It was clearly founded on Kennedy's firm belief in his country's unique ability—and responsibility—to provide leadership and the assumption that the nations of Latin America would accept the American model of success, recognizing the interdependence of democracy and economic growth and that only economic and social reforms can stem the tide of revolution.

Despite the buoyancy the Kennedy administration sought to give to its Latin American policy, the first two years of the alliance were devoted to dealing with internal institutional problems and, by extension, to retrieving the multilateral spirit that had been the driving force of Kubitschek's initiative. The endless internal debates in the administration and Congress, as well as the successive restructuring of the administrative apparatus of the alliance, was a lamentable waste of energy and precious time. This waste could have been avoided had there been less brashness in the New Frontier's early pretension to overcome any and every obstacle and had more serious attention been given to the experiences of the Brazilian plan at a critical moment in inter-American relations. While Kennedy's social rhetoric angered the conservatives, the absence of substantial accomplishments inflamed the reformers.

In addition, the implementation of each of the five social targets enumerated by Kennedy—land reform, jobs, housing, health and education—which gave the program its popular orientation, fell short of its ambitious goals. Somewhere, rather early on, as Chilean President Eduardo Frei would concede in 1964, the revolution lost its way. If the goals of the alliance were revolutionary, the means were not.

"NO SUCH WORDS SINCE FRANKLIN ROOSEVELT"

Still, to understand the hopes and general mood the alliance aroused we must look at how it all began. On March 13, Kennedy outlined his proposal in an address to the Latin American diplomatic corps assembled for the occasion in an unprecedented reception at the East Room of the White House. Most of the diplomats were in a state of enthusiastic expectancy. For more than a decade their governments had pleaded for greater attention and concern for the ferment in the region, most recently in the 1958 collective move led by Brazilian President Juscelino Kubitschek's Operation Pan America (OPA) proposal. But Washington's response had been slow and often grudging. Now a new US president was voicing many of their own grievances and promising to work with them toward bold solutions in a spirit of hemispheric solidarity unequaled since Roosevelt's time.

Kennedy began by recalling that the United States had urged recognition of the Latin American republics fighting for independence against Spain 139 years earlier to the week. He noted that the revolution which had begun in Philadelphia in 1776 and Caracas in 1811 was not yet finished: "for our unfulfilled task is to demonstrate to the entire world that man's unsatisfied aspiration for economic progress and social justice can best be achieved by free men working within a framework of democratic institutions."[15]

Now was the time, Kennedy said, to turn away from the failures of the past to a future "full of peril, but bright with hope." The task was to create an American civilization "where within the rich diversity of its own traditions, each nation is free to follow its own path toward progress." Then he added:

I have called on all people of the hemisphere to join in a new Alliance for Progress, a vast cooperative effort, unparalleled in magnitude and nobility of purpose, to satisfy the basic needs of the American people for homes, work and land, health and schools. Let us once again transform the American continent into a vast crucible of revolutionary ideas and efforts—a tribute to the power of the creative energies of free men and women—an example to all the world that liberty and progress walk hand in hand.[16]

Arthur M. Schlesinger Jr., who together with Berle and Richard Goodwin had helped draft the speech, captured the atmosphere of the White House in his memoir, *A Thousand Days*:

> It was an extraordinary occasion. The people in the East Room came suddenly alive as the young President spoke his words of idealism and purpose. There was strong applause. Goodwin and I circulated among the group as it dispersed. One found still a measure of doubt and cynicism, but most people were deeply moved. The Venezuelan ambassador took my arm and said urgently, "We have not heard such words since Franklin Roosevelt." The future of the hemisphere did seem bright with hope.[17]

Schlesinger's account correctly reflected the optimism and self-confidence of Kennedy and his collaborators in the opening months of the new administration, as well as the euphoric reaction of most Latin American envoys present at the White House, caught up as they were by the emotion of the occasion. A more detached assessment might have warned the Kennedy officials that the enthusiasm demonstrated by the diplomatic representatives in Washington did not necessarily guarantee that their governments would assume the same position. After so many false starts—most recently Washington's grudging reaction to OPA—many governments were less awed and more prone to retain the "measure of doubt" Schlesinger had detected even among some of the envoys who heard Kennedy's address.

In a message to Congress at noon the next day, Kennedy requested $600 million as the first installment for the ten-year program and urged early action on the new inter-American program. President Castro, who from the outset suggested that Kennedy's foreign aid policy was essentially intended to give the United States economic leverage to pressure and intimidate Cuba, assailed the plan as "an attempt to buy the conscience of Latin America." Speaking at a rally at Havana University, he said, "We'll see whether the conscience of Latin America can be bought for $500 million as Kennedy intends, or whether, as we contend, it cannot be bought at any price."

The White House ceremony breathed a fresh spirit. Few among the Latin American diplomats, even the most right-wing, had given high marks to the Eisenhower administration. In the eyes of the representatives of the liberal democracies, the departing government's poor performance in Latin America was attributed to the stodgy conservatism and dogmatic anticommunism of its Republican businessmen and corporation lawyers. By the same token, the men of Kennedy's New Frontier regarded themselves—and were much regarded by the media—as hard-nosed pragmatists, capable of a more imaginative and flexible approach, combining ardor for democracy and economic development with a tough stance against communist subversion.

Thus even as Kennedy was publicly proclaiming the need to speed reform and holding up his country's revolutionary past as a shared heritage with Latin America, he was preparing to go along with covert operations to unseat a revolution he considered to have gone awry, the Castro revolution, with a minimum of regard for the fact that failure in that dubious enterprise could seriously undercut the hemispheric unity the alliance was intended to foster, and that would be an essential ingredient for its successful implementation.

Of all the motives that fed the initiation of the alliance, anticommunism was the strongest. Cuba's choice of communism had unfortunately pushed its revolution and the whole notion of Latin America's social revolution into the realm of the Cold War. It led the United States to espouse, still somewhat awkwardly, the idea of promoting a program of social evolution and basic reform—backed by over $1 billion annually in loans and grants—to ensure that the irreversible new movements in Latin America were kept within the framework of representative democracy and allegiance to the West. Kennedy did not deny the direct link between the alliance and the policy of anticommunism. Criticizing the decision adopted by the Congress in the fall of 1962 to reduce the foreign aid program, he declared it to be senseless to make speeches against the spread of communism, voice regrets over the instability of Latin America, and then vote for a reduction of spending for the Alliance for Progress, throw up roadblocks in the way of the Peace Corps, and undermine efforts to stop communist influence in vital areas.

Whatever may be the case for or against the alliance in retrospective academic studies, the Kennedy program in its contemporary context had a healthy impact on Latin American public opinion. It provided evidence that the young president was implementing his campaign promise to reverse the Eisenhower administration's political rhetoric and economic policies of the preceding eight years. In 1954 Secretary of the Treasury George Humphrey set the tone of that policy, by making crystal clear to the Latin American countries that they had to look to private investment capital, not the US government, for help. He rejected their pleas for stabilization of raw material prices as a threat to the free market economy. In 1957 Humphrey's successor, Robert B. Anderson, again rejected Latin American requests for an inter-American bank as "unnecessary." Such a bank ultimately was set up during the last months of the Eisenhower administration and would play a major role in the Kennedy program.

On alliance strategy, conflicting views within the administration were quick to surface. In line with Kennedy's inclination to pursue a dynamic hemispheric policy, the prevailing view of such White House advisers as Schlesinger and Goodwin was that the United States had to exercise firm leadership in pressing for speedy, meaningful social and economic reforms in order to stem the spread of the Castro brand of radical revolution. Other experts counseled caution, arguing that by focusing mainly on its communist adversaries, Washington might be saddling the alliance with a potentially alienating "made in the USA" label that could be exploited not only by communists but by Latin American nationalists as well.

At the same time, Teodoro Moscoso, the Puerto Rican industrialist whom Kennedy had appointed to be ambassador in Venezuela and then recalled to name coordinator of the alliance, sought to disarm right-wing critics, stating, "In supporting the Alliance, members of the traditional ruling class will have nothing to fear." Rather, he cautioned, privileged groups "must choose between the objectives of the Alliance and exposing themselves to the destructive type of revolution of a Fidel Castro." To which his friend Rómulo Betancourt added the classic retort the advocates of the New Deal made to their right-wing critics: "We must help the poor . . . in order to save the rich." Of course, it was evident that the alliance involved a change and presupposed the acceptance on the part of the United States of certain old demands of the Latin American governments; but it was just as obvious that it was by no means a revolutionary solution capable of transforming the socioeconomic structure of Latin America.

In the words of Alonso Aguilar, the Mexican historian, the alliance "was, no doubt, a new weapon—to be used, however, within the framework of the old anticommunist strategy."[18] As far as rhetoric was concerned, the alliance did represent a determined effort from the start to present the Kennedy administration as fostering drastic social and economic reforms, which, compared to the recent past, loomed as revolutionary. For several months, especially in 1961 and 1962, Teodoro Moscoso kept repeating throughout the hemisphere that the alliance was the most important revolutionary instrument the peoples of Latin America ever had in their hands.

In 1962, at Punta del Este, Uruguay, where the multilateral charter of the alliance was formally consecrated, the hemisphere foreign ministers set forth the real problems and failures of Latin American development, often making accurate diagnoses. However, in Aguilar's assessment,

> they failed to resolutely confront the problems, to resolve to overcome the basic obstacles to progress and to call a spade a spade; the keynote was empty rhetoric, stereotyped phrases and tempting offers which did not suffice to conceal that the governments of the continent, fearful of the possibility of

real revolutionary change, were trying to protect their interests by means of superficial adjustments which would not seriously affect them.[19]

Even some of Kennedy's staunchest allies remained ambivalent about the US plan. Former Costa Rican president Jose Figueres sent a somewhat ambiguous message to Latin American leaders, stating, "We consider this Alliance a realistic defensive measure on the part of the United States government . . . in the protection of her liberties and with a view to her own interests." For his part, Secretary of State Dean Rusk declared: "The Alliance constitutes a concrete part of an indivisible whole . . . it rests on the concept that this hemisphere is part of Western Civilization which we are pledged to defend."

The success of the alliance appeared increasingly remote even as early as a few months after the approval of the resolutions at Punta del Este. One of the first voices to question the wisdom of a vigorous US stewardship of the alliance was that of Albert O. Hirschman, a professor of economic relations at Columbia who had been invited by the Kennedy administration to participate in the preparatory work for the ministerial-level meeting called to draft the alliance charter. In an article published in the May issue of the *Reporter*, Hirschman wrote:

> Many influential intellectuals and policymakers of Latin America, like their Asian or African counterparts, want to chart an independent and somewhat unpredictable course between the two principal power blocs. . . . We must learn how to cooperate with the increasingly influential groups of new nationalists who wish to experiment with new forms of social and economic organization and recoil from any outspoken commitment to us.[20]

The Hirschman article was a realistic reflection of the Latin America rejection of the idea that "Uncle Sam knows best." Ironically, the kind of US leadership and prestige Kennedy was trying to reassert after the Bay of Pigs was precisely what Brazil and the other Latin American countries had sought—and not received—from Eisenhower in response to Operation Pan America. President Kubitschek, who was strongly committed to the West, had expected that the United States would be stirred to seize on the long-range development program to regain its traditional position of hemisphere leader, keep communism out of the hemisphere and restore the central position inter-American affairs had in Washington's foreign policy during the Roosevelt years. A decade later, President Janio Quadros of Brazil was no longer prepared to accept that his country's destiny be subordinated to the whims of US officialdom.

TO LEAD, OR NOT TO LEAD?

During the first few months of the Kennedy administration the Latin American policy commanded top-level attention, perhaps as a smoke screen to conceal and eventually offset the Cuban enterprise. After the Bay of Pigs fiasco efforts were redoubled to make up for the blunder and lost time. In quick succession, Kennedy dispatched Adlai Stevenson and Edward (Ted) Kennedy, the president's youngest brother, to reassure the hemisphere governments that the Cuban episode had not derailed the alliance and that plans were in place for far-ranging financial assistance and commodity price stabilization arrangements. These were to be announced at the impending Punta del Este conference in Uruguay scheduled for August to draft the alliance charter.

The provisions of the Charter of Punta del Este were bold and far-reaching. The drafters were not afraid of the word "revolution," although most of them represented governments which were far from revolutionary. Some US observers found the word disquieting—but not Secretary Dillon, who had been a forceful advocate of an enlarged and more generous Pan Americanism for a dozen years. He argued that the United States should not rest until the millions who still lived with hunger, poverty and despair throughout the hemisphere had their demands met. Whereupon Ernesto "Che" Guevara, representing Cuba, reminded the delegates that they had Cuba to thank for this sudden US generosity and prophesied the failure of the whole enterprise.

Faced with social revolution, the foreign ministers of America offered a formula of gradual evolution, of institutional reform to strengthen democratic institutions, accelerate economic and social development, stimulate land reform, ensure fair wages, abolish illiteracy, modernize tax systems and proceed with the integration of Latin America. The charter established the objectives and methods of the alliance, indicating that the estimated minimum growth in per capita income of 2.5 percent per year would be achieved through development programs, economic integration, stable prices for basic exports, public housing and health programs and agrarian, fiscal, educational and public administration reforms.

Some greeted the proposals with hope—others with anger. Hope was the exultant response of the millions of landless throughout Latin America. The large landholders reacted with anger, mixed with disbelief. They could not comprehend that anyone would be so foolish as to upset the normal and proper balance of society. After outlining these ambitious goals, the Declaration to the Peoples of America affirmed "the conviction . . . that these profound economic, social and cultural changes can come about only through the self-help efforts of each country." But it recognized that such self-help "must be reinforced by essential contributions of external assistance." Then followed the US pledge "to provide a major part of the minimum of $20 billion" over a ten-year period, and "over a billion dollars" during the first year of the alliance. With this, there was the promise of the participating nations "to devote a steadily increasing share of their own resources to economic and social development, and to make the reforms necessary to assure that all share fully in the fruits of the Alliance for Progress." The declaration closed with a brave peroration:

> Conscious of the overriding importance of this declaration, the signatory countries declare that the inter-American community is now beginning an era when it will supplement its institutional, legal, cultural and social accomplishments with immediate and concrete actions to secure a better life, under freedom and democracy, for the present and future generations.[21]

"Thus was the Alliance born in ecstasy—and with a fairly precise budget," recalls historian Hubert Herring.[22] The financial goals were specific: a total investment in Latin American development during the decade of the 1960s of at least $100 billion; of this total, 80 percent would come from the Latin Americans themselves. This left 20 percent, or $20 billion, to come from external sources, about half, about $10 billion, from US public funds.

In the meantime, the administration went ahead with two emergency projects, a plan to rush aid to Brazil's destitute northeast, where some 20 million people were threatened with starvation on account of a drought, and a $50 million loan to help rehabilitate the Bolivian economy. Kennedy himself, in a trailblazing gesture, used his first trip to Europe as president a month after the Cuban incident to brief key NATO allies on his reform program for Latin America and press them for greater cooperation. He asked French President Charles de Gaulle and British Prime Minister Harold Macmillan to support new stabilization agreements to help countries facing foreign exchange shortages and balance of payments difficulties increase long-term economic development credits, reduce protective barriers against Latin America's basic products and avoid other protective measures designed to favor exports of Europe's former African colonies over those from Latin America. Kennedy made plain his view that broader European cooperation was essential for his reform program to succeed.

During the same European trip, the president also served notice to Premier Nikita Khrushchev that no real relaxation of the Cold War was possible if the Soviets continued to use Cuba to promote discord in the inter-American alliance. In response to the Soviet leader's bitter denunciation of US aggression against Cuba, Kennedy held to his position that communism on the island was "intolerable" and that the Cuban issue would not be "negotiated" in return for a Western withdrawal in some other East–West trouble spot. Any settlement of the Cuban question, he insisted, had to be made within the framework of the inter-American alliance and with the full knowledge of all its members. White House officials emphasized that it was the first time a US chief of state had given such high priority to Western Hemisphere problems in top-level European meetings.

A WORTHY OBSTACLE COURSE

Almost from the beginning the fundamental working arrangement of the alliance ran into difficulties. In theory, the program was a multilateral affair: a panel of economists, the "Nine Wise Men," drawn from Latin America as well as the United States, were appointed to study all plans, and the final allocation of loans and grants was to be a joint decision of all the member states. In practice, the United States increasingly assumed the right to decide on the projects into which its considerable dollars were going. Money earmarked for the alliance was handled by the Administration for International Development, and the chief officer for the allotment of funds became the US coordinator. Teodoro Moscoso, an architect of Puerto Rico's successful industrialization program, held this post until 1964 and made a valiant effort to be loyal to the multilateral ideal. But there was constant pressure from the US Congress and the Department of State for firm unilateral control.

This issue was addressed at a meeting of all the representatives of all the nations in Sao Paulo in November 1963. There it was decided to appoint an Inter-American Committee for the Alliance for Progress (CIAP), headed by Carlos Sanz de Santamaría, a former minister of economy and foreign affairs of Colombia.

CIAP was empowered to analyze the various projects proposed by the various countries and to make recommendations for the assignment of funds. The injection of this new voice in the decisionmaking councils of the alliance had a tonic effect, making way for more multilateral pressure as an offset to the preponderant influence of the United States. Nonetheless, the fact that Washington was supplying the lion's share of the funds made US approval of any project necessary. But CIAP helped return the alliance to a more broadly based all-American effort. Still, it was unable to achieve either the political thrust or the truly multinational character entailed in the earlier Brazilian initiative.

The Latin Americans' protest against what they considered excessive US control of the alliance is illustrated by the "tie-in" policy, under which recipients of US loans and grants were obligated to purchase 60 percent of the equipment and machinery involved in a given project from the United States, even if they could save money by making the purchases elsewhere. For example, when Bolivia was granted a loan to modernize mining equipment, there was bitter resentment that Bolivians were not free to save money by making purchases in Japan and Germany. In defense of this policy, US officials were quick to point out that the critics did not give due weight to the precarious US balance of payments position and the natural disposition of Congress to come to the defense of the country's exports.

The alliance blueprint combined the traditional trend toward a more cooperative regional effort under a strong leader with a new trend toward modernization of the government through the use of a new loyalty not only to the nation but to the regional effort. The dominant sentiment behind the plans was econometric, technocratic; invariably it would clash with the region's endemic nationalist sentiments. Essentially, the Kennedy administration in the dawning 1960s led the way in the modernization of Latin America's institutions. But it was unable to revolutionize the life of the common people overnight. The alliance inevitably encountered deep resentment in its effort to institute reforms, from advocates of the status quo on the right and from revolutionaries of the left. The right feared destabilization; the left argued that only by breaking the influence of foreign capitalism could Latin America develop as independent nations. Allende echoed the Marxist conviction that Western capitalism was using the backward countries as a source of profit to bolster the capitalist system.

To make an immediate impact, Kennedy and Moscoso picked the Dominican Republic as a chief "showcase" of alliance programs and strengthening of democracy. Meanwhile Sasha Vollmann, a Romanian-born labor organizer who lived in the United States, was sent from Washington to be a political adviser and to show Juan Bosch how to stay in power. He helped set up a political institute for the training of labor leaders and propagandists and taught Bosch how to secure mass support. One key to the decline and failure of the alliance was in the way it faced political and economic problems and how it dealt with them. Almost three decades later, when economic development has become a major field of scholarly study and government activity, we can easily forget how recent is our new knowledge. In the early 1960s the models were mostly the Marshall Plan experience in the reconstruction of Europe, Eurocentric and US patterns of analysis. Modern economic science was being applied to underdeveloped areas, which were simply called "backward," with little discrimination or regard for their own characteristics. Capital and trained skills were seen as the first requirement, with building of infrastructure, hydroelectric plants, iron works, and transport and communications a close second. Lacking a clearly articulated plan and efficient administration, however, the new US government achieved a mixed record.

Perhaps the most effective instrument of alliance policy has been the Inter-American Development Bank, whose first president, Felipe Herrera, exercised strong leadership. Theoretically, Herrera and his aides were free to pursue the multilateral ideal that was basic to the original alliance philosophy. But in practice they were subject to US pressure, and bilateral considerations influenced their operations. Private capital, both domestic and foreign, has failed to behave according to the bold prospectus of Punta del Este. Latin American capital was expected to stay at home, to be plowed back into the economic development of the several countries. In fact, Latin Americans who made profits found it expedient to move their funds, legally or illegally, to the shelter of United States or Swiss banks. How much money fled? Senator Wayne Morse was perhaps only guessing when he observed that as much local capital had left Latin America as the United States had put in since the beginning of the Alliance for Progress. The wealthy classes were not willing to invest in the future of their own countries. Morse's guess was confirmed by official and unofficial reports from Colombia, Chile, Argentina, Brazil and elsewhere.

US investors, for their part, were expected to put at least $300 million of new money into Latin America each year. But in actual practice, as with the Baker plan to deal with the Latin American debt in the 1980s, the net annual flow of new US capital to Latin America fell far behind the anticipated sums. For the first five years of the alliance, it averaged only $91 million. Furthermore, the net increase in total US direct investments in Latin America from 1961 to 1965 was only 13.8—the lowest percentage of increase of investment in any major area in the world in that period. US direct investments in Europe increased by 79.5 percent, in Africa, 78.9 percent and in Asia, 45.8 percent.

David Rockefeller, president of the Chase Manhattan Bank, said in Caracas in February 1964 that the alliance was faltering "because private investors have been reluctant to put their funds to work." A future secretary of commerce, John T. Connor, noted, "Would you invest in an atmosphere of rising anti-Americanism, unpredictable new taxes, revolutions that occur at the rate of two or three every few months, falling profits, and runaway inflation?"[23]

Some US corporations, for example, Sears, Roebuck, did invest there. In the 1960s Sears stores in Latin America had annual sales of over $100 million.

As one of its fundamental aims was to sell an ever-larger share of the products of the country in which it was operating, by 1966, for example, 99 percent of the merchandise sold in Sears stores in Brazil and Colombia was made in local factories.

In 1961 the framers of the alliance had set the goal for annual per capita economic growth at 2.5 percent. But the fact is that the rate for 1960–1965 averaged only 1.7 percent a year—and was actually less than it had been in the decade before the alliance was born. Perhaps the greatest single obstacle to increased productivity was a steady rise in the region's population. Another obstacle was the lagging tax reform, so earnestly prescribed by the alliance. The proposal that those who earn the most would pay their honest share was, of course, received as an affront by the more affluent.

Alliance members pledged to "improve and strengthen democratic institutions," but this gesture toward free elections, legally installed governments and an end to coups d'etat proved idle. Not only did the savage dictatorships of Stroessner in Paraguay and Duvalier in Haiti continue to plague the hemisphere, but there was a fresh series of overturns of constitutionally installed regimes—each a body blow to all that the alliance stood for. Presidents evicted by the military in the years 1961–1966 included Arturo Frondizi in Argentina in March 1962; Manuel Prado in Peru, July 1962; Juan Bosch in the Dominican Republic, December 1962; Ydigoras Fuentes in Guatemala, March 1963; Emilio Arosemena in Ecuador, July 1963; Villeda Morales, Honduras, October 1963; Joao Goulart in Brazil, April 1964; Victor Paz Estenssoro in Bolivia, 1964; the junta in Ecuador in March 1966; and Arturo Illia in Argentina, June 1966. Of these eight countries, only Peru and the Dominican Republic made a start toward constitutional ways in 1967.

Washington's continued hostility toward Havana, Latin American nations argued, was deepening political divisions across the hemisphere and unnecessarily complicating the already difficult task proposed by alliance reforms. Though the administration sought to create the impression abroad that the Cuban issue had become subordinated to the needs of the alliance, the internal debate was not about whether to relax pressure on the Castro regime but rather over what tools to use to dislodge it—multilateral diplomacy in the Organization of American States, collective economic measures or covert action, including assassination, if necessary.

If the failed Bay of Pigs invasion represented only a temporary domestic setback to the Kennedy administration, it had far deeper and more lasting repercussions in Latin America. In some countries, the covert operation not only rekindled fears of "Yankee interventionism" and put in doubt Kennedy's leadership qualities, but it vitiated much of the early promise aroused by the alliance. Four days before he was struck by an assassin's bullet, Kennedy had told a group of Latin American writers and artists in Miami: "I support the Alliance for Progress more strongly than ever before. . . . I do not discount the difficulties— but the greatest danger is not in our circumstances or in our enemies but in our own doubts and fears."

ALIANZA PARA EL PROGRESO

In his inaugural address on January 20, 1961, Kennedy spoke of the alliance as if it were the most important single foreign policy issue of his administration, just as he did during the election campaign. The prompt and warm response he received from Latin American leaders like Venezuelan President Rómulo Betancourt helped fan the enthusiasm of the president and some of his closest aides for the initiative. The State Department bureaucracy, on the other hand, remained skeptical. Over the years it had seen many bold campaign promises, particularly in Latin American affairs, evaporate into thin air once an administration was in office; it proved to be less than eager to strike out in new directions.

Another, perhaps more compelling reason for Kennedy to stress his eagerness to improve hemispheric relations was the imminent unleashing of a covert operation designed to oust the Castro government in Cuba, which the Eisenhower administration had set up a year earlier and Kennedy had decided to carry out. In mid-February Kennedy had entrusted the drafting of the speech to Richard N. Goodwin, a young lawyer who graduated first in his class at the Harvard Law School and then clerked for Justice Felix Frankfurter on the Supreme Court. The president was prepared to ask Congress for a big commitment: to finance his ten-year development program for Latin America. As Goodwin recalls it, Kennedy told him:

> I don't know if Congress will give it to me. But now's the time, while they're all worried that Castro might take over the hemisphere. I'm worried myself. Not about Castro particularly, although we have to do something about him, but if people think they have to choose between communism and not eating, they'll go for communism. Wouldn't you? I would.[24]

The scene described by Goodwin is reminiscent of the manner in which Dean Acheson in 1947 used the threat of Soviet expansion to scare Senator Arthur Vandenberg into pledging Republican support for the Marshall Plan. Perhaps

Kennedy had that antecedent in mind when he stopped Goodwin at the door of the Oval Office. "One more thing," the president said. "I don't want this to be an anti-Cuban speech. Just throw Castro in with the other dictators. I don't want them to think the only reason we're doing this is because of Cuba."[25]

That would be precisely what many Latin Americans thought when a month after Kennedy unveiled the alliance, the United States launched the Bay of Pigs invasion. Goodwin had been among those in the administration who had sensed the adverse effect the Cuban adventure was likely to have on Kennedy's broader Latin American policies. But like most of the other members of the New Frontier team, he felt either too inexperienced or seduced by the certitudes of the advice proffered by the CIA and Defense Department to contest it and swim against the tide. For the month it took to prepare the president's speech on the alliance, the brunt of Latin American policymaking, at least the most visible part, seemed to fall to Goodwin. As he relates it,

> Responding to the urgency of Kennedy's direction, I convened a series of White House meetings to discuss and refine the work of the Latin American task force. Our objective was to distill the lengthy, detailed recommendations into a major presidential address. The conferences were conducted with a confused informality that would have been inconceivable a year later, when bureaucratic lines had hardened. . . . Ten or twenty people crowded around at the conference table in the "Fish Room" at the White House. . . . The lone representative of the State Department (no Rusk, no Bowles, no Ball, not even a Bundy) was the assistant secretary of state for Latin America, Tom Mann, a holdover from the Eisenhower administration, who sat in silent acquiescence as we condemned and prepared to overturn the policies he had so faithfully administered.[26]

No Rusk, no Bowles, no Ball. Even under Kennedy, winning top-level interest for Latin American problems in a sustained way seemed difficult. The president sought to correct that by calling attention to the hemisphere during his first year in office through his many White House statements and press conferences, and via messages to other American heads of state.

Although he was no economic radical, Kennedy did not share the Republican aversion to state enterprises as wasteful, either in terms of running up deficits or stifling individual incentive. The Kennedy team was mindful that most Latin American governments supported the blueprints elaborated by the UN Economic Commission for Latin America because they had become convinced that at a time of rapid expansion of the economies of the industrial countries, only the intervention of the state could be sure to defend their markets from being overwhelmed by the competitive forces of the United States and the European powers.

However, during its last two years, the Eisenhower administration began to accept the views of a small faction of State Department experts, led by Undersecretary C. Douglas Dillon and supported by the president's brother, Milton Eisenhower, according to which the private sector alone was not sufficient to meet the region's economic development needs. Political and economic fences had to be mended, the argument went, requiring a more flexible economic policy. Partly out of this conviction, partly to stave off the far more ambitious plans envisioned by Kubitschek's OPA, the Eisenhower administration endorsed the creation of the Inter-American Development Bank with an initial congressional appropriation of $500 million and other government-sponsored development ideas contained in the Act of Bogota of 1960. By late 1960, the ground had been laid for what Adolf Berle, a principal architect of the alliance, called a "moral Marshall Plan." Whereas the Marshall Plan had merely attempted to restore a war-torn European society to a former level of achievement, the alliance was charged with constructing a new economic order, without abruptly unseating the old. Even more remarkable, in retrospect, than Kennedy's formula for a "peaceful revolution" was the limited nature of the investment he believed necessary to accomplish the goals.

NOTES

1. *Jornal do Brasil,* November 23, 1960, p. 4.

2. John F. Kennedy, "A Democrat Looks at Foreign Policy," *Foreign Affairs,* October 1957, p. 44.

3. Jerome I. Levinson and Juan de Onis, *The Alliance That Lost Its Way: A Critical Report on the Alliance for Progress* (Chicago: Quadrangle, 1970), p. 53.

4. Quoted in Richard N. Goodwin, *Remembering America: A Voice from the Sixties* (Boston: Little, Brown, 1988), p. 147.

5. Speech, White House, March 13, 1961.

6. Schlesinger, comments in pamphlet published by Book-of-the-Month Club, 1959.

7. Interviews with Oscar Camilión, undersecretary of foreign affairs in the Frondizi government (1958–1965), Buenos Aires, November 1964; secretary of defense in the Menem government (1993–1995), New York, United Nations, September 1994.

8. The United States consistently turned a deaf ear to these mediation efforts, as can be seen from the following memorandum of a conversation between Secretary of State Christian A. Herter and Brazilian Foreign Minister Horacio Lafer in Washington, August 12, 1960: "With respect to Cuba, the Brazilian Foreign Minister agreed that this is the most serious problem in the hemisphere. The Secretary explained the United States view that the hemisphere problem posed by Communist penetration of Cuba is of far more importance than the bilateral problems of Cuba with the United States, mentioning specifically that the latter are principally the expropriation of property and the propaganda and insults directed toward the United States.

"In this connection the Secretary stated the appreciation of the United States Government of Brazil's offer along with Mexico and Canada to provide its good offices in trying to aid a solution of the bilateral problems. Because of the greater importance of the hemisphere problems, the Secretary said that it appeared necessary first to seek a solution in this area and subsequently the United States would be anxious to avail itself of any opportunities to find appropriate solutions to the bilateral problems. The U.S. does not intend to bring up its bilateral problems with Cuba at San Jose, although there is of course a possibility that such action may be forced by Cuba if it follows through with its apparent intent of accusing the U.S. of economic aggression."

9. "Preblemy mira i sotsializma," September 1962, quoted in *Soviet Image of Contemporary Latin America: A Documentary History, 1960–1968* (Austin: University of Texas Press, 1971).

10. Goodwin, *Remembering America,* pp. 169–170.

11. Goodwin, *Remembering America,* p. 173.

12. Gary Wills, *The Kennedy Imprisonment: A Meditation on Power* (Boston: Little, Brown, 1981), p. 36.

13. Anna Kasten Nelson, "President Kennedy's National Security Policy," *Reviews in American History,* March 1991, p. 2.

14. Goodwin, *Remembering America,* p. 137.

15. *New York Times,* March 14, 1961, p. 1.

16. *New York Times,* March 14, 1961, p. 1.

17. Arthur M. Schlesinger Jr., *A Thousand Days: John F. Kennedy in the White House* (Boston: Houghton Mifflin, 1965), p. 205.

18. Alonso Aguilar, *Pan Americanism: From Monroe to the Present: A View from the Other Side* (New York: Monthly Review Press, 1968), p. 119.

19. Aguilar, *Pan Americanism,* p. 119.

20. Albert O. Hirschman, *Reporter,* May 1963, p. 17.

21. Levinson and Onis, *Alliance That Lost Its Way,* p. 351.

22. Hubert Herring, *A History of Latin America: From the Beginnings to the Present* (New York: Alfred A. Knopf, 1955), p. 767.

23. Quoted by Herring, *History of Latin America*, p. 932.

24. Goodwin, *Remembering America,* p. 147.

25. Goodwin, *Remembering America,* p. 148.

26. Goodwin *Remembering America,* p. 151.

Chapter Seven

LYNDON BAINES JOHNSON

When Lyndon Baines Johnson reached the White House, Latin America watched anxiously to gauge whether his commitment to the region would match that of his predecessor. "We know of no more important problems anywhere, any time, than the problems of our neighbors," Johnson declared at his first formal press conference as president. "We want to see our relations with them be the very best."[1] But he also announced the appointment of Thomas C. Mann, a fellow Texan, as his top official for Latin America. Mann, a career foreign service officer who was assistant secretary of state under Eisenhower, had been shunted aside by Kennedy for being out of sympathy with that administration's antiauthoritarian goals. At the time of Kennedy's assassination, Mann was serving as ambassador to Mexico, where he had established a reputation as a severe critic of Kennedy's policies; in fact, he had become the putative leader of the hard-line faction in the foreign service.

Johnson evidently felt that his first task was to reassure a world shocked by the assassination that there would be, as he phrased it, "continuity in transition." Nevertheless, from the outset he was eager to put his own stamp on foreign policy, where he reputedly lacked the sureness that he had demonstrated on the domestic front as Senate majority leader. Vietnam was already a simmering issue and demanded his immediate attention; but as a Texan who had championed the rights of Mexican Americans, he claimed to have a special affinity for Latin American affairs. Not surprisingly, his approach was paternalistic, very much in character with Johnson's expansive, domineering personality.[2]

Johnson was aware of dissatisfaction expressed about the uneven performance of the alliance. Businessmen had complained that Kennedy's revolutionary rhetoric was scaring private capital away, that radical pressures were increasing, and that the communists were reaping the fruits. Worst of all, Castro, linked by some to the Kennedy assassination, continued to thumb his nose at the United States, adding insult to injury.

These impressions were conveyed to Ambassador Mann. In his new post as assistant secretary, Mann promptly let it be known that there would be a return to the tough national security policies that he had championed under Eisenhower and Dulles. He made plain from the outset that there would be none of the favoritism the Kennedy White House had shown to the Democratic left; there would be no more inhibitions about supporting the right or the military where they were perceived as being the more effective bulwark against communism.

Mann knew that Johnson, as Senate leader, had generally sided with the Eisenhower administration on national security and foreign policy issues, often to the dismay of the more liberal wing of his own party. He also knew that a conservative posture was a matter of good politics in preparation for the presidential race that was only a year away. With Dean Rusk relatively uninterested in Latin America, Mann established himself as Johnson's principal and undisputed voice on hemisphere affairs. He was not only assistant secretary for Latin America, but also coordinator of the alliance program, the post that had been held by Teodoro Moscoso. Thus Mann combined in his office both State Department and AID activities.

While pledging that his new team would press ahead with the Alliance for Progress, Johnson made plain there would be less talk about revolutionary change and a mission to promote democracy and more emphasis on effective government and sound economic policies. The shift was disclosed by Mann in an off-the-record talk with US envoys to Latin America who had been summoned to attend three days of briefings at the State Department in mid-March 1964. The immediate effect of the new policy would be "to eliminate such deterrents against coups d'etat as were used by the Kennedy Administration," wrote Tad Szulc in the *New York Times* the next day.[3] Kennedy's policy, the article recalled, was to deny diplomatic relations and economic aid to newly created military regimes, unless they offered firm and convincing assurance of restoring democratic rule within the foreseeable future.

> Mr. Mann's views were considered as representing a radical modification of the policies followed by the Kennedy Administration under the Alliance for Progress. President Kennedy believed that economic and social development under the Alliance must move hand-in-hand with the development of democracy and that, therefore, the United States had the duty actively to encourage the practice of democracy and refuse its help to regimes that had overturned representative democracies. . . .
>
> To implement this concept, the Kennedy Administration broke diplomatic relations for varying periods with Argentina, Peru, Guatemala, Ecuador, the Dominican Republic and Honduras, when democratic regimes there were

overthrown by military coups d'etat. . . . The impression made by Mr. Mann's remarks was that the United States would no longer embark on such policies. . . . Diplomats who attended last night's session said that in his entire presentation Mr. Mann made no mention of the Alliance for Progress.[4]

Two influential Democratic senators reacted to Mann's presentation by insisting that the United States intended to continue to fight for the preservation of democracy in Latin America as well as the other goals of the alliance. Hubert H. Humphrey of Minnesota and Wayne Morse of Oregon, the feisty chairman of the Senate Subcommittee on Latin America, reminded the diplomats that Congress did not look with favor on governments that shot their way to power. Nonetheless, a scholarly assessment of the Johnson administration characterized the Johnson–Mann policy as follows:

> The two Texans agreed on a business-oriented anti-Communist approach, avoiding disorder even at the cost of takeovers by the military within the country. No less than thirteen governments south of the United States would be taken over by the military during those years.[5]

By comparison with Kennedy, whose efforts at reaching foreign policy decisions with dispassionate detachment were reflected in the cerebral attitudes and methodological approaches of technocrats like McNamara and Bundy, Johnson's responses to crisis situations seemed as impulsive and intensely personal as his overall management of the government. Johnson and his advisers belonged to what might be called the "Munich generation" of liberal internationalists still haunted by the idea that the democracies failed to stop the Nazi aggression in the 1930s.[6]

Johnson considered himself the true populist, personally able to understand the plight of Latin America's appalling poverty and inequality. He therefore rejected their complaints that he was vain, proud, contemptuous, intolerant and so on. On the other hand, he aroused admiration and even affection among those who liked his candor and earthy Texan style. But Johnson's charm coexisted with a volcanic temper that could easily be brought into eruption by a remark he interpreted as a personal slight or an action he considered injurious to US interests. These traits can be illustrated by the way Johnson describes "three Latino" crises in his memoirs.

JOHNSON'S THREE LATINO CRISES—PLUS ONE

Latin America seems to want to avenge US neglect by drawing attention to itself in providing each new administration with a full-blown crisis even before it can be settled. Such an early crisis, no matter how limited in scope, is promptly perceived as a test of US will, at times compelling the new administration to aggrandize the problem to show that it will not be intimidated by a potential or actual foe, no matter how small. Not infrequently, this emphasis on looking tough and protecting US credibility has led to serious distortion. Roosevelt had his "crisis" baptism with the fall of the Machado regime in Cuba; Truman was confronted with the Perón dictatorship and its reluctance to abide by hemispheric security commitments in the final year of World War II. Eisenhower came into office confronting the hemisphere's most acute financial crisis since the end of the war, but ignored it until the CIA warned that communists were plotting to seize Guatemala; Kennedy had the Bay of Pigs. Johnson would not be spared either.

The three crises that Johnson cites in his memoirs are the violence in Panama over the sovereignty of the Canal Zone, the threat by Cuba to cut off the water supply to the US naval base at Guantanamo, and the landing of US marines in the Dominican Republic. One he failed to mention at all was the military coup in Brazil.

CRISIS 1: PANAMA

In January 1964, just six weeks after Johnson took office, violent clashes erupted between Panamanian students and police and troops stationed in the Canal Zone. At issue was the festering controversy over sovereignty. Two dozen Panamanian high school students were killed and some 300 wounded after an incident prompted by the flying of the US flag—without the Panamanian flag beside it—over the Canal Zone. The official US casualty figures were four soldiers dead and dozens wounded. Johnson's immediate reaction was to blame communist agitators as well as the Panamanian authorities who, he assumed (not inaccurately), were out to exploit the situation on behalf of their long-stated goal of getting the United States to yield full sovereignty of the canal to them. US intelligence reports seemed to give empirical support to Johnson's views.

Actually, it was not Castro agents but American high school students who violated a presidential directive that Panama's flag be flown alongside the Stars and Stripes. Nor had there been anything "obviously well-planned" about the demonstration.

When this writer arrived in Panama forty-eight hours after the rioting broke out, the first "anti-American" perorations came not from communists but from the Panamanian ambassador to the United States and the deputy minister of foreign affairs, Miguel ("Mike") Moreno and Mariano Oteiza, respectively. Both were representative members of Panama's ruling elite, friendly to the United States and diehard anticommunists. In their private law firms, they represented leading American banks and airlines, but they were moved by the deep nationalist feelings that can stir a small country when it feels its sovereignty tarnished and insulted by a big power.

It was therefore not strange to see the two elegantly attired officials march in lockstep with thousands of demonstrators, most of them in shirtsleeves or bare chested, to protest the incidents in the Canal Zone. This information was conspicuously absent from the reports sent by the US embassy in Panama to Washington, which was determined to associate the events with "communist agitators." Nor did the information reaching the White House take into account the importance of tiny Panama to the other American republics as a symbol of Bolivar's struggle to bring independence and unity to their countries. Most school books in the region still record the Liberator's words:

How beautiful it would be for the Isthmus of Panama to be for us what Corinth was for the Greeks! O that some day we may have the good fortune to install there an august congress of representatives of republics, kingdoms, and empires for consultation and discussion about the high interests of peace and war with the nations of the other three-quarters of the world.[7]

Had Johnson read these texts he might have recognized some analogies between Bolivar's dreams and his own romantic vision of a Great Society extended to the rest of the hemisphere through a vast common market for which he would work so arduously at the meeting of presidents at Punta del Este in 1967. But in the opening months of 1964, historical antecedents were not as important as reasserting a strong presidency at home and US authority abroad. It must have been a matter of particular consternation that Johnson's first and most visible Latin American challenge came from the smallest of the hemisphere republics, one that had been dependent on the United States politically and economically since its inception.

In a telephone call to Johnson immediately after the outbreak of violence, President Rodolfo Chiari asked for "a complete revision of all the treaties which affect Panamanian–US relations because what we have at the present time is nothing but a source of dissatisfaction." He recalled that he had come to Washington in 1961 and had talked with President Kennedy about treaty revisions, but since those conversations "not a thing had been done to alleviate the situation." Johnson replied that "violence was no way to settle grievances."

Apparently Chiari hoped to use the disturbances to force the United States into a new round of treaty talks. I doubted that he would halt the attacks on the Canal Zone or restore diplomatic relations until he had done everything possible to achieve his goal. Having failed through diplomacy with President Kennedy, Chiari was going to try to exact a new treaty from me by force.[8]

A report by Thomas Mann, who flew to Panama with a fact-finding mission, conveyed the impression that the demonstrations and the anti-US sentiment were being stage-managed by the Chiari government. That not only ignored the whole history of US–Panamanian relations, but also the more urgent and relevant fact that Chiari in fact wielded little power, that he was heading a minority government that most likely would have been incapable of organizing a rally even if it wanted to. There was also no reference in Mann's dispatches to the impending election campaign in the United States.[9]

In quick succession, the Panamanian government broke off diplomatic relations with the United States and brought the dispute before the United Nations and then the Organization of American States. The maneuver took Washington by surprise because no OAS member, except for Cuba, had vaulted over the regional body to go directly before the world organization where it clearly could count on broader Third World sympathies. Finally, however, and after considerable discussion over jurisdictional procedures, Panama sought OAS help by accepting the good offices of the Inter-American Peace Committee. A somewhat different picture emerged in Johnson's memoirs:

> Since the summer of 1963 the Central Intelligence Agency had been warning us that we should expect difficulties in Panama late in 1963 or early 1964. Fidel Castro, working closely with the Panamanian Communist party, had been sending guns, money and agents into Panama. Demonstrations were likely. An attempted coup against the legal government was possible. If that happened, we expected the canal and the zone to become special targets.[10]

The prospects for solving the conflict were not helped by the fact that Panama was less than two months away from presidential elections. Demands for a complete revision of the Panama Canal treaties had for years been a central campaign issue; Chiari, who had been accused by the opposition candidate Arnulfo Arias of being a Yankee pawn, was virtually compelled to sever diplomatic relations with Washington. His own party's candidate, Marco Robles, said that had it not been for Chiari's prompt move, he would have lost the election. Johnson meanwhile knew he had to show himself intransigent to prevent the Republicans from turning the crisis into political hay. Senate Republican leader Everett Dirksen sensed an election issue in the making: "To give an inch would be equivalent to telling every small country that all they had to do was break off relations, attack our embassy, and demand whatever they wanted."[11]

"The first foreign crisis of my administration began only six weeks after I had taken office," Johnson wrote in his memoirs. Although in public he assumed the patient attitude of a schoolmaster dealing with a truant boy, in private he was heard to discuss Panama and the Panamanians with undisguised scorn. "I'm not going to be pushed around by a *** country no bigger than St. Louis," he repeatedly told his inner circle.

Almost three months would pass before Panama resumed diplomatic relations with the United States after arduous efforts to find a formula acceptable to both parties. Johnson wrote:

> In January 1964, the Inter-American Peace Committee of the OAS tried to negotiate the matter and failed. In March Panama took the problem to the OAS Council. Some progress was made, but in the end the council also failed. I rejected several proposals which, in an effort to paper over the gap, would have involved substantial US commitments before the negotiators even met. . . .
>
> I had no idea . . . how long it would take to work out our differences. The negotiations were still going on when I left the White House. But as of April 3, 1964, a new mood had developed, the immediate crisis had been overcome, and reasonable discussion was possible.[12]

As it was, once Johnson felt he had reduced the Panamanian government to size, that he had been able to assert his will, he named a high-level team headed by veteran troubleshooter Ellsworth Bunker to begin to consider new treaties. And he appointed Robert Anderson, a Republican who had been secretary of the Treasury in the second Eisenhower administration, to lead a technical commission to study the feasibility of a second sea-level canal. Both the treaty negotiations and the feasibility study took longer than expected—it would be eleven years after he left office until President Carter and General Omar Torrijos were able to sign the new treaties, after a bruising domestic battle waged by the Carter administration to obtain their ratification by the US Senate.

From the outset, and perhaps unavoidably, the Panama crisis was cast by official Washington largely in terms of the Cold War. For most Latin Americans, however, the canal still loomed as a legacy of the days of Teddy Roosevelt and manifest destiny and a violation of the sovereignty of a sister republic.

In a number of ways Panama was a harbinger of the stubborn attitude Johnson would demonstrate in Vietnam. Domestic press coverage of Panama prefigured a pattern of reporting that would be repeated in successive decades: as long as violence and diplomatic quarrels prevailed, the US media followed events there; as soon as a compromise was reached, the Panama situation dropped from sight. There was rarely any follow-up, and perhaps because Panama was such a small country, no effort was made to come up with an in-depth assessment of how Johnson had dealt with his first foreign crisis. This was a shame, for it might have served as a pilot model of how Johnson was to approach subsequent foreign policy challenges, most notably Vietnam.

Johnson's stubborn streak was dramatically illustrated when he peremptorily rejected a settlement worked out by the Organization of American States because he interpreted the English text differently from its Spanish original. Yet the very next day Johnson instructed Richard Goodwin to prepare a conciliatory statement he would read at his next press conference that, in fact, resulted in Chiari's immediate acceptance of a renewal of the talks and a quick settlement. Johnson simply had to have things on his own terms and in his own time. While the storm over the OAS communiqué was indeed an unnecessary "minicrisis," the unresolved canal issue would increasingly be cast by Latin American critics as a major test of US intentions toward relations with Latin America as a whole. Yet Johnson refused to see it as such. He saw the situation not as a symptom of the deteriorating hemisphere relations, but simply as the result of tensions with Castro and international communism. This blinded him to many other factors in the situation—the nationalist forces inherent in the region, their moorings in past historical grievances, and social and political forces that were seeking recognition.

For a man so adroit at political maneuvering, his indifference to the requirements of the Panamanian government for its own political survival is remarkable. The Chiari administration needed to claim victory in its quest for a treaty revision, which he saw as a duplicitous gambit to make him and the United States look silly, not an essential ploy to win the next election. Similarly, the uprising in the Dominican Republic by young military officers eager to restore the constitutional government overthrown by a coup of a handful of reactionary generals working in tandem with business interests, Johnson saw as a personal challenge to his efforts to keep the hemisphere quiet while he faced the awesome task of dealing with the deteriorating situation in Vietnam and keeping the Russians at bay in Europe.

Similarly, when the Argentine government of a mild-mannered country doctor, Arturo Illia, canceled US contracts to exploit the country's oil resources, Johnson regarded it as an unfriendly act, perhaps even associating it with memories of the wartime anti-Yankeeism of the Argentine military. Ironically, the great hero of the ruling Radical party (as well as of Illia) was Franklin D. Roosevelt, Johnson's political mentor, who had won the heart of Latin Americans in part through his sympathetic reaction to Mexico's nationalization of the oil companies in 1938. Government ownership of natural resources was an integral part of the political platforms of most liberal parties in Latin America. In fact, the military detested the Radicals; when they finally seized power in Buenos Aires in 1966 and ousted Illia, ostensibly to restore the economy to private initiative, few tears were shed in Washington beyond the conventional professions of hope of an early return to constitutional rule. But the underlying attitude, which everybody in Latin America knew well, was colored by an implacable determination by the US government that anything was better than "another Cuba."

CRISIS 2: SITCOM AT GITMO

The second Latin American crisis listed in Johnson's memoirs was a threat by Cuba to cut off the water supply to the Guantanamo base. It was a comparative noncrisis. Having from the beginning blamed Castro communism for the Panama riots, he understandably believed that the confrontation was with Castro himself. It concerned the seizure of four Cuban fishing boats near some islands in the Florida Keys and the detention of their crews by the US Coast Guard—and Castro's threats to retaliate by shutting off the water pipes leading to the naval base at Guantanamo. This type of incident had become a periodic feature of US–Cuban tensions, stirring a few days of headlines and some meetings in the crisis room of the Pentagon. In the event, the outcome invariably was uneventful—though much paper was expended in the process.

CRISIS 3: THE DOMINICAN INTERVENTION

Far more serious was Johnson's third crisis—his April 1965 decision to land the marines in the Dominican Republic, which he failed to mention in his voluble book. In its review of salient foreign policy issues for 1965, *The United States in World Affairs*, an annual publication of the Council on Foreign Relations, said:

> Washington's reaction to the crisis that erupted in the Dominican Republic in the last week of April . . . seemed at the time to confirm the worst misgivings about the new trend of US policy—impetuous and doctrinaire anti-Communism; reckless reliance on military force, impatience with contrary opinion: putting action ahead of calculation.[13]

The judgment that Johnson's Dominican invasion had significantly added to America's negative image abroad was a distinctly retrospective one. At first, reactions in the United States were favorable. Walter Lippmann backed the president's Latin American policy wholeheartedly. Although critical of US policy in Vietnam, US action in the Dominican Republic, he argued, could be defended on the old-fashioned diplomatic ground that the Caribbean republic lay squarely within the US sphere of influence. The *New York Daily News*, which had fully accepted the Vietnam War at the time, was fulsome in its praise of the Dominican move, saying Johnson was "a man of destiny, assigned by fate to clean up all or most of his inherited messes and thereby start world communism toward its downfall."

The Castro takeover in Cuba was invariably mentioned as having taught the United States to take preemptive action. Moreover, nobody could quarrel with the stated reason for the move—the protection of US citizens in the midst of a civil war. Former president Eisenhower immediately endorsed Johnson's move, as did senators Fulbright, Mansfield, Church and Morse, who had already turned against Johnson's Vietnam policies. Clearly, no one understood what was happening.

Some in Congress believed that the wisest course for the United States was one of restraint and patience. Less than a year earlier, Senator Hubert Humphrey had written a reasoned defense of the alliance, suggesting that US national interest was better served by joining battle with communism on the economic and social front than through military means. But by April 1965, he had become Johnson's vice president and toned down his criticism. Nevertheless, in a private conversation with this writer the following December, he confided that he believed that the Dominican invasion was "a terrible mistake." The only consolation, he then felt, was that he was certain that it represented "definitely the last time we land the marines anywhere in Latin America."

The reaction from Latin America was loud and immediate. Several countries called for a consultative meeting of the Organization of American States. The Peruvian foreign minister declared that the intervention was "the most severe blow inflicted upon the inter-American juridical system in recent years." *Jornal do Brasil*, one of the continent's most influential newspapers, wrote, "This is the end of the OAS." It was not too long before much of the US press and the US Senate began to turn against the intervention, having found little evidence to substantiate the administration's allegations that communists were dominating the rebel movement in the Dominican Republic.

But in Johnson's mind the communist threat remained real. It was feared that communists would move into the "vacuum"—a term frequently and often erroneously used when dictators fell—and that they would exploit Dominican grievances and make the country inhospitable to US interests.

On April 28, four days after the young officers ousted the provisional government of Donald Reid Cabral, Johnson ordered an initial contingent of 400 marines to land in Santo Domingo to calm the disorder. It was not lost to the Dominicans, however, that the marines installed themselves at San Isidro, the air base of the counterrevolutionary forces headed by Brigadier General Elias Wessin y Wessin, an ambitious, fiercely conservative member of the old Trujillo army. Two days later they were followed by another 1,700 Marines along with two battalions of the 82nd Paratroop Division.

The State Department announced that US forces had been dispatched to the island "to protect United States nationals and foreigners whose lives are in danger." In fact, no one was quite sure what was happening. The young officers, disenchanted with the conservative government of Donald Reid and the continuing influence of the old right-wing generals of the Trujillo era, wanted to restore Bosch. The US ambassador, W. Tapley Bennett Jr., who had been in the United States when the uprising occurred and returned only on April 27, trusted neither the young officers nor Bosch. When the rebels that afternoon sought Bennett's help to negotiate a settlement, he refused. Instead, in an episode reminiscent of Sumner Welles's reaction to the revolt of the progressive noncoms in Cuba in 1933, the envoy urged Johnson to send the marines to protect the evacuation of foreigners.

The next day, after demonstrators had ransacked the AID mission in downtown Santo Domingo and subjected the embassy to sniper fire, Bennett sent a new message recommending that "serious thought be given in Washington to armed intervention which would go beyond the mere protection of Americans and seek to establish order in this strife-ridden country." Revealing his true fears, Bennett then added,

> All indications point to the fact that if present efforts of forces loyal to the government fail, power will be assumed by groups clearly identified with the Communist party. If the situation described above comes to pass, my own recommendation and that of the Country Team is that we should intervene to prevent another Cuba from arising out of the ashes of this uncontrollable situation.[14]

This hypothetical scenario, according to Johnson, led him to order more than 22,000 troops to land in the Dominican Republic that very night. He later wrote:

> The last thing I wanted—and the last thing the American people wanted—
> was another Cuba on our door step. At the same time, the action suggested
> by the Ambassador would be a grave step. I wanted to know much more
> than I did then before taking such drastic action.[15]

More likely these words were written with the benefit of hindsight brought
about by criticism that the action had been hasty and taken without adequate
consultation with the other Latin American governments. The administration
had, in fact, brought the matter before the OAS the same day but the organization could reach no decision when what was needed, in his opinion, was
swift action: "There were many expressions of regret but few proposals for effective reaction to Dominican developments. The OAS ambassadors would
not commit their governments to anything without thorough consultations."[16]

This reflected Mann's impatience, which he so often expressed in private—
the OAS was too slow, too indecisive to deal with crises when the United
States called for support. If the United States was to live up to its responsibility
of keeping communism out of the Dominican Republic, it had to act alone,
no matter what custom or the appropriate juridical instruments dictated. In an
attempt to defend the move from criticism that the United States should not
have acted unilaterally, Johnson suggested that there were precedents set by the
inter-American community and by Kennedy. He wrote:

> Very much on my mind at the time—and, I am sure, in the minds of all my
> principal advisers—was the formal determination reached by all members of
> the OAS at the Ministers of Foreign Affairs meeting in Punta del Este in
> January 1962. "The principles of communism are incompatible with the
> principles of the inter-American system. . . ."
>
> Clear in my memory were the words of President Kennedy less than a week
> before his death: "We in this hemisphere must also use every resource at our
> command to prevent the establishment of another Cuba in this hemisphere."[17]

He was mindful of another bipartisan experience under Eisenhower when the
marines went ashore in Beirut in 1958 to stabilize Lebanon. Johnson, then
Senate majority leader, had rallied his forces in support of the president. "A
number of people, then and later, thought the Communist threat in the Dominican Republic was overstated," Johnson acknowledged.

> I did not and do not think it was. Nor do I believe that the majority of the
> involved governments and competent analysts believe, in retrospect, that
> the danger was not desperately serious. . . . I would like to believe that in all

three of the major Latin American crises we faced—in Panama, Guantanamo, and the Dominican Republic—we not only successfully met the challenge but took steps to prevent a recurrence of the trouble.[18]

To further justify the intervention, Johnson deliberately cited the recommendations of "senior civilian and military advisers," who were mostly holdovers from the Kennedy administration such as Robert McNamara, Dean Rusk, McGeorge Bundy, and Walt W. Rostow. "The recommendations made to me by my senior civilian and military advisers on April 28 and 29, were unanimous," he asserted.

> In the Dominican crisis of 1965, those who recommended the course of US policy were not divided into "hawks" and "doves." They were a group of informed and dedicated Americans who on April 28 were united in their belief that action was necessary if American and other foreign civilian lives were to be saved. They were united on April 29 in deciding that action was required if the citizens of the Dominican Republic were not to fall under the control of a small Communist minority and lose control over their own political destiny.[19]

Those who were truly informed about the Dominican Republic thought no such things. The fact is that the dedicated officials Johnson referred to knew little about Latin America or the degree of communist infiltration in the Caribbean. Something else was at work in the Cabinet Room in 1965, and it was best described by the Johnson cabinet's own secretary, Harry McPherson. The young Texan suggested that the principals—Rusk, McNamara, Bundy and the president himself—were all part of a generation haunted by Munich and the specter of appeasement. That accounted not only for the invasion but also for the readiness the Johnson administration exhibited in shifting away from Kennedy's early efforts to suspend military assistance to nonconstitutional governments. "Unless one was prepared to risk the extension of Communist power into the nations that did not choose to be controlled by it, one had to support the giving of arms to those nations, and hope that reforms would come after."[20]

Latin Americans, while not indifferent to the lessons of European history, tended to bring another perspective to the analysis of the Dominican crisis. It related more directly to the intrinsic struggle of the Dominican people to free themselves from the legacy of one of the most vicious and longest dictatorships in the hemisphere's history and to do so without outside interference. This reaction was summed up in an editorial of the prestigious inter-American journal *Politica*, published in Caracas under the sponsorship of Rómulo Betancourt's Acción Democrática party.

Because it reflected a wide spectrum of Latin American opinion, the editorial, titled "The Drama of Santo Domingo," is reproduced here almost in its entirety. Holding the marines responsible for arresting the Dominican Republic's progress toward democracy, it said:

> Clumsy and misinformed, precipitous, that measure by the United States has set back the history of inter-American relations to a period which already was in the process of being liquidated. The policy of the Good Neighbor inaugurated by Franklin D. Roosevelt, had substituted the one of the Big Stick wielded by the other Roosevelt in the entire Caribbean. . . . A policy of cordial relations and mutual assistance initiated with the Alliance for Progress proposed by President Kennedy, was smoothing out the misgivings, always present in the negotiations and treaties between our countries and the United States, even though some extremist groups, for strategic reasons, mouthed the anti-imperialist slogans to which past generations were devoted during the first decades of this century.
>
> The unilateral United States intervention in Santo Domingo is not only in violation of the principles consecrated in the Charter of the Organization of American States; it represents a mortal blow to the inter-American juridical system which, now bruised, demands a total renovation. The peoples of the continent have watched with alarm the act of force of the United States and suspect the arguments that pretend to justify it. If the doctrine expressed by President Johnson, namely, that the United States power will be exercised wherever a United States citizen may be in order to protect him, the only way to avoid aggressions would be by preventing citizens from that country to go to other countries.

The Johnson doctrine, combined with a policy designed to prevent the improbable establishment in the Americas of communist strongholds comparable to the one in Cuba, would represent a permanent threat of intervention to any of the Latin American countries, since in all of them there existed communist groups that posed a threat of protracted war until they achieved power. In Chile, if Allende would have won the election instead of Frei, the application of this principle would have led to US intervention.

AN UNMENTIONED CRISIS:
THE BRAZILIAN COUP OF 1964

Amazingly, in his memoir Johnson completely ignored another early and critical move in his Latin American policy: the sympathetic treatment, and swift recognition, of the military coup that ousted the chaotic Brazilian government of Joao Goulart. The bloodless coup unleashed forces that kept the military in office for more than a decade and led to a period of harsh, systematic repression, something that had been virtually unknown in Brazilian history. From a larger perspective, given Kennedy's militant efforts to discourage dictatorial regimes, the Brazilian episode marked another shift in the roller coaster of US policy toward Latin America and the beginning of a new rapprochement with authoritarian regimes favored by Mann. Nonetheless, in Johnson's 636-page book the only mention of Brazil is a recognition of the support that country's military gave to his Dominican adventure by sending General Hugo Panasco Alvim, a heavily decorated veritable Colonel Blimp, to take command of "this temporary peacekeeping force"—the euphemism given to the contingent made up principally of 22,000 marines.

What hemispheric concern was generated by Goulart's overthrow was focused on the institutional rupture in Brazil's long tradition of constitutionalism, rather than on the fate of the deposed president. Internally, Goulart's Labor party had been faltering ever since Vargas fell a decade earlier, and though it continued to enjoy a mass following in the far-flung rural areas and among the industrial workers, they were poorly organized. Goulart had deeply alienated virtually every other sector of Brazil's political spectrum. His blatant bid to strengthen presidential powers with the help of the left fatally alienated the powerful governors who were becoming the kingpins of Brazilian politics. In addition, both military leaders and the business community were rankled by Goulart's radical concessions to labor—including a 70 percent increase in army salaries—which fed inflation and left his administration economically exhausted. Hence his overthrow in March 1964 by an army coup did not come as a surprise.

Yet Washington's undisguised acclaim and swift recognition of the military regime headed by General Humberto Castelo Branco, the former chief of staff, less than a year after Kennedy had made the suspension of diplomatic recognition a penalty to unconstitutional governments, struck many Latin Americans as ominous for the democratic evolution of the hemisphere community.

Since the earliest stages of the postwar era, when Acheson formed the mixed US–Brazilian Economic Commission, Brazil loomed as the most important Latin American country for the United States next to Mexico. Brazil is potentially the wealthiest nation in the southern hemisphere, since its natural resources surpass those of Canada. Economically and geopolitically, Brazil is so important that from Washington's perspective the advent of military rule led by seemingly moderate generals, with the support of such trusted civilian economists as Roberto Campos and Delfim Neto, was one of the most momentous events to occur in Latin America during the 1960s. Studies by the Central Intelligence Agency, the Rand Corporation, the Brookings Institution, and most think tanks suggested that political instability was nowhere potentially more dangerous than in the Brazilian subcontinent.

The idiosyncratic rule of Quadros and Goulart's populist nationalism might have made Mann and others associated with the Eisenhower administration reflect on how they had misjudged the Kubitschek era. But there was no time to engage in much reflection, let alone acknowledge past mistakes and learn from them. The exquisite irony that key civilian members of the Kubitschek administration—who had been suspected of harboring communist sympathies—played prominent roles in the coup and as advisers to the military was never appreciated by Washington policymakers. Yet that was precisely the case with Schmidt and other top figures of the Kubitschek government.

The United States viewed Goulart's leftist sympathies with alarm, and his highly publicized journeys to Cuba and China fed US misgivings about Brazil's loyalty to the "hemisphere idea." In April 1964 the armed forces turned Goulart out of office and installed their candidate, General Castello Branco. The United States moved quickly. Within forty-eight hours, Secretary Dean Rusk, urged on by the US ambassador to Brazil, Lincoln Gordon, a Kennedy appointee, led the American republics in extending official recognition to the new military regime. With it came a commitment to help it govern. Goulart had left the economy a shambles, with all the classic symptoms of raging inflation and mounting foreign indebtedness. For years financial prudence seemed to call for a period of domestic austerity, but no leading politician had the will or the authority to institute such a program. The military government had both and strong US support as well. From 1960 to 1964, AID funding to Brazil had been $178 million. For 1965 to 1971, the figure was $1.1 billion. In the hearings the Senate Foreign Relations Committee held on US–Brazilian relations in December 1971, Chairman Frank Church reported that overall US aid to Brazil since 1964 had been around $2 billion.

Brazil meanwhile embraced the stringent economic policies insisted on by the International Monetary Fund as a precondition to obtaining stand-by loans in support of her balance of payments. On the political front, political expression was reduced to two official parties; dissent was rewarded with prison or exile. By 1972 Amnesty International had collected over a thousand documented cases of political torture since the onset of the military regimes. Conservative commentators in the United States nonetheless were pleased; a boom was in the making, a "Brazilian miracle." Roberto Campos, the minister of economy, was compared to Ludwig Erhard, the architect of West Germany's spectacular economic recovery. "The results were electric," wrote Benjamin W. Rowland.

Investor confidence was restored and foreign capital flowed into Brazil in unprecedented volume. By 1968, Brazil was riding a boom. From 1968 to 1972, Brazil's economy grew in real terms at the rate of eight to nine percent per year. Inflation sank to the historically moderate level of around 20 percent. In her international economic policy, Brazil seemed to be falling in step with the general Western prescriptions. There was a major tariff reform which won general approval.[21]

But for all these stunning economic successes, few in the United States were willing to cite Brazil as an example of successful Alliance for Progress policy. The taint of political repression was too strong—even though it paled alongside what the military in neighboring Argentina was inflicting on the people. Some were inclined to argue that Brazil demonstrated the alliance's moral bankruptcy. In a few short years, the ebullience that had once accompanied the alliance was gone. Under Johnson, official rhetoric took on a new and guarded form.

JOHNSON AND THE ALLIANCE:
PUNTA DEL ESTE, 1967

In reconstructing the Alliance for Progress, the Johnson administration followed the principles laid down by President Kennedy. Unfortunately, by 1964 the guidelines were left to his successor in the form of a bureaucratic structure dominated by the United States, with little left of the multilateral and essentially political thrust that had animated Kennedy's early model, Operation Pan America. The resulting program, most Latin Americans felt, had been coopted by the economists of the Agency for International Development and the Inter-American Development Bank, so that it began to resemble a haphazard collection of bilateral foreign aid projects instead of a cohesive, long-range, incremental plan to achieve regional development.

As an expression of Johnson's personality, it indicated the breadth of his social concerns—and also something of his vanity and paternalism. To their dismay, the president and his team felt as if they were laboring under the shadow of the Kennedy aura, constantly subjected to unfriendly media scrutiny. Some of the newcomers felt that they were shadow-boxing against a ghostly legacy, with the media asking, "How would Kennedy have done it?" and invariably giving the late president higher marks. While this bias was certainly true in a few instances, especially in the field of Latin American affairs, the Johnson White House tended to be oversensitive about its scope. In any event, it created resentments that did little to improve the administration's media relations.

Once the Kennedy imprint on the alliance had been cast aside with the downgrading of the program's emphasis on political democracy and a reemphasis on "practical" solutions to accommodate the complaints of the private sector, the Johnson team found itself laboring under the burden of autocratic regimes ill disposed to meaningful reforms. Consequently, confrontation came to dominate their thinking. This led them to put a greater premium on economic development, especially the formation of a common market, regardless of the political nature of the participating regimes, without much reference to democracy. Culminating with the Punta del Este summit of 1967, Johnson became more conservative, increasingly relying on private investment capital, as well he had to in light of the drain the escalating fighting in Southeast Asia was placing on US public resources.

To many Latin Americans, in the three years after his election, Johnson became more conservative, increasingly reliant on the private sector and completely absorbed in the political and economic consequences of the Vietnam War. Above all, they realized that the draining effect of the escalating conflict in Southeast Asia on the US economy made any effort to revive the alliance politically implausible.

The disillusionment that spread among the Latin American reformists was reflected in a resolution adopted by the Fifth Congress of the Venezuelan Confederation of Workers on November 26, 1964. It said in part:

> The workers of the Americas in general, and particularly the Labor Confederation of Venezuela, had welcomed with warm sympathy the brilliant Kennedy initiative of the Alliance for Progress. Unfortunately, after the tragic death of President Kennedy, the program lost steam and never succeeded in incorporating the voice of labor in its planning and execution.[22]

A more serious source of discord was created when Congress, under the Johnson administration in January 1964, decided to impose conditions on all aid projects: no project would be approved that would have an adverse effect on the US economy, discourage private enterprise or bar the participation of small US business. Furthermore, the Hickenlooper amendment provided that no grants would be made to any country that did not sign an investment-guarantee agreement with the United States, a reaction to the recent expropriation by the Goulart government of Brazil of ITT. The Johnson administration, sensitive to the growing reservations of Congress and the private sector, was ready to apply the brakes to public spending. Thomas C. Mann, Johnson's chief Latin American policymaker, had long been chary about the postwar economic development strategies adopted by the major republics in line with the recommendations of the UN Economic Commission for Latin America (ECLA), which leaned heavily on statism. ECLA favored industrial promotion policies to substitute domestically produced industrial hardware and raw materials for imports. In order to import capital goods and raw materials for their new domestic manufacturing plants, they incurred large debts in short-term, high-interest loans and suppliers' credits. By the end of 1964, Latin American countries owed close to two-fifths of the $33 billion aggregate public indebtedness of developing countries.[23] At the same time, the average price of all Latin American exports, excluding petroleum, fell 18 percent in the four years before the alliance. Only large increases in commodity export volume held earnings steady.

NOTES

1. *The Johnson Presidential Press Conferences* (New York: Earl M. Coleman Enterprises, 1978), introduction by Doris Kearns Goodwin, 1:11.

2. Doris Kearns Goodwin and Johnson staffers Liz Carpenter, Wendy Marcus and Harry McPherson, interview by author, 1978.

3. "U.S. May Abandon Effort to Deter Dictators," *New York Times*, March 15, 1964, p. 1.

4. "U.S. May Abandon Effort," p. 2.

5. Vaughn Davis Bornete, *The Presidency of Lyndon Baines Johnson* (Lawrence: University Press of Kansas, 1983), p. 172.

6. A situation well defined in Clark Clifford, *Counsel to the President: A Memoir* (New York: Random House, 1991): "Memories of Munich and appeasement were still fresh, especially in the minds of Secretary of State Dean Rusk and President Johnson" (pp. 403–404).

7. Translated from Simon Bolivar, *Carta de Jamaica* (Mexico: Centro de Estudios Latinoamericanos, 1978), p. 29.

8. Lyndon B. Johnson, *The Vantage Point: Perspectives of the Presidency, 1963–1969* (New York: Holt, Rinehart, & Winston, 1971), p. 183.

9. A subsequent memoir of a Johnson official who accompanied Mann on the mission was more insightful: "I never failed to leave [Panama] without a sense of foreboding. Our two peoples would never be at peace, so long as we occupied part of Panama's land" (Harry McPherson, *A Political Education* [Boston: Little, Brown, 1972], p. 223).

10. Johnson, *Vantage Point*, p. 180.

11. "Panama Suspends U.S. Tie and Charges Aggression," *New York Times*, January 10, 1964, p. 1.

12. Johnson, *Vantage Point*, p. 180; and interviews with Ernest Goldstein, White House counsel, and Harry McPherson, assistant secretary of the army, during research for book on Panama for Fondo de Cultura Economica, Mexico, 1974–1975.

13. *United States in World Affairs, 1965* (New York: Harper & Row, 1966), pp. 67–68.

14. Quoted in Johnson, *Vantage Point*, p. 197.

15. Johnson, *Vantage Point*, p. 198.

16. Johnson, *Vantage Point*, p. 198.

17. Johnson, *Vantage Point*, p. 201.

18. Johnson, *Vantage Point*, pp. 204–205.

19. Johnson, *Vantage Point*, p. 201.

20. Harry McPherson, *A Political Education* (Boston: Little, Brown, 1972), p. 259.

21. Robert W. Osgood, *Retreat from Empire? The First Nixon Administration* (Baltimore: Johns Hopkins University Press, 1973), p. 260.

22. *Cuadernos Americanos* (Mexico) 5 (1980).

23. Jerome Levinson and Juan de Onis, *The Alliance That Lost Its Way: A Critical Report on the Alliance for Progress* (New York: Quadrangle, 1970) p. 132.

Chapter Eight

RICHARD MILHOUS NIXON

In the wake of the euphoria of the Kennedy administration and the disappointment of the Johnson years, Latin America went through another of those cyclical phases marked by a general disillusionment with democracy and a turn toward extremist solutions on the left and the right. A socialist–communist coalition brought Salvador Allende Gossens to power in Chile as the hemisphere's first freely elected Marxist president. For Washington it raised the disquieting prospect of an ally of the Cuban revolution becoming established in the southern end of the continent. More common, however, was the reassertion of the right, with the return to military rule and a recrudescence of police excesses, torture of political prisoners, repression of criticism in the press and the concomitant resort to counterviolence by the radical left. This was, to varying degrees, the scenario in Argentina, Bolivia, Brazil, El Salvador, Peru, Nicaragua, Paraguay and Uruguay.

In the United States, the dangerous polarization was widely seen as not only underscoring the failure of the Alliance for Progress but also raising more fundamental questions: Just how important is Latin America in terms of Washington's global interests? Were the conditions that brought about the special hemisphere relationship and culminated with the Good Neighbor policy still relevant? Might a more prudent policy in a world of increasing global interdependence call for retrenchment rather than expansion of Washington's inter-American obligations?

Everywhere the military stood in the wings waiting for the weakened democracies to make a false step. Everywhere the ancien regime and its military allies was bent on provoking an explosion. This was equally true of Bolivia, Colombia and Panama. In these years of neglect and weakened inter-American ties a policy of repression and broken promises of illusory reforms stirred even the great mass of the populations in Peru to something close to rebellion. Warnings and remonstrances went for a time unheeded. There was rioting in the big cities. A sort of official terror saw its dawn in Argentina with the massacre at the Ezeiza airport, which went almost unnoticed. Leftists, for the most part unarmed, who had come to greet the return of Perón were fired on by paramilitary forces. More than 370 people were killed and over 1,000 injured and arrested. The news of this outrage did not receive attention until a report a decade later demonstrated the collusion between right-wing Peronists and the army.

The next years saw a steady crescendo of outrages. Every murder from the left led to fresh murders on one side or the other. Each side in this feud sought to outdo the other in ruthlessness. Domestic criticism of past policies ranged across the political spectrum. Conservatives in Congress who had never favored the long-range assistance programs for Latin America redoubled their opposition. Liberal Democrats who had sought to keep the Alliance for Progress spirit alive were now questioning some of its original assumptions—that Latin America enjoyed a new breed of democratically oriented military leaders, that economic reforms would necessarily strengthen the political center. Disenchantment was pervasive. The staggering cost of the Vietnam war had practically scuttled Johnson's Great Society program and further soured the country's mood on foreign aid.

THE NIXON ADMINISTRATION

After the national convulsion over Vietnam forced Johnson's resignation and contributed to Hubert Humphrey's defeat, a Republican administration was elected. It promised to replace "confrontation" with "conciliation," both in national and international affairs. In foreign policy President Richard Milhous Nixon would devote himself to the pursuit of what his national security adviser, Henry Kissinger, dubbed the "structure of peace." Eventually this included the liquidation of the Vietnam conflict, a dramatic opening toward Communist China, and a step-by-step effort to reduce tensions with the Soviet Union. Latin American policy was essentially put on hold until the administration found it necessary to intervene, covertly at first, to preempt the rise to power of the leftist coalition headed by Salvador Allende in Chile in 1970. When that failed, it initiated the destabilization of the Allende government.

Nixon, like his predecessors, regarded the crux of international order in the Cold War as peaceful coexistence between the United States and the Soviet Union. It was partly with a view to containing and moderating Moscow's behavior that he sought rapprochement with China, thereby diffusing the bipolar concentration of power that had prevailed at the height of the East–West tensions. In the context of this new emphasis on global power relationships,

Latin America would again be relegated to the lesser role it played during the Eisenhower presidency.

Paradoxically, no US president since Franklin Roosevelt came to office with greater firsthand experience in Latin American affairs than Richard Nixon. In addition to his extensive journeys to the neighbor republics as Dwight Eisenhower's vice president in 1955 and 1958, he continued to follow developments in the hemisphere with keen interest.[1] It was an interest, however, that stemmed preeminently from his concern with a worldwide communist conspiracy, most specifically from his violent reaction to the Cuban revolution. After Nixon encountered Fidel Castro in April 1959, he turned into one of the most uncompromising foes of the Cuban revolution in the Eisenhower administration.

That Cuba no longer seemed to obsess him was not due to any diminution in his animosity toward Castro, but rather to the pressure on his administration to end the war in Vietnam, the changing world constellation, and, not least, his new self-image as an experienced world leader. Nixon had worked hard to cultivate this image, especially after his ignominious defeat in the race for the California governorship. He sought desperately to rebuild his political fortunes. The "new Nixon" was no longer a provincial anticommunist but a statesman with foreign policy expertise, wise in the nuances of international communist conspiracy and uniquely qualified to counsel and lead the free world in its struggle for survival.

During the six years Nixon was in office he never again set foot in Latin America except for a one-day trip to the border of Mexico for the inauguration of the Amistad dam on September 8, 1969. In Latin America his absence reinforced the belief that since the humiliating physical attacks he experienced in Lima and Caracas in 1958, Nixon harbored a deep resentment toward Latin Americans.[2] The US media reflected little of this inter-American disenchantment; there was not much interest in hemispheric news. The focus of Nixon–Kissinger diplomacy was away from the Third World to the established centers of international power. As vice president a decade earlier, Nixon had steadfastly advocated foreign assistance as an integral part of the worldwide defense strategy against communism; as president he seemed to yield to the realpolitik advocated by Kissinger—as long as a nation did not impinge on US security concerns, it received little political attention.

Nixon's "low profile" approach to the hemisphere was sometimes referred to as "no profile." To most Latin Americans this policy recalled the barren years of the Eisenhower administration. The intervening Democratic administrations had at least attempted to placate the developing world through economic concessions. Nixon wasn't even prepared to do that.

EARLY INTEREST, BUT BRIEF

President Nixon displayed some interest in hemispheric affairs early in his first term. In retrospect it might be said he wanted to get the issue out of the way, never to return to it. In contrast to the early stages of the Kennedy administration with its expansive rhetoric, task forces and disorderly debates, Nixon brought to the White House a very different environment. Not unlike Lyndon Johnson, he and Kissinger tended to be secretive in the formulation of fundamental policy decisions, expecting them to be swiftly and effectively implemented by an unquestioning and loyal bureaucracy. Academics and the professional foreign service, whom he bullied, loathed and denigrated him. Leaders of his own party and a good number of foreign affairs specialists looked on him as a man with prodigious skills, but rarely with affection or much loyalty.

And yet under Nixon, Latin American policy in a way achieved greater coherence than it had in years. One obvious reason was that his plans for Latin America were less ambitious than those of his predecessors. Another reason was that since they did not merit direct attention from the White House, Nixon and Kissinger were content to leave hemispheric affairs to the State Department. Only when they perceived a new threat of communism, as in Chile with the advent of the Allende government in 1970, did the White House seize direct control with Nixon's favored style of covert crisis management.

Nixon appointed Charles A. Meyer, a political moderate and former vice president of Sears, Roebuck, as assistant secretary for inter-American affairs. Meyer brought to the job great tact, civility, and considerable sensitivity to Latin American customs gained from years of working in South America. He quickly developed a relationship of trust and mutual respect with Secretary of State William Rogers, who, like his predecessor, Dean Rusk, had little experience in Latin American affairs and relied heavily on his deputy. Meyer personally was much more popular in Latin America than the administration's policies. He lasted the four years of Nixon's first term, a record for a position that was notorious for its rapid, often rancorous turnover.

With Meyer on board, Nixon seemed to hold out an early promise of far-reaching revision of diplomatic strategy. Weeks after assuming office, he asked Governor Rockefeller to make an extensive fact-finding trip to Latin America. In April, the president pledged new approaches as part of a ringing reaffirmation of hemispheric friendship before the Organization of American States. In June he promised to give serious consideration to a list of complaints about US trade and aid policies from the foreign ministers of Latin America. Days later he received a state visit from the president of Colombia. In September Rockefeller delivered his much awaited report, *Quality of Life in the Americas.* It received great fanfare in the press but little notice from Nixon himself.

On October 31, 1969, Nixon spoke before the annual meeting of the Inter-American Press Association. Obviously stunned by the novelty, a *New York Times* editorial writer called it one of the most important speeches "ever delivered on Latin America by a President of the United States." The president proclaimed "a vigorous effort" to reduce tariff barriers erected by industrialized nations against Latin American products. He pledged to press for "a liberal system of generalized trade preferences for all developing countries, including Latin America."[3] The Latin American countries were delighted. What they did not know was that the State Department had cautioned Nixon against promising the generalized trade preferences on the grounds that Congress, in its protectionist mood, would never grant them. It never did. Hence all the rhetoric and activity on Latin America turned out to be little more than a frantic dress rehearsal for a play that would never have an opening night. Instead, Nixon and Kissinger sought accommodations with Moscow and Peking while combating communism in regional theaters, such as Indochina and the Middle East, and individual countries like Chile.

MORE AND MORE ARMS FOR THE MILITARY

In June 1969, Frank Church, chairman of the Senate Subcommittee on Western Hemisphere Affairs, held hearings that revealed widespread displeasure with US military policies and programs in Latin America going back to the Kennedy administration. He noted that since the signing of the Charter of Punta del Este in August 1961, there had been fifteen cases of the forcible overthrow of Latin American governments, excluding Cuba. "One of the questions we are seeking to answer in these hearings is the relationship, if any, of the US military activities to this sad state of affairs."

The answer from one of the witnesses, Ralph Dungan, a former special assistant to President Kennedy, was unequivocal: "Our present method of relating to the military society should be abandoned immediately. This means an immediate end to our military assistance program and the large missions which are justified by it."

Another witness, George Cabot Lodge, a Republican and the author of a book on Latin American economic development, was equally blunt. "We have failed to recognize," he said,

> that governments derive their legitimacy and capability solely from the power and organization upon which they rest. In Latin America this power

and organization is often the military, or the oligarchy; it is rarely the majority of the nation. US military and economic assistance to governments, therefore, constitutes intervention by the United States on behalf of the power and the organization of the regime in office.[4]

Appearing for the administration, Assistant Secretary of State Meyer sought to mollify the subcommittee, pointing out that the amount of money allocated to US military assistance programs to Latin America had already been reduced by almost 75 percent from the 1966 level of $80.7 million to the 1970 request of $21.4 million. The number of US military advisers in the region, he said, had decreased to 500 from 800 in 1966, a reduction of more than 35 percent. Yet he defended the continuation of a reduced level of military aid, particularly in the counterinsurgency field. He echoed the rhetoric of both Kennedy's Alliance and Nixon–Kissinger realpolitik. "Inasmuch as the threat of an external attack is unlikely and the danger of formidable insurgencies is today reduced," Meyer remarked,

legitimate questions arise as to the desirability or need to continue with a military assistance program to Latin America. Although today insurgent forces are not a direct threat to the governments in any of the Latin American countries, they do continue to represent, in varying degrees, a nucleus which can be further supported from outside in the event of deteriorating economic or social conditions. . . .

One primary purpose of our military assistance program has been and is to help our Latin American neighbors attain socioeconomic development by systematic evolution rather than in the volatile atmosphere of destructive revolution. Therefore, this program is a concomitant of the broader reform programs in such areas as education, land reform and the like, which are the top priority objectives of our participation in the Alliance for Progress. The Department of State and Defense both continuously work together to insure that this relationship prevails, as it should.[5]

THE ROCKEFELLER MISSION:
WHAT TO DO WITH THE DEMOCRATIC LITMUS TEST?

While congressional critics pressed for a broad reassessment of US policies, President Nixon was considering the choices. The approach he inherited from the Johnson administration emphasized development and fiscal stability along lines promoting capitalism and free enterprise. It made the degree to which a specific government was willing to pursue such policies rather than its political orientation the chief determinant of US assistance. As during the Eisenhower years, the contention was advanced that in the short run, military regimes could be more effective than democratically elected ones in promoting economic development in which democracy could later take root.

Another view, which had animated Kennedy's Alliance for Progress, and which most members of Congress still preferred, held that Washington should stress social change and the strengthening of representative democracy over economic progress.

In the first months of his administration, Nixon sent Governor Nelson Rockefeller on a special fact-finding mission to Latin America. His expertise in hemispheric affairs might generate new guidelines for Nixon's inter-American policy. In addition, his close association with Nixon's most influential foreign policy adviser, Henry Kissinger, meant that the mission's recommendations would receive top-level attention. It was an extensive journey to sixteen countries (excluding Cuba and Chile; Peru and Venezuela declined to invite the mission) accompanied by a score of economists, political scientists and management specialists.

In the end, the Rockefeller task force turned out a conventional, uninspiring report. In essence, it recommended turning back to the Eisenhower–Dulles approach of shoring up military measures to fight communism and leaving economic development to the private sector, reverting to the cherished Eisenhower formula of "trade not aid."

Some political observers suspected that Rockefeller, the standard bearer of the moderate wing of the GOP, still smarting from the humiliating defeat he had suffered at the hands of the Goldwater conservatives in 1964 in his quest for the presidential nomination, was perhaps more interested in asserting his credentials as a tough cold warrior than in addressing the current problems of Latin America.

To a striking degree, Rockefeller's effort seemed designed to certify the failure of the Alliance for Progress, noting at times with undisguised relish that the supposed threat of communism to the hemisphere had remained unabated and that what was now needed was continuing US military aid to keep it at bay. Reporting a dangerously worsening economic, social and political situation, Rockefeller said that the United States had allowed "the special relationship with the other nations of the Western Hemisphere to deteriorate badly."

"At the moment," he observed,

there is only one Castro among the 26 nations of the hemisphere; there can well be more in the future. And a Castro on the mainland, supported militarily and economically by the Communist world, would present the gravest kind of threat to the security of the Western Hemisphere and pose an extremely difficult problem for the United States.[6]

With its emphasis on national security considerations, the Rockefeller report was warmly endorsed by those who had become thoroughly disenchanted with the Alliance for Progress. This seemed to portend the change of heart among some early liberal advocates of the alliance that would have a crucial impact on some of the underlying theories of the US–Latin American relationships. It also anticipated the more pronounced defections and rightward shift of other repentant liberals such as Norman Podhoretz and Jeane Kirkpatrick who would exercise a decisive influence in the Reagan administration's foreign policy.

What contributed to this shift was the inauspicious reception that greeted the mission. In Montevideo, for example, demonstrations and firebombings led the mission to move its talks with the Uruguayan government to the isolated beach resort of Punta del Este. In the worst incident, terrorists set fire to the General Motors building in the Uruguayan capital, causing $1 million in damages. Pamphlets found on the scene denounced "the agent of Yankee imperialism, Nelson Rockefeller."

The Brazilian administration surrounded the visitors with a phalanx of combat troops and plainclothes policemen. "The efficiency of the security arrangements," reported the *New York Times*, "prevented any hostile acts, but suffocated any friendly gestures as well."

While Rockefeller stressed concern over Brazil's press censorship, purges of students and faculty in universities, and the closing of Congress by the military-dominated regime headed by General Artur Costa e Silva, he was impressed by the Brazilian president's vehement protestations that US public opinion was misled. He noted that Brazil's economic progress had made great strides in the five years since the military ousted the leftist government of President Joao Goulart.

The formula for success, as described by Minister of Planning Helio Beltrao, was "to replace demagoguery with work, subversion with order and improvisation with projects." He did not mention that this formula had been accompanied by the virtual destruction of political party activities and progressive suppression of the right to dissent or organize labor or student groups.

Costa e Silva reiterated to Rockefeller the doctrine that Latin America is the object of internationally directed subversion from Moscow, Peking or Havana, which the mission had already heard from the military who controlled the authoritarian regimes of Argentina, Peru, Paraguay and Bolivia. The Brazilian also reflected the great resentment arising from criticism by the United States of their political methods. He pointedly warned the US visitors that Washington could expect the Latin American leaders to react with "a heightened nationalism" whenever Washington suspended arms sales or attached conditions to military aid such as restrictions on the purchase of sophisticated equipment.

It took the Rockefeller group three months and four fact-finding trips to prepare its report. "We went to visit neighbors and found brothers," it began.

> We went to listen to the spokesmen of our sister republics and heard the voices of a hemisphere. We went to annotate, to document, and to record. We did so; and we also learned, grew, and changed.[7]

One thing the Rockefeller mission apparently learned that had not changed, however, was the supposed threat of communism to the hemisphere and the need for continuing US military aid to keep it at bay. "Forces of anarchy, terror, and subversion are loose in the Americas," Rockefeller declared. "Clearly, the opinion in the United States that Communism is no longer a serious factor in the Western Hemisphere is thoroughly wrong." Not surprisingly, the report concluded that the United States could have no qualms in dealing with the military regimes if it wished to avoid the spread of communism and insurrection in Latin America. Military regimes, he argued, should be viewed as a "transitional response" to the political and social instability afflicting the region. These regimes, he found, were "often becoming a major force for constructive social change in the hemisphere." A decade later, Jeane Kirkpatrick would refine this notion into an elaborate political theory that seeks to differentiate "authoritarian" regimes of the right that ostensibly are open to democratic change from left-wing "totalitarianism" that can be ousted only by force.

THE ROCKEFELLER REPORT: POLITICAL FOOTBALL

The report was delivered to President Nixon on September 4. It declared that what was at stake in Latin America was the "moral and spiritual strength of the United States in the world, the political credibility of our leadership, the security of our nation, and the future of our social and economic progress." The report proposed an immediate program of action:

1. The establishment of a civilian-directed Western Hemisphere Security Council to combat subversion
2. Increases in US grants for the training of security forces and sales of military equipment to Latin American countries

3. Reform of the Washington bureaucracy through a major reorganization of US agencies dealing with Latin America rather than through new programs for the region

Rockefeller proposed a new cabinet post, secretary of Western Hemisphere affairs, to coordinate all government policies involving the Americas; an Institute of Western Hemisphere Affairs to take charge of the economic and social aspects of development; greater involvement of the White House establishment of yet another Economic and Social Development Agency to replace the Agency for International Development; an Institute for Education, Science and Culture; and, reflecting the concerns of a previous Rockefeller commission, the creation of an Inter-American Institute of Natural Resource Conservation to address ecological problems. If the members of the mission knew that most of the proposed institutions already existed as part of the structure of the Organization of American States, it was not reflected in the report. Nixon, however, knew.

The president's interest in the mission had waned markedly since he first appointed it. Early in September the White House said that the contents of the report would remain secret until the document had been thoroughly discussed by the president and the National Security Council and, further, until Nixon had made a major speech to unveil his Latin American policy late in October. The announcement came as controversy began to stir around the Rockefeller mission based on leaks ostensibly stemming from members of the mission's staff. Liberals in Congress were concerned over the stringent anticommunist tenor of the report, while conservatives feared that any recommendation to expand aid to Latin America conflicted with the new administration's commitment to fiscal retrenchment.

In an unusual move, the president prevailed on Rockefeller to summarily cancel a private discussion of the report in New York to which the governor had invited eighty-seven business leaders, bankers and scholars. Nixon, long believed to envy the wealthy governor's ready access to the banking and academic community, was not about to be upstaged. In turn, Rockefeller, sensing that the presidential request could be construed as a rebuff, asked the *New York Times* not to run a story that he said contained erroneous details about the report. Rockefeller wrongly identified David Bronheim, a former Kennedy administration official who accompanied the mission, as having given a reporter [this writer] a "biased account" of its contents. Bronheim, who had served as legal counsel to the alliance, at the time was executive director of New York's Inter-American Center run by the governor's brother, David Rockefeller.

Rockefeller's suspicions were totally without foundation.

Bronheim, as much as other former Kennedy aides, had long before subsumed their initial enthusiasm for the alliance to the practical frustrations generated by its imperfections. They were genuinely interested in trying a new strategy and remained loyal, if not entirely uncritical, members of Rockefeller's task force. Actually, the information was supplied by Senator Jacob Javits, a New York Republican and friend of Rockefeller's, who was keenly interested in the improvement of inter-American relations. After receiving a call from Rockefeller complaining about the story, James Reston, the newspaper's executive editor who did not know the source of the story, agreed not to publish it. Significantly, Rockefeller failed to mention to Reston anything about Nixon's request that he call off his discussion group in New York, though this may have been the major reason why he was so eager to have the story quashed. The president's reasons for putting a lid on the Rockefeller recommendations were more difficult to assess. It was never quite clear if the president wanted to distance himself from the more controversial aspects of the report or if he was suspicious of the motives behind Rockefeller's New York conference. Conceivably, Nixon did not wish to allow Rockefeller the opportunity to gain publicity for himself or create the impression that the New York governor was setting up a rival foreign policy establishment to the official one in Washington.

Nixon finally upstaged Rockefeller by holding up the report until the end of October when he made a major foreign policy speech, giving the mission's recommendation second billing. He welcomed the group's broad strategic arguments—which in any case coincided with his own thinking, such as the need to maintain a vigilant attitude against communism, avoid any appearance of interfering with the internal affairs of the other republics by penalizing undemocratic regimes and broaden trade relations.

Nixon did not adopt the hard-line anticommunist rhetoric of the Rockefeller report. Nor did he adopt the recommendations for government reorganization that were certain to meet strong opposition from an economy-minded Congress. Predictably, the president did endorse the leading role of the private sector in economic development, though he added, "Each government must make its own decision on the place of private investment, domestic and foreign, in is development process."

Ultimately, the only Rockefeller proposal the administration sent to Congress (and that with a singular lack of enthusiasm) was a request for implementing legislation to establish the position of undersecretary of state for Western Hemisphere affairs. Though it briefly enjoyed some bipartisan support thanks to the long-time advocacy of senators Hubert Humphrey and Jacob Javits, the

Senate was in no mood to enlarge the federal bureaucracy and the bill was duly shelved.

Jerome Levinson and Juan de Onis wrote that Rockefeller's recommendations essentially reflected "a strategy of timely adaptation of economic policies and flexible accommodation to the emergence of a new military and a growing entrepreneurial class." They added:

> Underlying his report was the assumption on which US policy in the hemisphere has traditionally been based: that the United States must continue to dominate Latin America and that any basic change in the established structure of Latin American society would be detrimental to the security interests of the United States. . . . Although Rockefeller condemned the paternalism that he felt had permeated the development assistance program, his report expressed a much more fundamental paternalism—a belief that the government of the United States has the ultimate responsibility of maintaining order in the hemisphere.[8]

On balance, with the Rockefeller mission Nixon fulfilled his campaign promise, reiterated by Meyer in the Senate hearings, that "all of our policies and activities in Latin America should be examined periodically to evaluate their net utility and their consistency with changing conditions." At the same time he avoided any dramatic innovations and budgetary increases, in line with the administration's conviction that "balanced attention to Latin American needs in the totality of their national personalities is a desirable objective." With the Rockefeller mission out of the way, the president made plain that the conduct of Latin American policy was squarely the responsibility of Meyer, forestalling the rivalry and disarray the Kennedy administration had created by the lingering presence of the Berle task force and several influential members of his White House staff.

MORE TRADE, LESS AID

On trade, Rockefeller was more in line both with Nixon's own thinking and the new administration's capabilities, given the fiscal drain caused by the Vietnam War and the manifest reluctance of Congress to continue providing foreign aid to Third World countries, including Latin America. The United States, the report recommended, must lower its tariffs to grant Latin American exports preferential treatment, embark on a "generous" refinancing of the huge foreign debt of hemisphere countries and do away with "impediments in the flow of economic aid."

Trade expansion, of course, offered the supreme advantage of ensuring access to foreign exchange with a minimum of outside control. But how could Latin America with its stagnating primary economies and overpriced industries compete favorably in the world at large? For years the Europeans had been building a preferential trading system among themselves and with their former African colonies that was hurting Latin American exports to the region, a problem that would become even more acute in the 1990s.

Concerning the United States, Latin America, having seen its once unique relationship with that country gradually subsumed to the category of just another "less developed" region of the Rostow paradigm during the Johnson administration, was now experiencing the additional difficulties arising from the shifting focus of the Nixon–Kissinger diplomacy away from the Third World to the centers of international power. Though a decade earlier, as vice president, Nixon had been steadfast on foreign assistance as an integral part of the worldwide defense against communism, as president he grew ever more pragmatic. Soon it became clear that the interest evinced by the preceding Democratic administrations in placating the Third World through economic concessions declined significantly.

According to some critics, as disastrous as this shift might have been for US political influence in the Third World, it was a policy highly favored by US business interests. This thrust, combined with a return to greater fiscal prudence, was not without justification; the inflation that had seized the US economy as a result of the escalation of the Vietnam War showed no signs of abating and was undercutting the competitiveness of US exports while the outflow of dollars going into the world's financial markets left the balance of payments "precarious to the extreme."

Accordingly, of the new Third World economic policies announced by Nixon, nearly all contained special concessions for US private enterprise. Business was treated to a greatly expanded investment guarantee program. Increased supplier credits from the Export-Import Bank encouraged US export expansion, with little regard to how the Third World would be able to pay.

To complicate matters, the Nixon policy evolved just as economic nationalism was also spreading to the Latin American regional movements. In its Decision 24, the Andean bloc announced a regional investment code that placed foreign investments at a distinct disadvantage to domestic capital. In sensitive areas such as banking, mining and retailing, the Andean group announced that new foreign investment would be prohibited altogether. In all other areas foreign investors would be limited to minority participation in local enterprises, a practice modeled after Mexico's long-standing foreign investment code.

Even more disturbing to the Nixon administration was the wave of expro-priations of key US corporations that had begun to spread across Latin Amer-ica in the late 1960s, accompanied by little indication, in some cases, that the Latin Americans were inclined to pay the "prompt and just" compensation called for by the Hickenlooper amendment. According to one estimate, from 1958 to the beginning of 1971, some $2 billion in US property was expropri-ated by Latin American governments, a sum exceeding all the expropriations in the hemisphere, including those effected by the Castro regime in Cuba, during the preceding decade.[9]

The Nixon administration was determined to act resolutely to counter this trend. As had been the case with the Eisenhower administration, the new strat-egy appeared to tie US interest in gaining a favorable climate for overseas cor-porations to growing Latin American interest in trade expansion. But there was little evidence of success.

FROM VIÑA DEL MAR TO THE WHITE HOUSE: THE GRAND REMONSTRANCE

In May 1969, the Special Latin American Coordinating Committee (CECLA), a group formed in 1963 to promote the common interest of Latin America at the United Nations Commission for Trade and Development, met in the Chilean resort town of Viña del Mar to draft a document sharply critical of US economic policies. It was called the *Consensus of Viña del Mar*. Chilean foreign minister Gabriel Valdés, the chairman of the meeting, was designated to per-sonally deliver the document to President Nixon on behalf of the Latin Amer-ican countries.

The elaborate statement of grievances recalled nothing so much as the cele-brated episode in English history known as the Long Parliament's Grand Re-monstrance, the long statement of grievances against Charles I. Nixon's curt reaction to Valdés's representations strikingly anticipated the way he would re-spond to the Watergate scandals in his second term and echoed Charles's high-handed dealings with Parliament.

The president's meeting with Gabriel Valdés was as frigid and acrimonious and perhaps as unfortunate for inter-American relations as any single en-counter since the three-hour session Nixon, as vice president, had in his Senate office with Cuba's Fidel Castro a decade earlier. A Chilean aristocrat whose cavalier manner can easily be mistaken for arrogance, Valdés made plain he was speaking on behalf of twenty-one governments as he warned the president of "growing and harmful resentment" against US policies throughout Latin

America. United States aid, he charged, was directed more toward the growth of affluent areas than toward assisting the poorer nations.

The 6,000-word Viña del Mar document called for more effective inter-American cooperation and for the curtailment or elimination of many US barriers to Latin American exports, both primary and manufactured. It also deplored the existence of "political and military conditions" for US aid. The report urged the United States to adopt "operative measures" to assist hemispheric development in such fields as international trade, financing, investment, transportation and scientific development.

After leaving the Oval Office, Valdés gave newsmen what amounted to a sharp rebuttal of the Nixon administration's contention that nothing benefited the Latin American economies more than private US capital investments. "Private investments," he declared, "have meant, and mean today, for Latin America that the amounts that leave our continent are many times higher than those that are invested in it. Latin American leaders are convinced that Latin America gives more than it receives." Then the Chilean foreign minister added pointedly, "No solidarity can be based on these realities."

Valdés was equally forceful in his presentation to President Nixon, made in the presence of the envoys of all the twenty-one republics, Secretary of State William P. Rogers, Assistant Secretary Meyer and Kissinger. In his statement, read to President Nixon during a forty-minute meeting, the Chilean foreign minister listed in particular the disagreement of the Latin Americans with the economic assumptions that guided US economic policies in the region. The developed nations, he said, rather than aiding Latin America, were being aided by Latin America. The amount of private earnings repatriated to the United States in 1968, he contended, was five times the amount of private US investments in Latin America during the year. It was the dawning of an argument that would surface again with a vengeance in the 1980s in connection with Latin America's huge foreign debt payments.

"All that can be said has been said; the time has come for action." Valdés's parting words were interpreted by some of those present at the White House meeting as preempting a reply by Nixon. According to one Latin American diplomat, the president winced. Kissinger then approached the Chilean foreign minister to express his displeasure at his remarks and to invite him to continue the discussion at a Blair House breakfast the next day. The breakfast would be the scene of an extraordinary exchange of more than casual importance to US–Latin American relations.

"There is nothing strikingly new in the memorandum that Chile's Foreign Minister has delivered to President Nixon or the message President Lleras of

Colombia has brought to Washington," the *New York Times* said in an editorial on June 15.

> What is new is the sense of urgency—even of crisis—that inspired 21 Latin American nations to hammer out a 6,000 word list of criticisms of United States trade and aid policies and as a set of "new bases" for inter-American cooperation.
>
> Americans need to be disabused of the notion that the Alliance for Progress has failed because lazy Latins simply squandered billions provided by an over-generous Uncle Sam. In the Alliance's first seven years, the United States furnished $5.8 billion, mostly in loans, and the Latins had paid back $2.8 billion of it before the end of that period. Also, most of the money had by law to be spent in this country.
>
> Americans need reminding that despite many set-backs, Latin America managed in those seven years to invest $150 billion in development against an Alliance target for the first decade of $80 billion. And Latin self-help provided nearly 90 percent of that investment total.
>
> Americans also need to be reminded that Washington's actions in Latin America are sometimes contradictory and often at variance with its official message. Colombia's example is by no means unique. Trying valiantly to lessen its dependence on coffee exports, Colombia increased rice and corn production, partly through American credits. Then it found it could not export these products in competition with American rice and corn or it would imperil an agreement by which it got American wheat on deferred-payment terms.
>
> These are the kinds of American practices and attitudes, so little noted in this country, that cool off Latins on the Alliance for Progress and on Washington's inflated rhetoric about Pan Americanism. The Latins have now stated their case. As Chile's Gabriel Valdés said on emerging from the White House, "all that can be said has been said; the time has come for action." The Administration should heed those words.[10]

WARMER RECEPTION FOR LLERAS

By contrast with the chilly reception accorded to Valdés, Nixon and his aides went out of their way to be friendly to President Carlos Lleras, though he too had strong criticisms to make of US foreign aid procedures, trade policies and prevailing attitudes of investors. But unlike Valdés, he believed in cooperation, not confrontation, with Washington, and Nixon appreciated that. After two days of meetings in which Lleras reiterated to US officials many of the points of the Viña del Mar document, Nixon bade him an official White House farewell, declaring that his two days of wide-ranging political and economic discussions with the Colombian president marked a "major step forward" in the development of new US policies in Latin America. "Without you," he told the departing Lleras at the White House portico, "we would not have moved as far as we did."

In his quiet but forthright speech delivered in English to the National Press Club, Lleras conceded that a certain amount of protectionism is justified as a means of "promoting employment." However, he cautioned, after a certain point it is no longer a legitimate instrument of economic policy but an "obstacle to human solidarity, a perpetuation of privilege and inequality." "We receive plenty of advice on the need to increase and diversify our exports," the president said. "But when it comes to developing new exports one is confronted systematically with the vested interests of the industrialized nations."

He cited as typical obstacles US quotas for Latin American sugar, textiles and petroleum, as well as "administrative restrictions" on the import of Latin beef and tropical food. Between 1960 and 1967, Latin American exports to the United States rose from $3.3 billion to $3.7 billion; as a share of total exports they declined from 41.2 percent to 32 percent. In the same period US exports to Latin America grew from $3.4 billion to 4.2 billion; as a share of total exports they slipped from 45.2 percent to 42.1 percent.

"It is not true that Latin Americans are incapable of organized, disciplined behavior," Lleras declared. "The fault is to be found with international rules of the game which take from the poor and give to the rich."

NOTES

1. Because of the dramatic denouement of Nixon's South American trip of 1958, his successful, five-week first goodwill trip to Central America is rarely mentioned, not even in the sympathetic 633-page biography by Jonathan Aitken (1993).

2. Thirty-three years later, on the eve of the retirement of General Vernon Walters, who had been Nixon's interpreter on the 1958 South American trip, Nixon wrote to him: "You and I have faced death together and that gives us a special bond" (Jonathan Aitken, *Nixon: A Life* [Washington, D.C.: Regnery, 1993], p. 252). "After eight years as Vice President I had become fatalistic about the danger of assassination" (quoted by Dr. Fawn M. Brodie, *Richard Nixon: The Shaping of His Character* [New York: Norton, 1981], p. 491). See also Tom Wicker, *One of*

Us: Richard Nixon and the American Dream (New York: Random House, 1991), pp. 207–212.

3. Department of State *Bulletin,* November 17, 1969, pp. 409–414.

4. James Watson Gantenbein, *The Evolution of Our Latin-American Policy: A Documentary Record* (New York: Columbia University Press, 1950), p. 407.

5. Congressional Record.

6. *The Rockefeller Report on the Americas* (New York: Quadrangle, 1969).

7. *Rockefeller Report on the Americas.*

8. Jerome Levinson and Juan de Onis, *The Alliance That Lost Its Way* (New York: Quadrangle, 1970), pp. 315–316.

9. *New York Times,* April 16, 1972, sec. 4, p. 3.

10. *New York Times,* June 15, 1969, sec. 4, p. 4.

Chapter Nine

GERALD FORD

Previous chapters argued that the effect of Washington's overarching preoccupation with the East–West rivalry was to focus attention on the strategic element of foreign policy, notably the struggle against communist subversion. For Latin America, this single-minded concentration was both excessive and misleading. The primacy and centrality of the Cold War in US foreign policy led to the development of rival doctrines and policies among the Latin American allies. Some moved toward neutralism, joining ranks with the so-called Third World countries of Africa and Asia. Others, notably the countries ruled by the military (i.e., Argentina, Brazil, Chile, El Salvador and Guatemala), veered decisively to the right; they not only resorted to traditional authoritarian methods of suppressing constitutional government and civil liberties but allowed the emergence of fascistic paramilitary organizations. Using anticommunism as a self-serving justification for seizing power and claiming to draw ideological inspiration and practical training from the US military assistance programs, these governments inevitably ended up confronting Washington with the allegorical dilemma of the sorcerer's apprentice: the student daring to outsmart the master.

The ideological underpinning of this new and ruthless repression was a theory that became known as the doctrine of national security, a concatenation of old-fashioned right-wing anticommunism with the new counterinsurgency and internal security techniques promulgated by military theorists and conservative propagandists across the continent. By the mid-1970s, this campaign to reduce subversion had expanded in fierceness and in scale, victimizing not only insurgent groups but hundreds of civilians suspected of opposing military rule. Human rights groups and church organizations raised an outcry, which led to formal investigations by the UN and OAS human rights commissions.

These human rights concerns were invariably rebuffed by US military and political officials. They argued that the critics did not understand the nature of communist subversion and the particular characteristics it assumed in Latin

American societies, which were not politically mature enough, and therefore not ready, to assume the obligations and benefits of constitutional democracies of the Western alliance. Moreover, the sorcerer's apprentices who were developing close ties with right-wing groups in the United States began to suggest that the US government had itself become vulnerable to leftist infiltration and had better be on guard. The common danger was held to be détente.

In this atmosphere of polarization, very few Latin American leaders held to the democratic principles of the inter-American system with any degree of conviction.

ENTER FORD

The inauguration of President Gerald R. Ford brought a measure of political and psychological relief to Washington from the traumas of the final months of the Nixon presidency. Ford, lacking the mandate of election, had to move cautiously; his first priority was to restore the nation's confidence in its own government. Like Lyndon Johnson after the Kennedy assassination, he had to reassure the world of the continuity of US foreign policy. In his first statement as president, Ford announced he had asked Henry A. Kissinger to stay on as secretary of state, just as Johnson had done with Dean Rusk. General Alexander Haig agreed to remain as his deputy in the White House.

Richard Reeves, a highly regarded Washington reporter, wrote of those first days of the new administration, "While President Ford happily posed for happy photographers, Alexander Haig and Henry Kissinger ran the country."[1] Indeed, for the next two years Kissinger, as far as anyone could tell, had absolute control over foreign affairs. "Take that up with Dr. Kissinger," was Ford's standard reply when foreign policy questions came up in the Oval Office.[2] When Ford went to Martinique to meet French president Giscard d'Estaing, the French press began to refer to Gerald Ford as "the man who is accompanying Henry Kissinger."[3]

Many observers considered Ford a mediocre figure who was likely to further reduce public esteem for the executive branch, which had already declined markedly as a result of Vietnam and Watergate. He seemed to inspire the same negative media appraisal that bedeviled Truman immediately after Roosevelt's death. But Ford's popularity with the public soared. He conveyed an image of decency that stood in stark contrast with the deceptions associated with his predecessors. Ford projected himself as unaffected, amiable and open—a perfect contrast to Nixon. Although he demonstrated an unfortunate tendency to misspeak and stumble in public, he maintained consistently high ratings in opinion polls. His views on foreign policy, on the rare occasions when they emerged, turned out to be sensible and untainted by strong personal or ideological prejudices and dislikes such as Nixon harbored for Cuba and Latin American leftists in general. Where Latin America was concerned, the Ford administration's first year provided breathing space to reconstruct a national consensus but did not present any dramatic foreign policy initiatives.

Kissinger, both as a Harvard professor and an adviser to Governor Nelson Rockefeller in the 1950s and 1960s, had vigorously propounded the need for restoring the bipartisan cooperation in foreign policy that had characterized the immediate postwar years. Yet in the Nixon administration he was always ready to condemn his Democratic critics while the president refused any meaningful consultation with the congressional opposition. With President Ford, however, the secretary of state seemed more disposed to practice what he preached, the more because of the new readiness of Congress and the public to challenge the executive. This confrontational mood, in the words of one commentator, stemmed from "a common feeling that the earlier 'bipartisanship' and 'consensus' served basically to choke off the wider debate which, had it gone forward, might have prevented Washington's over-involvement in Vietnam."[4]

A decade later, Arthur M. Schlesinger wrote that

in foreign policy the resurgent Congress had its way on a number of specific points. Some of its actions—such as the restraint on CIA intervention in Angola and elsewhere, the insistence on human rights, the resistance to arms sales and to nuclear proliferation—were an improvement over what the executive branch would have done on its own.[5]

Partly in a move to win the bipartisan congressional support he had always considered indispensable for a successful foreign policy, Kissinger chose as his assistant secretary for inter-American affairs an affable, articulate Washington lawyer, William D. Rogers. Rogers had been legal counsel and then deputy director of the Alliance for Progress in the Kennedy administration. He was offered the job of assistant secretary when Kissinger became secretary of state during the second Nixon administration in 1973 but turned it down; he did not admire Nixon and objected to covert operations against the Allende regime in Chile. That obstacle was removed for him with Nixon's resignation. Asked during his confirmation hearings how he would respond if Kissinger were to order another covert exercise in Latin America, he flatly assured the Senate foreign relations committee, "I would resign, of course, immediately."

Although Democrats sought advice from Rogers during the McGovern campaign, he had moved toward the more conservative wing of the party and did not cause discomfort to the Ford administration. Insiders maintained that it had been "like-mindedness" that prompted Kissinger to bring Rogers back into the government more than any publicly stated penchant for bipartisanship. Indeed, by the time he returned to the State Department in 1974, a decade after his service under Kennedy and Johnson, Rogers had visibly tempered the idealism that had infused his advocacy of the alliance with a hard-headed pragmatism. However, he continued to believe that Latin America and the United States should enjoy a special relationship based on a conviction that "of all the developing countries, the Latins had more favorable social and economic conditions than any of the others (in Africa, Asia and the Middle East) to effect a rapid transformation to join the modern industrial world."[6] He also acknowledged that the neighbor republics shared the democratic Western values of the United States.

In due course the new assistant secretary came to realize that since Kissinger had neither great expertise nor genuine interest in the region, he had to force him to pay attention. Rogers did. Eventually the seventh floor of the State Department had more foreign service officers with Latin American experience than at any time since the Kennedy days, among them Viron Vaky and Luigi Einaudi. The secretary himself, accustomed to being the administration's man in motion, began to take time off from his shuttle diplomacy in the Middle East and southern Africa to add Latin America to his globe-trotting schedule. "When it came to get him to attend those laborious, endless meetings of the Organization of American States foreign ministers you had to drag him kicking and screaming," Rogers recalled years later. "It was a constant battle, but after a while he began to genuinely enjoy the meetings with the Latin Americans."[7]

In quick succession, Kissinger agreed to some moderate changes that became salient features of President Ford's Latin American policy. They ranged from seeking improvements in relations with Cuba and human rights to a new emphasis on economic development assistance and strengthening bilateral ties with what Rogers described as "the major countries, beginning with Brazil and Argentina." Unfortunately the new policy orientation failed to produce significant results, partly due to the ingrained ennui about Latin America that was Nixon's legacy, partly to circumstances. Nonetheless, Rogers believes there were major developments in four areas: Cuba, human rights, economic development and diplomacy.

Rogers met several times with Gonzalez Parodi of the Cuban foreign ministry, and insofar as a cloud of secrecy could be penetrated, agreement appeared to have been reached in principle. The effort came to naught, according to Rogers, when Cuban troops became involved in the civil war in Angola to back the Soviet-supported government against the rebel forces of Jonas Savimbi, who was backed by the United States and South Africa. "Still," says Rogers today, "it was the first time since we broke relations that an approach was made to Cuba without preconditions or a formal agenda."[8]

Rogers also argued for a more emphatic definition by the Ford administration of its commitment to human rights. Public outcries had erupted around the wave of brutal repression unleashed by the hemisphere's military dictatorships, particularly in Argentina, Chile and, to a somewhat lesser extent, Brazil. Communism had long provided a ready excuse for authoritarian rulers to persecute leftist and liberal critics; in the mid-1970s it began to include every trace of political opposition.

The Nixon administration generally accepted the official explanations of the offending governments, blaming "individual excesses" of the armed forces on the provocation of radical extremists. Rogers, with the resolute backing of Vaky and Einaudi, persuaded the Ford administration to adopt a more militant position in defense of democratic rights, and it moved successfully to reverse the previous administration's negative view of the Inter-American Human Rights Commission by nominating a US representative to the commission. The appointment of Thomas Farer, a Rutgers University law professor known for his criticism of the Nixon administration's human rights record, was intended to send a clear message to the inter-American community that a new era was dawning.

After President Ford came to the White House, Rogers recalled that the State Department and Treasury began to consider more flexible approaches to foreign assistance, especially toward Latin America. According to Kissinger, however, Nixon had already been contemplating a more forthcoming economic assistance policy. In his unabashedly self-serving style he wrote:

With the prestige of the Viet Nam settlement and the improved relations among the superpowers, the Nixon Administration could turn confidently to the Third World. We planned a new approach to Latin America and intended to use that as a point of departure for a new pattern of cooperative relations between industrial and developing nations.[9]

The implication is that the new approach fell apart during the Watergate debacle and was subsequently revived by Ford. While Nixon's intentions remain undocumented, the Mexican initiative could not easily be dismissed. Significantly, it was first launched by President Luis Echeverria Àlvarez at the UNCTAD meeting in Santiago, Chile, early in 1973, only months before the OPEC oil embargo dramatically underscored one of the plan's underlying premises: the essential frailty of international economic relations and the vulnerability of states to be held hostage to economic interests.

Under the circumstances, the Ford administration thought it prudent to present the United Nations General Assembly with a counteroffer, promising the Third World wider access to long-term development capital, the promotion of economic growth through market stability of commodities and a more readily available transfer of technology. "Developing countries that have been most successful and that no longer require concessional aid, especially in Asia and Latin America, have relied heavily on borrowing in capital markets," Kissinger told the assembly.[10]

Another change, according to Rogers, was the gradual replacement of Nixon's "low profile" policy with one of active courtship of the countries Rogers identified as "the main players" of the Latin American scene—Brazil, Argentina and Mexico. A whole new vocabulary surfaced in official statements, recalling Kennedy's rhetoric more than Nixon's. In their speeches, Kissinger and Rogers played down the strident anticommunism and once more recalled the concurrence of the US revolutionary tradition and ideals with those of Latin America—an attempt to find a link between the struggle for liberty and human rights and the economic improvement of the hemisphere.

At the same time, the new team substantially reversed the hostility that the Nixon administration demonstrated toward attempts by the Latin Americans to create their own subregional groupings independent of the United States. Under Nixon, officials used rhetoric reminiscent of the tough, inflexible policy Dulles had instituted toward the nonaligned bloc, particularly countries that made their neutrality into an ideological justification for flirting with Washington's foes. The Ford team deliberately eschewed this stance. Accordingly, when the Latin American countries met in Panama in October 1975 to adopt a Mexican–Venezuelan plan to create the Latin American Economic System (Sistema Economico Latinoamericano—SELA) without the United States— but including Cuba—Kissinger astonished many by welcoming the move as "a new possibility for cooperation among the nations of Latin America on common regional problems and projects," and he promised US support "as its members may deem appropriate."

This sensible US diplomatic endorsement represented, at last, a recognition of the kind of self-assertion that had been in the air in Latin America since the 1950s. Rogers and Vaky were more familiar with it than many in the administration. This attitude was reflected in the opening speech of the Panama meeting by Nicolas Ardito Barletta, that country's minister of public planning. Pointedly describing Latin America as "a mosaic of pluralist experiences, from the diversity of its resources, geography and historical traditions, as well as its economic and political systems," Barletta observed that despite the enormous potential of the region's resources, "we lack communications, means of transportation and access to natural resources and producers and consumers in our own markets." In Havana, Cuban Premier Fidel Castro praised SELA as "the antithesis of the Alliance for Progress."

Yet the transition did not always proceed as smoothly as the new team had hoped. Just as the Ford administration was moving on various fronts to establish a friendlier climate of relations, Congress in January 1975 passed the US Trade Reform Act, which denied most favored nation privileges to Ecuador and Venezuela because those countries belonged to the Organization of Petroleum Producing Countries (OPEC). The action brought unforeseen repercussions for the inter-American system.

Public demonstrations in Venezuela protesting the law prompted the government to announce that it would not attend an impending meeting of hemispheric foreign ministers that month in Buenos Aires. In a gesture of solidarity, Argentine foreign minister Alberto Vignes suspended the meeting, claiming that the congressional action "by its rigidity and unfairness damages fundamental interests of the Latin American countries." A special meeting of the OAS Council then voted unanimously to condemn the move; only the US delegation abstained.

An attempt to explain the congressional action to the OAS envoys as a manifestation of the public outrage over the Arab oil embargo was a fiasco. At a special meeting at the State Department, Rogers and the head of the US mission to the OAS, ambassador William Maynard, a former Republican congressman who had worked hard to restore US–Latin American friendship, promised that the Ford administration would do everything in its power to amend the legislation to exempt Ecuador and Venezuela from its punitive consequences. But Kissinger did not attend the meeting and Rogers arrived late, so it was portrayed in the Latin American media as a complete failure.

While there was general agreement that Kissinger had succeeded in at least bringing a new style to the inter-American dialogue, considerable concern remained over rumblings and pressures emanating from the hemisphere's military and the security forces. In October, for example, senior US and Latin American officers ended a meeting in Montevideo with a resounding declaration pledging to wage an "aggressive fight" against leftist subversives and seek the removal of "Marxist-oriented governments" from inter-American security organizations, in what was interpreted as a veiled threat against the reformist regimes of Peru and Panama. The newspaper *El Nacional* of Caracas quoted one delegate as describing the meeting as "an exhumation of the best arsenal of the Cold War."[11]

BANQUO'S GHOST AND THE KISSINGER PUZZLES

Official recognition of the need for a strategic change toward Latin America was long overdue. The mood of discontent had for years been hovering in the background like Banquo's ghost, concealed from the US public by the loud controversy over Vietnam and other period distractions. Latin American officials who criticized the Nixon administration for generally ignoring the region had more than enough reason to complain. Nixon's rueful benign neglect alternated with CIA militancy in destabilizing the Allende regime in Chile, leaving the inter-American alliance in a desultory state—and a vigilant Congress filled with distrust. This policy did not differ remarkably from that of the past; what rankled Latin American pride most was the historic rationale Kissinger had advanced with brutal candor to Gabriel Valdés in 1972, when he proclaimed the region of peripheral importance to the Western alliance.

There is a strange discrepancy between Kissinger's record as scholar and as statesman. His theoretical writings suggested that if anybody was prepared to deal with the looming problem of Third World grievances, it should have been Dr. Kissinger of Harvard. Back in 1965, he correctly predicted that though the United States was the greatest donor of concessional aid in relation to Europe and Japan, it would be Washington's lot to suffer the Third World's resentments.

"Over the next decades," he wrote, "the United States is likely to find itself increasingly engaged in the Far East, in Southeast Asia and in Latin America." The European allies or Japan were unlikely to see a vital interest of their own in these areas. What is difficult to understand is how little prepared he was as national security adviser and secretary of state when these involvements actually came to pass in the 1970s with the anticipated results.

Another discrepancy that puzzled Latin American officials and scholars familiar with Kissinger's broad understanding of Europe and the problems it faced in its alliance with the United States was his apparent reluctance to cast a similarly sympathetic eye on the problems of the inter-American alliance. In dealing with NATO in *The Troubled Partnership*, for example, he criticizes what he considers to be Washington's tendency to force the Atlantic alliance into a US mold:

Security for the United States has involved the defense of geographically remote areas based on coordinating the efforts of many threatened countries. We therefore have expected our Allies to fit themselves into an over-all strategy essentially devised in Washington. States have been judged according to their contribution to a Grand Design, with relatively little concern for their history or tradition. Attempts by our allies to adjust their positions relative to each other have been considered out dated nationalism.

However, a society rarely draws its inspiration from serving as a contributor to an over-all division of labor; more usually its cohesiveness reflects a sense of shared historical experience and the conviction that it represents a more or less unique set of values. An alliance cannot be vital unless it conforms, at least to some extent, to the image which the states composing it have of themselves. The test of any coalition is its ability to relate the common effort to the values, aspirations and national peculiarities of the individual allies.[12]

The contrast between Kissinger's capacity to vividly represent the European dilemmas vis-à-vis the United States and his belated, almost begrudging recognition that the Latin American allies may be afflicted by similar concerns is remarkable. Throughout his writings, Kissinger expressed a profound understanding for the difficulties confronting the NATO allies. Perhaps reflecting an empathy natural to his European background, he stated, "A society which has suffered severe shocks cannot find fulfillment in the Grand Design of others without risking its identity. Before it can decide what it wishes to become, it has to rediscover what it is."

This could have been written by a Mexican historian or statesman to explain his country's reluctance to become enmeshed in the successive schemes advanced by the United States for the inter-American alliance over the years. Similarly, Kissinger rarely applied to Latin America, with the possible exception of Brazil and Mexico.

One of his former associates in the department recalled hearing Kissinger remark after an early trip to Mexico, "I don't think there exists a more venal country in the whole world." Ironically, the timing of the visit coincided with the tenure of a foreign minister who was known for boasting that "Henry Kissinger is my best and most trusted friend." The implication was that Kissinger had been won over to the cause of Mexico because of the minister's personal magnetism, a prerogative that in Mexico is left to the president to the peril of any usurper. Another department official who held senior positions in the Ford administration said that by the time Kissinger acquired a deeper interest in Latin America he was already out of government representing affluent Latin American clients.

Rogers gives a very different account of Kissinger's progressive involvement with Latin America. Acknowledging that Kissinger had practically ignored the other American republics prior to his service in government, Rogers contends that once he acquired firsthand experience in the region he became "fascinated." When almost a decade later, in 1983, President Reagan asked him to head a bipartisan commission to study the Central American crisis, Kissinger told friends that "in certain respects" he felt more at ease with Latin Americans than with most other foreign officials.

It is not quite clear whether this was intended as diplomatic hyperbole or represented a genuine sentiment. In the complex relationship between the Monroeist tradition and even the more enlightened Good Neighbor or partner approaches, the representatives of the Colossus of the North have found it hard to surrender their right to patronize the Latin American, just as many Europeans cling to their tradition of superiority in relation to the New World. Kissinger, like other European immigrants to the New World, may have felt liberated by the openness, the responsiveness, the warmth, the uninhibited natural candor, that give a special human quality to Latin America and can conceivably add to the variety of life for so experienced a world traveler as the former secretary of state. Others who have known Kissinger over the years tend to be skeptical. More likely, they contend, his interest can be measured in direct proportion to the amount of adulation exhibited by Latin American officials, who tended to be charmed when not intellectually overwhelmed by the urbane university professor turned diplomat.

KISSINGER: THE YEAR OF LATIN AMERICA, 1976

How to account for this remarkable metamorphosis? Whatever motivated Kissinger to discover Latin America for himself, it represented a striking change in his cosmology compared to his first years in government, when only Europe and Asia seemed to matter to him. Theodore Draper, an incisive commentator on US politics and foreign policy who knew Kissinger from the time both men served in the army, recalls that even as a Harvard professor Kissinger had devoted himself almost exclusively to Europe and to European–US relations. "In book after book and article after article," Draper wrote,

> he had taught that the fate of the United States was bound to be decided in or with Europe. In this view he had not differed from official American policy, at least until the Johnson administration, which had departed from it in deeds if not words.[13]

Yet by the time Kissinger became President Nixon's national security adviser, the president had already made it plain that "Asia, not Europe or Latin America," was the area of the world that would be "most dangerous" to the United States in the final third of the twentieth century.[14] He saw the United States as "the great Pacific power" propelled westward, as "partners," not as "conquerors." Asia was where "the greatest explosive potential is logged." That position had been taken by Nixon as presidential candidate in an article in *Foreign Affairs* (October 1967).

The rhythm of history, as Kissinger put it, had dictated that the focus of both crisis and change is shifting: from Europe to Asia. Europe having been rebuilt and the Soviets "contained," he urged that the United States reserve its main energies for Asia "to reach out westward to the East, and to fashion the sinews of a Pacific community," a harbinger of his preoccupation with an "honorable" solution for Vietnam and the subsequent opening to China. As Draper put it,

> Once they [Nixon and Kissinger] decided on a course which put American interests all over the world at the mercy of such an intangible nuance as "honor" in Vietnam, their freedom of action and even their field of vision were hopelessly restricted elsewhere. . . . The price of the Vietnam war was paid not only in Vietnam; it was paid all over the world.[15]

Accordingly, Latin America was once again remitted to the waiting list after China, Russia and Vietnam, especially while Nixon and Kissinger were contriving the delicate operation that led to the opening toward Communist China. Kissinger's sense of the practical, knowing who is the boss, contradicts most other transactions with Latin America. In the first volume of his memoirs, *The White House Years*, Kissinger relates that in 1972 he told the leaders of South Vietnam, "We have fought for four years, we have mortgaged our whole foreign policy to the defense of one country."

That passage acknowledges, albeit indirectly, the complaints Valdés and other Latin American leaders made over the years suggesting that the United States was repeatedly and routinely subordinating Latin American interests because of its involvements elsewhere in the globe, whether it was Berlin, Korea, Taiwan or Vietnam.

Kissinger's speeches to the foreign ministers' meeting and during travels to Latin America, mostly crafted by Rogers and Einaudi, in the three years he served in the Ford administration contain some of his best statements about inter-American relations. Yet save for a few quotations in specialist studies, they have been neglected, even in his own collected works. That neglect, by a man who confesses to being anything but self-effacing, is in itself significant. For example, the appearance of two volumes of his memoirs might have been an occasion for a reappraisal of his role in hemispheric affairs, but this did not happen. More often than not it is the fate of gentle and small nations to be overshadowed by more formidable contemporaries.

Indeed, compared with the time and attention paid to the Middle East and the more forceful shift of policy toward the crises in southern Africa, the Ford administration's approach to Latin America remained largely symbolic. Nevertheless, the wit, sharpness of observation and compelling worldview Kissinger brought to his speeches and press conferences were not without a positive effect south of the border. Many Latin American political leaders and scholars seemed pleased that after Nixon virtually ignored hemispheric affairs for seven years, Kissinger finally was acknowledging the need for rethinking Latin American policy.

Compared with the skepticism that greeted Kissinger's presentation at Tlatelolco in 1974, his subsequent visits to South and Central America elicited a more appreciative response, especially in official circles. Though in Brazil and Costa Rica student demonstrators protested Kissinger's role in Chile, as far as the governments were concerned, the "new dialogue" promised at least psychological results. In some countries the mere presence of such a formidable man, a man privy to the highest official circles of the world, had the effect of bestowing on them a graduation present that certified their passage to political adulthood.

Kissinger capitalized on his immense celebrity. He believed, plausibly enough, that his brief trips would help overcome the Latin American displeasure with the Nixon administration's "low profile" policy. He so much as acknowledged that there had been past mistakes and misunderstandings, noting, however, that they were caused as much by Latin America's failure to understand Washington's burdens as a superpower as by the slowness with which the United States had responded to the region's "impatient" demands for more equitable economic conditions. On the delicate matter of the "low profile" policy, he rationalized away almost seven years of relative inattention to Latin America by arguing that far from having abandoned the "special relationship" that had once governed inter-American relations, US diplomacy had sought to integrate it into a broader network of global interdependence.

What used to be a simple perception of hemispheric uniqueness and a self-contained exclusive relationship has become enmeshed in the wider concerns we all now have in the rest of the world.

A NEW VOICE FOR THE "NEW DIALOGUE"

In February 1976, after a long silence, Kissinger found his voice on the entire range of US–Latin American questions, including pronouncements on what had gone wrong in the past. In a thoughtful address in Venezuela, he traced some of the difficulties to "conceptual misunderstandings," others to the need of bringing a "global" dimension to hemisphere problems, and still others to mutual failure to fully understand the limitations each side had. At times, his rhetoric began to sound Rooseveltian. "The United States," he asserted,

> values its bilateral ties with your countries without any intention of pursu-
> ing them in order to break up your regional solidarity. We want to preserve
> our hemispheric ties and adapt them to the moral imperatives of this era—
> without hegemony, free of complexes, aimed at a better future.[16]

In a candid reflection on the outcome of the Tlatelolco conference two years earlier, Kissinger conceded that his call for a "new dialogue" in the midst of the world oil crisis had led to "misunderstandings," that "as it was conducted, it only partially met the psychological requirements of our modern relationship." "The United States," he explained in retrospect,

> was prepared to work with the other nations of the hemisphere to improve
> and perfect the undeniable community that has existed under the name of
> the inter-American system for almost a century. Yet the explicitness of our
> approach to the concept of community led many in Latin America to think
> that the United States wanted to maintain or create a relationship of hege-
> mony. This misunderstanding obscured the reality that the hemisphere was
> in transition, between dependence and interdependence, between consolida-
> tion and political growth, and that the old community based on exclusivity
> was being transformed into a more open community based on mutual inter-
> ests and problem solving.[17]

Kissinger went on to develop an interesting, slightly self-conscious explanation of how his remarks might have been further misconstrued by his use of the singularity of each Latin American country, perhaps not quite realizing that it had become a favorite cliché of postwar US policymakers. Recalling an address to the Latin American foreign ministers attending the United Nations General Assembly a few months earlier, the secretary explained that he had sought to pledge that both in specific negotiations concerning the world energy crisis, and "in all aspects of our relations," the United States would remember that "each Latin American country was different and we would be responsive to the distinctive national interests of our friends in the hemisphere." The remarks, he pointed out, had raised "contradictory speculations," adding,

> The explicit introduction of global considerations into our Latin American policy was variously interpreted as implying either that the United States denied the existence of a special relationship with Latin America or that it sought to build on that relationship to constitute a new bloc in world affairs. . . . In this hemisphere the legacy of our history is a tradition of civilized cooperation, a habit of interdependence, that is a sturdy foundation on which to seek to build a more just international order. And it is absurd to attempt to create a broader world community by tearing down US–Latin American relations.[18]

Yet addressing a meeting of foreign ministers in Caracas, he seemed to be reformulating the old Pan American themes:

> The U.S. has always felt with Latin America a special intimacy, a special bond of collaboration, even in the periods of our isolation from world affairs. Even now when our countries are major participants in world affairs, when our perception of contemporary issues are not always identical there remains particular warmth in the personal relationships among our leaders and a special readiness to consider the views of our neighbors![19]

This sudden enthusiasm for Latin America increased once he left the government and devoted his diplomatic and public relations talents to his consulting firm, Kissinger & Associates, which in quick succession acquired important clients in Argentina, Brazil, Chile and Mexico.

Rogers (who became Kissinger's legal counsel in private life as well as a partner at Kissinger Associates) gave a final assessment of the Ford administration's Latin American policy in a speech in New York on December 6, 1976, a few weeks before Jimmy Carter was sworn in. The speech sounded like a eulogy for Kissinger.

Among the accomplishments he listed were the progress made on a Panama Canal treaty, removing Cuba as a source of friction with the other Latin American republics, consolidating relations with Mexico, the expansion of trade and accelerated development of technology appropriate to the region's needs.

> We have dealt with the Cuban trade and recognition problems and removed Cuba as an item of conflict from the inter-American agenda. We are dealing

with the Panama Canal issue. We are talking seriously with other governments of the region, both in the OAS and bilaterally, about the expansion of
trade and accelerated development of technology appropriate to the region's
needs. And we are leading no crusade. We are not taking over the region's
problems for ourselves.[20]

NOTES

1. Richard Reeves, *A Ford, Not a Lincoln* (New York: Harcourt Brace Jovanovich, 1975), p. 71.

2. Haynes Johnson, White House correspondent, *Washington Post,* interview
by author, Washington, D.C., April 1975.

3. Haynes Johnson, interview by author.

4. Stephen S. Rosenfeld, "Pluralism and Policy," *Foreign Affairs*, January 1974,
p. 266.

5. Arthur M. Schlesinger Jr., *The Cycles of American History* (Boston: Houghton
Mifflin, 1986), p. 289.

6. Quoted by Robert F. Kennedy in the introduction to William D. Rodgers,
*The Twilight Struggle: The Alliance for Progress and the Politics of Development in
Latin America* (New York: Random House, 1967), p. xiii.

7. Interview by author, Washington, May 1989.

8. Interview by author, Washington, May 1989.

9. Henry A. Kissinger, *Years of Upheaval* (Boston: Little, Brown, 1982), p. 6.

10. Text of Kissinger speech, Free World Forum, 1988. In possession of the
author.

11. Emilio O. Rabasa, Mexican foreign minister, interview by author, 1975.

12. Henry Kissinger, *The Troubled Partnership: A Reappraisal of the Atlantic Alliance* (New York: McGraw-Hill, 1965), p. 41.

13. Theodore Draper, "Kissinger," *New York Review of Books.*

14. Theodore Draper, *Present History* (New York: Vintage, 1984), p. 233.

15. Draper, *Present History*, p. 233.

16. Henry Kissinger, speech, Caracas, Venezuela, February 17, 1976.

17. Kissinger, speech, February 17, 1976.

18. Kissinger, speech, February 17, 1976.

19. Kissinger, speech, February 17, 1976.

20. William D. Rogers, speech, New York, December 6, 1976.

Chapter Ten

JIMMY CARTER

Democratic and Republican administrations have experienced a curious parallelism in regard to their Latin American policy. Practically every incoming president since Harry Truman began by proclaiming his dedication to a new, more understanding approach to inter-American relations. Yet soon after coming to power, each administration seemed compelled, or merely allowed itself, to be diverted from these good intentions: Truman and Eisenhower were diverted by their overarching concern for Europe and Asia; Kennedy by Cuba with its Bay of Pigs and missile crises; Johnson by the Panama crisis and the invasion of the Dominican Republic, not to mention the Vietnam War; Nixon by global geopolitics and his covert attempts to destabilize the Chilean government of Salvador Allende.

Thus a succession of openings to improve hemisphere relations began with a compelling idea—occasionally even a passionate leader and a sense of mission—but invariably ended in retreat and disillusionment. In each case high-sounding, long-range goals were replaced by short-term improvisations in the name of necessity rather than design. Truman held out his Point Four program. Eisenhower tried, belatedly, a "new partnership." Kennedy launched the Alliance for Progress. Johnson hoped to expand Great Society programs to the rest of the hemisphere. Nixon sought, very briefly, to revive a "new partnership."

Of all of the postwar presidents, Carter actually seemed to have a deep-seated attachment for Latin America. Spanish was his one foreign language, and he and his wife had traveled to Mexico and Brazil. Moreover, he saw in Latin America a special opportunity to apply, as Gaddis Smith put it, "the philosophy of repentance and reform—admitting past mistakes," and to make the region a "showcase for the human-rights policy."[1] Indeed, his campaign speeches were studded with echoes of noninterference in the internal affairs of others and references to mutual respect, the cardinal principles of Roosevelt's Good Neighbor policy.

Another persistent theme was that "we should get away permanently from an attitude of paternalism or punishment or retribution when some of the South Americans don't yield to our persuasion." It was meant to suggest that under his administration there would be no covert operations such as the overthrow of Arbenz in Guatemala or the destabilization of Allende in Chile. "Our commitment to human rights," he told the nation in his inaugural address, "must be absolute, our laws fair, our national beauty preserved; the powerful must not persecute the weak, and human dignity must be enhanced."

"As President," Carter later wrote in his memoirs,

> I hoped and believed that the expansion of human rights might be the wave of the future throughout the world and I wanted the United States to be on the crest of this movement.[2]

Laudable as this goal was, a big question remained: How far can outside forces influence the acceptance of human rights without violating a nation's sovereignty? The issue had been debated by generations of inter-American jurists. To make a human rights crusade the centerpiece of a new US policy required supreme diplomatic skills, especially since the Latin Americans understood that this campaign, like nearly everything else, was really nothing more than another extension of the Cold War. Washington's chief target was the abuse of civil and political rights in the communist world; this concern for democracy and freedom would only be credible if it applied equally against the dictatorships in the noncommunist world. Gaddis Smith has argued that "in Jimmy Carter's case there was considerable substance and sincerity behind the rhetoric."

Yet unlike the expectations and even enthusiasm that Latin Americans normally displayed when the Democratic party emerged victorious, Carter's accession to power in 1977 was greeted with as much skepticism and uncertainty as hope. To most Latin Americans—just as to most North Americans before the 1976 primaries—Carter was an unknown quantity. And as a Southerner he was not so much seen linked to the Roosevelt and Kennedy policies toward the region as to the Johnson administration's ambiguous Texas style.

Furthermore, the Latin American governments had come to regard the proclamation of a new approach to the region as a seasonal ritual for an incoming administration. It would be discarded and forgotten at the first appearance of crisis in another part of the globe. Had not Nixon come into office a decade earlier intent on shaping a new approach to inter-American relations only to remit hemispheric affairs to the periphery of his global strategy? And did not Carter recall Nixon's publicized move to involve the experienced Nelson Rockefeller in the formulation of a new hemisphere agenda, by turning for help to the Commission on United States–Latin American Relations?

The commission, a private, bipartisan and multinational group of prominent citizens cochaired by Sol M. Linowitz, a former US ambassador to the Organization of American States, and Galo Plaza, former president of Ecuador, came up with recommendations that tended to be bland, often proffering conventional wisdom dressed in overblown language, with its criticism tempered by the optimism of those who believe there is a rational solution to every problem. Most Latin American governments, therefore, demonstrated little confidence that the new Carter agenda would differ much from Nixon's. "There are not many or clear differences that can be identified between the policies of the Republicans and the Democrats," wrote Francisco Martinez de la Vega:

> In contrast with the policies of Kissinger, there are now constant references to Latin America, vowing to abandon the traditional anti-democratic policies. Carter cultivates a new attitude; the test will come in his relations with Chile, Argentina, Brazil and other military governments. . . . Is Carter truly a purifier and renovator of the routines of the Empire, or only a new mask, appropriate to the circumstances? Tradition compels to skepticism and distrust.[3]

Nonetheless, few presidents had come to office under more auspicious circumstances, with a political establishment eager to purge itself of the stigma that lingered in the aftermath of the Nixon administration. Few presidents had been more active in their first year. Yet somehow Carter was unable to give effective expression to the spirit of renewal he had promised to bring to Washington.

THE GEORGIA STYLE: PARADOXES AND CONFUSION

Latin Americans were generally disconcerted by Carter's philosophy and style: a Democrat who did not seem to believe in a central role for government; a former governor of Georgia who professed populist beliefs but held to fiscal policies applauded by conservative Republicans; and a born-again Southern Baptist, that peculiarly American brand of Protestant fundamentalism. Carter had pledged to restore morality and reason to a political landscape tainted by scandals—a promise that must have sounded strange to the ears of hemispheric officials who for almost a decade had experienced the politically expedient global power maneuvers of the Nixon-Ford-Kissinger brand of realpolitik. Carter apparently saw himself as divinely ordained to redeem the ship of state, which had been tarnished by what he understood as a total disregard for the principles and values of the republic.

The Carter administration's departure from traditional Democratic positions was conspicuously underscored by the early formulations of Latin American policy. Influenced by the staff of the Linowitz commission, notably by executive director Abraham F. Lowenthal, it sought to drastically tone down the special relationship theme of the Latin American policies of the Kennedy and Johnson administrations. Paradoxically, it equally rejected the low profile policy of the Nixon-Ford-Kissinger years with their readiness to support authoritarian regimes on the grounds that they ensured the law and order necessary to combat communism.

As Lowenthal put it, the Carter administration "reformed the rhetoric of US policy by purging from official pronouncements any mention of a 'special relationship,' a concept that in the past had so often masked paternalistic, discriminatory, or interventionist treatment. Instead, the new administration announced that it would deal with Latin America in a broad, global context."[4]

That was, of course, the very context that Kissinger had used to justify his low profile policy toward Latin America, which had been so vigorously resented by the Latin Americans in the early 1970s. Moreover, without the influence implied in the special relationship, Washington would be deprived of the practical leverage required to influence authoritarian regimes to change their ways, another contradiction the Carter administration evidently did not take into account. For all its rhetorical flourishes and even its sincere exertions on behalf of human rights, the Carter administration, by subordinating hemispheric relations to a vague global vision, was unable to bring forth a defined Latin American policy of its own; consequently, strategic confusion and tactical improvisation prevailed.

Two campaign declarations—the vow to give up paternalism and the acceptance of the Linowitz commission's recommendation to give priority to the Panama problem and the observance of human rights—suggested clarity of purpose. But behind the superficial clarity of these moves lay considerable confusion, which became clear early on in the Carter presidency. How, for example, did it propose to reconcile the renunciation of paternalism and intervention with the desire to impose moral values and judgments on other nations? Carter seemed supremely confident in his ability to mesh principle with practice—to the engineer it was all a matter of method, precision, logic and planning.

The problem of implementing such goals as the settlement with Panama and a stricter observance of human rights was symptomatic of a larger problem within the Carter administration: the division among top administration officials, notably Cyrus Vance's State Department, the Pentagon and Zbigniew Brzezinski's National Security Council, on the one hand, and increasingly strained relations with Congress, on the other. This resulted in fluctuations, contradictions and a general impairment of the effectiveness of Carter's foreign policy.

"An air of bustle, confusion—and self-importance—permeated the corridors and offices of the Carter transition team," wrote Haynes Johnson, a perceptive observer of the Washington scene.[5] The new team was determined to turn the Nixon legacy upside down, and even announced that they would dispense with the advice of old experts. Instead, Carter brought in a young Harvard graduate, Robert Pastor, as a special adviser on Latin American affairs. At the time he was named to the White House post as Latin American expert of the National Security Council, Pastor's experience consisted of a weeklong trip to Panama where he wrote an article on the inequities of the Panama Canal treaty and a stint as assistant to Lowenthal at the Linowitz Commission.

Moreover, though Carter himself demonstrated considerable personal interest in Latin American affairs, his administration displayed an air of lighthearted inexperience with overall foreign policy. This clearly impaired the achievement of his objectives, either by exacting a staggering political price for victory as in the case of the ratification of the Panama Canal treaties, or of compounding difficulties through inner conflicts and indecision as in the strategy of dealing with authoritarian governments or the mounting crisis in Central America.

At the same time it must be acknowledged that far from indulging Nixon-like backroom conspiracies on the domestic front and secret diplomacy in foreign affairs, the Carter administration was perhaps the most open in recent history. Instead of pursuing the expedient policies of the Nixon administration toward authoritarian regimes so long as they were anticommunist, Carter revived the moralistic Wilsonian ethos and confronted them head on. He explained:

> I feel very deeply that when people are put in prison without trials and tortured and deprived of basic human rights, that the president of the United States ought to have a right to express displeasure and do something about it. I want our country to be the focal point for deep concern about human beings all over the world.

Progressive forces in Latin America greeted his forthright defense of democracy as a refreshing change. They waited in vain, however, for this outspoken condemnation of repression to be incorporated into a broad strategy that would resuscitate the economic and social development plans of the Kennedy administration that Johnson had abandoned partly because of the imperatives of the Vietnam War.

CARTER'S FOREIGN POLICY PRIORITIES: HUMAN RIGHTS AND PANAMA

The Carter administration's insistence on making human rights the central consideration of his hemispheric policy was not just a reaction to the brutal repression and torture that erupted across the hemisphere in the early 1970s. Human rights had already become a critical issue in US relations with the Soviet Union, especially in regard to the restrictions encountered by Soviet Jews wishing to emigrate to Israel or the United States. In the face of Moscow's protestations of interference in its internal affairs, Congress overwhelmingly approved the Jackson–Vanek bill to withhold trade and economic assistance to the Soviet Union so long as the regime continued denying exit visas to those wishing to leave. It followed, then, that a coherent policy required not only the condemnation of the Soviet regime but also the denunciation of human rights violations of the resident dictatorships of Latin America.

Carter's embrace of the human rights issue as an international cause coincided with a period of systematic, brutal repression and torture in countries such as Argentina, Brazil, Chile, El Salvador and Guatemala, perhaps unprecedented in Latin American history. "One can surmise," wrote Arthur Schlesinger approvingly,

> that Carter, seeking to give American foreign policy a moral content it lacked in the Nixon years, arrived at human rights as the perfect unifying principle. This principle tapped the most acute contemporary concerns as well as the finest American traditions. It promised to restore America's international moral position, so sadly eroded by Vietnam, Watergate, support of dictatorships, CIA assassination plots, and so on.[6]

"Our commitment to human rights must be absolute," Carter declared during the presidential campaign. Yet practical questions remained. Was it wise for President Carter to make human rights a salient foreign policy issue at a time when the industrial nations were being pressed by the developing countries for drastic concessions on trade and economic development assistance in the stagnated north–south dialogue? What did the United States gain by abandoning the "special relationship" concept with Latin America in favor of a field of global politics in which Washington had even less influence? Was it realistic to expect that the United States, facing severe economic difficulties, could effectively, to recall the words of A. A. Berle Jr., exercise its power and resources to further "a general advance in civilization"?[7]

It soon became evident that the Carter administration would hedge on its lofty human rights goals in the face of vociferous right-wing attacks that cynically defended the dictatorships by adopting their specious arguments—that radical terrorism made state terrorism a necessity for the survival of "democracy." Though Carter implemented his policy in the case of such flagrant violators of human rights as Argentina and Chile by withholding economic and military aid, in the final days of his administration he ended by yielding to its critics in the case of El Salvador, fearing that insurgent forces would turn that country into another Nicaragua. Fear was often compounded by inexperience and ignorance.

The global approach to human rights in particular and to foreign relations in general received its rationale from National Security Adviser Zbigniew Brzezinski and two other influential academics, Lowenthal and Albert Fishlow, an economist on the National Security Council. They maintained that "the long-standing thrust of US policy toward the region has become increasingly irrelevant. Not only is the hegemonic presumption no longer helpful, the scope for regional policies of any kind has inevitably narrowed."[8]

The Lowenthal–Fishlow argument was predicated on the well-intended assumption that an activist Latin American policy inevitably leads to paternalism or "the hegemonic presumption." At times it seemed that nobody had made a final decision whether to deepen US ties with Latin America or dissolve them. Unlike Kennedy, Carter had no substantive program to help him bring about the changes needed to improve inter-American relations—meaning no consistent and comprehensive political, economic or social strategy to deal with hemispheric problems, aside from the emphasis on human rights.

There was also no coordinated action with hemispheric allies and no apparent unity of purpose. Both of these proved politically difficult to command at home and diplomatically impossible to coax. Unlike Kennedy's Alliance for Progress, which used the incentive of substantial long-range economic assistance to induce governments to adopt economic and social reforms, Carter was bereft of any such leverage. Nor was Carter's Panama strategy a model of well-prepared or even well-informed policymaking. Though Panama topped the Linowitz Commission's list of urgent and unresolved matters, it possibly overestimated the importance that Latin America gave the canal problem and underestimated the extent to which the protracted conflict was seen as a manifestation of a deeper divergence between Washington and the rest of the hemisphere. By rallying behind Panama's demand for a revised treaty, the Latin American governments were sending Washington a message that conceivably had less to do with that country's sovereignty claims than with the region's accumulated grievances for having lived in the shadows of the mainstream of US foreign policy concerns since World War II.

Unintentionally, by attaching such overarching importance to the Panama settlement, Washington provided Latin America with a political cause. Ever since the 1964 clashes in the Canal Zone, the dispute had aroused widespread emotional responses in Latin America for its David and Goliath quality. Negotiations were begun in 1964 but interrupted repeatedly by foreign and domestic considerations such as Vietnam, Watergate and, in 1974, internal political changes in Panama, just after draft agreements had been approved by the two governments. That year, General Omar Torrijos and the National Guard annulled the elections that would have given the government to the perennial populist candidate, Arnulfo Arias.

The negotiation process fired Panamanian nationalist sentiment to new heights. That it did not explode into new riots and anti-US violence was a tribute both to the skills of the Bunker–Linowitz negotiating team and Torrijos's determination to secure an agreement, his hold over public opinion and the effectiveness of his National Guard. Things did not go as smoothly in the United States, where fierce opposition to the treaties did not make it possible for Carter to bring them up for Senate ratification until 1977, after a bitter national debate.

A BRUISING PANAMA CAMPAIGN

President Carter decided that a settlement with Panama over the future status of the canal would be the administration's first objective in Latin America. As Carter saw it, the choice made sense for four reasons. First, negotiations had been going on sporadically since 1964 and were at a dangerous stalemate; there was a sense that, if denied a settlement, Panama might precipitate new violence and even destroy the canal. Second, the issue was bipartisan. Presidents Johnson, Nixon and Ford had been committed to a settlement in principle and their negotiators had done much of the necessary groundwork. Third, Carter believed that successful negotiations would have such a positive impact in Latin America that they would be seen as heralding the beginning of a new era. And fourth, a settlement would be, in effect, a gracious apology by the

United States for past wrongdoing and thus was compatible with Carter's emphasis on the need, in the words of Gaddis Smith, for a "moral cleansing" of foreign policy.

Vance, who as an assistant secretary of defense in the Johnson administration had been directly involved in the Panama crisis of 1964, moved swiftly. He appointed an expert team of Sol Linowitz and Ellsworth Bunker to take the principles enunciated in the earlier Kissinger–Tack agreement as the basis for negotiation and dispatched them to Panama less than two weeks after Carter's inauguration.

From the outset, the septuagenarian Bunker adopted an informal style reminiscent of Cordell Hull's shirt sleeves diplomacy at the Montevideo conference four decades earlier. Over long discussions on sun-drenched Contadora Island combined with fishing trips in the Pacific waters, he developed a close working relationship with Torrijos, who delighted in the veteran diplomat's colorful anecdotes. Commenting on the atmosphere of trust and informality that prevailed in the Contadora meetings, Torrijos once confided to this writer that "I felt like I was talking to my grandfather. I had total confidence in his good-faith."[9]

More than that. From the moment he began negotiations with Kissinger during the Nixon administration, Torrijos indicated a romantic belief in the good faith of the people of the United States. "The United States public," he said in an interview in 1974, "is by nature generous and fair-minded."

I am convinced that once it is presented with the facts of how Panama was coerced into yielding sovereignty over the canal in the first place, there will be no question about rectifying that gross injustice. The trouble is that the people of the United States were never apprised of the true history of the canal.[10]

Ironically, US presidents from Eisenhower to Carter did not seem to share that confidence. Just as Eisenhower had been slow in recognizing the legitimacy of Panamanian grievances concerning the salaries paid to its workers in the Canal Zone, Johnson, who commanded a much wider following in Congress than Carter did, was convinced that neither public opinion nor the Senate was prepared to endorse a revised treaty if it called for the termination of US sovereignty over the canal.

Not so Carter. Dismissing past inhibitions, he decided to challenge Congress, no matter how bruising a battle it would take, to secure Senate ratification of Panama's demands for sovereign rights over the canal. He believed that resolving the dispute with Panama would give him the key to a new relationship with all the other nations of the hemisphere. He calculated that the fight was worth it. Consequently his administration expended an enormous amount of time and energy to secure the two-thirds majority needed for ratification by the slimmest of margins.

In retrospect, it may have been a Pyrrhic victory. For the few weeks of acclaim it gained Carter in Latin America, ratification was in no way commensurate with the damage it caused him on the domestic front. The bitter debate it unleashed in the United States was eagerly seized on by his Republican critics, notably California Governor Ronald Reagan, whose impassioned rallying cry, "We bought it, we paid for it, it's ours and we're going to keep it," kindled the kind of chauvinistic fervor that would help sweep him into office four years later.

GOOD INTENTIONS POORLY EXECUTED

To observers outside the government, the chief result of the inexperience of the Carter White House in Latin American affairs was disorientation and ideological chaos. For example, though Carter saw himself as responsive to the sensibilities of the neighbor republics, on the critical matter of consultations with the Latin American allies on major world issues affecting the hemisphere his record was no better than that of previous administrations.

Robert Pastor, Carter's Latin American specialist, acquired a reputation for what one veteran Latin American diplomat called a "take it or leave it" attitude. With Kissinger Latin Americans could justly complain about lack of interest in their region; Brzezinski and his team were seen as overly zealous in proffering advice. In neither case was there an abundance of constructive dialogue.

Pastor received intensive empirical training, learning much from costly mistakes caused by inexperience and lack of genuine interest by senior officials. Also, like Goodwin before him, his White House position ineluctably pitted him in bitter policy and jurisdictional disputes with the State Department. Yet while Kennedy sought to avert further friction by shifting Goodwin into the State Department, Carter kept Pastor at the White House working for Brzezinski, who was no more interested in hemispheric affairs than Henry Kissinger had been.

Again like Goodwin, Pastor would become a central figure in several controversies. Pastor was the author of a notorious letter signed by Carter in the midst of the Nicaraguan civil war commending Anastasio Somoza for an improvement in his government's human rights record at the very moment when a State Department negotiator was in Managua seeking the portly dictator's resignation and the formation of a coalition government. Ironically, the real reason for the letter had less to do with the situation in Nicaragua than with the administration's zeal to secure ratification of the Panama canal treaties.

A new hitch developed when Representative Charles Murphy, chairman of the House Maritime Committee, warned Pastor that if the United States pursued its efforts to remove Somoza from office, he would do his utmost to block the Panama treaty legislation. Murphy had been a close friend of Somoza since the two were cadets together at West Point; they were also said to have been partners in a Nicaraguan shipping enterprise. It is significant that Murphy got involved in the Panama debate after the Panamanian government had impounded two Somoza-owned vessels.

In a desperate attempt to neutralize the committee chairman's opposition, Pastor used the occasion of a momentary lessening of repression in Nicaragua to have Carter send off the letter—with a copy to Murphy. The maneuver had an ironic twist when Murphy became involved in another conflict of interest scandal and was indicted and convicted, forcing his withdrawal from Congress.

But the damage was done, and it was considerable: the letter was interpreted by Somoza—and all Nicaragua—as a vote of confidence from the United States. Accordingly, the dictator, far from heeding the advice of the State Department and the Pentagon that he leave the country, dug in his heels. He ordered the National Guard to redouble the fight in a futile attempt to quell the uprising, succeeding only in tragically prolonging the civil war, leaving thousands more casualties before the regime collapsed. Ultimately, Somoza was forced to flee to Paraguay and was assassinated a few weeks later by a Sandinista commando.

Another tragic result was that having spearheaded the military victory, the most radical elements of the opposition, the Sandinista Front, totally dominated the coalition that came to power. The State Department mediator pleaded with the Sandinista leaders to work as equals with the conservatives who had opposed Somoza in preparing for free elections. But the opportunity for moderation had been squandered when Somoza clung to power, encouraged by the Carter letter. Heady with their military victory, the young Sandinista leaders saw no reason to heed the advice of the United States, a country they held responsible for aiding and abetting the Somoza dynasty for almost four decades. The Nicaraguan revolution entered into a relentless collision course with Washington, much as Cuba did under Castro two decades earlier.

Though Pastor drew sharp criticism from State Department officials and some members of Congress, he never lost Carter's confidence. He remained at his post at the National Security Council to the end of Carter's term, despite many differences, some of them quite stormy, with Assistant Secretary of State Terrence Todman. After failing in his reelection bid against Ronald Reagan in 1980, Carter invited Pastor to become the director of the Latin American and Caribbean program at Emory University's Carter Center in Atlanta, where he has consolidated his reputation as a Latin American expert, in both political and academic circles. Some of the congressional resentment turned out to be long lasting. When President Clinton wanted to make Pastor ambassador to Panama in 1994, the nomination was effectively blocked by Senator Jesse Helms, who was on his way to becoming chairman of the Foreign Relations Committee.

NICARAGUAN POLICY:
TWISTING, TURNING AND HESITANT

For more than three decades, the relationship between the United States and Nicaragua followed the pattern, so fervently deplored by Carter at the beginning of his administration, of embracing "any dictator who joined us" in opposing communism. Yet when his administration had an opportunity to rectify the situation, it bungled masterfully. In fact, Washington emulated, step by step, the mistakes made in its relations with revolutionary Cuba two decades earlier to the benefit of absolutely no one. During the first year of the Carter administration, Nicaragua plunged into civil war. Somoza's National Guard responded to guerrilla attacks with the indiscriminate bombing of villages, mass arrests, torture and executions. As with the Cuban revolution, the State Department proceeded cautiously. At first the administration deplored Cuban support for the Sandinistas more vigorously than Somoza's violations of human rights. It took prodding by liberals in Congress led by New York Congressman Ed Koch and Massachusetts Senator Edward Kennedy to get the administration to hold back economic aid. This was a light slap on the wrist for Somoza's atrocities—reminiscent of the admonitions that Eisenhower leveled at the Batista regime of Cuba when it was already moribund. But when Somoza made what some observers called "a cosmetic gesture" toward easing repression, aid was released to him almost immediately.

In his history of the Carter administration, Gaddis Smith characterizes its policy toward Nicaragua as "a grim comedy of mixed signals: diplomatic pressure to curb atrocities and accept mediation of the civil war; withholding and restoring aid; and personal congratulations from President Carter to Somoza over insubstantial concessions."[11] The crisis kept growing, nonetheless, and the year 1978 opened with the murder of Pedro Joaquin Chamorro, the liberal editor of *La Prensa*, Nicaragua's leading newspaper and a critic of Somoza. His assassination rallied business opposition and provoked a general strike against Somoza, who responded with more repression. A senior foreign service officer with considerable experience in the Caribbean wrote:

> With a sinking sense of *deja vu*, I watched us repeat in Nicaragua our Cuban mistakes of twenty years earlier. Conceptually, we understood in 1978 as in 1958 that our best course was to encourage moderate forces to fill the developing power vacuum. The Carter administration *said* that was what it intended to do, but like the Eisenhower administration, failed utterly to carry through.[12]

In mid-1978 the United States, with the full backing of the Organization of American States, launched a negotiating process carried on by an international mediation panel. Some progress was made in the search for a moderate solution, but crucial mistakes in the Carter White House derailed the process. First, in June 1978, against the advice of the Department of State, Carter sent Somoza the letter commending him for considering certain steps toward greater respect for human rights.

Such congratulations were decidedly premature. None of the steps had actually been taken—and most never were. Worse, the letter concluded by inviting Somoza to continue discussing his constructive actions with the US ambassador. Somoza understandably interpreted the letter as a sign that he continued to enjoy US favor and that Washington would not insist on his relinquishing power. Only a firm show of determination by the Carter administration might have convinced Somoza to step down. "But when in the fall of 1978 push came to shove in the negotiating process," writes Wayne S. Smith,

> the administration failed to shove. By October, the international mediation panel, which was headed by my old office companion from Havana, Bill Bowdler, together with the Nicaraguan *Frente Amplio de Oposición*, had worked out a peace plan. Somoza was to resign and turn power over to a government of national unity including representatives of all sixteen opposition groups—the Sandinistas being only one of the sixteen. . . . [The plan] could have worked if Somoza had resigned and given it a chance. Somoza, however, would have resigned only under US pressure. But the US failed to press him, and allowed the whole negotiating process to collapse. From that point forward, we really had no policy in Nicaragua. We simply drifted.[13]

With a peaceful solution ruled out, Somoza's opponents turned to armed struggle. The civil war escalated, and it became clear that those with arms in hand would have the inside track to power once it was over. That meant the Sandinistas, for they were the principal armed group. By failing to throw its weight decisively behind the peace plan, the Carter administration not only lost its best chance of bringing about a satisfactory solution in Nicaragua but also increased the chances that the Sandinistas would end up in power—exactly what the US did not want.

In the words of Alfonso Robelo, then a leader of the Frente and later a leader of the Nicaraguan Contras:

> If at that moment, in October, November, December of 1978, they [the US] had been ready to put pressure on Somoza, like saying, "Okay, forget it, you're not going to have a sanctuary in the States." . . . Somoza would have stepped down and a different thing would have happened. We lost the best opportunity we had at that time. . . . After that, the Broad Opposition Front was left with nothing and the only people who had initiative were those in the violent mode, the FSLN.[14]

The Carter administration acted against the advice of its most informed senior diplomats. Both Viron P. Vaky, the assistant secretary of state for inter-American affairs, and William Bowdler, his deputy, urged that the United States encourage Somoza to resign. But both were ignored. Why? According to Wayne Smith,

> For a variety of reasons, some reflecting misjudgment; others, however mistaken, based on solid moral principles. For one thing, by the time negotiations had reached the crucial point, the NSC, inexplicably, had convinced itself that Somoza could survive the crisis. While we might not like him, the council reasoned, it would be foolish and probably futile to pressure him. The NSC's Latin American adviser asked me in September 1878 if I agreed with Pete Vaky that Somoza could not last. When I replied that I did, that in my view Somoza was finished, whether his final demise came in two months or two years, the adviser replied that both Vaky and I were dead wrong. "The problem with all of you," he said, "is that you see this as a replay of Cuba in 1958. But it isn't. The Cuban army wouldn't fight; the National Guard will, and since it will, Somoza will be able to hang on."[15]

Smith agreed that the guard was better led, so the process might take longer, but it too would lose heart as it realized it was fighting the Nicaraguan people as a whole. State Department diplomats argued to no avail. Until it was far too late, the National Security Council went on expecting Somoza to survive. Even in June 1979, only a month before Somoza's final defeat, Pastor was still predicting that the Nicaraguan dictator would weather the storm.

Despite his theoretically absolute devotion to human rights, President Carter, prodded by Brzezinski, continued to worry primarily about communism. In a June 1978 discussion with the presidents of Panama, Mexico, Costa Rica, Colombia and Venezuela, the talk was about human rights, but also "about how to constrain Cuban and other communist intrusion in the internal affairs of Caribbean and Latin American countries, and how to encourage freedom and democracy in Nicaragua and minimize bloodshed there."

Some State Department officials not directly involved in Latin American affairs were opposed to pressuring Somoza, partly to maintain a noninterventionist posture required by the OAS charter, partly out of fear that such action would bring the wrath of Somoza's powerful conservative friends in Congress down on the department. One of these officials was Anthony Lake, the director of the department's policy planning staff, who apparently influenced Vance to abstain from intervening. "For a mix of reasons, we did nothing," observes Wayne Smith.

> With negotiations paralyzed, the fighting grew steadily more intense during the first half of 1979. This was neither a bloodless coup nor a comic-opera revolution. It was a full scale civil war with heavy fighting all over the country, great destruction, and high loss of life. Somoza soon lost the upper hand. Despite desperate measures such as the indiscriminate bombing and shelling of heavily populated areas, he was on the ropes by the middle of June 1979.[16]

Only in late June did the United States attempt to get a handle on the situation. The new US ambassador in Managua, Larry Pezzullo, was sent in to tell Somoza that Washington expected him to resign. Bill Bowdler meanwhile helped hammer out a last-minute agreement between the opposition and the authorities regarding modalities for a transitional government. The US aim was the same in June and July 1979 as it was in the fall of 1978—to avoid a Sandinista-dominated government. But what might have worked the previous year would not hold together now. It was too late. The Sandinistas had grown too strong and gained too much momentum.

At this point Brzezinski also got into the act. A meeting of OAS foreign ministers took up the Nicaraguan situation in late June. The Department of State wanted the OAS to call for a cease-fire, followed by Somoza's resignation in favor of a transitional government. Brzezinski, however, insisted that Vance also propose the creation of an OAS peacekeeping force to move into Nicaragua as soon as Somoza left. The area specialists knew this proposal would not fly. It harkened back to the special force created in 1965 to support the US invasion of the Dominican Republic, and no Latin American country ever again wanted to endorse armed intervention against a sister republic, even under the shield of collective action. Vaky, Bowdler and Pezzullo all warned against it. Brzezinski, the East–West specialist, wasn't listening. Neither was President Carter.

Secretary Vance presented the US alternative: formation of an interim government of national reconciliation acceptable to all major elements of the society, the dispatch by this meeting of a special delegation to Nicaragua, a cease-fire, an OAS peacekeeping presence to help establish a climate of peace and security and to assist the interim government in establishing its authority and beginning the task of reconstruction, and a major international relief and reconstruction effort.

The OAS peacekeeping force was the crux. With the antecedent of President Johnson's request for a similar force to give a multinational veneer to the US invasion of the Dominican Republic, not a single Latin American nation supported it and "the Vance plan died the moment it was presented." Neither the administration nor Congress was prepared to send a purely US "peacekeeping" force to do the job, not while memories of Vietnam still lingered.[17]

Somoza resigned on July 19 and fled the country. The Sandinistas took Managua, and the National Guard surrendered. The United States decided to work with the new junta, controlled by the Sandinistas but including some nonradical opponents of Somoza. Diplomatic relations were established on July 24 and the United States sent emergency food and medical aid. For the remaining eighteen months of the administration, while Washington was preoccupied with events in Iran and Afghanistan, Nicaragua received little attention. US policy was, in President Carter's words, "to maintain our ties with Nicaragua, to keep it from turning to Cuba and the Soviet Union." The Sandinistas had their own agenda, and pleasing the United States was not on it. They followed a Cuban model of politics, accepted Cuban advisers, alienated many Nicaraguans who had once cooperated with them, and helped set the stage for the limited covert war initiated during the Reagan administration.

The Carter administration, by trying to find a middle way between Somoza and the Sandinistas, incurred the criticism of both sides in Nicaragua and the right and the left in the United States. To the dismay of American liberals, Nicaraguan policy was dominated by Cold War considerations more than by the protection of human rights. After the Sandinista victory, the Carter administration accepted what it was unable to prevent and extended economic aid. And yet, to critics on the right in the United States, the episode was another defeat—another consequence of weakness and an ill-advised human rights policy. Jeane Kirkpatrick, for example, accused the Carter administration of bringing down both the shah of Iran and Somoza, staunch anticommunists and friends of the United States. She wrote that "the American effort to impose liberalization and democratization on a government confronted with a violent internal opposition not only failed but actually assisted the coming to power of new regimes in which ordinary people enjoy fewer freedoms and less personal security than under the previous autocracy—regimes, moreover, hostile to American interests and policies."

SALVADOR NIGHTMARE

The small, densely populated country of El Salvador, on the Pacific coast of Central America, had never attracted the same attention from the United States as Nicaragua. Since 1932, El Salvador had been governed by an alliance of reactionary landowners and the military. They mouthed the rhetoric of anticommunism while denying democracy and using force to crush dissent. "Here was a textbook case for the application of foreign policy based on human rights," according to Gaddis Smith. Any hope that El Salvador might return to democracy was dashed in February 1977 with the fraudulent election of General Carlos Humberto Romero as president. In the same month, government troops fired on a crowd of demonstrators, killing an undetermined number. As in the case of Nicaragua, Congress prodded the Carter administration by questioning the wisdom of sending military aid to such a regime.

The administration responded by blocking an Inter-American Bank loan to El Salvador. The Salvadoran government, however, offended by US criticism, refused military aid before it could be denied. In August, while Patricia Derian, assistant secretary of state for human rights, went to investigate the situation firsthand, Terrence Todman, assistant secretary for Inter-American affairs, signaled to Romero and others like him that the United States understood the "cruel dilemma between a government's responsibility to combat terrorism, anarchy and violence, and its obligation to avoid applying any means which violate human rights." As a gesture to US concern, President Romero suspended martial law and the United States restored economic aid. Two months later Romero enacted legislation making criticism of the government a crime, in effect suspending all civil rights.

At the same time, Salvadoran right-wing terrorist groups—the feared death squads—became more active. In October 1979, there was a brief moment of rejoicing for US diplomats. Younger, seemingly more liberal officers overthrew General Romero and established a junta that included moderate civilians. Deputy Secretary of State Warren Christopher proclaimed, "El Salvador has a new government pledged to open the political system, to pursue urgently needed economic reforms and to respect human rights." The junta proved powerless to end the killings. Its land reform program, encouraged by the United States, was blocked by the far right. The death squads continued unchecked, and their brutality may have created more implacable revolutionaries than they killed.

On March 24, 1980, the archbishop of El Salvador, Oscar Arnulfo Romero, was murdered while celebrating mass in his cathedral. Death was the price he paid for daring to speak out against the government and the right. He was one of an estimated 9,000 to die in political violence during 1980 at the hands of both the right and the left. By 1980, El Salvador had become the most difficult issue in US relations with Latin America. But in the year of Afghanistan, Americans held hostage in Iran, and President Carter's battle for reelection, that said little about El Salvador's priority in foreign policy as a whole. The president, the secretary of state and the national security adviser had little time for El Salvador. (Neither Vance nor Brzezinski address El Salvador in their memoirs.) The United States muddled along—extending aid with each sign of hope and restricting it in response to new atrocities.

Human rights advocates struggled in the State Department and seemed to be losing out to those who put first emphasis on suppressing terrorism. Some suggested training the Salvadoran army in "clean counterinsurgency," in preference to the dirty, uncontrolled terror of the right-wing death squads. When Salvadoran soldiers in December 1980 murdered four American Catholic missionaries, three nuns and a woman lay worker, President Carter suspended military aid once again and sent a special mission headed by William D. Rogers, undersecretary of state in the Ford administration, to investigate and report. The junta promised it would spare no effort to find the murderers and bring them to justice. But on returning to Washington after a three-day visit, the Rogers mission told President Carter that they had heard "hand grenades and automatic rifles going off all during the night as people were being killed. They don't have anybody in the jails; they're all dead. It's their accepted way of enforcing the so-called law."

In January 1981, two American advisers to the ill-fated land reform program and a Salvadoran official were murdered by a death squad while they drank coffee in a San Salvador hotel—and the Carter administration resumed sending military aid to the government. After that, the situation was in the hands of the Reagan administration.

MEXICAN FUMBLE AND CUBA

During the campaign, Carter criticized his Republican predecessors for neglecting Mexico and promised to be different. He considered it a happy coincidence that Mexico's new president, José Lopez Portillo, a former finance minister believed to be friendlier to the United States than his predecessor, Luis Echeverría, was inaugurated only one week before his own term began. Initiating what would become a custom of naming her his special cultural envoy, Carter sent his wife, Rosalynn, to attend Lopez Portillo's inauguration. The following month the Mexican president became the first head of state to visit the Carter White House. The visit was cordial but left no lasting impact on US–Mexican relations. In subsequent years relations improved somewhat in contrast with the clashing views held by Echeverría and Nixon on everything from relations with Allende's Chile to divergent approaches toward the Third World's economic development problems.

Surprisingly for one who had criticized Republican neglect of the neighbor republic, Carter waited until his last year in office to make his first trip to Mexico City, in February 1979. By then, differences were simmering over a range of issues—the sale of Mexican natural gas, control of illegal narcotics and water pollution. These became compounded by divergences over Carter's Central American policy, particularly the resumption of military sales to El Salvador combined with his growing suspiciousness toward the Sandinistas, who enjoyed a warm relationship with Mexico.

Moreover, Carter's goodwill visit was marred by an unfortunate faux pas. During a toast at the opening of his first state dinner at the National Palace, Carter recalled how an attack of Montezuma's revenge had spoiled a jogging spree at Chapultepec Park the first time he visited Mexico. In a country famous for its fierce national pride, the innocent remark quickly found its way into the catalog of anecdotes Mexican officials love to tell, claiming real or imagined slights to their country by the leaders of the powerful neighbor to the north. Commenting on Carter's maladroit performance, the scholarly quarterly *Cuadernos Americanos* wrote, "Seldom had a high-ranking official undertaken a Latin American tour under such inauspicious circumstances."[18]

Washington expressed its concern about Cuba's newly acquired allies in the region, Granada and Nicaragua, in a classical way: major new air and naval maneuvers were to be staged just off the Cuban coast in October, culminating in a mock amphibious landing at the Guantanamo naval base. Carter, even before Reagan, seemed determined to remind the world that the Caribbean remained the Mare Nostrum of the United States. "Measures so strongly reminiscent of earlier gunboat diplomacy could not but offend other Latin American countries, even those made nervous by Cuba's new alliances in the region," reflected Wayne Smith. "Friends such as Costa Rica, the Dominican Republic, and Honduras, for example, relied on US assurances of support in the face of their more powerful neighbor, Cuba. Their natural inclination was to support us, but given the history of US interventions in the region, not even they could endorse the landing of marines."[19]

In sum, added Smith, "it seemed to me that we could accomplish more with diplomacy than with military demonstrations. The Cubans would not accede to threats, but they might respond to calm reminders that if relations between us were to improve, both sides had to behave prudently and take the other's security interests into account."[20]

NOTES

1. Gaddis Smith, *Morality, Reason, and Power: American Diplomacy in the Carter Years* (New York: Hill & Wang, 1986), p. 110.

2. Jimmy Carter, *Keeping Faith: Memoirs of a President* (New York: Bantam, 1982), p. 144.

3. "Es Carter, realmente, un depurador y renovador de las rutinas del Imperio, o sólo una nueva Máscara apropiada a las circunstancias? La tradición obliga al esceptisimo y a la desconfianza" ("Nueva Cara del Viejo Imperio?" *Cuadernos Americanos*, March–April 1977).

4. Abraham F. Lowenthal, *Partners in Conflict: The United States and Latin America* (Baltimore: Johns Hopkins University Press, 1987), p. 42.

5. Haynes Johnson, *In the Absence of Power: Governing America* (New York: Viking, 1980), p. 37.

6. Arthur Schlesinger, *Cycles of American History* (Boston: Houghton Mifflin, 1986), p. 97.

7. Quoted in Samuel Flagg Bemis, *The Latin American Policy of the United States* (New York: Harcourt, 1943), p. 391.

8. Abraham F. Lowenthal and Albert Fishlow, *Latin America's Emergence: Toward a UN Response*, Headline Series 243 (New York: Foreign Policy Association, February 1979), p. 26.

9. Interview by author, Contadora Island, Panama, June 1974.

10. Interview by author, Hotel La Siesta, Panama, August 1974.

11. Smith, *Morality, Reason, and Power*, p. 119.

12. Wayne S. Smith, *The Closest of Enemies: A Personal and Diplomatic Account of UN–Cuban Relations Since 1957* (New York: W. W. Norton, 1987), p. 173.

13. Smith, *The Closest of Enemies*, p. 174.

14. Quoted by Smith, *The Closest of Enemies*, p. 174.

15. Smith, *The Closest of Enemies*, pp. 174–175.

16. Smith, *The Closest of Enemies*, p. 176.

17. Gaddis Smith, *Morality, Reason, and Power*, p. 121.

18. *Cuadernos Americanos* (Mexico), 1980, p. 58.

19. Smith, *The Closest of Enemies*, p. 190.

20. Smith, *The Closest of Enemies*, p. 190.

Chapter Eleven

THE REAGAN ERA

A Chronicle of an Administration Foretold

No postwar president came into office with a worldview more emphatically announced than Ronald Reagan. Nobody could have had any doubt where he proposed to go or what his objectives were. In the 1980 presidential election campaign, Reagan forces accused the incumbent Carter Democrats of having mishandled everything, from causing a catastrophic erosion of US military and economic power to dangerously undermining the nation's strategic position in the hemisphere by helping the Sandinistas gain power in Nicaragua. At the root of the nation's problems, Reagan's campaign contended, were two factors: the administration's reluctance to "put US interests first" and its unwillingness to eliminate an excess of federal regulatory powers. All that Carter held dear was derided by the Reagan campaign: détente with the Soviet Union, arms control, nonintervention, improving social conditions in the developing world and, above all, human rights.

Central to the Reagan campaign's foreign policy framework was the conviction that the Soviet Union was the focal source of all regional trouble spots, be it Central America or the Middle East. In some of the bluntest language heard in Washington since John Foster Dulles, Reagan proclaimed his willingness both to threaten and to use military force to curb Soviet expansion. Portentously for Latin America, the GOP platform deplored "the Marxist Sandinista takeover of Nicaragua and the Marxist attempts to destabilize El Salvador, Guatemala and Honduras." It mattered less that military despots ruled in much of the hemisphere or that Argentina, Brazil and Mexico stood on the verge of bankruptcy, having accumulated the largest foreign debt in their history.

In fairness, Carter did not leave his successor with a particularly auspicious inheritance. In Latin America he achieved temporary acclaim for concluding a new Panama Canal treaty and taking an assertive stance on human rights. But relations with Argentina, Brazil, Chile and Mexico lay in shambles, while the Caribbean and Central America seethed with violence. At home, the public perception of vastly increased Soviet strength and a reduced confidence in the capacity of the United States to defend its strategic interests as evidenced by the crises in the Persian Gulf and Central America virtually cried for tough talk by the Reagan campaign.

Unprecedented participation in the 1980 election campaign by articulate conservative intellectuals who emerged as an influential ideological force in Republican ranks offered the possibility of a compelling political debate. They had the advantage of being able to challenge Carter's frequently incoherent and moralistic foreign policy objectives by applying realpolitik with sufficient intellectual rigor as to come up with some vital arguments. However, the debate quickly became perverted by extreme partisan rhetoric that led both Republicans and Democrats to distort the position of the other with such efficacy that they ended up painting themselves into corners they might not have chosen in more sober moments. Charges and countercharges were traded; pertinent issues such as the Latin American economic crisis and the region's struggle to recover democracy went begging, often leaving the field to the Christian right.

The intellectual foundation for the GOP assault against the Carter administration's Latin American policy was largely inspired by a heretofore little-known academic, Jeane Kirkpatrick, a political science professor at Georgetown University and senior fellow at the conservative American Enterprise Institute. In her article "Dictatorships and Double Standards," which appeared in the December 1979 issue of *Commentary* magazine, she held Carter's policy responsible for undermining the regimes of Somoza in Nicaragua and of the shah of Iran, and helping militant radicals come to power. Kirkpatrick also took issue with "the pervasive and mistaken assumption" that the United States could help induce democratic alternatives to established autocracies. She dismissed as "sentimentalism" any exceptional concern for human rights while the United States was locked in a mortal struggle with the forces of communism and often seemed more offended by those who denounced the horrors of torture and repression than by those who were responsible for them. The rise of the Sandinistas, she maintained, was the fault of those in the Carter administration who had fought with greatest zeal to protect freedom and democratic rights in Nicaragua and not the fault of the brutality and corruption of the Somoza regime.

With Kirkpatrick and such other neoconservative mandarins as Irving Kristol, Norman Podhoretz, Constantine Menges and George Will leading the onslaught, the Carter administration was held to be vacillating, inconsistent, too embroiled with such "peripheral" issues as apartheid, Third World poverty and with moralizing to foes and allies alike to focus on the principal challenge to Western civilization: Soviet communism. Human rights considerations, according to this argument, accounted for US failure to bolster the faltering regimes of the shah of Iran and President Anastasio Somoza of Nicaragua, leading to the humiliation the United States was subjected to by the radicals who took their place. Carter was also held to be responsible for alienating such "friendly" regimes as those of Argentina, Chile, El Salvador, Guatemala, South Africa and South Korea with a steady stream of public recriminations and foreign aid sanctions in reprisal for repressive policies listed in the catalogues of horrors issued by Carter's State Department, Amnesty International and other rights organizations. Finally, it was an issue stealthily fostered to undermine US resolve to stand up to communism. Combined with persistent suggestions about "leftist dupes" in high places infecting the Carter administration with revolutionary ideology, the campaign effectively revived the "soft on communism" charge of the 1950s draped in a more sophisticated political science rhetoric.

These views were long shared of course by the conspiratorial world of influential Latin American rightists, who had established close links to Senator Jesse Helms and the burgeoning right-wing US think tanks. They believed that Carter, like Kennedy before him, lent himself to an "international campaign" aimed at discrediting "traditional authoritarian regimes" with the connivance of leading "liberal" newspapers, leftist scholars and human rights militants and an assortment of liberal "dupes" they suggested were manipulated by Moscow and Havana. Indeed, there were people in the White House and in Congress, as epitomized by Senator Helms and aide Roger Fontaine, who subscribed to the crusade advocated by the military and the ultra-right in Latin America to advance "Christian values" and eradicate communism and other left-wing ideas, no matter how perverse the means might be.

Understandably, Reagan's victory was greeted with jubilation in the officers' messes and conservative salons across the hemisphere. But cheer as they may, there would be a limit to the US tolerance of the excesses of the more extreme Latin American military, no matter how blind Reagan might have been toward them. Once Congress and the public discovered how far removed their own democratic values were from the Latin American brand of rightism, there was little chance that they would indefinitely consent to helping regimes that consistently allowed torture and murder in the name of national security and empty promises of reform. Soon the issue of human rights would come up again, compelling the administration to change course.

Initially, however, the prominence of foreign affairs issues in the presidential campaign paved the way for a significant redirection of hemispheric policy. Sincere doubts among moderate Republicans and influential conservative Democrats about the viability of Carter's approach coexisted in expedient, if uneasy alliance with the shrill anticommunism of the so-called new right. At times, Reagan's hyperbolic language about Cuba, the Sandinistas in Nicaragua and the insurgents in El Salvador sounded as excessive as the speeches crafted by the John Birch Society. Indeed, by linking all revolts against injustice to communism and, conversely, by condoning state repression as a shield for democracy, Reagan foreshadowed a drastic rethinking of the foundations of Carter's Latin American policy.

On taking office, the Reagan administration lent weight to those expectations, reversing much of what Carter had set out to do—punish military regimes guilty of violating human rights, maintain a modicum of civilized contacts with Cuba and remain relatively open minded about the course of the Sandinista revolution. One of its first actions was to lift the sanctions that had been imposed by Carter on Argentina, Chile, Guatemala and El Salvador because of political and human rights abuses. US embassy officials in those countries insisted that Washington remained committed to human rights, and that the only change was a shift of tactics—from the Carter administration's activism to Reagan's "silent diplomacy." Very few believed it.

By the same token, when Secretary of State Alexander Haig announced soon after taking office that in the new foreign policy "international terrorism will take the place of human rights in our concern," he served notice that tough talk would from now on be reserved for Soviet totalitarianism and not wasted on rhetoric that would alienate "friendly autocrats," such as the Argentine and Guatemalan military regimes. Nor would a dubious human rights record be allowed to stand in the way of Reagan's plans to provide generous military support to the military autocrats of Argentina, El Salvador and Guatemala, as long as they pledged to fight communism. To do this, Washington had to free itself from the restraints of the multilateralism required by the treaties and conventions of the Organization of American States (OAS) in order to pursue an unfettered unilateral policy whenever it deemed that was required to defend "national security."

It often seemed that for Reagan, Latin America symbolized the restoration of US self-affirmation, of the redemption of a proud heritage the Republicans blamed Carter for dissipating. Not since Roosevelt and Kennedy was Latin America as an issue projected as being so central for United States national security. The critical difference under Reagan, of course, was that while Roosevelt and Kennedy held up hemispheric relations as an intrinsic value and as an example to the world of peaceful cooperation and friendship, Reagan's driving force was to use Latin America as a means to dramatize the peril of communism and its implications for the national security of the United States.

Like Richard Nixon, whom he admired, Reagan had an instinctive interest in Latin America, perhaps engraved in his memory from the Roosevelt years when he was a Democrat. His goal was to persuade the neighbor republics to accept a kind of "older brother" relationship. Fundamentally, his policy wound up being influenced by economic rather than altruistic motives. As a "big business" Republican, the president was apprehensive about the debt and gave Treasury Secretary Baker a free hand to find ways of exorcising the specter of countries like Mexico, Brazil and Argentina from forming a debtor cartel. Taking a page out of the Nixon strategy, the administration sought to dislodge Brazil from the others by forming closer financial and commercial ties.

Perhaps the most positive idea put forward by the Reagan camp during the election campaign was the creation of a North American common market with Mexico and Canada. The plan for a treaty was dropped in a matter of months, after the State Department persuaded the White House staff that there was too much opposition in both neighboring countries and Congress, though President Bush would resurrect it in 1991 as the North American Free Trade Agreement (NAFTA). Nonetheless, early in his administration, Reagan moved toward a policy of political rapprochement with Canada and Mexico. During his first meeting with President José Lopez Portillo, at Ciudad Juarez in January 1981, Reagan assured the Mexican leader that his views would increasingly be taken into account, in recognition that "we have a shared interest in a peaceful solution of the region." The president also promised that Mexico, Venezuela, Costa Rica and Colombia would be "consulted" in the search for political solutions—a purely rhetorical attempt to placate Mexico's critical stand toward his Central American policies, which he had no intention of changing.

The rapid deterioration in relations between the United States and Nicaragua, the military assistance provided to the Salvadoran army, irritating differences with Mexico and a manifest propensity for ignoring the region's paramount multilateral forum, the Organization of American States, were some of the factors that gave a particularly bleak and discouraging appearance to the Reagan administration's conduct of hemisphere relations. Even a Congress that was usually indifferent to foreign policy issues became alarmed over how Reagan's covert war against the Sandinistas was bringing about increasingly severe domestic and foreign criticism, culminating with the World Court condemnation of the use of the CIA in the mining of Nicaraguan ports.

REAGAN'S THREE
LATIN AMERICAN CONUNDRUMS

The Reagan administration's policy toward Latin America was characterized at the start by three features. First, it focused obsessively on a single issue and a single contingency—the threat of the expansion of Soviet-Cuban influence, particularly in El Salvador and Nicaragua—and a vehement desire to roll it back. Second, it sought to replace Carter's emphasis on human rights with a renewed emphasis on counterinsurgency, both overt and covert, across the hemisphere and on a close relationship with the Latin American military. Third, viewing inter-American multilateralism as a hindrance to US interests, it moved resolutely to assert its right to unilateral action.

Central America provided an early test of the new administration's foreign policy aptitude, both in style and consistency. It also began inauspiciously with several drearily familiar episodes relating to human rights. It might still be recalled how during his confirmation hearings before the Senate Foreign Relations Committee, Haig sought so desperately to justify the repressive record of the Salvadoran military that he wound up making light of the brutal murder of four US religious workers. Similar embarrassment was caused by Washington's determination to ignore the human rights violations occurring in Argentina and Chile. In El Salvador, the administration spurned negotiations with the opposition, discounting prevailing anticolonialist, nonaligned tendencies within both civilian and guerrilla organizations.

Eventually the administration's Central American policy fell into a kind of splendid disarray, plagued by the divided councils of the State Department on the one hand, and the White House and the National Security Council on the other. Central to the success of the latter was the Cuban American National Foundation, which was the most effective lobby in Washington among the otherwise diffuse Hispanic groups. Dedicated to the single-minded purpose of overthrowing the Castro regime, it coincided with the goals of Reagan's hardliners of subordinating all other objectives in the region to the eradication of communism.

Shortly before retiring, Secretary of State George P. Schultz, in an interview to the *New York Times*, was not reluctant to give high marks to the administration's overall foreign policy performance, from improved relations with Moscow to virtually every area in the world—with one exception: Central America. In an unusually candid admission, Schultz characterized the state of affairs as "very depressing" and a "tortured experience." It was the only segment of the interview where Schultz indicated that he thought the United

States might have done better with a different approach.[1] Though he had defended Reagan's tough policy toward the Sandinistas, it was well known in Washington that right-wing officials, including White House national security advisers who wanted the "Contras" to seize power, had pressed the administration to avoid any diplomatic compromise.

Whether the Central American republics, for decades the scene of ghastly brutality, rigged elections and military coups, represented an appropriate test case for the administration's belief in the paramountcy of military solutions for the region raised doubts not only among its critics but also among top civilian and military officials of the Pentagon. These officials worried that less than a decade away from Vietnam, the public was far from ready to endorse new military adventures abroad.

Soon the Reagan administration encountered a small but restless opposition in Congress to its proposed militarization of the Salvadoran crisis as well as reservations from many of its allies, including Canada, Mexico, Colombia, Venezuela and key European countries such as France, Spain, West Germany and Italy. By 1983, unable to reconcile itself to the fact that its Central American policy had neither popular support nor the backing of Congress, Reagan appointed a bipartisan commission headed by Henry A. Kissinger to study the whole gamut of Central American problems, accompanied by a blaze of publicity in the hope of recovering bipartisan consensus in time for the upcoming presidential elections. The travels and hearings of the commission and a proliferation of background briefings orchestrated by the White House guaranteed public attention would continue to be focused on Central America when, in fact, a tremendous accumulation of events happening elsewhere in the hemisphere was waiting to be understood.

One of the practical effects of the Kissinger commission was a return, if ever so tentative, to a more balanced approach, combining military assistance with economic aid and continued support for social reforms. The result was the Caribbean Basin Initiative, a tax-incentive investment program largely coordinated by Puerto Rico. After a slow start, it showed significant financial and political successes, becoming a long-range catalyst for regional investments and trade. Ultimately, however, democratic revival in South America gained importance as a force that could moderate the Reagan administration's more aggressive impulses. In turn, however, the Latin American political negotiating position was hampered by a portentously ballooning foreign debt, especially in the case of the heavy players—Argentina, Brazil and Mexico.

The prevailing mood at the end of Reagan's first term suggested greater division between Washington and Latin America than at any time since the 1950s.

It now seems obvious that Washington's increasingly imperious unilateralism was helping propel an independent Latin American position in international policy backed by Spain and certain West European governments.

The Latin American stand offered a determined challenge to the obsolete but still obtrusive Monroe Doctrine, dusted off by men in Washington with the patronizing theory that the whole of the American continent was the backyard of the United States. Commenting on the diverse signals emanating from Reagan's State Department and the White House, Flora Lewis, a *New York Times* foreign affairs analyst, wrote at the time, "It's hard to remember when there was more confusion in the world about the signals sent from Washington."

By early 1984, the Reagan administration realized that its Latin American section at the State Department had so fallen into disrepute, both in Congress and with the Latin American chancelleries, that it was compelled to call home Harry Shlaudeman, who was serving as ambassador to Argentina. The presence of Shlaudeman, who eventually became coordinator of the Kissinger Commission, thus provided a reassuring face to the Latin American governments and the members of the congressional foreign relations committees.

An early embarrassment was the peremptory dismissal of Robert White, US ambassador to El Salvador, a career foreign service officer. Appalled by an abundance of evidence linking right-wing paramilitary death squads to the assassination of scores of moderate and leftist political leaders, including four US nuns, White spoke out publicly in favor of halting further military aid until the culprits were found and prosecuted. For his stand, White, a veteran diplomat who had played a major role in bolstering Christian Democratic President Jose Napoleon Duarte against radicals of the left and right, was summarily removed from his post and subsequently forced to resign from the foreign service. It went almost unnoticed that his successor, Deane Hinton, soon reached similar conclusions—that as long as the dismal human rights record of the Salvadoran security forces was not corrected the government could not establish a credible argument for its democratic intentions.

The White dismissal was a revealing example of how those in Washington who seek to apply broad ideological concepts and model solutions to all problems, wherever they occur, would collide with the empirical observations and practical arguments of those who are concerned with the particulars of the case. Meanwhile, the unsolved murders of US citizens and the continued civilian killings in El Salvador caused many to question the emphatic US backing for the government there. There is no denying the horror of these incidents, and the Reagan administration repeatedly insisted it had cautioned the Salvadoran authorities that the incidents were unacceptable. These rhetorical warnings were glaringly contradicted, however, by an uninterrupted flow of military aid and close relations between the intelligence and military officials of the two countries and the close relations between the Salvadoran military and US intelligence and counterinsurgency specialists. US military assistance, which had been completely cut off in 1977, was partially restored by Carter— to the tune of $10 million—and would be tripled by the end of the first year of the Reagan administration; Haig also instituted a program of military advisers to help train the Salvadoran military in counterinsurgency tactics. Consequently the Salvadoran authorities learned to doubt the seriousness of Washington's admonitions. But for too long the deception was accepted by much of the US media and Congress.

However, repudiating the errors or failures of the previous administration was hardly enough to assure wisdom and success in defining and implementing a new policy. More significant, however, seemed to be the public perception that the radical measures propounded by Reagan's conservative ideologies, contrasted with their portentous tolerance of right-wing dictators and disregard in hemispheric relations for the same human rights considerations used to anathemize the Soviet Union, were inimical to the national values of the United States. Finally, in Latin America at least, the conflict in El Salvador looked like a genuine civil war and not a communist conspiracy.[2]

FROM THE MEKONG DELTA TO
NICARAGUA AND EL SALVADOR
(OR THE PERIL OF SCOFFING AT HUMAN RIGHTS)

The Reagan administration, determined to prove President Carter wrongheaded for applying human rights sanctions against military dictators, swiftly resumed aid to military dictatorships, euphemistically renamed "friendly authoritarians." So zealously did the new administration set out to implement Jeane Kirkpatrick's admonition to formulate "a morally and strategically acceptable, and politically realistic" program for dealing with nondemocratic governments supposedly threatened by Soviet-sponsored subversion that, to its great embarrassment, it wound up painting itself into a corner along with such nasty allies as the Argentine, Guatemalan and Salvadoran generals.[3] Soon it would have to pay the consequence for ideological overreach as the military clients predictably proved to be unmanageable.

Barely a month after Reagan's inauguration, Undersecretary of State James Buckley went before the Senate Foreign Relations Committee to request lifting the legislative ban enacted under Carter on US military assistance to the generals in Argentina. Two months later the administration's sanguine hopes for the usefulness of its flexible new human rights criteria received a chilling denial. Significantly, the administration combined the shakeup with an announcement that it would send 100 military advisers to a new base in Honduras to train 2,400 troops from El Salvador. Yet all along, Haig's successor, George Schultz, the new secretary of state, insisted that "we will not, repeat not, Americanize the conflict there." However, by 1983, as the Reagan administration was preparing for reelection, the position was far less clear. A broader, retrospective analysis suggests that a different course had to be steered, allowing pragmatism to seep back into the policymaking mainstream of both the White House and the State Department.

Just as during the Carter years, the specter of Vietnam was invoked by policymakers, critics and the media alike. Indeed, given the composition of the team directly in charge of implementing Central American policy, it was easy to conclude that much of the Reagan administration's basic thinking about the regional conflict, and its distortions, was a direct product of Washington's Indochina experience, as many of the key officials charged with implementing policy had made their careers either in Vietnam or Cambodia. They ranged from Assistant Secretary of State Thomas O. Enders, the former ambassador to Cambodia, and Office of Central American Affairs Director Craig Johnstone in Washington, to ambassador John D. Negroponte, to his deputy chief of mission, to his political officer. All had made their reputations in Southeast Asia during and after the war. Some old Latin American hands in the department suggested this "gang that blew Vietnam" was trying to correct the mistakes of the Mekong Delta in the hills of Honduras and Nicaragua.

Even some of Washington's closest allies were weary of the possible fallacies that can come from misapplied analogies. "What my country doesn't want, is the Vietnamization of Central America," warned Edgardo Paz Barnica, Honduran foreign minister.[4] And yet as soon as these Indochina veterans, notably Enders, talked about negotiations or diplomatic rather than military solutions, they were denounced by the hard-liners on the National Security Council and the CIA as "cookie pushers" and eventually shoved aside. Meanwhile, the unsolved murders of United States citizens and the continued killing of civilians in El Salvador caused many to question US backing for the government there.

Confronted with incontrovertible evidence of the horror of these incidents, no further evasion seemed possible and the Reagan administration time and again claimed it had informed the Salvadoran authorities that the incidents were unacceptable. As has been said, these warnings were contradicted, however, by an uninterrupted flow of military aid and close relations between the intelligence and military officials of the two countries and the close relations between the Salvadoran military and US intelligence and counterinsurgency specialists; the result was that the Salvadoran authorities no longer believed in the seriousness of the warnings by administration critics.

Yet the administration, determined to prevail, defended its policy with the argument that there "has been progress" in the observance of human rights and that there would be more if the Salvadoran security forces were not faced with guerrilla provocation. When the administration finally admitted that there had actually been little or no progress, it launched one of those diversionary tactics at which it was becoming increasingly adept. The point, it argued, was that the Salvadoran government wanted not only to eliminate human rights abuses but also to implement land reform and take other steps to promote long-term economic and social progress.

The trouble was that the administration's insistently optimistic assessments and communiqués bred excessive expectations for early solutions. To assuage congressional critics, Reagan appointed a series of "mediators"—Richard Stone, a former Democratic senator from Florida, and Harry Shlaudeman and William Habib, two veteran diplomats, ostensibly with the mission to find a peaceful solution to the Central American conflict. In Habib, a consummate negotiator, some White House staffers may not have known they were getting an inveterate problem solver who took his mission in utmost earnest and could be relied on to find ways to make agreement possible. Not surprisingly, from the outset Habib found himself on a short leash; not only did his instructions give him little room for maneuver, but it soon became obvious that Reagan wanted no solution short of the complete capitulation of the Sandinistas in the case of Nicaragua and of the guerrillas in El Salvador. After resigning out of frustration, Habib all but acknowledged what had become manifest—that neither the White House nor the State Department had any patience left for dialogue, that they were too quick to jump to forceful solutions when what was needed was better understanding of the issues at stake outside of their superimposed East–West context.

In the end, the statesmanship of the Contadora nations and the Group of Eight, later known as the Group of Rio, stepped into the breach at the critical moment, and the errors of judgment and tactics of the Sandinistas enabled the outgoing Reagan administration to hand a relatively viable situation to President Bush and his team at the beginning of 1989. In another colossal blunder, the Reagan administration's clumsy, futile efforts to force the resignation of General Manuel Noriega, Washington's once-trusted ally, as head of Panama's defense forces by imposing an economic boycott on the tiny republic further deepened the disillusion with US policies.

An even more glaring example of what can happen when political expedience and considerations extrinsic to a region's interests are reflexively applied for ideological reasons was the Reagan administration's unfortunate flirtation with the Argentine military. Deaf to criticisms by human rights groups, the Reagan administration enlisted the Argentine junta for its crusade in Central America. With the administration's blessing, Argentine mercenaries joined Honduran troops and former Nicaraguan National Guard members in harassing the Sandinista government while regular Argentine army officers were sent to train Salvadorans in counterinsurgency techniques. This was an extraordinary step by the Argentine rulers, considering not only the country's long tradition of neutrality in foreign policy but especially the perennial indifference the country had exhibited in the past toward Central America.

Independent observers, however, believed that this outside intervention only strengthened the pro-Soviet Sandinista leaders, who were thus able to coopt Nicaraguan nationalist sentiment and attack not only the "Contras" but also the democratic opposition as traitors. Meanwhile, the Argentines turned out to be feckless allies for Washington; even before the Malvinas/Falklands war of 1982, Argentina's military was exchanging Soviet arms for wheat. Indeed, under the junta, Argentina became Moscow's leading trade partner in the developing world and in international forums the Soviet Union tenaciously blocked discussion of Argentine human rights violations. The Argentine–Soviet rapprochement reached such proportions that Antonio Cafiero, a former Peronist minister of economics, accused the junta's policies of creating structural dependence on Moscow. As the nation and its allies found out, ideological posturing encourages exaggeration and risks distortion, especially when each local crisis is deliberately turned into an East–West crisis involving the superpowers.

To the dismay of the new Reagan team, just as the new policy was being tested, the Alfred A. Knopf publishing house began to circulate galley proofs of a work by Jacobo Timerman, an Argentine newspaper editor who had achieved worldwide attention for his imprisonment and torture at the hands of Argentina's military rulers. Timerman was freed and expelled from the country after considerable pressure on his behalf by the Carter administration, several members of Congress, and the Israeli government. His book, *Prisoner Without a Name, Cell Without a Number*, gave a vivid testimony of his experience in the junta's prisons and the anti-Semitism displayed by his torturers.

Thus much of the US public learned for the first time what many Latin Americans had long endured as a rationale for the bizarre scenario painted by some of the ideological proponents of the "national security" doctrine, but most forcefully advanced by the Argentines: that they were fighting the West's first battle of World War III by cleansing the hemisphere of radicals tied to a vast international Soviet–Zionist conspiracy. Such an endeavor, the military argued, required draconian methods, for it could never be successful abiding by democratic practices.

Accordingly, while Central America at times looked like a tragic, insoluble maze, a more surprising situation awaited Reagan's decision to embrace Argentina's military rulers. Argentina's junta had been a particular target of the opprobrium of Carter's human rights activists, especially the State Department's Pat Derian, so that it became a highly risky, and ultimately ill-advised, test for the redemptive Kirkpatrick approach toward "traditional autocracies." Unaccustomed as they were to dealing with the sometimes mercurial Argentine behavior, Reagan officials discovered that their theoretical assumptions about "friendly autocrats" were way off the mark. That was established by the dramatic 1982 invasion and seizure of the Falkland/Malvinas islands by Argentine troops and their subsequent recapture by the British navy, after considerable losses of lives on both sides, derailed what Reagan foreign policy specialists expected to be a quick smoothing of relations with Buenos Aires. In many ways, indeed, this period must be counted as a low-water mark in the conduct of inter-American policy.

For its part, the Argentine military junta felt betrayed by a Reagan administration it thought would at least remain neutral, if for no other reason than a tacit recognition of the junta's quiet assistance in helping train the military in El Salvador and the Contras in Honduras. Most Argentines, however, were less hurt by Washington's action than by the support Britain received from all of the other countries of the European community, with the sole exception of Italy, who joined in an economic boycott of Argentina.

By contrast, the Organization of American States voted overwhelmingly to condemn Britain. With that, Argentina's long-cherished dream of being the lone repository of European civilization in South America was shattered, and the Argentines suddenly discovered a new and vital sense of identity in feeling as one with the other Latin American peoples. On the diplomatic front, what Washington strategists like to call a worst-case scenario had come to pass: forced to choose between its European and Latin American alliance, the United States resolutely sided with the former. The OAS stood by helplessly. (Another lesson of the South Atlantic war was that serious negotiation could not be entrusted to the machinery of the OAS, for it was likely to break down in a world crisis. The real victors were the unilateralists, as well as some Pentagon officials and exponents of military thinking who had never believed in the regional organization in the first place.)

This was the situation that greeted Argentina, Brazil and Uruguay just as those countries experienced the return of civilian governments. Along with

Colombia, Peru and Venezuela, they generated a new momentum in Latin American diplomacy to counteract US policies they felt were inimical to the long-range interests of the region. It clearly contributed to a shift in continental strategies: the formation of subregional blocs and a sudden warming of the personal relationship among Latin America's heads of state that would soon lead to a more informal style of diplomacy of considerable effectiveness.

In short, the Falklands/Malvinas war and the Timerman testimony stimulated a backlash in Congress, spurred by Senators Edward Kennedy and Christopher Dodd, against the State Department's attempts to justify removing human rights sanctions against Argentina on the grounds spelled out by Jean Kirkpatrick—that "traditional authoritarian" regimes are less repressive than "communist totalitarians." Having added fuel to the fire, Timerman clearly contributed to the first defeat of the administration's new human rights policy when the Senate Foreign Relations Committee voted 13–4 against Ernest K. Lefever, the president's nominee for the post of assistant secretary of state for human affairs. Lefever, a colleague of Kirkpatrick's at Georgetown University, had told the committee that he knew of only one flagrant human rights violator—the Soviet Union. The nomination was subsequently withdrawn. Two months later, Undersecretary of State Walter J. Stoessel assured Congress that the administration would continue to oppose human rights violations, whether by ally or adversary, and that the administration would reject a policy of selective indignation.

It should have been clear from the outset that a theoretical scheme constructed in such absolute terms, invoking "systemic differences" to justify greater forbearance for anticommunist autocrats, was almost certain to arouse not only an angry reaction from Democrats but unease among powerful moderate Republicans unwilling to consider the traditional revulsion against tyranny to be a liberal monopoly. Clearly more was at stake than the operational validity of a political theory or relations with Argentina and other "traditional authoritarians." First, it offered a dramatic practical illustration of how, by disregarding democratic institutions and legal methods in the name of fighting subversion, a state can easily slide into the moral anarchy of unrestrained repression—whether it is called authoritarianism or totalitarianism. Second, Timerman's revelations about the endemic anti-Semitism in the ranks of Argentina's so-called friendly authoritarians challenged some simplistic neoconservative propositions (that the Latin American military supported Israel while the left was pro-Arab) and posed extremely delicate questions for many Jewish neoconservatives who played a prominent part in defining and propagating the creed of neoconservatism as the Reagan administration's official ideology.

One can always overstate a position in such a way that it can be attacked as a myth, the sociologist Nathan Glazer noted,[5] and one can overstate the counterposition in such a way that it becomes a myth too. If Carter boxed himself in with the observance of human rights across the globe, often without the necessary leverage provided by an effectively structured and articulated foreign policy, then Reagan ideologues who seized on human rights as the embodiment of leftist subversion also came perilously close to their own dead end. But reality has a way of tempering zeal, even for the resolutely ideological Reagan administration.

Indeed, it was not long before the administration had to adjust to a more moderate interpretation of policy or else pay dearly for attempting to devalue a fundamental principle that was implanted in the Bill of Rights by the founding fathers and that was also a preeminent weapon in the psychological arsenal against communism: the observance of human rights. Just as in his relations with Moscow, Reagan was able to make an about turn from rigid hostility to an emotional cordiality, on human rights he ended up a virtual missionary— but only in the wake of the defenestration of the military by a tide of democratic upheavals across the hemisphere. Administration policymakers such as Elliot Abrams, Enders's successor, called it realpolitik, bending with the punches; others branded it cynical opportunism.

THE PERILS OF UNILATERALISM

From the Latin American viewpoint, one of the Reagan administration's most regressive features, and one that put in question the wisdom of US leadership, was a cavalier disregard for the rules guiding inter-American relations. The primary disregard was for the Charter of the Organization of American States with its provisions calling for multilateral consultations, the peaceful resolution of disputes and the ban on unilateral intervention. Certainly the notion of Washington "going it alone" did not sit well with the other members of the inter-American alliance. Nor did the Latin Americans, who did not share Washington's habit of viewing every problem through the lens of East–West confrontation, appreciate being treated as props against the background of Washington's showdown with communism. If the purpose of tossing aside the self-limiting provisions of the OAS charter on such sensitive matters as intervention and human rights (on the grounds of national security) was to instill fear in the foes of the United States, what it clearly accomplished was to distress its friends whose democracies relied on the rule of law.

Other complex, sometimes convoluted issues were dealt with on the ideological front. Clearly the question of whether a revolutionary regime will steer toward democracy or dictatorship was intertwined with thinking about intervention, whether through economic or military means. But there were divergent visions about this problem in Latin America and Washington. In Latin America, the major objection to intervention was not merely a matter of legal principle but the fact that it had often tended to advance the repressive alternatives, the loss of freedom, it ostensibly sought to forestall. It was not long before the administration, prodded by relentless congressional pressure and its failure to win a public consensus for its Central American policy, was forced into a tactical retreat. Even before Reagan moved to bring Henry A. Kissinger back to the scene by appointing him head of a bipartisan commission to reexamine Washington's policy in the region, it was compelled to recognize that protection of human rights and the improvement of economic and social conditions had to be reintegrated into the formulation of Latin American policy. Such an evolution was all too predictable.

Before Reagan's first term was over, the festering Central American violence and Washington's intransigent position toward the kind of political negotiation propitiated by Costa Rica and the other Contadora countries, together with its dramatic support of Britain in the Falkland/Malvinas war and the invasion of Grenada, suggested to many that the inter-American system had been nullified by the US global interests. However, the century-old system once again proved to be more resilient than expected. Its interment had been predicted at the time of the CIA's covert operation in Guatemala in 1954 and again when it sponsored Cuban exiles in the Bay of Pigs invasion. Still, the aggregate of Reagan's unilateral moves provided an irresistible target for his critics.

A GOODWILL TOUR THAT
REQUIRES DAMAGE CONTROL

President Reagan's first direct exposure to Latin America beyond Mexico came in a hastily arranged tour in December 1982, half a year after the region was shaken by Washington's support of Britain in the Falklands/Malvinas war. It was one of those whirlwind trips US presidents have become famous for—and the subject of satire in the Latin American media. In five days, Reagan visited Brazil, Colombia, El Salvador and Honduras and met with six heads of state. The administration clearly felt that a presidential trip was one way of making the best of an embarrassing situation. The attempt to ingratiate itself with the new Argentine rulers after its flirtation with the military while pressing ahead with its central goal, a military victory, if necessary, in Central America, brought mixed results.

While Reagan succeeded in developing a warm friendship with General João Baptista Figuerido, Brazil's de facto head of state, the president became the object of merciless ridicule in the Brazilian press for "misspeaking" his toast at a state dinner celebrating "the people of Bolivia" instead of Brazil. Later that evening Reagan compounded the error by explaining to the Brazilian chief of protocol that Bolivia had slipped into his remarks inadvertently "because that's where we're going next."[6] In fact, the next stop was Colombia.

The idea for the trip came from his new secretary of state, George P. Schultz, who had succeeded General Haig. Schultz, who had served on Nixon's cabinet, remembered Nixon's conviction that Brazil was central to US interests and was particularly eager to improve relations with that country. Moreover, Schultz wanted to bring some balance to what he suspected had come to be a skewed emphasis on Central America by extending the itinerary to include Brazil and Colombia as well as Costa Rica and Honduras as the focus of the whirlwind visit.

The closing phase of the goodwill tour, Reagan's eight-hour visit to Colombia, was marred by a tense encounter with President Belisario Betancur, who indulged in his characteristically outspoken criticism of Washington's Central American policy. Having been alerted of the Colombian president's remarks in advance, several Reagan aides proposed to overfly Bogota and proceed to the next stop, Costa Rica, but Reagan insisted in sticking to the schedule. It seems that nobody in the presidential entourage had alerted the president to the fact that Betancur, a progressive conservative, enjoyed wide popularity in Latin America, where no leader could match his eloquence, his grasp of inter-American relations or his intellectual energy. Hence the Bogota meeting turned out to be a sadly missed opportunity for a thoughtful dialogue.

Nevertheless, President Reagan returned to Washington, proclaiming "a successful trip." But after the stops in Bogota and San José, after the discomfort of his misstatements in Brasilia and the friction with Betancur, after the stalemate in the Central American conflict refused to yield, Latin Americans suddenly seemed to be paying less attention to US policy in the region than to their own. Aside from the president and a few White House reporters, there was little consensus that Reagan had swept triumphantly through the hemisphere.

DEMOCRACY SURPRISES WASHINGTON

The White House had to retreat from its ideological policies, confronted by the ineluctable challenge of how to manage change. When dictators fell one after another, in some cases out of incompetence and overreach, in others because of popular revulsion, the administration, to its credit, began to shift gears, at first imperceptibly—beginning with the restoration of human rights as a standard for good relations with Washington. By 1983 the observance of human rights once again emerged as a major criterion on which the United States made economic and military aid available to a neighbor republic. Even the hard-liner Elliot Abrams, making his last speech as assistant secretary of state for Inter-American affairs on January 13, 1989, was compelled to speak out on behalf of a more militant human rights policy.

The fact is that the ultra-right position advocated earlier by Abrams and other neoconservative ideologues was so far removed from traditional US policy it had no chance to survive. It seemed that Reagan's initial purpose was simply to undo "accommodating" Carter policies in the region and to reassert the primacy of the United States. All of this, simply to keep out communism, and, wherever possible, the liberal center as well. Instead of pursuing a policy that made human rights paramount, Haig and Kirkpatrick promoted the notion that the United States had to eradicate "communist terrorism" first—suggesting that the major hemisphere power was not capable of pursuing both goals at once. The new team in Washington had chosen—only temporarily as it turned out—the ultra-right as its natural ally in the name of national security.

The shift back to human rights was paired with demonstrations of greater flexibility in other orthodox Reagan positions: the easing of conditions to the enormous Latin American repayment schedule of a record debt load approaching $400 billion, and partial acceptance of the Latin American thesis that the United States must carry its share of responsibility for the burgeoning drug epidemic as the world's primary consumer of illegal drugs.

In Latin America, the advent of a new generation of democratic leaders in 1983 began a veritable carousel of bilateral and subregional summit meetings. This postwar generation was united by a common detestation of dictatorship and a striving to modernize obsolescent political institutions. The new reformers included Raúl Alfonsín in Argentina, Jose Sarney in Brazil and Julio María Sanguinetti in Uruguay, as well as Betancur in Colombia, Vinicio Cerezo in Guatemala, Oscar Arias in Costa Rica and Miguel de la Madrid in Mexico. While the conditions were not yet entirely propitious for a revival of the idea of Latin American integration, a renewed spirit of cooperation in foreign policy and on economic issues seemed to be gathering an irresistible momentum.

A primary political objective of these leaders was to find a peaceful solution to the Central American crisis and stem what they believed to be President Reagan's temptation to move in militarily. They were reacting as their ancestors did seventy-five years earlier to the corollary attached to the Monroe Doctrine by President Theodore Roosevelt to give Washington carte blanche to stage incursions into other republics in the event that he considered those governments to be in default of their constitutional obligations. They were also taking a new look at regional arrangements to find a path away from an inter-American system in which the United States held preeminent sway. But even within the administration, many Defense Department officials had become quite outspoken in their opposition to the hawkish posture of some of the administration's civilians in regard to Central America.

By 1985, one of the most experienced US military officers made an unusual public statement. On the eve of his retirement as commander of army and air force combat forces in the United States, General Wallace H. Nutting deplored talk about a possible invasion of Nicaragua, arguing instead for reform in language that recalled the rhetoric of the Alliance for Progress. "When we treat such regimes, from the outset, as delinquents, and try to 'destabilize' or starve them," he said, "we foster both unnecessary hostility and the kind of internal reaction that strengthens extremism, paranoia and repression."

Considering that the United States "have learned to live with Cuba for 25 years," he observed,

> instead of worrying about invading Nicaragua and throwing out the Sandinistas we should concentrate on developing the hemispheric idea of coalition, building strength through political reform and economic development in the surrounding countries. There is a strong urge for democracy all over Latin America. The military today in Latin America really are, I think, exhibiting a social conscience and acknowledge a need to change. If we don't support them, they won't make it.[7]

Nutting pointedly criticized those who talked lightly about an invasion, cautioning that overthrowing the Sandinistas would be "a major operation" requiring "multiple divisions and air support and sea support to go along with it." Ultimately, he observed, "maybe Nicaragua and Cuba, if they see everybody else better off than we are, then perhaps internal movements will generate and the problem will solve itself."

IDEOLOGICAL CERTAINTIES
VERSUS TRIAL AND ERROR

For all the early lurching, the Reagan administration scored no palpable political gains in the hemisphere other than scoring points with the right at home and abroad. It did not, however, serve the national interest, as it would soon discover. Having replicated many of the Cold War paradigms of the 1950s, when the Eisenhower administration could suborn right-wing dictators and keep them in the US camp, the 1980s confronted Reagan with the new realities spawned by the blurring of the East–West divide. Since the mid-1970s, Washington had to face increasing opposition of right-wing governments not only on human rights but also on such strategically significant issues as nuclear technology and arms sales—the kind of loss that in CIA jargon would become known as blowback.

In addition to the Argentine turnaround in the South Atlantic war, when the United States refused to sell Brazil a nuclear reactor, the military-dominated Brazilian regime signed a deal with a West German company, over Washington's public protest. Likewise, the Guatemalan military turned to France and Middle East suppliers when Washington halted military assistance because of that country's dismal human rights record. And on more than one occasion the Reagan administration endured the Salvadoran army high command thumbing its nose at its representatives. One bright spot during these years was that the Reagan foreign policy team was exposed to the sobering experience of learning by trial and error. Moreover, the political price of failed policies to the more fundamental strategic interests of the United States in relations with its European allies was disproportionately steep. For example, the shock waves generated by the human rights controversy further unsettled the already fragile consensus in NATO and Western Europe.

Hence, the decade of the 1980s may well be remembered as a watershed in this country's relations with Latin America. As with all watersheds, the topography is blurred, but the rough outlines emerge clearly. It was a little noticed conference in Caracas in the summer of 1986 that put the era in perspective. The event was the Ibero-American conference on the commemoration of the 500th anniversary of the Columbus voyage to the Americas. One of the items on the agenda was a request by the Christopher Columbus Quincentenary Jubilee Commission to become a full member of the "Iberoamerican" conference. In a semantic sleight of hand, the Spaniards thought that by calling it Iberoamerican they could confine the conference to Spanish-speaking republics of the New World and legitimately exclude the United States and other non-Hispanic countries of the Western Hemisphere. One glaring technical error was to set a precedent that broke the language criterion—to admit Haiti to full membership.

Mexico and Venezuela were the most vocal opponents to US membership, along with Panama, which was entering a grueling dispute with the United States at the time. The excuses and rationalizations to keep the United States out of its own hemisphere were a smokescreen to conceal what everybody knew—a deep-seated resentment with the Reagan administration's high-handed dealings in the hemisphere.

As the United States approached its fifty-first election, the inter-American outlook was more depressing than it had been since the dark and violence-ridden year of 1958. But unlike 1958, when Brazil rallied so many other states around Operation Pan America, in 1988, the Latin American leadership was politically paralyzed by a heavy debt burden. The fact that neither the new Bush administration nor the Nicaraguan junta reverted to the Cold War postures of Reagan and Ortega intimated that once the uneasy transition phase passed, it might be possible for the new US administration to take up again the inter-American ties that had been broken. The real question was whether the beginning of a Bush administration would see further progress in US–Soviet relations lead not merely to a wider East–West détente but also to a relaxation of tensions in the complex field of inter-American relations.

Previous administrations had not always been responsive to the urgency of the Latin American situation, but they rarely denied the existence of those problems or suggested that they could be willed away without major US support. The hemispheric version of "Reaganomics" seemed to do just that. Whenever possible, the Reagan administration pretended that change, especially revolutionary change, was not really inevitable; when change was undeniable, such as the popular repudiation of the military regimes of Argentina and Uruguay in the early 1980s and later in Chile and Haiti toward the end of its second term, it sought to take credit for the shift.

The peaceful removal of president "Baby Doc" Duvalier in Haiti and Ferdinand Marcos in the Philippines early in 1986, roughly at the midpoint of Reagan's second term, had far-reaching significance for US policy toward Latin America. It consolidated the inevitable shift away from the Kirkpatrick doctrine differentiating left-wing from right-wing dictators and led to a formal proclamation of support for "democratic revolution" and human rights.

The proclamation, contained in Reagan's March 14 message to Congress, seemed at first glance to restore the more balanced approach to human rights conforming to a humanitarian tradition in US policy, declaring that "the American people believe in human rights and oppose tyranny in whatever form, whether of the left or the right." This was in sharp contrast to Reagan's thundering denunciation of left-wing despots in Latin America while shamelessly courting the military as defenders of freedom during the first term of his administration.

Reagan had never before made such a statement, which sounded like something honed by the Carter White House. It reflected something more than a "shift of emphasis," which is how Elliot Abrams characterized the new position.

Administration officials had provided the text to major newspapers a day in advance of the message to Congress because, according to the *New York Times*, "the White House wanted to call attention to its newness and importance." However, some US observers as well as numerous Latin American diplomats were wary; they feared that overt pressure, even on behalf of democracy, constituted a dangerous precedent. According to Leslie H. Gelb, the *Times* national security correspondent and former State Department official,

> There would be no more double standard, it seemed to say on human rights, in tolerating dictatorships of the right but not of the left. And yet, this message is seen by many Administration diplomats as well as critics as being packed with pitfalls: in confusing anti-Communists with democrats in fogging over profound differences between political revolution and socioeconomic revolution; and in possibly misusing human rights as a cover for covert military aid without a clear sense of policy.[8]

Gelb contended that the success of the US role in distancing itself from Marcos "lay in President Reagan's style and his awareness of the limits of American power," which he applauded in comparison to the hypothetical performance of his predecessors, who would "probably have been far more intrusive than he in a situation involving an eruption of popular dissatisfaction with a dictatorship."

Gelb anticipated the policy of Reagan's successor, President George H.W. Bush, toward the coup that unseated the first freely elected president of Haiti, Father Jean Bertrand Aristide. While joining other members of the Organization of American States in declaring publicly that there was no alternative to the restoration of Father Aristide, the United States in fact was not overly distressed at his removal from power by the military.

Indeed, after civilians had achieved control and there was no political cost to the United States, the administration boldly proclaimed that it was in the business of fostering democracy by any means, so that whatever happened the Reagan doctrine would be preserved untouched.

REAGAN REPRISE

In retrospect, the Reagan era can be seen as the completion of two cycles. One, in a historical context, from an intense ideological reaction to the counterculture radicalism of the 1960s to a more traditional posture in its final years paving the way toward a moderate succession. Two, as its internal evolution progressed over the course of eight years, it unquestionably moved from focusing primarily on a single-issue anticommunism mode and a jingoistic impulse

to "go it alone," to a more balanced reliance on military strength and economic assistance to achieve political ends, approaching a more pragmatic posture than some of its most vociferous ideologues might have wanted.

Still, if the angry mood of the 1960s threatened the political consensus with
the radicalism of the New Left, the 1980s responded with its own brand of radicalism, the New Right. In both cases elements that historically had been on the
periphery of US politics broke into the mainstream. This was particularly true
in the case of the Reagan administration's Latin American policy, where right-
wing conservatives, prodded by the Cuban exile leadership in Florida, relentlessly monitored the professional foreign service for ideological purity.

But there is more to the initial passivity that greeted the Reagan foreign policy shifts. It has often been described as the triumph of image over substance.
Indeed, a new mood seemed to invade Washington, symbolized by Reagan's
vaunted affability and winning ways with the electorate which earned him the
sobriquet of "great communicator." This brought into public life a confusion
about the problems of reality and illusion even greater than that normally in-
jected into the political dialogue. Members of Congress and foreign statesmen
no less than the media were understandably perplexed about the discrepancy
between the president's ability to convey his political message and the easy way
he manipulated facts, adorning those that suited his reality, discarding those
that didn't fit.

A handful of critics deplored these distortions. Disturbed by the hyperbole
and misinformation that surrounded the Central American crisis by 1986, Viron P. Vaky, a former assistant secretary of state for inter-American affairs and
ambassador to Costa Rica, wrote:

> The language that fills government cables, memorandums, and reports has
> become language that avoids acknowledging its meaning clearly, and that
> leads those who speak it to avoid acknowledging that meaning them-
> selves. . . . How easy it is to substitute analogy and buzzwords for thought.
> Just say "vital interest" or "dominoes" and one can avoid the need for rigor-
> ous supporting analysis.[9]

In his analysis of Reagan's defense policies, *New Yorker* essayist John Newhouse
concluded that the president "had many sides," one of them being "the fanta-
sist, who confused illusion and make-believe with reality," a symptom that was
often particularly acute in regards to foreign affairs. Garry Wills, among others, noted the importance to Reagan's outlook—and political effectiveness—
not only of the illusory metier of a film star but also the experience he acquired
in broadcasting using voice and speech as manipulative art.

"President Reagan's indifference to reality is hardly news," according to James David Barber, author of *The Presidential Character*. "His criterion of validity is drama, not empiricism." Barber quotes David Stockman, director of the Office of Management and Budget, summing up the White House system: "Every time one fantasy doesn't work they try another one." Barber, recalling the time a reporter challenged Reagan about the veracity of one of his endlessly repeated anecdotes—how a black hero at Pearl Harbor ended segregation in the armed forces—the President replied: "I remember the scene . . . it was very powerful." What mattered to Reagan, Barber concluded, was the grace and theatrical force of a performance; as a lifelong practitioner of illusion, he was in no way embarrassed by its victory over the facts. What was surprising, he added, was the public's apparent acceptance of Reagan's "rationality." It may be that in 1980 he found the public fatigued with reasoning, ready for the release and comfort of fantasy.

To brand the Salvadoran FLMN forces and the Nicaraguan junta "thugs" and worse, while heralding the dubious Contra leadership as "the equivalent to our Founding Fathers" may have been the result of a verbal romp among the White House speechwriters; it was not considered funny to Salvadorans and Nicaraguans subjected to the firepower of US-supplied weapons. Admittedly, the Reagan administration did not always make the rhetoric of its doctrine immediately operational commensurate with its rhetorical intensity.

Yet earlier US hesitations about Soviet and Cuban intentions in the Western Hemisphere and former moderation about the scope of US interests were thereby dismissed. As during the Dulles era, the Reagan administration was calling for a "politico-military" offensive in El Salvador and Nicaragua aimed at altering the status quo by a military defeat of the FLNM and toppling the Sandinista regime. Washington's policy now had a clear vision, as seemingly unlimited power made it possible to attend to apparently endless interests. The Reagan administration was, in fact, attempting to annul almost half a century of hemispheric history.

A typical statement by senior officials at the time was that of Nestor D. Sanchez, deputy assistant secretary of defense for Inter-American Affairs, who wrote that in El Salvador, the Soviet Union "is abetting an assault on the security of this hemisphere more dangerous than the postwar threat to Western Europe."

Simultaneously, the Defense Department began to show great skill manipulating information, spending a disproportionate amount of time on fine details such as whether the United States should send twenty or twenty-five army doctors to El Salvador or if officers on training missions should or should not wear side arms. Yet Pentagon spokesmen remained strangely mute on such fundamental issues as the quality and amount of weapons that were being shipped to "friendly" Central American armies or the number of officers and troops that were being trained in US counterinsurgency warfare.

However much one may attempt to abolish history, it will not stay abolished. Beyond a certain point, the reality of what was happening could be denied only at the risk of disaster. Bit by bit the Reagan policy seemed to be unraveling; the civil war in El Salvador showed no signs of abating; the Sandinistas, far from yielding to US military pressure, forcefully denounced the Reagan administration before the World Court at the Hague. But Reagan was able to justify a veritable undeclared war with so-called covert operations, and the arming and training of the anti-Sandinista forces, both in the United States and in Honduras.

As is wont to happen, eventually the functioning of the US constitutional system, the system of checks and balances, began to reassert itself. Congress, which had become notably ineffectual in foreign policy ever since the post-Vietnam Tonkin Gulf resolution, gradually regained its voice. Having failed to challenge Reagan's swift raid into Grenada, it chose to draw the line on Central America and on human rights; there a growing bipartisan coalition insistently pressed the executive to be more responsive to the "advise and consent" role of the legislative branch.

Indeed, in Congress an increasing number of Republicans, some conservatives as well as most of the remaining liberals, joined a growing chorus of voices speaking out against retreating from the human rights issue in foreign policy. Senator Nancy Kassebaum took the lead in rejecting the notion that the advent of the Reagan administration signaled a US acquiescence to South Africa's apartheid, which she declared to be inimical to "the mainstream Republican philosophy."

Another respected Republican, Representative Millicent Fenwick, addressing a conference on European–US relations in Strassbourg, demanded that the West be more vigorous in articulating its values: "Human rights, the right to dissent, the right to speak and publish—that's what we want to defend and must say so." She received the only standing ovation given to a US delegate.

The battle lines were finally drawn after it became known that the administration had a hand in the mining of Nicaraguan ports and authorized a series of covert CIA operations that finally became public knowledge with the exposure of the Iran–Contra scandal. Those episodes demonstrated the falseness of many of the arguments advanced by the administration to explain its Central American policy. After the House of Representatives voted to cut off aid to the Contras, James Reston of the *New York Times* wrote:

We have our CIA spooks all over Central America, our warships off the coast of Nicaragua. We are not trying to overthrow the governments the Reagan Administration says it doesn't like there, but everybody knows that is precisely what we are trying to do by subversive warfare.[10]

Reflecting on the unraveling of the Iran–Contra scandal, Russell Baker, the *New York Times* columnist, summed it up very well: "When things really start to go wrong in Washington, the incredible becomes the commonplace."[11] That insightful comment bore an eerie resemblance to the final sentence summing up the surreal bureaucracy portrayed in Kafka's *The Trial*: "the lie is turned into the commonplace." As far as Latin American policy was concerned, it might be read as a fittingly contemporary footnote to the Reagan legacy.

NOTES

1. Elaine Sciolino, "Summing Up: Shultz Looks at His Tenure at State," *New York Times*, December 18, 1988, p. 22.

2. Carla Anne Robbins, *The Cuban Threat* (New York: McGraw-Hill, 1983), p. 270.

3. Jeane Kirkpatrick, quoted by Allan Gerson; interview by author, Washington, D.C., 1993.

4. Quoted by Christopher Dickey, "The Gang That Blew Vietnam Goes Latin," *Washington Post*, November 28, 1982, p. C1.

5. Nathan Glazer, "Culture and Mobility," *New Republic*, July 4 and 11 (double issue), 1981, pp. 29–34.

6. Marsilio Moreira, interview by author, Brazilian embassy, Washington, April 1990.

7. Richard Halloran, "General Opposes Nicaragua Attack," *New York Times*, June 30, 1985, sec. 1, p. 3.

8. Leslie H. Gelb, "Reagan and the Philippines: A Winning Style," *New York Times Sunday Magazine*, March 30, 1986, p. 31.

9. Viron P. Vaky, "Language vs. Thought," *Christian Science Monitor*, December 12, 1986.

10. James Reston, "Washington: Reagan on Subversion," *New York Times*, October 23, 1985.

11. Russell Baker, "Maybe Just Deserts," *New York Times*, November 29, 1986, p. A31.

Chapter Twelve

GEORGE H. W. BUSH
Return to Pragmatism

From the beginning, the Bush administration regarded its crushing victory over Massachusetts Governor Michael Dukakis in 1988 reason enough to seek more pragmatic solutions to foreign policy problems without having to worry much about the indignation it might incur with the Republican party's ideological right.[1] To Mexico and the South American countries Bush offered debt relief; in Central America, he opted for negotiation rather than military confrontation. Thus Latin America arguably became the first geographical region to directly benefit from President Bush's inaugural pledge to conduct a "kinder and gentler" government. The Bush administration also signaled its intention to turn away from the go-it-alone mood of his predecessor and move toward better collaboration with multilateral bodies such as the United Nations, the World Bank, the Inter-American Development Bank and the Organization of American States—except where national security considerations might be involved, as in the case of Panama.

The cardinal objectives of the Bush foreign policy were to end the Cold War, unite East and West Germany within the North Atlantic Treaty Organization (NATO), and place the United States as power broker at the fulcrum of what the president called "a new international order." In the event of a rapidly disintegrating Soviet Union that augured a wholly new correlation of world forces, Bush wanted to rid the US foreign agenda from conflicts such as the violence in Central America. For too long that regional conflict had not only diverted US attention from more vital hemispheric issues, but it had also poisoned the domestic political scene, particularly relations with the Congress.

With the fading Soviet threat, the legacy of Reagan's crusading spirit was being overtaken by a more traditional and moderate pragmatism. Secretary of State James A. Baker III clearly found a pragmatic policy, the kind that led to the endorsement of the peace negotiations sponsored by the Central American heads of state, to be the appropriate approach to further Bush's goal of welding together disparate political factions at home and among Washington's allies abroad, especially France, Germany and Spain, that had long been riled by the Central American imbroglio. A primary post–Cold War task would be to consolidate the democratic alliance and draw Eastern Europe into the fold.

Although not widely noted at the time, Bush had a personal stake in making Latin America a significant component of his foreign policy.[2] During his years as ambassador to the United Nations and director of the CIA he had developed warm personal relations with various hemispheric leaders. Accordingly, within the first five weeks in office the Bush administration removed all of the remaining obstacles that hindered progress toward a Central American settlement and set the stage for significant measures to alleviate the hemisphere's crippling debt burden.

Public attention, however, tended to be focused on the primary emphasis the new administration placed on readjusting East–West strategy and dawning notions of a "new world order."[3] Nonetheless, a new, more active and broadly conceived hemispheric relationship was slowly emerging, based on three key principles—the promotion of democratic rules, liberal economic reform and laying the groundwork for a regional common market—as central to the new administration's policy.

"Here in the Americas, we are building something unprecedented in human history—the world's first completely democratic hemisphere," Bush told Latin American heads of state—and meant it beyond a formal requisite diplomatic statement.[4]

Just as political convergence began to take hold in Washington, a similar softening of once-rigid ideological patterns that had colored both political and economic thinking was happening across Latin America. Whereas in Central America reconciliation was reached mainly because of weariness with violence and the growing conviction that military solutions were practically impossible, in South America the political mellowing was driven partly by shifting economic attitudes, from the protectionist statism of the 1950s and 1960s to a widespread embracing of free market approaches in the wake of the disastrous debt-ridden 1980s. Partly it was also due to the ineptness and an onset of corruption that had wormed its way into the bureaucracies of a number of social democratic governments (most notably Venezuela and Peru) that could no longer be truly differentiated from the right-wing autocrats they once denounced as inept and corrupt.[5]

Bush, true to his instinct for letting economics dominate his foreign policy strategy, quickly focused on measures to alleviate Latin America's huge foreign debt burden and help the momentum of the hemisphere's new democracies institute free market reforms and attract private investments. Thus along with the quest for a political settlement of the Central American crisis, the administration advanced a plan worked out by Treasury Secretary Nicholas Brady that offered debt forgiveness in return for far-ranging reforms that would subordinate the remaining protectionist and statist policies to the principles of free trade and liberal investment policies.

To provide financial backup to these reforms, the Brady and Baker plans envisioned a substantial increase of the US subscription to the Inter-American Development Bank to help establish a substantial multilateral investment fund that would provide an indispensable financial cushion in support of the bold restructuring programs initiated by an increasing number of countries, led by Argentina, Bolivia, Chile, Colombia and Mexico. The Brady plan was a big step forward from the plan developed by Treasury Secretary James A. Baker III, which simply allowed the governments and helped private bankers to provide more time and liberal terms for the repayment of the Latin American debt, which by 1989 had reached mind-boggling proportions. This was supplemented by a series of financial measures that significantly bolstered the lending capacity of the Inter-American Development Bank to help the privatization of deficit-ridden state enterprises and propel the region toward closer economic integration.

Notwithstanding these constructive moves, and in keeping with Bush's assertion that he had no use for "the vision thing," there were no discernible historical insights or a comprehensive geopolitical scheme that would place an overall hemispheric plan close to the center of US foreign policy. On the other hand, the absence of any great ideological scheme gave Central America the requisite political space to find its own solutions.

TEAMWORK AND
RECONCILIATION IN CENTRAL AMERICA

At the outset, Bush, like Carter and Reagan before him, tended to focus only on one issue, in his case how to get out of the Central American imbroglio. Thus from the outset both Baker and National Security Adviser Brent Scowcroft moved single-mindedly to end the protracted confrontation with Congress over aid for the Nicaraguan exile Contras and unconditional support for the Salvadoran military. A graduate of the Kissinger school of realpolitik from the Nixon White House, Scowcroft was prepared to be flexible, mindful that the administration had neither the votes nor the public support to continue Reagan's objective of a military defeat of the Sandinistas and the Salvadoran insurgents.[6]

Indeed, the absence of any great ideological scheme allowed space for Central America to find its own solutions. Thus if one constructive consequence was to emerge from the combined tragedies of Guatemala, El Salvador and Nicaragua it is that the Central Americans, both of the left and right, eventually became so disenchanted with Washington's inconsistent meddling that both sides chose to settle their differences through direct negotiations. The upshot was greater political moderation and self-reliance.

In line with the new pragmatism and consensus building, Bush appointed a former Carter White House aide, Bernard W. Aronson, to succeed Elliot Abrams as assistant secretary of state for Inter-American affairs.

Aronson's appointment was widely interpreted as a concession to bipartisanship on hemispheric policy. A labor specialist with excellent connections in Congress, he had already worked with the Reagan White House to promote the cause of the Contras in Nicaragua in their struggle against the Sandinista regime. But unlike some of Reagan's policymakers, Aronson believed that US aid to the anti-Sandinista groups ought to be conditioned to their showing civilized respect for human rights. Though he had drafted much of a 1986 speech in which Reagan said it would be a "a tragic mistake" for Congress to prohibit arming the anti-Sandinista freedom fighters, by 1989 he realized that after eight years of failed policies Washington had one realistic course left—to seek change through the diplomatic initiatives rather than on the battlefield.

Once the Central American situation began to settle down, Baker and his deputy, Lawrence Eagleburger, were content to leave Latin American affairs in the hands of Aronson and Luigi Einaudi, the permanent US representative to the Organization of American States. It was a well-functioning team; while Aronson's experience was strong on political negotiation but limited to Central America, Einaudi loomed as a respected expert on Brazil and South America.

Aronson and Einaudi shored up considerable support for Bush's hemispheric policy within the administration and in Congress, while Julius I. Katz and the Chilean-born Frechette spread the gospel of free trade among skeptical Latin American and Caribbean governments. Unlike previous administrations, there seemed to be no great fissures among Bush's foreign policy advisers. "We understood Bush's policies and one another," one of the officials recalled, "and one reason might have been that several of us had already worked together in the Ford administration."7

"We do not claim the right to order the politics of Nicaragua," Bush noted—an assertion he perhaps forgot when three years later he yielded to Senator Jesse Helms's pressure to withhold US aid to the government of Violeta Chamorro of Nicaragua in a futile attempt to force her to dismiss the Sandinistas, who still controlled the army and police.[8] But 1992 was an election year, when it seemed more important to the White House to consolidate the support of the Republican right than preserve the coherence of the country's foreign policy.

The Bush initiatives came in the midst of the democratic revival in Latin America, which had spurred the Reagan administration in its closing years to revert to proclaiming the virtues of democracy and abhorrence of dictators and violators of human rights. Thus in his inaugural address, Bush could reasonably assert, "We know how to secure a more just and prosperous life for man on earth: through free markets, free speech, free elections and the exercise of free will unhampered by the state."[9] Actually, the groundwork for the Central American accords was in large measure the labor of a Latin American consensus worked out by the heads of state of the region aided by what became known as the Contadora process, in recognition of the Panamanian island where the leaders met, supported by the so-called Rio Group made up of Argentina, Bolivia, Brazil, Chile, Colombia, Ecuador, Peru, Uruguay and Venezuela. There were also sporadic visits by the foreign ministers of France, Spain and other European Social Democrats who bolstered the Latin American opposition to Reagan's Central American policy. In fact, the continental movement in support of the forces favoring a negotiated solution began among the Latin American countries as far back as 1982. It was led by presidents Belisario Betancur of Colombia, Carlos Andres Perez of Venezuela and Oscar Arias of Costa Rica, and intended as a counterpoise to Washington's muscular unilateral pressures.

Soon after a new meeting of heads of state of Costa Rica, Guatemala, Honduras and El Salvador at Esquipulas, a small town in Guatemala, Bush called in congressional leaders and signed an agreement in support of the multilateral peacemaking efforts.

While Bush's more moderate policies won plaudits across Latin America, credit also went to Gorbachev's reformist regime as well as the sheer perseverance of the leaders of the Contadora movement and the shift of the Central American presidents led by Arias at the Esquipulas talks in Guatemala. These talks, which finally won Bush's support for Arias's "ballots not bullets" formula, culminated years of sporadic but increasingly effective resistance to the pressures and intimidation Washington had wielded in its efforts to eradicate the left-wing movements in Central America.

Most significantly, the active role of several Latin American governments to help bring peace to Central America was another example of how the region's leaders were increasingly disposed to coordinate their policies outside of the formal framework of the OAS. The United States, having once been the foremost champion of the inter-American system, for too many years had acted as though the OAS no longer served its security and political interests for anybody to take the commitment seriously any more. But Bush, unlike most of his recent predecessors, was willing to give multilateralism another chance; it was a policy that had Eagleburger and Einaudi as its most convincing proponents. Even in the nettlesome conflict with General Manuel Antonio Noriega, the administration first sought to move the OAS into action to remove his thuggish regime, but anti-interventionism was still too powerful a sentiment. Doubtless the ill-fated Dominican precedent of 1965 was vivid enough in memory to deter any attempt at sending another inter-American "peace force" into the field.

This inclination of the Latin Americans to present a united foreign policy front recalled 1958 and Kubitschek's Operation Pan America, a trend that peaked again in the late 1970s when Latin America moved uniformly in support of Panama's efforts to renegotiate the Panama Canal treaties with the United States. Specifically, it achieved an institutional voice in the early 1980s when Mexico, Colombia and Venezuela, with the support of Argentina, Bolivia, Brazil, Peru and Uruguay (to be known later as the Group of Eight before becoming the Grupo de Rio), acted as a backup to the initially somewhat dissolute round of talks of the Central American heads of state. The efforts culminated in a round of private talks at Caracas early in February 1989, on the occasion of the inauguration of President Carlos Andres Perez of Venezuela. Indeed, whenever the OAS faltered, the cohesion of the Rio Group was invoked as an effective instrument of regional collaboration.

It was not until the advent of the Bush administration, however, and the end of US obstructionism led by Abrams, Senator Helms and a handful of conservative Democrats, that the peace process bore fruit. Bush himself initiated the movement to mollify Congress with its Democratic majority when, as president-elect, he called on House Speaker Jim Wright. The message was that a Bush administration would endeavor to end the ideological and anti-Congress zeal of the Reagan administration officials like Elliot Abrams and place more emphasis on diplomatic efforts to find political solutions.[10] It was soon evident what the Bush administration wanted to do in the Caribbean and Central America: clear the decks for a total overhaul of relations with Mexico in order to bring that country into the North American Free Trade Agreement already concluded with Canada. How it intended to do so and the means at its disposal were not immediately evident.

To assist the hemisphere-wide trend of economic reforms designed to deregulate, privatize and open previously state-guided economies, the Bush administration made a farsighted decision: to bolster the resources of the Inter-American Development Bank as recommended by an economic study Bush requested from Brady after a meeting with the Peruvian, Bolivian and Colombian heads of state at Cartagena. The new policy was painstakingly assembled by Treasury Secretary Brady and Assistant Secretary David Mulford, with the quiet support of a new president of the Inter-American Development Bank, Enrique Iglesias, the worldly former director of the UN Economic Commission for Latin America and foreign minister of Uruguay. Mulford, a former New York banker, realizing debt-ridden Latin America's dire need to count on foreign capital to cushion these far-reaching policy changes, pressed hard to bolster the capital of the regional lending agencies. In the correct assessment of a scholar of inter-American affairs, the initiative "begged the question of its seriousness."[11]

The study proposed an enterprise initiative packaged as "a new partnership . . . to encourage and support market-oriented reforms and economic growth." However, it was announced in such a hurried, uncoordinated fashion that it almost passed unnoticed in the media, particularly compared to the wide publicity that greeted the Kennedy administration's launching of Alliance for Progress at a celebrated White House ceremony in March 1961.

Yet in retrospect, the initiative arguably provided a greater economic impetus for the region than any other postwar program. One immediate goal was to replenish the resources of the Inter-American Development Bank, almost doubling its capital from $34 billion to $60 billion. Following the same multilateral philosophy, the Clinton administration five years later would bolster the bank's capital by another $20 billion. His ultimate goal, Bush explained, was the creation of "a hemispheric free trade zone from Alaska to Argentina."[12] The initiative included practical and immediate steps, such as negotiating tariff reductions on products of special interest to the region, an official pledge to provide debt relief to some of Latin America's weakest economies and a $15 billion investment fund managed by the Inter-American Development Bank intended to facilitate privatizations, debt-for-nature swaps and free trade with Latin America.

The Latin American response was immediate and enthusiastic. President Carlos Andres Perez of Venezuela, a frequent critic of US policies, called the initiative "the most advanced proposal the United States has ever proposed for Latin America. It's revolutionary, historical." President Carlos Saul Menem of Argentina hailed it as "the most brilliant moment in our relations with the United States." The president of Uruguay, Luis Lacalle, was even more effusive: "When, after years of our complaining of neglect, the most important man in the world offers his hand, then, I think I should grab it—and the arm and the elbow and the shoulder, too."[13]

A year later, a president not normally given to great ardor in his speech, sounded more eager than ever about the enterprise in an anniversary speech that evoked a New World rhetoric not heard in a long time. "From the northern tip of Alaska to the southernmost point of Tierra del Fuego, we share common heritages," he declared, adding,

> And now, as democracy sweeps the world, we share the challenge of leadership through example. We can lead the way to a world free from suspicion and from mercantilist barriers, from socialist inefficiencies. We can show the rest of the world that deregulation, respect for private property, low tax rates, and low trade barriers can produce vast economic returns. . . . We can make our hemisphere's freedom first and best for all.[14]

In practical terms it loomed as an imaginative offer to the Western Hemisphere to build its own trading bloc from a North American base.[15] Though less publicized than the Alliance for Progress or NAFTA, it was comparable in scope and conception to Kennedy's program, though it actually bore greater resemblance to the "regional common market" plan Lyndon Johnson took to Punta del Este in 1964 but regrettably left in limbo soon afterward because of the all-absorbing pressures of the Vietnam War. Above all, the EAI and NAFTA focused on the importance of regional concentrations in international trade and investment at a time when Europe and the Pacific Rim were each well ahead in consolidating such arrangements.

Some years later, Mexico proposed the enlargement of the free trade area through the creation of NAFTA, taking a page out of Reagan's short-lived 1980 campaign proposals for a Canada-Mexico-US common market. Like Canadians, Mexican officials saw themselves "as living under the shadow of a giant absentminded neighbor, one with an irrepressible propensity to unilaterally place restrictions on its imports, with major consequences for foreign exporters."[16] For instance, in 1988 US government agencies were processing fifty-seven petitions to impose special duties on imports allegedly "dumped" in the United States, twenty-two petitions to impose countervailing duties on imports allegedly subsidized by foreign governments, twenty-nine cases alleging other unfair practices with regard to imports and twenty-five cases alleging other unfair practices with regard to US exports or other US international economic interests.[17]

Once Mexico decided to open its borders to more international trade, new teams of largely US-trained economic reformers were determined to find some means of having the United States think a little longer before moving to new restrictive action that might shake the Mexican economy. Most importantly, prominent intellectuals such as writers Octavio Paz and Carlos Fuentes saw positive implications for future US–Mexican relations, a drastic shift from the

time just a few years earlier that "Yankee cultural imperialism" had been the favorite demon of a preponderant sector of Mexico's intelligentsia. Suddenly
Mexicans had confidence in the strength of their own culture to stand up to
foreign inroads. "Perhaps we'll reverse the situation and re-colonize the US
Southwest," quipped Fuentes, but only half in jest.[18]

In fact, from the administration of Miguel de la Madrid on, Mexico's new
breed of "reformist" leaders had another concern that fueled their desire for a
North American Free Trade Association. This was a fear that the various
heroic measures to which they were already committed in opening the Mexican economy, such as the drastic reduction of tariff levels and the lifting of numerous restraints on the creation of foreign-owned subsidiaries in Mexico,
might be reversed by a future Mexican administration. "Like [Jean] Monnet in
Europe, the Mexican leaders hoped that their membership in a NAFTA might
bind future administrations to maintain the open regime that they were currently creating."[19]

Just as political convergence began to take hold in Washington, erstwhile
uncompromising ideological positions were swiftly changing across Latin
America. The change was driven partly by shifting economic attitudes, from
statism to the free market system, partly as a result of disenchantment with the
desultory record of the socialist models of Eastern Europe and Cuba. On a
more immediate level it also came as a reaction to the corruption that had
wormed its way into the administrations of some of the social democratic governments, most notably Mexico, Venezuela and Peru, to the point where they
could no longer be easily differentiated from the right-wing autocrats they had
denounced and displaced.

MEXICAN RAPPROCHEMENT

In an early letter to Mexican President Carlos Salinas de Gortari, Bush asserted
that he found "spiritual, intellectual and political affinities" between the two
countries. In turn, Salinas not only played a supportive role in persuading Washington to drop its obstruction of a negotiated Central American settlement—
the issue that had so strained US–Mexican relations under Reagan. Salinas did
something more: through a skillful and massive lobbying strategy in Washington, he virtually induced first the Bush administration and then Congress to embrace NAFTA, arguing that relations with Mexico were the economic and
political linchpin of US relations with all of Latin America.

In this campaign he often cited Carlos Fuentes's maxim that "Mexico is the
border between the United States and all of Latin America." Even when he
pressed for a North American Free Trade area with the United States and

Canada, originally a Bush idea, it was advanced as the first step in a hemisphere-wide enterprise. To help Washington push ahead with the project, Salinas saturated the United States with an intensive public relations strategy that overwhelmed even its most recalcitrant foes in Congress to the point where most observers began to take Senate approval for granted, albeit prematurely. When it fell to the Clinton administration to seek Senate confirmation, the new president had to wage a bruising battle to win a narrow majority, and in the process hone his skills in negotiating with friends and foes in both parties, so fractious was the debate.

One of the most memorable of the many virtuoso performances he regularly played to a wide variety array of US audiences—businessmen, politicians, scholars, labor leaders and so on—undoubtedly was his appearance before the gala dinner offered by the board of the Metropolitan Museum at the opening of a blockbuster exhibit entitled *Three Thousand Years of Mexican Culture*. In his hands cultural exchange became a metaphor for a newly honed modern Mexico that was bidding to the United States for broader capital investments, trade and political cooperation. "Cultural exchanges between our countries," he said,

> are not merely another topic on the bilateral agenda: rather, they are a means of facilitating broader prospects for cooperation. Questions of trade, migration, drug trafficking and ecology are challenges that we will be better equipped to meet through the meeting of our cultures, and through the appreciation for the creation of a neighborly spirit that is shown by those who look upon neighborly relations as a valuable opportunity. We belong to different cultures. Let us rejoice that it is so. . . . *This exhibition therefore also serves as a means of understanding the confidence that now leads Mexicans to open their doors to the world with a feeling of security: confidence and security that we derive from the enormous strength of our age old culture.*[20]

Significantly, Salinas made his speech in English—the first time ever that a Mexican head of state spoke abroad in public in a foreign language. Thus in his campaign, Salinas scored two notable triumphs beyond laying the groundwork for NAFTA's approval by the Clinton administration: (1) uniting for the first time the diverse and fractious Hispanic organizations, from the stanchly anti-Mexican Cuban exiles organizations in Miami to the populist La Raza of California, in support of the common market idea and (2) thwarting leftist criticism branding NAFTA a threat to Mexico's cultural identity by taking a leading role with Spain in the celebration of the 500th anniversary of the first Christopher Columbus voyage to the New World, an unprecedented move for a government that since the Mexican Revolution had specifically subordinated its Spanish influence to its Indian heritage.

Moreover, the Salinas government, breaking every precedent, gave the impression of an outright supporter of the re-election of George Bush—which forced the prompt replacement of the senior Mexican embassy officials in Washington after the election of Bill Clinton.

OVERKILL IN PANAMA

While Bush undoubtedly had greater foreign policy experience than any other president elected in at least half a century, domestic political considerations probably motivated his order to invade Panama. Having resisted moving against General Manuel Antonio Noriega for a full year after Reagan and his administration had made futile attempts to dislodge him either by negotiation or financial blockade, the White House was finally forced to yield to bipartisan pressures. Bush had already been subjected to right-wing criticism of his Central American policy, arguing that he had "abandoned" the Nicaraguan contras and had been insufficiently forceful in exercising global leadership. Conservative columnists like George Will began touting what they called the wimp factor.

Ironically, nobody did more to push the Bush administration toward intervention than the persistent criticism of congressional Democrats led by Edward Kennedy and Christopher Dodd, the two leading Latin American specialists in the Senate, who might have known how repugnant a further US intervention would be considered in the rest of the hemisphere. Instead, they made common cause with Republican Senators Alphonse D'Amato and Jesse Helms in a campaign denouncing Bush, which reached a fever pitch after the administration failed to come to the aid of an attempted palace coup staged by a handful of defectors of Panama's Defense Force in October 1989, two months before the administration finally ordered the invasion.

For almost two years Noriega had become a prime example of what the intelligence community called blowback—when the so-called clients of the US intelligence operatives subordinate Washington's interests to their own. In the case of Panama, the CIA and the Reagan administration had for years played cozy with Noriega, despite his proven involvement in the illicit drug market, on the grounds that he seemed to be a useful ally in the covert war against the Nicaraguan Sandinistas.

As should have been predictable to anyone familiar with the region, Noriega had a private agenda, and as soon as it was convenient he went out on his own. Thus by the time Bush decided to invade Panama and arrest Noriega, the

Panamanian strongman had been so effectively demonized by the US government and media that the question was, How had he been able to hold on to power as long as he did?

The die was cast by the popular outrage that followed the beatings Noriega's goon squads gave opposition leaders during the political campaign, and the coalition headed by Gustavo Endara prevailed easily in one of the cleanest elections in recent Panamanian history. The dictator's refusal to recognize the triumph of the opposition and the brutal repression that ensued earned him an instant hemisphere-wide reputation, making it easier for the United States to institute a destabilization process that culminated with the invasion of December 1989. The State Department entrusted its first step, the freezing of Panamanian assets, to William D. Rogers, senior partner of the prestigious Arnold & Porter law firm and a former undersecretary of state for economic affairs. "With these measures the Noriega regime will not survive more than three days, at the most a week," Rogers rhapsodized the day he announced the measures in the presence of leaders of the Panamanian opposition assembled in his office in Washington.

At the same time, the US representative to the OAS, Ambassador Einaudi, sought to persuade the hemisphere organization to use military force, if necessary, to "liberate" the Panamanian people from the Noriega scourge. According to most OAS members, since Panama was not threatening its neighbors, there was no juridical justification to dispose of Noriega, though nobody doubted the price Panamanians were paying to live under his repressive regime. Moreover, some diplomats wondered privately why Washington should become exercised over Noriega when the much bloodier repression and torture of the military regimes of Argentina, Chile, El Salvador and Guatemala had gone unpunished. That was when the Bush administration opted for unilateral sanctions, starting with the financial boycott.

At the time, observers in Washington believed Bush had to demonstrate that he too could be tough, though administration spokesmen insisted that he had been provoked by Noriega goon assaults against US servicemen and their families in Panama, which at the time numbered close to 40,000, and the threat the situation posed to the orderly transfer of the canal to Panamanian sovereignty by December 1999, as provided by the Torrijos–Carter treaties of 1977. As it turned out, the financial sanctions were a spectacular failure and should have served as a warning against future economic embargoes. Rogers blamed it on the loopholes left by State Department lawyers, rather than on the inventiveness of the Noriega regime, which paid public officials with chits they could use to purchase vital necessities.

Far more successful was the US government's campaign to blacken Noriega's image (after years of defending him from domestic critics). On the domestic front, it neutralized any significant opposition to the invasion in the United States but failed to convince Panama and the rest of Latin America. In fact, Noriega misdeeds were nowhere near as outrageous or so numerous as the atrocities that were being tolerated in El Salvador and Nicaragua with the connivance of the US intelligence agencies and the Pentagon. Still, the fact that the other American states voted unanimously to condemn the invasion was strictly a formality, for nobody was inclined to come out in defense of the abhorrent Noriega.

It is true that well before the decision was made to invade, Washington had hoped that the OAS would deal with the Panamanian situation, especially after Noriega's Panamanian Defense Force had annulled the presidential elections when opposition candidate Endara seemed to emerge victorious. But there was something incongruous about Washington invoking the sanctity of the ballot box in a country where a decade earlier it had aided and abetted in the fraudulent ballot counting that brought its candidate, Nicolas Ardito Barletta, to run the presidency.

In terms of producing real change, Panama turned out about as well as Iraq. In the latter the US succeeded in removing the threat to neighboring Kuwait but was unable to remove the autocratic regime of Saddam Hussein; in Panama Noriega was removed and with him went the terror. But the free elections of May 1994 returned to office the very party that since 1968 had governed hand in glove with the military, including Noriega, the Partido Democratico Popular. As William Greider pointed out, "the sequence of events with Iraq is exactly parallel to what Bush did in Panama."[21]

EAGLEBURGER'S REPRISE AND COLLECTIVE DEFENSE OF DEMOCRACY

If President Bush's response to the challenge of world leadership could be described by US scholars as "appropriately Wilsonian," his actions in relation toward Latin America were positively "Rooseveltian."[22] If during the Cold War years Washington's principal concern was how to prevent communism from taking root in the New World, by 1990 it was how to consolidate democracy and fuel economic prosperity with the free market system. In the intervening years, however, alliances were often made with little regard for the civility of military regimes and their intelligence agencies as long as they proved trustworthy in the struggle against communism. This meant that the vaunted inter-American goals of respect for democracy and human rights were remitted to the "see later" folder. In fact, their flowering came in the 1980s, with Latin America's surprising, spectacular democratic revival and the slow but relentless collapse of the Soviet Union.

Late in 1990, Bush made an extensive trip to South America, having previously visited Mexico and Central America several times. Reminiscent of FDR, his declared purpose at a time of uncertain international realignments was the construction of a "completely democratic hemisphere" as a primary policy goal. For some time Washington had made plain an increasing inclination to deal only with democracies, thereby discouraging military putsches or unconstitutional moves by elected governments, as was the case with Peru and Guatemala in the early 1990s.

On a multilateral level, the United States sought to put into practice the pledge of continental democracy by openly exerting pressure on the Organization of American States (OAS) to take a united stand in favor of democracy. This drive, which found wide favor, particularly among the Anglophone Caribbean nations, Colombia, Costa Rica and Venezuela, eventually led to the groundbreaking Resolution 1080 adopted at the OAS General Assembly at Santiago, Chile, in June 1991. The resolution gave the OAS secretary-general new powers that enabled him to deal, for the first time, with internal threats to constitutional government. In the future, the secretary-general could call an emergency meeting of the Permanent Council to ensure joint action by the member states whenever he determined there was a "sudden and unscheduled interruption" of the constitutional process. Multilateral sanctions could then be invoked to prompt the restoration of democracy.

Resolution 1080 would soon be put to a test under very different circumstances but with uniform success in Haiti, Peru and Guatemala. Experts considered Resolution 1080 to mark a return to the spirit of collective action, reminiscent of the Rio Treaty of Collective Security of 1948, which had been sundered by the ideological confrontations that began with Guatemala in 1954 and lingered with Cuba, the Dominican Republic and, most recently, Central America.[23]

Critical US support for the measure was stated in a historic, albeit little noticed, speech by Eagleburger to the foreign ministers assembled in the halls of the Chilean Congress. In an eloquent, often moving reaffirmation of US commitment to multilateralism and the OAS, the veteran diplomat reached back to the semantics of the New World and the Good Neighbor policy, characterizing the organization as a "noble experiment in hemispheric cooperation" that "has paid the price of our differences in terms of paralysis and wasted opportunities."

"I want to tell the truth," Eagleburger began in a low, solemn tone, facing the foreign ministers assembled in the old Congress Building of the Chilean capital. It was a speech that included a passage many had never heard a top-ranking US official speak before:

> I will not deny that my own country bears its share of responsibility for hav-
> ing tended to view our hemispheric relationships through the sometimes
> distorting prism of the Cold War. . . . But mistakes we made, the most seri-
> ous being a failure at times to take our hemisphere on its own terms and to
> deal with its problems in their own right.

For Enrique Bernstein, a senior Chilean diplomat, the speech brought back
memories of another OAS conference held at the nearby Hotel Carrera in
1959, in the midst of the Cold War, when his delegation sought to moderate
Secretary of State Christian Herter in the sole objective he brought to the
meeting: to obtain an inflexible commitment from the Latin American allies
to join Washington in proscribing "foreign ideologies" from the Americas.
Though Cuba was not mentioned by name, the US resolution was clearly a reflection of Washington's fears that the young revolutionary leader Fidel Castro
would turn the Cuban revolution into communism's bridgehead in the Western Hemisphere.

For those in the audience who remembered 1959, it was a poignant coun-
terpoint to hear another secretary of state concede three decades later that
Washington had perhaps overdrawn the scope of the communist threat and allowed the divisiveness of the Cold War to absorb its policy toward Latin America. To many it sounded as if a top-ranking US diplomat was deploring
publicly for the first time the dubious wisdom of Washington's postwar subor-
dination of Latin American affairs to the exigencies of the Cold War and need-
lessly dissipating the goodwill capital that was the legacy of the Roosevelt era.[24]

Barely three months after Santiago, Resolution 1080 received its first test
after the Haitian military ousted the island's first freely elected president, Jean-
Bertrand Aristide. Meeting in Washington, the foreign ministers used their
new powers to declare a diplomatic and economic embargo against the repressive military junta of general Raoul Cedars. But for effective results, the hemispheric community had to compel the United Nations to follow suit, for too
many European and African nations saw fit to elude the OAS embargo.

However, Resolution 1080 acted as a prompt and effective deterrent when
it was again invoked by the OAS to punish the military in Guatemala for
threatening to seize the government in 1993. The resolution also provided the
necessary juridical umbrella for the intervention of US and UN forces to restore the elected government of Aristide three years later.

In July 1995, Argentine Defense Minister Oscar Camilión, addressing the
first hemispheric defense conference, recalled the Santiago resolution as laying
the groundwork for an almost unprecedented period of democratic affirmation

across the hemisphere, and "a new willingness by the armed forces to play an unprecedented role in the defense of democratic institutions."[25]

Though it is rarely acknowledged, the OAS is the only multinational body explicitly committed to the principle of representative democracy, whereas the United Nations and other regional organizations establish no such condition, abiding instead by the principle of universal membership, which by and large was the criterion that prevailed at the founding meeting of the UN at San Francisco in 1945. At the Organization of American States, however, it is a principle that often stands in conflict with two other founding principles—self-determination and democratic practices.

"What if the peoples of a country choose to elect a socialist or autocratic government, as has been the case," argued Vicente Sanchez Gavito, for many years the Mexican ambassador to the OAS, in defense of his government's opposition to the ostracism of the communist regime of Cuba from the OAS.[26]

Santiago thus witnessed a sea change in inter-American policy. For Latin America it meant burying the historic fear that furthering democracy meant making countries vulnerable to extrinsic interference in their internal affairs. For the United States it meant abandoning, once and for all, the distressing notion that stability and hemispheric security were more effectively protected by autocrats and military dictators than by liberal, civilian governments.

But it was, above all, a juridical recognition that modernization had hit Latin America's institutional development, that the tide had turned against dictators and their bosses in the feudal oligarchies that had desperately fought to survive, especially in Central America. Even diehard ideologues began to discard the shibboleths of statism, dependency theory and old-fashioned racial arguments that kept whole Indian communities in bondage with the excuse that they could not adapt to the twentieth century. A significant aspect of this change was that it was helped, not hindered, by the newly found pragmatism of the US government.

"TO WHAT END?"—BEYOND PANAMA

A dramatic indictment of Washington's postwar approaches to Latin America is contained in a 1992 Rand Corporation analysis of the origins and conduct of US policy toward El Salvador.[27] It noted that after spending $5 billion in eight years, during which 75,000 Salvadorans had died, the United States had failed to achieve its main goal—to bring peace and democracy to the region. Significantly, the study was commissioned by the Department of Defense, perhaps a bit late. The scathing conclusions did not receive adequate notice if we take into account the magnitude of human suffering inflicted by the Salvadoran civil war. Most importantly, once again the nation faced the question posed in the mid-1960s by journalist and novelist Ward Just about the Vietnam War: "To what end?"

"To what end?"—that question must be asked about most of the missteps of postwar US policy in Latin America. Generally undertaken for a greater cause, they nevertheless brought a costly aftermath that ended up eroding US influence in the hemisphere, not to mention the moral leadership the United States had acquired during the Roosevelt era. Some of the notable milestones in this climb to disaster included (1) the overthrow of Arbenz, supposedly to free Guatemala from communism, which led to more than three decades of ruthless military repression until a civilian president was elected in 1991 to a bankrupt Guatemala; (2) the bungled Bay of Pigs, which undermined much of Kennedy's authority and the altruistic arguments on behalf of the Alliance for Progress; (3) the invasion of the Dominican Republic represented a throwback to the Big Stick policy and encouraged right-wing forces across the hemisphere; and (4) the failure of Reagan's ill-conceived, illegal efforts to reconstruct El Salvador and Nicaragua as stable, democratic allies; in addition, the obsessive attention he gave these issues overshadowed the far more serious financial and economic problems of Argentina, Brazil and Mexico.

Many of the policy disasters of recent years, such as the Guatemalan episode, the Bay of Pigs and the illicit funding of the Contras, stem, I believe, from a failure to view the region's situation correctly. Not only have the Cold War policies bequeathed to Washington a painful legacy, but also, behind the flawed thinking they have perpetuated, is a dangerous, misleading worldview whereby Latin America became a playing field for ad hoc decisions. Worse, it is a legacy littered with "unintended consequences," as we have seen in Cuba, Guatemala, Venezuela, Argentina and much of Central America. That such consequences as a forty-year civil war that has left some 100,000 casualties in Guatemala were not intended is a poor consolation for those who must suffer them. So is the fact that Richard Bissell, the CIA deputy director who conceived Operation Success in Guatemala, admitted publicly that "if I had to do it over again, I wouldn't."[28]

If there is a lesson in the fiascos and incomprehension that have bedeviled Washington's relations with Latin America in the past decade and more, it is that the administration must jettison the policies that were responsible for such a chaotic state of affairs. If the situation today is analogous to the dismal state of relations that confronted the first Roosevelt administration in 1933 and again President Kennedy in 1961, the goal in the twenty-first century must be to make a drastic detour and rebuild once more the spirit of hemispheric solidarity that those two presidencies accomplished. As long as Latin America remains as a continent more of shadows than of substance to US policymakers, Washington is likely to advance positions that are not seldom mistaken.

What is needed now, not only by US policymakers but also by liberal and conservative critics alike, is a period of detachment and unbiased reflection about recent hemispheric events in the larger context of history and diverse cultural perspectives, mindful that those who limit themselves to the practical approach to human affairs are the ones who, in Veblen's words, are content to repeat the errors of their predecessors.

Some of those questions concern the ability of the US government to maintain a long-range foreign policy. While congressional vigilance against disastrous or dishonest policies is indispensable, the fragmentation of opinion and frequently partisan concerns of Congress make cooperation with the executive branch difficult. The system of checks and balances aimed at protecting citizens from the victories of any one faction and from the threat of centralized power interferes with the executive's ability to act with authority, effectiveness and continuity on the world stage.

George H.W. Bush, with his passionate interest in foreign policy, his fascination for the world stage, chose to minimize those checks and balances, sometimes by ignoring them, other times by sidestepping them altogether. He did so even if it meant, for example, ignoring "advice and consent" provisions stipulated by the Constitution or ignoring clear signals from Congress about the unpopularity of his actions. True, the congressional posturing on Central America that began during the Reagan administration could be exasperating, but the administration's tactic of isolating and humiliating the legislative branch was a perfect recipe for fleeting policy spectaculars, not for lasting achievements. A perfect example was attacking Panama City without asking Congress to authorize such a warlike action.

Accordingly, one of the problems with the Bush administration was that the image makers who had caused so much damage to the government's credibility did not abide by Bush's more pragmatic impulses or those of the Baker State Department. Instead, they continued managing information and disinformation with abandon.

Late in 1990, roughly in the midterm of his administration, Bush paid a one-week visit to South America carrying his message of the linkage between economic growth through the prospective Enterprise for the Americas Initiative and the strengthening of democracy. The tour was warmly welcomed in Latin America and even won the plaudits of some of his critics in the United

States. In an article titled "An 'Abrazo' for Bush," Sol M. Linowitz, cochairman of the Inter-American Dialogue and a former ambassador to the OAS, wrote that Bush "is demonstrating understanding of the problems facing the hemisphere and the need to work together to forge cooperative solutions."[29]

This sentiment was widely shared by many Latin American leaders, particularly President Carlos Salinas de Gortari of Mexico and President Carlos Saul Menem of Argentina. The warm personal friendship these men felt for Bush was remarkable, considering the great pride the two countries took in their historical record of distancing themselves from US policies. Contrary to the vaunted hemispheric tradition of not mixing into another country's internal affairs, neither Salinas nor Menem made any secret of their hope that Bush would be reelected.

The sentiment was mutual. A touching postscript that illustrates both Bush's continued interest in Latin America and his sense of personal loyalty toward his erstwhile colleagues surfaced in the winter of 1996, when the State Department confirmed a Bolivian report that the US embassy in La Paz had refused a visitor visa to former president Jaime Paz Zamora, who was under investigation for alleged ties to the drug cartels. Bush promptly telephoned Robert Gelbard, the assistant secretary of state for international narcotics and law enforcement affairs. "What are you doing to my friend Jaime?" the former president was reported to have asked the official, a former ambassador to Bolivia. State Department officials speak of the incident in wonderment, stating that it reflected Bush's genuine involvement with Latin America and the region's officials, many of whom he had known from his years as UN ambassador.

Not surprisingly, it was with great dismay that most Latin American leaders witnessed the decline of Bush's popularity in the United States, as his ratings plummeted from the zenith of his popularity during the Gulf War of 1990 to the nadir reached in his last year in office. The debacle came after a series of domestic and foreign policy setbacks, from the public reaction to his decision to raise taxes to sidestepping the debacle in Bosnia and Haiti, not to mention having Japanese television provide a public spectacle of his getting sick at a state dinner offered by the Japanese prime minister in Tokyo.

Those who disliked the Bush era for continuing to cover up the illegal shenanigans the Reagan administration inflicted on Central America must admit that it was also an era of rectifications, imaginative policies and, on the whole, a good thing for inter-American relations. Bush, on becoming president, showed himself a friend of Latin America and eventually won the loyalty, and even the affection, of most hemispheric leaders. But the ineptness of his reelection campaign proved to be his political undoing.

The prestige of the Bush administration, once unsurpassed and seeming unassailable, was shattered forever. Ironically, the promising legacy of his Latin American policy initiatives would be picked up by a little-known governor from a remote state in the Ozarks, Arkansas. His name was William Jefferson Clinton.

NOTES

1. Peter W. Rodman, director of Department of State Policy Planning during the Reagan administration and President Bush's deputy assistant for foreign affairs, writes: "Among the contrasts most apparent to those of us who straddled both administrations were two factors that showed up vividly in Central America policy—the downplaying of ideology and the remarkably frictionless cooperation within the government" (*More Precious Than Peace* [New York: Scribners, 1994], p. 435).

2. A suggestive remark recalling FAR's invocations of the founding fathers by way of stressing US links with the other American nations was contained in Bush's State of the Union address of 1990 when he said, "This nation, this idea called America, was and always will be a new world—our new world."

3. In the midst of the crisis created by the Iraqi invasion of Kuwait in August 1990, Bush told a joint session of Congress: "Out of these troubled times . . . a new world order can emerge: a new era—freer from the threat of terror, stronger in the pursuit of justice, and more secure in the quest for peace. An era in which the nations of the world, East and West, North and South, can prosper and live in harmony. . . . Today that new world is struggling to be born." He repeated the phrase "new world order" a few days later in his call to the United Nations for joint action against the Iraqi aggression in the gulf: "What is at stake is more than one small country; it is a big idea: a new world order, where diverse nations are drawn together in common cause to achieve the universal aspirations of mankind—peace and security, freedom, and the rule of law."

4. Department of State Dispatch, June 24, 1992, p. 452.

5. One after another the region's most prominent Social Democrats were accused, impeached and often convicted of malfeasance of public funds, the most notorious being Alan Garcia of Peru, Carlos Andres Perez of Venezuela and various Sandinista leaders.

6. Robert Pastor, "The Bush Administration and Latin America," *Journal of Interamerican Studies and World Affairs*, Fall 1991, pp. 1–33.

7. Luigi Einaudi, deputy director of the Division of Policy Planning, US Department of State, interview by author, Washington, D.C., November 1, 1995.

8. Luigi Einaudi, interview by author, November 1, 1995.

9. In a speech before the Organization of American States Bush said: "The day of the dictator is over. The people's right to democracy must not be denied" (*New York Times*, May 3, 1989).

10. Robert Pear, "Bush Aides Speak of New Policy of Diplomacy in Central America," *New York Times*, December 20, 1988; "Bush Said to Plan No Early Contra Aid Move," *New York Times*, December 20, 1988, p. A7.

11. Robert Pastor, *Whirlpool: US Foreign Policy Toward Latin America and the Caribbean* (Princeton: Princeton University Press, 1992), p. 97.

12. President Bush's language accompanying the legislation to Congress to implement the initiative, September 14, 1990, Office of the White House Press Secretary.

13. "Bush's Trade Offer Gets a Warm Latin American Reception," *New York Times*, August 26, 1990, p. 23; "Bush to Press Trade on South American Trip," *New York Times,* December 2, 1990, p. 11.

14. Bush speech marking the first anniversary of the Enterprise of the Americas Initiative, delivered in Washington, July 27, 1991; published in Department of State Dispatch, August 8, 1991.

15. "The Contra War: 1981–1990," *New York Times*, June 28, 1990, p. 24.

16. Raymond Vernon, "Passing Through Regionalism: The Transition to Global Markets" (unpublished paper, October 20, 1995).

17. *Operation of the Trade Agreements Program*, 40th Report 1988, USITC Publication 2208 (Washington D.C.: United States International Trade Commission, July 1989), pp. 137–149, 191–203; quoted in Vernon, "Passing Through Regionalism," p. 10.

18. Interview by author, Cuernavaca, April 21, 1991.

19. Michael Gastrin and Leonard Waverman, "Extension of NAFTA to Latin America," in Alan M. Rugman, *Foreign Investment and NAFTA* (Columbia: University of South Carolina Press, 1994), pp. 276–301; quoted by Vernon, "Passing Through Regionalism," p. 11.

20. Metropolitan Museum, New York City, October 10, 1990 (emphasis added).

21. W. Greider, "No More Years: Why George Must Go," *Rolling Stone*, October 1, 1992, p. 19.

22. Peter W. Rodman, *More Precious Than Peace: The Cold War and the Struggle for the Third World* (New York: Scribners, 1994), p. 267; Tony Smith, *America's Mission: The United States and the Worldwide Struggle for Democracy in the Twentieth Century*, A Twentieth Century Fund Book (Princeton: Princeton University Press, 1994), p. 312: "President Bush's response to the challenge of world leadership was appropriately Wilsonian. Given the legacy of the Reagan years and that of Wilson and Roosevelt before him at other watershed moments, how indeed could it have been otherwise?"

23. For a thoughtful, detailed treatment of Resolution 1080, see Viron P. Vaky, "The Organization of American States and Multilateralism in the Americas," in *The Future of the Organization of American States* (New York: Twentieth Century Fund Press, 1993).

24. OAS Document, Santiago, Chile, June 3, 1991. This remarkable speech received unremarkable treatment from the US press, which ignored it.

25. Interview by author, Williamsburg, Virginia, and New York City, October 1995.

26. Conversation with author, Washington, D.C., 1961.

27. Christopher Marquis, "US Study calls Salvador Policy a Failure," *Miami Herald*, international ed., January 17, 1992.

28. Interview on *Frontline*, PBS, November 1988.

29. *Washington Post*, op-ed page, December 6, 1990.

Chapter Thirteen

BILL CLINTON AND THE POLITICS OF TRADE

George Bush's reelection bid against Bill Clinton in 1992 generated an exceptional tide of sympathy for the Republican candidate, from Argentina to Mexico. In the past Latin Americans routinely favored the Democratic candidates, whose platforms on economic and social reform they found more congenial than the Republicans'. Three reasons accounted for the shift: (1) the conviction that fiscal reform and free trade would spur the region's economic growth, fueled by Bush's Enterprise for the Americas Initiative; (2) the pragmatism demonstrated by the Bush White House in helping resolve the Latin American debt crisis and finding political solutions for Central American conflicts; and (3) the fact that Clinton had never been heard from on matters of hemispheric policy, other than for his initial reluctance to endorse the North American Free Trade Agreement (NAFTA).

In Latin America, as in other regions of the world, the Arkansas governor was perceived as a provincial with little interest in, or understanding for, the nuances of foreign policy. To offset this negative image, the Clinton campaign relied on a foreign policy team made up mostly of Carter administration veterans, headed by Warren Christopher, a former undersecretary of state, and academics and bankers such as Anthony Lake and Samuel R. Berger, who would head Clinton's national security staff. The Latin American advisers were a relatively low-profile group, compared to the generalists—Lake, Berger and Richard Holbrooke, who had true hands-on experience in the thicket of international relations.

The Latino advisory body was chaired by Sol Linowitz, a former Xerox executive who had served as ambassador to the Organization of American States in the Johnson administration and subsequently headed the US team that negotiated the final stages of the Carter–Torrijos treaties that gave Panama sovereignty over the canal. The campaign theme was a boilerplate reiteration of the Carter legacy—that Clinton would bring innovation, consistency and confidence to hemisphere policies through a stout commitment to democracy, free market economics and human rights as part of a global strategy. In the event, it showed neither innovation nor imagination.

This was unfortunate; it deprived the first US president elected after the Soviet demise of the opportunity to engage in a national debate about the future course of US foreign policy. It was a time that offered "a rare opportunity, an open but fleeting moment in world history," one that might have expanded the pervasive East–West orientation that continues to condition the world vision of Washington policymakers.[1]

Surely a national debate around the subject of a hemispheric system based no longer on ideological confrontation but on shared values and objectives could have prompted Washington to accord Latin America a more central role in the post–Cold War international constellation. Sadly, the failure to undertake a more imaginative Latin American policy was explained on the ground of ignorance of hemispheric history, traditions and personalities. Even White House and the Department of State experts privately acknowledged this was in good measure because there were "no experts in the top echelons."

Paradoxically, on the few occasions Clinton entertained Latin American leaders or on his rare visits to the other countries of the Americas, there seemed to be no limits to his lavish praise of the region. Again and again he underscored its almost uniform and emphatic embrace of democracy and free market reforms as a model to the rest of the world. But the emotional words were rarely accompanied by concomitant action, as was eminently demonstrated by his failure to live up to the pledge to bring Chile into the North American Free Trade Agreement (NAFTA) that the United States has with Canada and Mexico. That would be postponed to the last couple of months before he left the White House. Indeed, his first two years in office left much of the hemispheric agenda languishing on the proverbial back burner.

More hung in the balance than just a paralyzed trade expansion process; Latin America understood that Chile had been designated since the Bush administration to be the first to join NAFTA, not just because it had led the process of market opening but also because it had carried out a successful transition from military dictatorship to electoral democracy. As Bernard Aronson pointed out, after Congress refused to grant Clinton "fast-track" authority to negotiate with Chile, "the momentum for market reform, and also democratization, diminished in Latin America, and so did US leadership."[2]

This hesitation certainly belied the election campaign slogans suggesting a Clinton administration would restore a youthful "Kennedy spirit" to hemispheric relations along with Carter's conspicuous emphasis on human rights.

Throughout the campaign, the Clinton camp accused Bush of failing to restore democracy in Haiti after the military coup that deposed President Jean-Bertrand Aristide, of refusing to admit Haitian refugees to the United States and of hurting labor and the environment with his initiative to bring Mexico into the North American Free Trade Agreement (NAFTA) the United States had negotiated with Canada.

Once in office, however, it did not take long for Clinton and his advisers to realize that there was more to the Bush administration's Latin American policy than their campaign rhetoric had allowed. In quick succession, Clinton shifted positions to proclaim bold support of NAFTA, continue the ban on Haitian refugees and retain the ambiguous approach toward Aristide the State Department and CIA had developed under Bush.

As early beliefs that the post–Cold War world would be dominated by regional partnerships, a more equitable distribution of wealth and respect for human rights faded, economic expansion emerged as the Clinton administration's main tool to promote democracy. And when it seemed prudent to tread water rather than act on behalf of principle, that was the preferred choice, as was the case with a string of diplomatic appointments when they ran into opposition in the Foreign Relations Committee headed by Senator Jesse Helms, or policies toward Cuba and Haiti or the halting position on opening CIA files going back to the years Washington was in collusion with the military dictators of the 1970s and early 1980s.

Even though the young president from Arkansas continued to cite President Kennedy as his role model, more often than not his administration followed in the footprints of Carter. The criticism of Carter by two influential Democratic party foreign policy voices, Harry McPherson and Richard Holbrooke, could just as well apply to the early phases of Clinton's foreign policy: "Once the party of a positive, internationalist foreign policy, the party that had led the nation to meet its world responsibilities, the Democrats by 1980 had become identified with indecision, retreat and apology."[3] Indeed, twenty years later, an article in *Foreign Affairs* directed a similar comment to Clinton's foreign policy noting "the degree to which he departed from his initial idealism and embraced Realpolitik."[4]

The problem, of course, transcended Latin American affairs. Though Bill Clinton was recognized as one of the most intelligent heads of state in recent history and as having great political skills, his administration was afflicted by the image problem that haunted Carter: he confused people as to his real position, causing him to appear not so much well-balanced as vacillating, not so much wise as weak. Observers agreed that Clinton compromised on much and satisfied few. Policy often appeared to be spinning full circle.

Early on Clinton adopted a hard line toward Cuba, such as backing the Torricelli bill to further tighten the embargo, even though many of his advisers favored dialogue and easing relations. In fact, his position turned out to be more rigid than that of his predecessor. The Republican Bush administration, widely thought to favor a tougher approach toward the Castro government than the Democrats, had carefully begun to distance itself from Jorge Mas Canosa's influential right-wing Cuban-American National Foundation by opening the White House to more moderate Cuban exile leaders, such as Carlos Alberto Montaner and Eloy Gutiérrez Menoyo. Clinton, on the other hand, quietly and swiftly restored the primacy of Mas Canosa in a calculated bid to win the help of the Cuban exiles to wrest Florida from the Republican ranks—a ploy that paid off in the 1996 election.

When the subject of Cuba surfaced at a private luncheon Clinton had at the home of *Washington Post* publisher Katharine Graham at Martha's Vineyard in the summer of 1994 with novelists Carlos Fuentes and Gabriel García Márquez, the conversation promptly and politely turned to literature. The Colombian novelist had hoped to persuade Clinton to ease the blockade, but he realized early on that the Clinton administration's acquiescence to conservative pressures to tighten the embargo against the Castro regime remained undeterred. So much for bold new directions.

The hesitation and backsliding that became a hallmark of the Clinton style of governing also afflicted his federal appointments, as has been widely noted in the media in connection with the Supreme Court nominations and a whole series of ambassadorial appointments that were shot down by Senator Jesse Helms's Foreign Relations Committee. In Latin American affairs this was instantly brought out when the president tapped Mario Baeza, a black Cuban American Princeton graduate with a reputation as a brilliant New York lawyer, for the job of assistant secretary of state for Inter-American affairs. The surprise designation suggested that Clinton was indeed disposed to strike out in new directions. But the White House waffled the moment Baeza came under fire from Mas Canosa's Miami-based foundation, and his appointment was sent into oblivion.

In June 1993, after months of soul-searching, the administration submitted to the Senate the nomination of Alexander Watson, a respected career foreign service officer who most recently had been ambassador to Peru, after serving in many Latin American posts. He would head the Inter-American bureau until March 15, 1996, just short of Aronson's record of four years, plagued, like many of his predecessors, by inattention from the secretary of state and the White House. By the time he resigned, Watson had become thoroughly disenchanted with White House neglect.

Watson was succeeded by another career diplomat, Jeff Davidow, a six-footer with a gruff sense of humor. Davidow benefited from greater access to the White House with the help of Ambassador James Dobbins, a "Europeanist" who was brought from Brussels to become Latin American adviser on the National Security Council. They made an effective team, as Dobbins had the reputation of being a highly competent administrator "who knew how to get the attention of the President."[5] But beyond keeping the bureaucracy running and keeping Congress informed on the progress or regress of the war on drugs in Latin America, and putting out small brushfires here and there, nothing noteworthy happened until the end of 1994.

Latin America finally received serious, if only transient, notice when Clinton convened the Summit of the Americas for December 1994. The way it was announced was illustrative of how offhandedly the administration dealt with hemisphere affairs. Indeed little attention was paid to a hasty announcement made by Vice President Al Gore in Mexico of a forthcoming hemispheric summit, despite the fact that it would be the first in which the United States would participate since the Punta del Este meeting President Lyndon Johnson attended in 1964.

On a personal level, most Latin American leaders who called on Clinton in Washington or dealt with him in Miami and Santiago agreed that he projected himself as articulate, intelligent and openminded. Nor were they surprised at his general lack of understanding for the region. They expected nothing else.

THE UPHILL ROAD TO THE SUMMIT, DENOUEMENT AND RESURRECTION

The first harbinger of the drive to put an economic stamp on Latin American policy came the day after the Senate ratified NAFTA, when Vice President Gore flew to Mexico for a triumphal appearance before the Mexican Congress. In a speech to a cheering audience that included President Carlos Salinas de Gortari, Gore portrayed the agreement as the culmination of the first stage of a process begun by Bush that had profoundly altered the relationship between the two countries. Rejecting the old fears of Yankee imperialism, the Salinas government had enacted an unprecedented series of laws to open to the private sector and foreign investments an economy that for more than half a century had been firmly controlled by the government and exclusionary nationalistic regulations as part of his audacious goal "to bring Mexico into the First World," with the United States as its closest partner. But it was a couple of paragraphs inserted in the text at the last minute that captured the headlines in the news stories that appeared the next day: President Clinton would invite the heads of state of the Americas, save Cuba, for the first Pan American summit in almost three decades.

Considering the significance of the announcement to the whole hemisphere, it seemed odd that it would be made not by Clinton in Washington but by the vice president in Mexico, a country many Latin Americans already suspected of monopolizing US attention. At the same time, the message could not have been more imprecise. The fact that Clinton himself failed to make the announcement in Washington, where he at least commanded the attention of the White House press corps as well as space on his Saturday broadcasts, was a classic example of the kind of problems the Clinton administration had in getting its Latin American policy to the US public. Some attributed this gap to poor staff, but it was perhaps more a lack of genuine commitment at the highest level of the administration.

Barely two months prior to the summit the event appeared headed toward chaos, or so it appeared to the resident Latin American diplomats in Washington. Planning was in disarray, they reported. The White House was distracted elsewhere and swamped with internal troubles. Latin Americans complained that National Security Council expert Richard Feinberg, who was charged with drafting the agenda, wanted to turn the summit into a "moral crusade" against corruption and drug trafficking without paying adequate attention to the economic and trade interests that the Latin Americans considered the raison d'être of the conference.

Paulo Tarso Flecha de Lima, Brazil's blunt-spoken ambassador to the United States and a veteran of many inter-American negotiations, made no secret of his disdain for the White House agenda. He seemed to take special delight in criticizing Feinberg personally and threatened to ask that Brazil boycott the conference unless trade was made the centerpiece. Complaining that the Clinton administration was preoccupied "only with getting domestic mileage" out of the conference, he told me, "This is no more than a publicity stunt, a photo-op for domestic purposes; they care not a fig about our needs." The ill-prepared meeting, he said, was proof positive that Washington, aside from paying lip service to the reforms undertaken by the Latin American governments, failed to grasp the "enormous efforts and sacrifices" these governments had made in recent years by adopting US-sponsored reforms, often braving social and political backlash, in order to open their economies to the private sector. In a last-minute personal appeal to Clinton's chief of staff, Thomas "Mack" McLarty, Tarso declared, "We struggled to implant democracy and to reform our economies without any cost to the U.S. taxpayers, we are not supplicants, we seek equity."[6]

McLarty, instructed by Clinton to salvage the conference, went to work around the clock with a hastily organized Latin American task force headed by the Brazilian envoy. The group, joined by deputy foreign ministers and a group of hardy officials from the Department of Commerce and the Office of the Trade Representative, held a weekend meeting at Arlie House, an old plantation in nearby Maryland. With McLarty's folksy way of resolving conflicts, the deadlock over the agenda was broken with the US delegates agreeing to give priority to trade and economic issues, which the National Security Council and State Department advisers had relegated to the back burner of the agenda. McLarty, a successful businessman from Arkansas, made sure that trade would dominate the meeting.

At the summit Clinton gave a prodigious display of personal charm and political talent. He was in his element, projecting with irrepressible gusto his election battle cry, "It's the economy, stupid," onto a hemispheric scenario. The high point came when he obtained general agreement from the other thirty-three leaders to launch plans for a free trade zone from Alaska to Tierra del Fuego at the southernmost tip of South America by the year 2005. Though at the time this goal appeared to be faltering, the Free Trade Area of the Americas (FTAA) would become the main and probably most lasting achievement of the Latin American policy of Clinton's two terms in office.

Clinton portrayed the Miami summit as a pivotal event in the history of hemispheric relations. Flanked by thirty-three leaders of the Americas, he proclaimed that the plans laid out at the summit would create a market of 850 million people by 2005 and multiply US exports and jobs. The first concrete step would be to make Chile, Latin America's fastest-growing economy with the lowest tariff scale, the "fourth partner" of NAFTA prior to the next summit, scheduled to be held in Santiago, Chile, in 1998.

In what might be a forgivable moment of exhilaration Clinton called the concord of the conference "a miracle." In fact, it was not miraculous but the result of political and economic interests that had been converging for almost a decade. He also predicted that a "whole new architecture" of regional relations would stem from the conference. If it was meant to be an "architecture," however, it did not adequately supply the bricks and mortar on which to build a solid foundation; most of the projects and initiatives adopted in Miami were remitted to the OAS for implementation. But immediately an anomaly came to the fore: the White House team advancing the summit agenda with its new tasks for the OAS seemed unaware that the State Department was leading a drive to cut the organization's budget from $100 million to $80 million. But relieved governments said at least they were taking home some achievements.

To some the Miami summit was a case study of a good idea that risked being undercut by poor organization and staff work. In the words of a veteran Argentine diplomat, "The Clinton administration comes up with good ideas and means well; the problem is a chronically poor methodology."[7] He might have added that the methodology was poor because foreign policy goals in the Americas were continually deformed by the primacy of Washington's East-West orientation when they were not being diluted by domestic politics. Even members of the US government conceded that the Miami summit was "an event looking for a mission." Eventually the opening of wider trade relations became the central purpose of the US initiative.

To the dismay of Latin America, the central project of Clinton's initiative, the creation of an FTAA by 2005, stalled when Congress balked at giving the administration fast-track authority to fulfill its pledge to bring Chile into NAFTA by the end of 1997. That authority would have allowed the administration to negotiate trade deals without the risk of a line-by-line legislative veto. Seeking a trade negotiating authority enjoyed by every president since Gerald Ford, Clinton worked the phones frantically. He sent virtually his entire cabinet to roam the halls of Congress. Vice President Gore had called a fast-track defeat "unthinkable."

Yet the bill—supported by three former presidents, the congressional Republican leadership, big business, every prestige newspaper, and practically every mainstream economist—lost. Fast-track failed because Clinton did not have the support of two traditional Democratic constituencies, labor and the organized environmental groups, and not enough votes could be mustered from the Republican side. He failed, in the words of Peter Beinart, the editor of the *New Republic*, "because in the past six years a wave of nationalism has hit both parties substantially altering their character on issues like trade." This was due to the national passions unleashed by the "anti-Washington, anti-Wall Street fury unleashed by the candidacies of Ross Perot and Pat Buchanan." Others might suggest that it failed because Clinton did not see it as one of his foreign policy priorities, as with NAFTA or the Middle East, to which he would have given his undivided attention until he rounded up enough votes to push it through.

What struck Latin American leaders as paradoxical was that the US president who had convened the first inter-American summit in thirty-seven years should be so inconsistent in his policy directives. This belief was reinforced when Clinton became the first modern US president not to visit the region during his first term in office. It was not until May 1997, at the beginning of his second term, that Clinton headed south on his first official trip to Mexico and Central America. The year had been proclaimed by the White House as the "Year of Latin America," but this did not help him when he sought to win support to push through fast-track authority from Congress. Besides the embarrassment over the absence of progress on the FTAA, the president further disappointed his hosts by appearing more concerned with US domestic politics than with the conference he had helped create. "His mind was not only on what Congress was doing to the social security legislation but also on a forthcoming trip to China," a disillusioned member of the US delegation confided to a Chilean diplomat. Not having much to show for on trade, Clinton recommended measures to foster cooperation in consolidating democracy, expanding the role of civil society, developing education and combating narcotics and poverty. But Latin Americans surely focused more on what was missing from the speech than on his rhetoric.

What surprises, however, is that after a delay of almost six years, the United States and Chile decided on November 29, 2000, to launch the negotiations for a free trade agreement, barely six weeks before Clinton was to vacate the White House. It would have been encouraging to report that toward the end of his presidency Clinton had refocused on Chile to redeem his early promises, but that was not the case. "We were shamed into renewing the talks because of Chile's indignant reaction to the sudden free trade negotiations with Singapore and Jordan," State Department officials acknowledged a month later.[8]

A terse statement by Clinton merely noted that the United States and the government of Chilean President Ricardo Lagos would make a new effort to reach an accord that "reflects our mutual commitment to advancing free and open trade and investment in the Americas and around the world." Perhaps not by accident the statement came only days after the United States had entered into similar negotiations with Singapore, touched off by a casual promise Clinton made to President S. R. Nathan at a golf course during a conference of financial heads.

The sudden move infuriated the Brazilian government of Fernando Henrique Cardoso, which had labored hard to bring Chile into Mercosur, the common market made up by Argentina, Brazil, Paraguay and Uruguay. Brazil had hoped to strengthen its bargaining position by presenting a united front among the Mercosur countries and associate members like Bolivia, Chile and eventually other Andean countries when time came to negotiate the establishment of a Free Trade Area of the Americas with the United States.

Just a few months earlier, in late August, Cardoso attempted further to consolidate this "united front" by finally giving in to a long-held conviction that Brazil should take the lead in forming a South American subregional group.

He did this by convening the first conference ever of only the heads of state of the twelve South American countries in Brasilia on August 31, 2000. Behind this carefully laid out plan was the clear expectation of speeding agreement to link Mercosur with a yet foundering Andean common market. But that idea soon fell apart, given the reluctance of Brazil's neighbors to tolerate what some feared would be the formal emergence of another hegemonic power in the hemisphere. "Our future hinges on having access to the US market, not with Brazil," President Jorge Batlle of Uruguay told me as he attended the Millennium Summit of the United Nations barely three days after the Brasilia meeting adjourned.[9] Chile's renewed bid to join NAFTA only appeared further to vacillate the Brazilian plan.

PRAGMATIC SHIFTS AND POLICY STUMBLES

The president finally matched the rhetoric to his Latin American amigos by making his first trip to Latin America and the Caribbean four months into his second term. The discrepancies between words and action should not have surprised anybody. From the outset of his administration, Clinton's foreign policy was marked by fluctuations and contradictions. In 1992, for example, he could tell the United Nations not to neglect its obligations to protect democracy around the globe. The following year he returned to warn that the organization cannot police every trouble spot in the world. But by 1994, addressing the world forum again, he reverted to the "defense of democracy" argument after Washington was compelled to send US troops to Haiti and Bosnia. Once the determined advocate of an assertive multilateralism, the rule of the World Court and other measures to regulate the international community, the United States increasingly became a reluctant participant. In another retreat, he declined to join Canada in its otherwise successful bid to get worldwide support for the convention against the use of land mines as well as various international treaties to protect the environment.

Similar contradictions afflicted his Latin American policies. On the one hand, there was a dissolute and protracted negotiation to restore the Aristide government in Haiti, and an analogous ambivalence when it came to sanctioning the Peruvian regime of Alberto Fujimori for its corruption and violation of human rights. On the other hand, the administration developed an unflaggingly close relationship with Mexico and generally friendly relations with the government of Brazilian president Fernando Henrique Cardoso, except for some tiffs over trade restrictions. Still, decisive leadership from the White House in the foreign policy field was not readily forthcoming. Perhaps the Clinton administration was so set on reelection that it rarely challenged the Republicans on matters of foreign policy.

By the end of the 1993–1996 term, however, the Clinton administration envisioned US leadership—and US exceptionalism—in world affairs hinging on expanding trade, successful peacekeeping and the strengthening of democratic institutions and human rights around the world. Secretary Christopher put it succinctly:

> In this time of accelerated change, American leadership must remain constant. We must be clear-eyed and vigilant in pursuit of our interest. Above all, we must recognize that *only* the United States has the vision and strength to consolidate the gains of the last few years, and to build an even better world. . . . Without American leadership, thugs would still rule in Haiti, and thousands of Haitian refugees would be trying to reach our shores. The Mexican economy would be in free-fall, threatening our prosperity and harming emerging markets and the global economy.[10]

The statement anticipated a key foreign policy message of Clinton's reelection campaign: the United States as "the indispensable" nation. Since his first term in office, he stated in his second inaugural address, "America stands alone as the world's indispensable nation."[11] Once again, "our economy is the strongest on earth." If the phrase failed to ignite public pride, its bombast succeeded in alienating friends and foes alike.

America's growth statistics justified a degree of smugness, both in the country at large and in the Washington establishment. Had not the British historian Paul Kennedy, a Yale professor, forecast a gloomy prognosis for US economic and political hegemony in *The Rise and Fall of the Great Powers*, an acclaimed best-seller? Yet in the dozen years since the book appeared in 1988, the United States had won the Cold War as well as two wars in the Middle East and the Balkans. At the same time, the impressive roar of the economic "tigers" of Japan and the rest of Asia turned to pleas of help to Washington and the international banks. Commenting on the US scene in the light of Kennedy's foreboding, a veteran columnist of the *Financial Times* cautioned, "The dramatic turnaround should give pause to anyone considering making grand forecasts."[12]

Not surprisingly, then, Christopher's successor, Madeleine K. Albright, instructed by Clinton to wed foreign policy to public policy, repeated the "indispensable country" notion incessantly in her assertive drive to galvanize US public support behind the administration's foreign policy agenda and in the resolute rhetoric in international forums. Whereas from the former she expected to win congressional backing for a less restrictive budget for the State Department and the foreign aid program, from the latter she hoped to earn recognition for what she considered was Washington's deserved leadership.

In either case, the administration's tendency to build its policy around the notion of an expanding global economy kept Latin America's aspirations of greater political recognition on the sidelines.

Thus nothing very dramatic happened on the Latin American policy scene during Clinton's watch at the White House. The thrust of White House interest was concentrated on the economic field, focused on trade and the generation of jobs in the United States. Political leadership could be left to Brazil or Mexico, if they wanted it, or so the White House reasoning went.[13] The upshot was that in Latin America, as elsewhere, Clinton acquired the reputation of indecisiveness and inconsistency that continued to haunt his presidency at home and abroad.

Toward the end of his first term, the *New York Times* characterized Clinton's foreign policy as having shifted from the idealism that had made human rights a crucible of his foreign policy to more "pragmatic" and "politically astute" approaches "more reminiscent of his Republican predecessor than of the last Democratic President."[14] By the end of his second term, another commentator noted that in his handling of foreign policy, Clinton illustrated "the degree to which he departed from his initial idealism and embraced realpolitik."[15] A front-page *Washington Post* headline over a retrospective analysis of the Clinton administration went further: "Policy and Politics by the Numbers: For the President, Polls Became a Defining Force in His Administration."[16]

Another area of Clinton roller coasting showed up in its efforts to curb drug trafficking. Having at first objected to "militarizing" the war against drugs, Clinton finally bowed to Republican pressure in Congress by appointing a five-star general, Barry McCaffrey, the US "drug czar." Though in his confirmation hearings General McCaffrey promised that 75 percent of his first budget of some $9 billion would go into "prevention and treatment" of drug abuse, five years later he had doubled his annual budget to $20 billion with most of the money going into enforcement.

Likewise, the general, a former head of the Southern Command, became the most passionate advocate within the administration on behalf of a congressional drive launched by conservative Republicans to "militarize" the war on drugs in Colombia. It led to the passage of the controversial $1.3 billion Plan Colombia. With most of the money going into military training, equipment and armed helicopters used more for "counterinsurgency" purposes than hunting down elusive drug laboratories, the project immediately touched off bitter protests both in the United States and across Latin America and Europe. The issue of narcotics ballooned under the Clinton administration to the point where at least in Congress it rivaled the status enjoyed by communism during the Cold War, the only wake-up call capable of drawing legislators' attention to hemispheric problems.

From the reversal of the Haitian refugee policy to the steady shift away from his early promise to make multilateralism and UN peacemaking the cornerstone of Washington's post–Cold War policy, to his critics these and other flip-flops made Clinton look like a man who would bargain any principle away. Too often his foreign policy seemed guided not by domestic interests but by the latest opinion poll.

On Haiti, it took a belated White House order, prodded by the Congressional Black Caucus, to move the troops into the island to restore the freely elected government of Aristide. And that only after the ignominious episode of the USS *Harlan County*, the vessel carrying a lightly armed force whose purpose was to train a civilian police force that backed down in the face of Tonton Macoutes bullies who made scary noises but would have scattered like scared rabbits had somebody given the order to shoot over their heads.

The circle of the administration's capitulation to the Miami-based Cuban lobby was completed when the president signed the Helms-Burton bill after opposing it while it was being debated in Congress. It immediately nettled some of Washington's closest allies—Canada, the European Union and the nations of Latin America and the Caribbean. At times the president seemed temperamentally incapable of consistency. Observers agreed that Clinton compromised on much and satisfied few.

The media seemed determined not to let a single flaw in the Clinton administration go unnoticed, perhaps a reaction to past criticism that it had been too lenient with Reagan and Bush. But administration complaints that never before had a sitting president been so unfairly castigated by the news organizations and columnists lacked the perspective of US history. Harry Truman and Lyndon Johnson had made the same claim with far better reason.

It is also true that Clinton faced a world vastly different from that of his predecessors. Not only had the end of the Cold War left the United States in a position of unprecedented military and economic power, but it also emerged as a kind of postmodern pioneer, leading the world in higher education, scientific research and advanced technology that called for entirely new mind-sets, both in confronting domestic problems and formulating international relations. All eyes were on Clinton—the former Arkansas governor who ran on a purely domestic platform was viewed skeptically throughout the hemisphere.

There was also a pervasive disenchantment that, with the Cold War won, the US government still seemed more concerned with Moscow and its former territories than with Latin America.

By the time his reelection campaign began, the US chief of state, who had convened the first inter-American summit in almost thirty years, incongruously became the first president since Calvin Coolidge to fail to tour the region during his first term in office, even though he had visited and revisited Europe, the Middle East and Asia. The closest he came to Latin America was a four-hour visit to Haiti. Nor did he even call on Puerto Rico, though Governor Pedro Rosselló had recently been named vice chairman of the Democratic Governors' Caucus. For a man so gregarious and outgoing, he displayed an unusual disconnect when it came to Latin America.

"Something I need to take on even more," Clinton said in an interview, "is trying to figure out a way to make the American people believe, not just episodically but instinctively, that there's no longer an easy dividing line between foreign policy and domestic policy, that the world that we're living in doesn't permit us that luxury any more."[17]

That insight had long been common currency among professional diplomats and academic foreign policy experts. It revealed that Clinton, who had campaigned on domestic economic issues, during his early tenure in the White House had yet to define a conceptual structure of US foreign policy and a strategy to explain its themes for public discussion at home and abroad. It did not take long for some voices to warn that the opportunity to do this by expanding the opening provided by Bush's NAFTA and the Enterprise for the Americas Initiative was in danger of being wasted.[18]

That task had to await the departure of his publicity-shy Secretary Christopher and the arrival of his successor, Albright, who began her tenure with a determined effort to develop a broader foreign policy constituency at home and greater acceptance for Washington's policies abroad. The new secretary proved to be even more Eurocentric than her predecessors. It was not until 1996 that Albright, still as US ambassador to the United Nations, paid a surprise visit to Bolivia; her goals were to explain to the heads of state attending a Rio Group meeting the reasons behind the administration's Cuban policy and to pursue her successful campaign against the reelection of Boutros Boutros-Ghali as the world organization's secretary-general.

On the upside, Clinton's quick intelligence and convivial personality helped him develop close contacts with other world leaders, and in time he acquired a surer footing in international affairs, especially during his second term, when much of his domestic program was preempted by the Republican-controlled

Congress and a host of ethical problems about finances and his private life took some luster away from his image and credibility at home. Perhaps he concluded that exercising a stronger role as the leader of the world's only remaining superpower would compensate for his perceived domestic weaknesses and the embarrassment caused by the Lewinsky affair.

Still, there were times when something lighthearted, almost frivolous, seemed to creep into Clinton's conduct of foreign policy. That is what a considerable number of diplomats and scholars thought when he finally scheduled his first trip to Latin America in May 1997, his fifth year in office. He spent two days in San José, Costa Rica, for a meeting with the heads of state of the five Central American countries and the Dominican Republic (Panama did not attend).

A trip to South America followed in October, when he spent one day in Venezuela, two in Brazil and three full days in Argentina, which his aides explained was a gesture reciprocating president Carlos Menem's professions of "carnal relations" with the United States, an attitude unprecedented in the history of Peronism. The cozying up to Menem, whose government was reputedly one of the most corrupt in recent Argentine history, strained relations with that country's neighbors, especially Chile, after Clinton announced it had consented to Menem's plea to become a "major strategic non-NATO ally," a status heretofore enjoyed only by such strategically significant countries as Israel, Egypt and Japan.[19] It was a minor concession in practical terms, as it only made it easier for Argentina to acquire weapons, most US surplus, but the gesture carried a powerful political impact, particularly in Brazil and Chile, countries that considered themselves worthier democratic allies than Menem, who was regarded as a clever upstart. State Department officials conceded privately that the whole thing had been "an embarrassing mistake" in that without formal consultations or department approval, Menem and his foreign minister, Guido di Tella, had talked the US embassy into sending their request to Washington.

During an unofficial visit to the United States, Menem had "profusely thanked" Clinton for agreeing to his letter, to which Clinton smiled and assented without knowing what it was about. When Menem left the White House meeting he told Argentine newsmen he had succeeded in his bid to obtain "extra-NATO status," after which neither the White House nor the State Department thought it would be wise to disavow him.

To make matters worse, word leaked out, and Secretary of State Albright was asked about the Argentine claims when she was leaving her office with the visiting Chilean secretary of foreign affairs, José Miguel Insulza. They had just discussed the sensitive issue of the Clinton administration's decision to restore to Latin American governments the right to buy US military equipment, which had been banned during the Carter era.

As if it was not already embarrassing enough for the Chilean minister to hear the secretary adorn the decision made to please the US defense industry by claiming that Chile had asked the ban to be lifted so that it could buy modern US fighter planes, a statement Insulza denied on returning to Chile, Secretary Albright claimed to know nothing about endowing Argentina, Chile's neighbor, with extra-NATO ally status but said nobody would mind. However, Insulza's face turned crimson.

Whenever Clinton made a promising approach to Latin American affairs, he would stumble, mainly over obstacles of the administration's own making. With the singular exception of Undersecretary of State Thomas R. Pickering, a former ambassador to El Salvador, few of his top foreign policy advisers had extensive experience in Latin American affairs or, worse, cared much about them. Nor did anybody, from Albright to Samuel "Sandy" Berger to Strobe Talbott, possess the kind of passionate commitment that would have been necessary to take the region from the sidelines and move it onto the main playing field.

Occasional visits from a Latin American head of state or tea with David Rockefeller or Sol Linowitz, two aging senior statesmen, reminded the president that he needed to overcome the conspiracy of complacency that surrounded Latin American policy, but since the demise of the Kennedy administration there had never been a sustained effort to accomplish this. They would remind him of the importance of being ahead of events in foreign policy, prompt him to return to the rhetoric he had so skillfully employed in Miami, but that impetus never lasted very long.

Still, at the end of the Clinton administration Albright would defend its Latin American policies, stating that the president and she had made more trips to the region than any previous US leaders, as if miles traveled were a surrogate for a coherent policy. Perhaps what discouraged many Latin Americans and baffled foreign policy observers was Clinton's failure to consolidate the gains made in Miami with the obligatory Latin American trip before his term was over, thus passing up another opportunity for the kind of personal diplomacy he excelled in—and that Latin Americans hold in high esteem. Instead, in February 1996, nine months before the elections, Clinton scheduled a one-day visit to Tijuana, Mexico, to meet with President Ernesto Zedillo, who was confronting deep-seated political and economic problems. The immediate reason was to proclaim renewed US–Mexican friendship and lend support for his reform program.

By the end of his first term Clinton had met with his Mexican colleague only three times, compared to Bush's eleven sessions with Zedillo's predecessor, President Carlos Salinas de Gortari, in Mexico, Canada and France, as well as the United States. However, until the trip to Mexico was announced in February 1996, the White House said there were no plans for Clinton to visit Latin America before the election, even though trips had been scheduled to Spain, Russia and Japan. "Remember that the President spent three days on the summit in Miami," one official said ruefully. "That should be the equivalent of one trip to Latin America."[20] It was not, so far as Latin Americans were concerned.

If throughout his administration Clinton considered the Summit of the Americas initiative to have been the "summit" of his Latin American policy, it must be recognized that after the exhilaration the presidential rhetoric brought to the Miami meeting, little of note took place after the conference. The summits provided little in the way of a coherent vision of the role the hemisphere was to play in the total framework of US foreign policy. There was not even a road map of how further to expand NAFTA or hitch together the different trade groups of the region. A measure of the complexity of the negotiations yet to come is that nobody knows whether nations will be able to join the new club individually or in groups, or whether the US Congress will ratify each treaty separately or all together. "What we have is a flight plan that will keep us busy for years to come," said Mexican Foreign Minister José Angel Gurria. "How to get there will be the biggest issue to be resolved."

THE PLUS SIDE

The Clinton administration's first outstanding foreign policy success on the hemispheric front stemmed from his pushing ratification of NAFTA for Mexico through a recalcitrant Senate and then using his executive power to approve a $12.5 billion credit to save the Mexican peso from collapse after Congress refused to authorize an appropriation to ease the neighbor country's financial crisis. A similar maneuver helped back Brazil's financial reforms. Significantly, these efforts were led not by the State Department but by the compelling arguments presented by Treasury Secretary Robert E. Rubin and the teams at Commerce and the Office of the Trade Representative, backed by powerful business and banking interests.

The direction of hemisphere policy had already shifted to the administration's economic team, where it remained to the end of a Clinton presidency whose foreign policy was based on the premise that economic globalization was inevitable. In retrospect it appears NAFTA was the one issue on which

Clinton countenanced no compromise. When Lane Kirkland, the president of the AFL-CIO, offered to support the president's cherished health plan before a sharply divided Congress if he would drop NAFTA, Clinton did not budge. NAFTA passed; health care did not. By December 1993, it appeared that Clinton's leadership in the bipartisan effort on behalf of NAFTA might usher in a more decisively hemisphere-oriented foreign policy.

The bruising fight to the finish line to bring relief to the Mexican economy, at a time when that government was facing profound internal dislocations, scandals and a rash of unsolved political killings, recalled Carter's bitter, politically costly struggle to win approval of the ratification of the Panama Canal treaties that would return the canal to Panamanian sovereignty by the year 2000. But then, fearing negative domestic reactions, he never showed up at the transfer ceremonies on December 15, 1999, to the dismay of the Panamanians.

Meanwhile, the president took advantage of his first trip to Latin America in May 1997 to urge the Central American governments to be patient while his administration sought to give the region some of the benefits enjoyed by NAFTA through a measure known as the Caribbean Basin Initiative Enhancement Act. It finally passed, four years later, almost overshadowed by Mexico's efforts to create its own common market with the Central American countries through an imaginative regional industrial development plan president Vicente Fox dubbed From Puebla to Panama.

Some Central Americans groused at the slow pace of US policy, pointing at the rapid progress made by what emerged as the most successful economic regional arrangement other than NAFTA, the Mercosur common market among Argentina, Brazil, Uruguay and Paraguay, which Chile and Bolivia were invited to join. Established as a trading bloc by the Treaty of Asunción in 1991, at the behest of Brazil and Argentina, it quickly acquired great geostrategic importance to Brazilian foreign policy. Brazilian foreign minister Celso Lafer called it "a symbol of a new South American presence in the post–Cold War."[21]

The Brazilian–Argentinean understanding, according to Lafer, lies at the heart of Mercosur, "just as the understanding between Germany and France stood as the cornerstone for the construction of the European Community."[22] This time, however, Latin America would not wait. The rise of a globally integrated transnational economy run by private corporations bigger than most countries propelled the Latin American countries and the Caribbean to move swiftly into a series of subregional free market arrangements, rather than mark time until Congress decided to authorize the expansion of NAFTA.

By the year 2000, six years after Clinton pledged before the first Summit of the Americas in Miami to bring Chile and other reform nations into the North

American Free Trade Agreement (NAFTA), the promise remained unfulfilled. The administration backed down, after a combination of Republican protectionists and Democratic labor congressmen voted against giving the administration a "fast-track" to negotiate the agreements. "Had the president really pressed for it, he could have had the votes," I was told by Senator Paul Coverdell, the late chairman of the Senate Foreign Relations Western Hemisphere subcommittee, late in 1997.

Although Latin America stood ready as in no time since the 1940s to give new life to the hemispheric alliance, Washington left the field to Spain. Between 1990 and 2000, Spanish banks, communications conglomerates and hotel conglomerates and heavy industries had outstripped US investments in at least five major countries, Argentina, Brazil, Chile, Peru and Colombia, not to mention Cuba.

Still, some experts considered Clinton's relatively low-key foreign policy to be appropriate to its time, "when there is little to gain in foreign policy and much to lose," according to Stephen M. Walt, professor of international relations at the John F. Kennedy School at Harvard University. "The American people recognize this and have made it clear they want neither isolationism nor costly international crusades. Bill Clinton is nothing if not sensitive to the vox-populi, so he has given his fellow citizens the foreign policy they wanted," Walt wrote.[23]

NOTES

1. Carnegie Endowment for International Peace, *Changing Our Ways* (Washington, D.C.: Carnegie Corporation, 1992), p. 1.

2. Bernard Aronson, "A Hero in Mexico," op-ed, *Washington Post*, July 20, 2000.

3. "A Foreign Policy for the Democrats," *New York Times Sunday Magazine*, December 1983, p. 18.

4. Stephen M. Walt, "Two Cheers for Clinton's Foreign Policy," *Foreign Affairs*, March–April 2000, p. 78.

5. Ambassador Davidow, interview by author, Mexico City, April 1999.

6. Interview by author, October 1994.

7. Argentine ambassador Guido di Tella, interview by author, Washington, D.C., July 1994. Di Tella subsequently served as foreign minister from October 1994 through 1999.

8. Two State Department sources, interview by author, Four Seasons Hotel, Washington, D.C., December 12, 2000.

9. Interview by author, New York City, September 5, 2000.

10. "Leadership for the Next American Century," lecture by Secretary of State Warren Christopher at the John F. Kennedy School, Harvard University, Cambridge, Massachusetts, January 18, 1996.

11. Transcript of Clinton's second inaugural address, *New York Times,* January 21, 1997, p. 14.

12. See Gerald Baker, "The Future of America: Liberty's Triumph," *Financial Times,* December 23, 1999, p. 12.

13. Numerous interviews and conversations with James Dobbins, national security adviser; his successor, Arturo Valenzuela; and Jeffrey Davidow, Peter Romero and other assistant secretaries of state, 1994–2000.

14. Steven Erlanger and David E. Sanger, "On Global Stage, Clinton's Pragmatic Turn," *New York Times,* July 19, 1996, p. 1.

15. Walt, "Two Cheers," p. 78.

16. "The Clinton Years: Story of a Survivor," *Washington Post,* December 31, 2000, p. 1.

17. "Clinton Years," p. 16.

18. Reports of Inter-American Dialogue, WOLA (1993); Benjamin Gilman, chairman, House International Affairs Committee, interview by author, April 1994, published in *Diário Las Américas,* Miami.

19. "U.S. Hails Argentina's Role as Ally," *Financial Times,* October 17, 1997, p. 5.

20. Richard Feinberg, director for Latin America, National Security Council, addressing the annual meeting of the Latin American Studies Association, Sheraton Hotel, Washington, D.C., September 29, 1995; also see Raymont, "Favorecen a Clinton los acuerdos de paz," *Diário Las Américas* (Miami), October 1, 1995, p. 1.

21. Celso Lafer, "Brazilian International Identity and Foreign Policy," *Daedalus,* Spring 2000, p. 217.

22. Lafer, "Brazilian International Identity," p. 218.

23. Walt, "Two Cheers," p. 79.

Chapter Fourteen

EPILOGUE

In his insightful 1928 *Foreign Affairs* article, Franklin D. Roosevelt wrote:

In our century and a half of national life there have been outstanding periods when American leadership has influenced the thought and actions of the civilized world toward international good will and peace; and there have been moments—rare ones, fortunately—when American policy either has been negative and sterile, or has earned for us dislike or fear or ridicule. . . . The outside world almost unanimously views us with less good will today than at any previous period. This is serious unless we take the deliberate position that the people of the United States owe nothing to the rest of mankind and care nothing for the opinion of others so long as our seacoasts are impregnable and our pocketbooks are filled.[1]

The decade following the collapse of the international system as it had evolved during the Cold War, along with the fall of the Berlin Wall, promised to be one of those "outstanding periods" of American influence FDR understood so well to be the challenge of US leadership. Perhaps a similar realization sent President Clinton and Secretary of State Madeleine Albright to proclaim to the world that the United States was now the "indispensable nation," an infelicitous term even if true. The implied faith in the country's moral superiority fueled unnecessary resentment. By the end of the century the exercise of US leadership was turning sour. Absent the imperatives of the Cold War, a growing indifference to the rest of the world became apparent.

Once the determined advocate of the World Court and other measures to regulate the international community, the United States increasingly became a reluctant participant. The Reagan administration had correctly assessed US public opinion that remained predictably muted in the face of Washington's rejection of World Court rulings when it stood accused of mining Nicaraguan waters. Similarly, when the Clinton administration, one of the first sponsors of an international court to prosecute crimes against humanity, ended up voting against it, as it did in the case of the convention against the use of land mines and various treaties to protect the environment, public reaction was notable for its absence.

The post–Cold War years came close to winding up "on the debit side of the ledger," as FDR might have put it. In some parts of the world US policies began to earn the "dislike or fear or ridicule" Roosevelt attributed to Latin American reaction to the Hoover era in the 1920s. In that respect the nations of the Western Hemisphere differed from other regions in the world, where fascination with the extraordinary US economic growth cycle and the stratospheric level of the stock market muted past criticisms of its foreign policy.

Undoubtedly statistics justified a degree of smugness, both from the country at large and the Washington establishment. Had not the British historian Paul Kennedy, a Yale professor, made a gloomy prognosis for US economic and political hegemony in *The Rise and Fall of the Great Powers*, an acclaimed best-seller? Yet in the dozen years since the book appeared in 1988, the US had won the Cold War as well as two wars in the Middle East and the Balkans. At the same time, the impressive roar of the economic "tigers" of Japan and the rest of Asia turned to pleas of help to Washington and the international banks. Commenting on the US scene in the light of Kennedy's foreboding, a veteran columnist of the *Financial Times* cautioned, "The dramatic turnaround should give pause to anyone considering making grand forecasts."[2]

After the threat of Soviet aggression disintegrated along with the Berlin Wall, the United States confronted a new juncture that offered a unique opportunity for an imaginative, comprehensive and long-range policy for Latin America. The way was open to the kind of change the region had clamored for ever since the end of the Good Neighbor policy and the short-lived Alliance for Progress. First Bush and then Clinton held out such hopes with their Enterprise for the Americas and the Free Trade Area of the Americas, respectively. But neither marshaled the required political muscle behind these initiatives, which were allowed to languish. The result, however, was not necessarily unfavorable to the region, as it learned to rely more on itself and the countries began to find their own responses to the requirements of globalism by quickening their quest for investments and markets in Europe and Asia.

Likewise, George W. Bush continued the ritual of making Latin America a personal priority. He said so himself.[3] As a former governor of Texas, a state that for years has taken pride in its "special relationship" with Mexico, his commitment initially seemed to acquire greater credibility. Indeed, it received an early boost when Bush made a preinaugural trip to the home of Mexican President Vicente Fox in Guanajuato. To give the visit a more intimate touch, Fox took the US visitor to his mother's house. Nonetheless, Bush remained true to the tradition of dropping the region from his agenda as soon as more urgent issues arose. It was not long before domestic issues stemming from the Iraq crisis, together with a host of economic uncertainties, once again remitted Western Hemisphere matters to the dubious warmth of the proverbial back burner.

Some early Latin American commentators initially thought that in his "rapprochement" with Mexico Bush might follow in LBJ's footsteps, and the Mexican–US talks become the bilateral relationship that the US president felt most comfortable with. In fact, the highest Washington official of the Bush administration to develop an affable, sustained relationship with his Mexican counterparts was Robert B. Zoellick, the US trade representative. But most of the Bush administration's political appointments to the Bureau of Inter-American Affairs were bitterly disappointing to most Latin American governments.

Roger Noriega was the man technically in charge of diplomatic relations with Mexico and the rest of Latin America. He was a former aide to the arch-conservative Senator Jesse Helms, whose witch hunts of alleged leftists in the Carter and Clinton administrations had so thoroughly discredited him with most Latin Americans that some democratic leaders in the hemisphere either opted to deal directly with Secretary of State Colin Powell, a man widely respected as a moderate, or put a wide range of relations with Washington on hold except for the most routine issues.

When he was sworn in, Noriega sought to distance himself from his blatantly reactionary record by vowing that he would devote his major efforts to defeating the new enemy, corruption. Nonetheless, the assistant secretary of state for Western Hemisphere affairs remained obsessed by Cuba and those who favored bringing the island back into the regional fold. This presaged tense relations with some of the major countries—Argentina, Brazil and Chile. Soon he denounced Argentina's president Néstor Kirchner, a Peronist, first for being "soft" on Cuba and later for not taking more stringent measures against labor rallies protesting Argentina's "neoliberal" economic policies forced on the country by the International Monetary Fund (IMF). Not surprisingly, his ill-considered remarks brought a sharp rejoinder from Argentine Foreign Minister Rafael Bielsa: "If Mr. Noriega is concerned about what is happening in our country, the Argentine government is sick and tired with his intrusions into the internal affairs of Argentina." "That official," he complained, "speaks about Argentina as a 'backyard,' showing no restraint about meddling in the internal affairs of other countries."

Of course, Latin America was not the only arena in which the Bush administration seemed incapable of moving away from the tried-and-failed policies of the twentieth century.

What more moderate and more experienced US officials, such as Secretary of State Colin Powell, understood is that in this new millennium there is no alternative to fostering goodwill and hoping for alliances among neighbor nations while building bridges to the newly expanded European Union. The old divisions and the quest of power politics have little meaning today and do not fit in with the new global environment. But old habits die slowly. Yet clearly the interests and activities of states overflow their boundaries and are worldwide. No nation can isolate itself or be indifferent to the political or economic fate of other nations.

"Co-operation can only be on a basis of equality and mutual welfare, on a pulling-up of the backward nations and peoples to a common level of well-being and cultural advancement, on an elimination of racialism and domination," wrote Jawaharlal Nehru more than half a century ago. "No nation and no people are going to tolerate the domination of and exploitation by another, even though this is given some more pleasant name. Nor will they remain indifferent to their own poverty and misery when other parts of the world are flourishing. That was only possible when there was ignorance of what was happening elsewhere."

Nonetheless, in one sense, Latin America ended the century in hugely better shape than might have been imagined fifty years ago. Few then would have believed that midway through the second half of the century the mercurial political topography of the hemisphere would have become transmogrified by elected regimes that embraced democracy and the free market as their ultimate goals. The tradition of coups d'état, military dictatorships and boom-and-bust economies seemed on the way to becoming things of the past.

Indeed, alliance, convergence and coalitions have become the watchwords of the democracy construction that is engaging Latin American politics these days. The heads of state that attended the installation ceremonies in March 2000 of President Ricardo Lagos, who won the election as leader of Convergencia, a coalition of Christian Democrats and Socialists, offered the clearest indication of the new trend. There was Fernando de la Rúa, whose centrist Unión Cívica Radical had enlisted the support of the leftist FREPASO alliance; Jorge Batlle of the Uruguayan Colorado party, who had just defeated a powerful leftist challenge by enlisting the support of his traditional rivals; Fernando Henrique Cardoso of Brazil, who had worked overtime to pound together support for his legislation from the most diverse political sectors of the Brazilian Congress.

Common interests as well as their personal and political affinities have led these leaders to persuade Lagos to move closer to the Mercosur rather than continue waiting for the United States to beckon him into NAFTA, a goal Clinton was unable to fulfill due to the hostility of his own party toward the regional economic group. This impetus toward regional integration and bilateral comity suggests that prior to globalization the nations of the Americas are ensuring their future by first traversing a period of regionalization. If this is insufficiently understood by Washington or the country at large, it is because the drug cartels, the insurrection in Colombia, Cuba and the alarms over imagined Chinese threats against the Panama Canal have combined to obscure the remarkable political and economic progress taking place in Latin America.

At the turn of the century, Latin America had not done badly for itself. The shift toward democracy that began in the 1980s had consolidated, leaving Cuba as the only outright authoritarian government. A sweeping agenda of economic and social reforms had restored growth to Argentina, Brazil and Uruguay and most of the Andean countries, though the lives of a huge majority of their population were, in the pungent words of Thomas Hobbes, "nasty, brutish and short," still awaiting what the great economist Simon Kuznets called "modern economic growth," meaning a cumulative rise in real per capita income.[4]

In the perspective of the past half century, by the beginning of the 1990s, a mood of rapprochement with the United States was sweeping Latin America not experienced since the Roosevelt era. The region's support of President Bush's Enterprise for the Americas Initiative and its sequel under Clinton signaled the new impetus of democratic and capitalist aspirations. But it was not as swiftly recognized and reciprocated as the neighbor governments had hoped. Since the mid-1980s, when military dictatorships, torn by corruption and weakened by demonstrable inefficiency, began to leave the field to democratically elected governments, Washington's Cold War behavior shifted; no longer afraid of communism, it began to demand respect for human rights from its friends and allies.

Still, the Washington establishment, like a person who spent too many years in a cast, remained deformed by old Cold War habits, focusing on Europe and Asia and paying occasional lip service to Africa. Meanwhile, Latin America was taken for granted as "our own backyard," a condescending phrase that is not calculated to win friends. Ten years before Bosnia, the United States invaded Panama to remove a drug-running dictator who once worked for the CIA and then sent troops to Haiti with UN endorsement, making the intervention in defense of democracy in the Americas a trailblazer for the latest concept in international jurisprudence. But not enough was made of this point.

Toward the end of the Bush administration and, sporadically, during Clinton's two terms, attempts were made to address inter-American relations, but never was there the kind of serious committed initiative that the Latin Americans had hoped for and that might have placed the region in a more central position of US foreign policy, as the Good Neighbor policy had been. The Bush II administration, absorbed by the war on terror, hewed to the same pattern.

Nonetheless, in Latin America, hopes remain high that a new hemispheric alliance would be forged on the eve of a new century that heralded a period dominated by rival regional blocs before the competition yielded to the global marketplace envisioned by the World Trade Organization. In more recent times this process has been accelerated by the combined influences of the United States replacing Europe as the training ground of much of the Latin American elites and the impact of electronic media on the popular culture—to the shame of those who have been expounding learned essays on the "inadaptability" of Latin cultures to modern institutions.

The current process of modernization in Latin America consists of trying to catch up with the more dynamic parts of Western society. Political modernization, as Theodore Geiger observed thirty years ago, means essentially the achievement of changes in attitudes, norms and relationships that can reduce or offset the importance of such inbred particularism, paternalism and *personalismo* that used to typify much of Latin American culture so that these inherited characteristics no longer exercise the decisive influence on political institutions and procedures.[5]

Washington's acknowledgment of these changes, if indeed they penetrated the upper layers of the policymaking establishment, was largely confined to ceremonial rhetoric and academic papers. Politically, what was needed was more focused attention and modernizing ideas brought to the faltering regional system, of which the Organization of American States (OAS) was its undistinguished and frequently maligned emblem. Why is it so difficult for the changes in Latin America to have a greater impact on US policymakers?

Ironically, the financial and business communities have a more realistic picture, judging by the spiraling trade and investments registered during the last decade. Trade and economic considerations alone make a compelling argument for future administrations to propel Latin America to a commanding place in its foreign policy scheme. By the year 2020, US exports to the region are projected to be $240 billion, an amount greater than US exports to the European Union and Japan combined. But there are other considerations that Washington no longer can ignore. One, of course, is the growing Latino (or Hispanic) presence in the United States and its corresponding potential for political influence. Another is the increasing importance of regional alliances, be they for the sake of maintaining peace or regional common markets, such as NAFTA, Mercosur and the Central American Free Trade Zone. By contrast, policy discussions and debates in Washington sound more like a continuation of old arguments than a genuine rethinking or reformulation of the subject. The threat of communism disappeared, only to be replaced by fear of a new collective enemy, such as the threats of drug traffic and Islamic terrorism. The techniques learned against communism were polished, expanded and applied to the new crusade against illicit drugs, both at home and abroad.

New techniques were developed and applied against the coca growers of Bolivia and Peru and the drug cartels of Mexico and the Caribbean. They included the emplacement of DEA and covert US agents; the gathering and evaluation of secret intelligence; and, as in the case of Colombia and Panama, military training and supply of weapons to their respective police forces. But these measures and a whopping antidrug budget of $1.6 billion failed to stem the flow of drugs, and soon people talked about pouring good money after bad.

Clinton was reluctant to devote much time or effort to foreign policy in his first term but made an about-turn during the second. Perhaps he found redemption for his scandal-ridden administration in foreign policy initiatives, a strategy Nixon discovered while he was vice president. He tirelessly ventured two weeks into Africa, toured China and made enormous efforts to bring peace to Northern Ireland and the Middle East. Latin America received little more than passing attention, ostensibly because, in the words of aides, "there are no conflicts or crises, so relations there don't require constant attention."[6]

Latin diplomats do not share that benign assessment. Instead, they complain bitterly about "apathy," "indifference," and "neglect," as they have practically since the day Franklin Roosevelt died. These are not gratuitous complaints, as the advocates of globalism (or "world civilization," the more elegant term Arnold J. Toynbee gave this phenomenon half a century ago) have practically displaced the regional perspective that dominated much of the US past. How did Washington respond to the changes taking place in the hemisphere?

The best the Clinton administration could conceive to guide its Western Hemisphere policy was a new literature of trade with inspiring phrases such as "our historic democratic journey towards a future built on free trade," as Al Gore put it in a technocratic speech to mark the first anniversary of the Miami summit.[7] But the "spirit of Miami" quickly faded from the Washington scene. Clinton's hemisphere policy was based not so much on an orderly, comprehensive weltanschauung, an understanding of the Latin American component in US history, but mostly was steered by the winds of circumstance. A border problem with Mexico, threats to Colombia's political stability, a visit by a Latin American leader here, a brief trip to the region there. Good "photo-ops" but poor foundations for a true policy overhaul.

The Clinton administration's policy was highlighted by various summits; all sounded good and were well intended. But they lacked the kind of conviction he displayed in moments of crisis, such as in Kosovo, the Middle East or the ratification of NAFTA or in dealing with the Mexican and Brazilian debt problems by finding ingenious ways of circumventing a recalcitrant Congress. As a result, the United States has had to face the criticism that in a time when great constructive ideas were needed in the task of preparing the hemisphere to deal with the challenges of globalization and the technological opportunities of the upcoming century, Washington displayed a unique failure of imagination and resolve.

Perhaps Clinton was diverted by other issues. Or perhaps, as James McGregor Burns has pointed out, for the man who wanted to model himself after FDR, Clinton had chosen the wrong philosophy, centrism or pragmatism. He did lots of little things incrementally rather than embrace a vision of history and the world and construct truly innovative policies capable of charting new routes. In retrospect it is evident that Clinton was not prepared to provide the bold, transformational political leadership required to fashion such a policy. It also demanded far more focused attention and involvement in the region from the top levels of the National Security Council and the State Department. That may be true for much of the world. I would argue however, as a believer in New World exceptionalism, that the seat-of-the-pants policy should not be applied to Latin America. In a way the southern half of the continent is as predictable as its northern cousins. There was a kind of presidential tragedy because he would never make the changes that would have been required to change the public attitude toward Latin American policy.

Significant underlying assumptions intrude surreptitiously into the public discourse to hamper better understanding and, therefore, a closer relationship with Latin Americans. One is the Washington establishment's overarching concern with Europe and Asia, which persistently relegates Latin American affairs to the proverbial back burner; the other is a conspicuous lack of understanding and, therefore, full appreciation of Latin American cultures and their affinity for their US counterparts.

The answer lies less in geopolitics or economics than in cultural perceptions. Starting with the notoriously prejudiced high school textbooks of the nineteenth century, it became a habit to disparage the countries "south of the border." It is a constant predicating of differences, from the old shibboleth that the southern half was colonized by gold-grubbing, exploiting and lazy Spaniards, while the north reaped the virtues of the Puritan ethos that colored the life of its hard-working Pilgrims.

Commentators such as Howard Wiarda,[8] Carlos Rangel[9] and, most notably, Lawrence E. Harrison[10] have perpetuated this cultural burden theory. But the larger point is that these socioeconomic commentators, working with the concept of cultural theory, fortified, with a mass of erudition, all the ancestral prejudices US society had about Latin America. They unearthed inherent behavior patterns—obsolete theories Franz Boas, Margaret Mead and Ruth Benedict long ago laid to rest. They forgot the rise of the middle class, and they made the workings of democracy in Latin America practically impossible to understand.

Nonetheless, those stereotypes have endured, even if in a slightly modified and updated version. They perversely surface in congressional debates and frequently hover as an unspoken subtext in much of the US–Latin American official discourse. Now it is perhaps no longer the coarse image of the "lazy Mexican" sleeping under his sombrero or a pistol-packing caudillo subjugating his people or the "latifundista" exploiting his Indians.

These stereotypes were replaced by a new set tailored to fit the times: the drug kingpins, money launderers and former generals and other military officers whose reign of terror has finally been given official recognition as crimes against humanity. As the United States speeds helter-skelter toward a new electronic millennium, Latin American culture is thought to have little affinity for modernity. The underlying myths, however, have to do with the children of Spain being "un-American," ill-equipped to deal with the laws of capitalism, liberalism, civility. Why did they fail to achieve the success that produced the American dream? Here lies the real intellectual tragedy of our time, that we endowed such basic prejudices the garb of economic or cultural theory.

Octavio Paz once told me Washington's inability to comprehend the process of change in Latin America and the opportunities to refashion the hemispheric relationship represented "a failure of the imagination," especially imagination irrigated by an understanding of hemispheric history, including a keener grasp of America's own origins, if we are to reclaim once more the notion of the commonality of the New World nations. But that will not happen unless there is the political will and leadership capable of overcoming the difficulty of changing the entrenched structures and ideas that have become ossified in Washington's thinking since the Cold War and the danger of remaining culturally blind to what is happening in the rest of the hemisphere.

But it also stems from lack of effective political leadership, a leadership based on conviction, commitment and consistency that is capable of generating fundamental changes in public attitudes and policies. It is perhaps true, as the various occupants of the White House and their staffs have maintained in recent years, that the majority of the people of the United States care little about and know less what goes on south of the border, at least beyond Mexico. Yet nothing prevented them from using the nation's leading bully pulpit as a forum of public education in the effective manner in which FDR sold the nation the Good Neighbor policy. Roosevelt did this by not missing a single opportunity to remind Congress and the country of the importance of the Good Neighbors.

It must also be noted that his commitment was based on knowing Latin America firsthand. Thus empirical knowledge of the region should be a prerequisite for our political leaders; otherwise Latin America would be reduced to a collection of statistics and GNP charts to the occupant of the White House; to understand a region with any degree of depth one must have been there. In the case of the Americas, we know it to be a continent full of bustling, creative peoples, who not only produce industry but also have a culture rich in music, art and wonderfully ingenious and lively communities that resist abstract definition. And it is in this culture that we find the strongest links, not in "the economy, stupid."

In that sense, we do well to recall the counsel advanced in the late 1960s by Theodore Geiger, chief of international studies of the National Planning Association of Washington: "The major conceptual and attitudinal changes needed by both the United States and Western Europe are explicit acceptance of the fact that Latin America is part of Western civilization, and the consequent willingness to behave accordingly toward Latin America."[11] It is in fact more than that if we are to believe J. Hector St. John de Crevecoeur, Germán Arciniegas, Frederick Jackson Turner and Walter Prescott Webb.

There would be nothing essentially novel in such a change in the Western, especially the North American, way of thinking about Latin America.

> In effect, it would mean reverting to the conception of Latin American society that prevailed until the end of World War II; since then, preoccupation with "development" has obscured the significance of sociocultural similarities and differences. Reversion to the older way of thinking would contribute more than any other possible change toward making the relationship between these different parts of Western civilization less conflicted and more beneficial to all concerned.[12]

The magnitude of this lost opportunity recalls the farewell speech by Senator William Fulbright, who, like Clinton, came from Arkansas, when he noted that "history casts no doubt at all on the ability of human beings to deal rationally with their problems, but the greatest doubt on their will to do so. The signals of the past are thus clouded and ambiguous, suggesting hope but not confidence in the triumph of reason. With nothing to lose in any event, it seems well worth a try."[13]

We should, I believe, harness the interest that has mushroomed in US financial and commercial circles to generate the political dynamism required to develop a comprehensive new approach that gives priority consideration to the region, creating a resurgence of the interest it once enjoyed during the first two terms of Franklin D. Roosevelt.

By contrast, those who participated in the Roosevelt administration had a much more penetrating understanding of the global implications of its Latin American policy. James F. Byrnes pointedly told the *Herald Tribune* Forum six months after FDR's death: "Inter-American cooperation is not unconnected with worldwide cooperation among the nations. Regional arrangements, like the Inter-American system, which respect the rights and interests of other states and fit into the world system can become strong pillars in the structure of world peace."[14]

In the last decade of the twentieth century there still existed a vast reservoir of goodwill in Latin America toward the United States, perhaps greater than at any time since the Good Neighbor. To nurture it would have made sense not only to boost the commerce and investments the Clinton administration was so keen in furthering, but also in terms of the affinities we share in our histories and cultures. But by his second term the Latin American leadership had clearly come to the conclusion that Clinton would not be another Kennedy, let alone another Franklin Delano Roosevelt. This would have required a thorough geostrategic rethinking of Latin America's role in the world, predicated on a new awareness of the actual and potential importance the region still holds for US interests and tradition.

It does not help, of course, to have a US secretary of state, born in Czechoslovakia, proclaim the United States to be "a European nation." One is then tempted to recall in rebuttal Giovanni Papini's disdainful remark, aptly made at the height of fascism in the 1940s, dismissing the Americas as "the repository of the rejects of Europe," not to mention Smith's disdain for American creativity.

When it becomes incorporated into foreign policy, this Eurocentric view results in a rigid, unimaginative, traditional approach. What will be necessary to break away from this postwar Washingtonian habit will require nothing less than a different way of viewing the world, or, perhaps, simply recapturing the spirit of the Great Frontier, that shared experience of the New World. It is possible through leadership, as the two Roosevelts showed in politics.

I close with an insight I heard years ago from Francisco Fernández Or-dóñez, the late foreign minister of Spain, who had come to Washington in a futile attempt to talk President Reagan into adopting a more moderate stance in the Central American crisis. After a small dinner at the Spanish embassy, he invited me for a walk. Visibly frustrated, he gave me an off-the-record account of his meeting with the president. It was not very flattering.

"He doesn't understand the first thing about Latin America," Ordóñez mut-tered. Then, in a more mellow voice he added, "Perhaps it doesn't matter. Be-cause to understand Latin America you need to love Latin America. And to love it you need to know it. And in your government, very few people have taken the trouble to get to know it."

In the advent of this new century it would be fitting for the next adminis-tration to confront the economic, social and psychological challenges of glob-alization by reformulating the US practice of differentiating itself from Latin America. The United States should attempt to see in the New World what the early navigators and Founding Fathers expected to see. This should not be a cause for surprise or disdain, for it is inherently difficult to grasp what is unfa-miliar. The real test comes later, with the capacity to abandon the standard im-ages and inherited preconceptions to understand that the Americas are a new world and a different world, for it is this difference that is overwhelmingly ob-vious to observers from the sixteenth century to this day. "Everything is very different," wrote Fray Tomas de Mercado in his book of advice to the mer-chants of Seville; "the talent of the natives, the disposition of the republic, the method of government and even the capacity to be governed."[15]

But how to convey this fact of difference, the uniqueness of the Americas to those who are not aware of it either because they know not their own history or are too imbued by its Eurocentric version? One obvious way is to restore the frontier vision of the American reality and revive the American consciousness of its existence. As Prescott Webb suggested in his neglected *The Great Frontier* half a century ago: "It is the American frontier concept that needs to be lifted out of its present national setting and applied on a much larger scale to all of Western civilization in modern times."[16] No idea could be more relevant to the twenty-first century.

NOTES

1. Franklin Delano Roosevelt, "Our Foreign Policy: A Democratic View," *Foreign Affairs* 6 (July 1928): 573–586.

2. See Gerald Baker, "The Future of America: Liberty's Triumph," *Financial Times,* December 23, 1999, p. 12.

3. See *Harvard Magazine*, January–February 2002, p. 25; John H. Coatsworth, *Latin America and the World Economy Since 1800* (Cambridge, Mass.: Harvard University Press, 1998).

4. Martin Wolf, "The Curse of Global Inequality," *Financial Times*, March 17, 2000, p. 8.

5. Theodore Geiger, *The Conflicted Relationship: The West and the Transformation of Asia, Africa, and Latin America* (New York: McGraw-Hill, 1967).

6. Arturo Valenzuela, interview by author, Executive Office Building, Washington, D.C., January 6, 2000.

7. Text of remarks by Vice President Al Gore, Washington, D.C., December 12, 1995.

8. "Much of the history of Latin America all the way to the present may be understood in terms of the institutions and behavioral patterns that Catholic, feudal, authoritarian, patrimonial Spain carried with her to the Western Hemisphere" (Howard J. Wiarda, *Dictatorship, Development, and Disintegration: Politics and Social Change in the Dominican Republic* [Ann Arbor, Mich.: Xerox University Microfilms, 1975]), 1:17, 19.

9. Carlos Rangel, *Del buen salvaje al buen revolucionario* (Caracas: Monte Avila, 1982).

10. Lawrence E. Harrison, *Underdevelopment Is a State of Mind: The Latin American Case* (Cambridge, Mass: Center for International Affairs, Harvard University, 1985); *The Pan-American Dream: Do Latin America's Cultural Values Discourage True Partnership with the United States and Canada?* (New York: Basic Books, 1991).

11. Geiger, *Conflicted Relationship*.

12. Geiger, *Conflicted Relationship*.

13. Geiger, *Conflicted Relationship*.

14. James Byrnes, "Neighboring Nations in One World," October 31, 1945.

15. *Summa de tratos y contratos* (Seville, 1571), quoted in J. H. Elliott, *The Old World and the New* (Cambridge: Cambridge University Press, 1970), p. 21.

16. Walter Prescott Webb, *The Great Frontier* (Boston: Houghton Mifflin, 1952).

INDEX